# Rich/Poor Man's Guide to Pittsburgh

plus

## "I Love Pittsburgh! Pull-Out Sightseeing Guide"

### EIGHTH EDITION

by Dorothy A. Miller

**New Pittsburgh Publications**
Publishers of "Pittsburgh Walking Map & Guide"
and "Pittsburgh Pleasures Events Calendar"
Box 81875, Pittsburgh, PA 15217

## A WONDERFUL TOWN

Welcome to the 8th Edition of the *Rich/Poor Man's Guide* designed to help you discover all of the wonderful things that make Pittsburgh such a special place.

For 15 years the Guide has shared with more than 150,000 readers Pittsburgh's hidden secrets...its unique restaurants, ethnic cuisines, romantic hideaways, beautiful river views.

Scenically set at the Point of three rivers and rated one of the U.S.'s most liveable cities, Pittsburgh is a fascinating blend of ethnic heritages, big corporations, sophisticated cultural attractions, champion sports and—the city's hall-mark—friendly people...a big city with a small town feel.

This new 8th Edition—completely revised and expanded to 250 pages—includes scores of new eateries in Pittsburgh's swiftly-changing restaurant scene. We've also added 10 Terrific Day Trips, new Coffeehouses, a greatly expanded Budget Eats section, the latest in riverfront fun and scores of new things to do including the Warhol Museum, Heinz Architectural Center and the new Regional History Center.

Visitors tell us the best thing about the city is its variety of ethnic cuisines. We've gotten an enthusiastic response to our Famous Pittsburgh Food...*and* the Outdoor/Riverside Dining sections.

People from all over the world, amazed at Pittsburgh's beauty, have written to tell us how much the *Guide,* our *Walking Map* and the *Pittsburgh Events Calendar* have helped them discover real Pittsburgh.

Our readers come from all walks of life...natives keeping up with city changes, business executives, young profession-als, new high-tech workers, students, people temporarily stationed here, former 'Burghers, conventioneers, visitors, tourists—they all fell in love with the city.

Let the Guide help you fall in love with Pittsburgh and discover the secrets of what makes it such a "wonderful town"—a great place to live, work and visit!

# TABLE OF CONTENTS

I Love Pittsburgh
Pull-Out
Sightseeing
Guide

Visitor's Special
5 Easy Ways To Fall
In Love with the City

RENAISSANCE II
BUILDING WATCHER'S
GUIDE

# HOW TO USE THIS GUIDE

It starts with you! This 8th Edition of the *"Rich/Poor Man's Guide"* is divided into 19 sections with numbered tabs on each page for quick, easy use To get the most from the Guide begin with:

**REVIEWS & RICH MAN'S DINING**
Sections 1 & 2. These restaurants and experiences of the city are all special Pittsburgh places with extraordinary cuisine and atmosphere or unusual ethnic food. To help you discover the city's best these sections are indexed by:

> **Geographic Area**
> **Type of Cuisine**
> **Connoisseur Dining**
> **Nights of Romance**
> **Fabulous Buys**
> **Shopping/Experiences of City**

All other tabbed sections are easily found in the Table of Contents.

**GENERAL ALPHABETICAL INDEX**
can be found in the back of the Guide

**COMPANION PIECES**
The *Guide* and the *I Love Pittsburgh! Pull-Out Sightseeing section* are best used in conjunction with the *Pittsburgh Walking Map & Guide,* an invaluable aid in getting around the city and the *Pittsburgh Pleasures Events Calendar* with listings of 850 things to do in Greater Pittsburgh and 13 color photos of the city. **For suggestions in planning a special day/night in Pittsburgh or a celebration within your budget call us at 412-681-8528**

### KEY

| | | | |
|---|---|---|---|
| AE | Amer Exp | Inexp | Under $10 |
| CB | Carte Blanche | Mod | $10-$20 |
| D | Discover | Exp | $20 & over |
| DC | Diner's Club | (dinner per person) |
| MC | Master Card | | |
| V | Visa | | |

♿ Accommodates wheelchairs entrances, tables, restrooms

# REVIEWS, RICH MAN'S DINING
## (By Category)

## GEOGRAPHIC

*This is an independent publication, not connected with or financed by any business establishment. Prices, checked up to the eve of publication, are subject to change, as are policies and management. All opinions expressed are the author's.*

# Poor Man's Tips—Save Money Dining

**A La Carte:** A la carte ordering is becoming more and more acceptable in the more casual, economical dining of the '90s. (It's probably what the restaurant staff do on their nights out.) Sharing and sampling several dishes can be fun. Some restaurants have a modest plate charge. Ask!

**Always Ask:** If you don't understand a menu item or a foreign language menu, the server is usually glad to assist you. If you question a charge on your check...don't be shy. They'll respect your alertness. A comfortable, satisfied diner returns.

**Hidden Costs:** Don't hesitate to ask the cost of verbal daily specials. Also watch for hidden costs on extras i.e. special dressings, appetizers. Ask if they're extra. In some night clubs the price of drinks rises with the entertainment and it pays to order when the band's not playing.

**Specials:** Take advantage of the Guide's Early Bird dinners, fabulous buys and bargain brunches. Shop around to save.

**Wine:** There's a wise saying, "If you can afford the bottle, you won't like it." House wines by the glass or carafe are often the best buy—many are excellent.

**Tips:** Tips are part of the service worker's salary. What's fair? Regular service, 15%, special service, 20%, so-so, 10%.

# Tipping For The Rich Man's Feast

Pittsburgh restaurants are less formal than many other cities'. Some fine restaurants automatically add a 15% gratuity to your check, continental style. But tipping well is still the best insurance that your fabulous feast will be a nght to remember and you'll be greeted warmly on your return. The cast in a fine restaurant usually includes:

**The Maitre d':** Everything revolves around the maitre d', the gentleman—usually tuxedoed—who greets you at the door. He chooses your table, seats you and insures your dinner is a sucess... and other staff members take their cue from him. Most Pittsburgh restaurants say tipping head waiters is not necessary except for unusual service. But you can insure a very special evening by slipping him a folded $5, $10 or more.

**Wine Steward: (Sommelier)** Also an important person in making your evening a sucess... recognized by the by the tasting cup and medallion around his/her neck. Helps you select the right wine, insures it's properly served. For special service tip 5%-20% cost of wine.

**Waiter:** Minimum 15%-20%. A portion is shared with the busboys.

# RESTAURANT REVIEWS

Pittsburgh is a diner's town with one of the largest number of restaurants per capita in the country. Here are some of the city's most unique, exciting eateries...plus shopping and experiences of the city...all special Pittsburgh places with charm, great cuisine, ethnic touches. The reviews tell you When to Go, What to Order, What to Wear for city's best values.

## Abate

**Italian Feast, Fabulous Prices**

*Waterworks Mall, Freeport Road, Fox Chapel. Mon-Thur 11:30-11, Fri & Sat til 11:30-12. Sun 9am-11pm, Brunch 9-2. AE,D,MC,V.* **781-9550.** 🦽

We resisted this restaurant's seafood reputation for years only to succumb to its superior pasta. A big, rambling room with a high noise level, it's immensely popular for its well-priced menu. Best seats in the house are in the glass-fronted patio where ceiling fans and white patio furniture give an airy, informal feel. Pizza lovers and snackers can get closer to the wood-fire hearth ovens in an outer room with quick service at high stools. In any case there are a lot of wonderful dishes here at great prices. Expect crowds and children—this is also a family favorite.

**When To Go:** Anytime is fun time.

**What To Order:** You can get anything here (including a Bloody Mary & other mixed drinks at $2.95.) A big menu features pizza, pasta, salads, soups, fish, seafood and chicken entrees—and great desserts—many of them for take-out. Everything's served with delicious chewy hearth bread. You'll be tempted to take one of the big crusty loaves home—it's that good! Entrees include Shrimp Scampi, Broiled Seafood Platter, Virginia Spots and several versions of chicken.

But our favorites are some of the best pastas in town happily available in regular or smaller "piccolo" servings...just enough when paired with a dynamite salad. We heartily recommend the **Angel Hair with Lobster & Mascarpone Cheese**...a delicious blend of spinach, mushroom, cheese, cream...only $5.95...perfect with the big $2.95 **House Salad** —roast peppers, zucchini, red onions and provolone. Try it with our favorite dressing, the low-cal Tomato Italian...one of the best we've ever tasted. Other good selections are the **Chicken Caesar** or the **Hot Chicken Salad**, both $5.95. Interesting appetizers include the foccacio—pizza dough from the hearth oven with Italian cheeses, sun-dried tomatoes, basil & prosciutto, $4.95.

For "best dessert" we nominate the **Raspberry Chambord Cheesecake** ($3.75) also available for take-home. P.S. There's a lot to like here...including big bargains on **Shrimp Feast Day** Wednesdays and a big line-up of "Light Dining for Heart" offerings.

**Prices:** $3.95-$13.

**What To Wear:** Anything goes.

**Recommended:** Italian Cuisine, Seafood, Fabulous Buys, Sunday Brunch, Late Supper.

**Chic Italian,
Townhouse
Setting**

## Abruzzi's

*52 S 10th Street, South Side. Mon-Thur 11:30-10, Fri & Sat til
11. Sun 4-9. AE,MC,V.* **431-4511.**
This charming South Side townhouse is the home of another
of the city's favorite Italian kitchens...this one from Abruzzi
in central Italy. On the site of the former Sarah's Restaurant
near the 10th St Bridge, close to Downtown and Station
Square, it's sure to gain a big following. Why? The friendly
and unpretentious welcome of Tony and other Masci family
members, a counterpoint to the simple yet stylish decor...a
great dining environment. The cuisine also has the right combination of sophistication and simplicity. Inside the gray
townhouse's welcoming doorway is a snazzy mirrored bar/
waiting room, urbane yet warm and inviting, giving this restaurant a 'Pittsburgh style' all its own.

**When To Go:** Fun for dinner, cosy by the chimney fireplace.

**What To Order:** It's an extensive menu with lots of difficult dishes alongside
some old Italian favorites...lamb, steak, chicken, veal and
even rabbit entrees and several seafood dishes. The many
versions of chicken include a Chicken Saltimbocca stuffed
with prosciutto and provolone, Chicken with Peppercorns in
port wine, with Sun-Dried Tomatoes & Mushrooms. Our
favorite was a delicious **Pollo Arresto Abruzzese roast
whole chicken in wine & garlic**...really good for $12.95
and of the veals...a tender **Scallopini** for $14.95. Chef
Johann Meinke has a real fine Italian hand in the kitchen.
Another good entree idea is sharing the **Zuppa Di Pesce**,
traditional Italian seafood soup with shrimp, scallops, clams
and mussels paired with **outstanding house salads with
honey Dijon dressing** and an appetizer i.e. the zucchini or
Italian cheeses and meats.
But the **pasta dishes turned out to be the treasure of
the house**...simple yet subtly seasoned...cappellini, linguini,
fettuccini, penne, mafalda (a flat, wavy noodle), fusili (cork
screws) with scores of sauces—Olive Oil & Garlic, Sweet
Peppers or Meat Marinara for $8.95, Shrimp & Hot Peppers
$13.95, up to a seafood pasta for $17.95. Equally good are
the Italian staples—manicotti, cannelloni, eggplant Parmesan, gnocchi and stuffed shells...all in the $8-$9 range.
And this is a place to have dessert...delicious homemade
canoli and rum cake.

**Prices:** $8.75-$19.95, appetizers for less.

**What to Wear:** Suit yourself. Dress or informal.

**Recommended:** Italian Cuisine, Late Supper.

## Baum Vivant

**NY Ambience For Haute Cuisine**

### Baum Vivant

*5102 Baum Blvd, Oakland. Lunch Mon-Fri 11:30-3. Dinner Mon-Thur 5:30-10, Fri & Sat til 11. Reser sugg. AE,CB,D, DC,MC,V.* **682-2620.**

This jewel-like little room with a sophisticated NY ambience has been home to a succession of fine restaurants, the latest—and hopefully the last—the creation of restaurateur Toni Pais, former maitre d' of the famed La Normande. Its urban elegance...from the welcoming canopy over the lighted doorway to the glamorous bandbox interior, is a fitting setting for exceptional dining. Toni has created an intriguing menu of extraordinary Italian and Portuguese dishes. And the service...perfectimento! This is a special place for intimate, couples dining or a luncheon tete-a-tete.

**When To Go:** Lunches are more economical, dinners doubly elegant.

**What To Order:** This is definitely 'high table' ($17.95-$26) but the creative culinary juices are flowing—Bass with Fresh Fennel and Eggplant, Filet of Beef with Foie Gras, Steak with Roasted Shallots and Chestnuts. Steepest in price are the delicious **Lobster Flambe** with Tarragon Creme Fraiche, Lamb Tenderloin wrapped in Spinach and Phyllo and a Portuguese Mariscadada—Shellfish Bouillabaise...all around $24-$25. Less expensive are an unusual **Pork Tenderloin and Clams in Red Pepper Sauce** and **Chicken Santa Fe** with peppers and corn ($18). There are wines to match, perfect with the complimentary appetizer that begins your dinner—mouth-watering herbed pate with toast. And owner Pais also often dispenses an almond liqueur after dinner. You can savour the cuisine at more economical lunches. Don't miss the zesty soups...hallmark of a great restaurant—smooth **Roasted Yellow Pepper Soup**, cold **Caldo Verde** ($4.50) wonderful with fabulous breads served with herbed cream cheese. You can pair a soup with **Salad Vivant** (feta, pecans, red onions) or a divine **Angel Hair with Hot Italian Sausage** and tomato basil ($6-$7). Other adventurous items include Italian Sausage in Puff Pastry, Goat Cheese Tart with tomato/fennel salad and Lobster Cakes with Vanilla Sauce ($8-$11). This restaurant is obviously for gourmet food lovers. Put it on your special occasion list.

**Prices:** Lunch $7-$10.50. Dinner $17-$27.

**What To Wear:** It's a smart, sophisticated crowd.

**Recommended:** Continental Cuisine, Connoisseur Dining, Night of Romance, Rich Man's Guide, Late Supper.

**Riverside Fun
On Floating
Barge**

## Boardwalk, On the Water

1

*15th & Smallman, Strip District. Enter thru parking lot under bridge at 15th St. 7 days.* **281-1600.** ♿

One of the liveliest scenes in town—night or day—is this floating 420-ft entertainment center on barges anchored 30 feet from the Allegheny shore. Heralding the city's "riverside renaissance," the Boardwalk is phase one of a $50 million complex planned for a 12-acre site between the Veterans and 16th St Bridges.

Fun for all ages, it's a wonderful place to take your guests to appreciate the beauty of our rivers. In the summer under the stars with the lighted city in the background...or with holiday decorations reflected in the night waters...it makes you proud to be a Pittsburgher! Within walking distance of town, the bi-level complex contains two restaurants, a disco, a banquet hall and a handsome patio deck...an exciting scene in summer with two bars, a splash pool and boat docking on all three sides. The gay nautical flags over the wide ramp entrance spell out the letters S T R I P in code. A half-mile Riverwalk stretches the length of the project to a 60-slip Yacht Club marina next door and water taxis and shuttles connect to Pirate and Penguin games. Plans are underway for an additional bar/grill, jazz club and an oldies club.

**Where To
Eat/Party:**

**Crewsers** *7 days 11-12, Bar til 2. Sun Brunch 10-2. AE,MC,V. Reser sugg 8 or more.* **281-3680.**
Big 250-seat restaurant, 150 more on outdoor patio, with a great river view, nautical theme, glass walls sliding open for summer breezes. Grilled fish/steak, sandwiches, pasta. Two bars. Informal or dress-up fun. Mod. $7.95-$16.
**Buster's Crab** *Mon-Sat 5-12. (Sun summer).* **281-3683.**
Informal fresh fish/seafood restaurant & raw bar; beautiful topside view. Clams, mussels, crab claws, oysters, peel & eat shrimp plus pastas, salads, surf & turf, Seaman's Baskets with fries/slaw ($8.95-$20) plus all you can eat Crab Legs, $13.95.
**Patio Deck** Eat under the stars on the open air deck/bar where you can watch river fun, boat docking. Two outdoor bars, service from Crewsers. Bands add to summer fun at Tues Splash Party, Thur Oldie Night, Sun Rock Party & steel band Sat-Sun 2-5.
**Donzi's** *Wed-Thur 8-2am, Sat 5-2am. AE,MC,V.* **281-1586.**
Big, glitzy, upscale Euro-style nightclub. Dancing to DJs/live bands. Cocktails/dancing. Cover $2-$5. Mod-Exp.

**What To Wear:**  Spiffy/casual in summer.

**Recommended:**  American Cuisine, Seafood, Night of Romance—Patio, Brunch, Pgh After Dark.

## Brandy's

| | |
|---|---|
| Romantic<br>Late Night<br>Eatery | **Brandy's**<br>*Penn Avenue & 24th Street, Strip District. Mon-Thur 11-1am,,*<br>*Fri & Sat til 2am, Sun 3-11. Parking lot on corner. AE,D,DC,*<br>*MC,V.* **566-1000.**<br>The restaurant that started Pittsburgh's wave of new eateries has settled in as a favorite for businessmen and late night snackers. (A Brandy Van brings hotel guests to and from downtown.) The city's first after-hours restaurant with class, Brandy's is all charm from its remodeled three-story brick facade to the unique interior with its flickering fireplaces, skylight roof, hanging plants and old time bar...one of the best ambiences in the city. |
| **When To Go:** | Business lunch, Late snacks, breakfast Fri-Sat til 2am. |
| **What To Order:** | Just five minutes from town, Brandy's lends itself to a relaxing lunch. Besides fish, beef, chicken entrees, there's a good Spinach & Bacon Salad for $4.75, and hearty hot sandwiches—a popular Crabmeat Devonshire, Hefty Ham, Roast Beef—all served with fries and slaw. For lunch we recommend $5-$6 daily specials, Italian, Greek and Cajun dishes such as **Stuffed Eggplant, Blackened Red Fish, Stuffed Peppers, Shellfish.**<br><br>Dinners range from $12 to $18 for surf & turf but you can get snacks for much less. Still a good lunch/late nite buy are the juicy half pound **Brandyburgers** around $4-$5—especially the cheese-bacon specials. And you can dessert on heady 151 proof **Brandy-laced Rum-Raisin Ice Cream** concoctions in a huge 17-oz snifter $3.75. You won't need a drink with these.<br><br>A new addition at Brandy's is an outdoor concrete patio facing Penn Avenue. It's gay green & white umbrellas and a colorful skyline mural make for fun summer dining with the help of an outdoor grill and a light menu from $4-$7. This is a 'good-weather' after-theatre stop.<br>Try out the unique **Human Jukebox** (25c song, 5/$1)— you can call in to a record connoisseur with a collection of 250,000 all-time greats from as far back as 1922. And Friday nights you can join in the friendly barroom sing-a-long. |
| **Prices:** | Lunch $3.25-$7, Dinner $12-$18, Breakfast $3.25-$5.25. |
| **What To Wear:** | Casual best, informal or 'suit' the occasion. |
| **Recommended:** | American Cuisine, Night of Romance, Outdoor Dining, Party Rooms, Late Supper. |

| | |
|---|---|
| **Theatre Bistro Draws Raves** | **Bravo! Franco** |

**1**

*613 Penn Avenue, Downtown. Mon-Thur 11:30-9, Fri & Sat til 11. Sun 4-8 some show nights. Reser. AE,D,MC,V.* **642-6677.** ♿

A "first nighter's" favorite, this sparkling little restaurant across the street from Heinz Hall is ideal for catching pre/post performance dinner. The gleaming interior, a miniature Heinz Hall with red accents, chandeliers, mirrors, shiny brass, is always crowded with business lunchers and people on their way to and from the theatre. It's superb cuisine and high style have earned it rave reviews and a long, successful run. Be sure to get reservations as it's often SRO on busy nights and owner Luigi Caruso hates to turn people away at the door. The service is fast and deft...insuring you'll make your curtain on time.

**When To Go:** Downtown Lunch, Before/After Theatre.

**What To Order:** This is Classic Italian beautifully served with some starring dishes...a famous fried zucchini...delicious focaccia...wonderful pastas and antipastas, grilled chicken, fish, a crusty steak Siciliano...and some of the city's best veals. Pastas are $13.95...half order $6.95; seafood, veal and chicken $14.95 to $20 and over. Veal comes in many ways—piccata, marsala, Parmigiana, alla Romano with peppers, mushrooms and onions.

But our favorite way to eat here is to savour small course by small course...the delicious **Chicken Pastina Soup** ($1.75), then one of the fine salads...the beautifully constructed **House Salad** ($2.95) wonderful with generous dollops of blue cheese dressing or the robust **Salad Italiano** with mozzarella, reggiano and fresh basil. Then a small order of the day's pasta ($6.95)...or for the hungrier...the delicious **Capellini with Salmon, Tomatoes & Cream** ($13.95). This kind of eating leaves you room to appreciate "la dolci vita"—Italian sweets (dolci) too good to bypass...Cannoli, White Chocolate Cheesecake, Mascarpone Mousse, Creme Caramel, Tiramisu, Berries with Zabaglione, Gelato (smooth Italian ice-cream). One of the world's pleasures is savoring a fine Italian dessert with espresso or cappuccino laced with Galliano.

There are smaller luncheon portions of the same wonderful food and a late night menu with appetizers, soups, salads and hot and cold antipastas from $5-$9.

**Prices:** Lunch $5.75-$8.25. Dinner $12-$20.

**What To Wear:** Downtown/Theatre attire.

**Recommended:** Italian Cuisine, Connoisseur Dining, Late Supper.

## Cafe Allegro

**Inspired Riviera Cuisine**

### Cafe Allegro

*51 S 12th Street, South Side. Dinner Mon-Thur 5-10, Fri & Sat til 11. Sun 4:30-9:30. Reser. MC,V.* **481-7788.**

With cuisine that is truly 'allegro'—lively and inventive—this little restaurant has brightened the entire Pittsburgh dining scene. A family affair of gusto and love, Allegro is an intimate two-story restaurant tucked away in South Side's old Market Square. The mood is pleasant and romantic, the tables white-clothed, flower-bedecked. And the food... inspired by the French/Italian Riviera...often transcends. There's a light touch and terrific new tastes here with a sure use of herbs and spices.

**When To Go:** A lovely long dinner, weekday or weekend.

**What To Order:** A complimentary hors d'oeuvre, which might be anything from pate to roasted peppers, gets your meal off to a happy start...along with smiling service. Tempting main entrees—unique versions of salmon, chicken, pork, lamb and veal ($17-$23) change weekly. But we've never been able to get beyond the superb and affordable a la carte dishes. Ranging from a modest $4-$12, soups, vegetables, salads, pastas, appetizers of unforgettable tastes make for delightful eclectic dining...the cafe goer's favorite way to eat. There are rare dishes from which to choose...Red Pepper/Tomato Soup, Shrimp Bisque, Grilled Eggplant and an incomparable **Portabello & Roasted Sweet Pepper Salad...one of the city's best**—with fresh mozzarella and balsamic vinaigrette ($6). Another wonderful offering which can be shared is the **Vegetable Platter**—new potatoes and seasonal vegetables Allegro style, redolent with herbs and spices. **Watch for the Swiss Chard cassorole** exquisitely seasoned with tomatoes, wine and fennel, topped with toasted cheese and bread crumbs...a dish fit for a king! You can also share a **Riviera Antipasto Plate** ($12) marinated mussels, caponata, roasted herb goat cheese, smoked trout. The pastas, available in full or half orders ($6-$12) fit beautifully into an a la carte meal. (Don't miss the **Pasta del Sole** in a creamy sauce with sun-dried tomatoes, Romano cheese.)

The desserts are in a class by themselves. Our hats are off to Chef Joseph Nolan for his fine touch in this small kitchen and the Cardamone family for proving that uncommon cuisine can be had for reasonable prices.

**Prices:** Dinner $8-$23.

**What To Wear:** Something nice. This will be an occasion you won't forget.

**Recommended:** French/Italian Cuisine, Connoisseur Dining, Night of Romance, Vegetarian Fare, Fabulous Buys, Late Supper.

| From the Terrace on Craig Street | **Cafe Azure** 1 |
|---|---|

**Cafe Azure**

*317 S Craig Street, Oakland. Lunch Mon-Thur 11:30-2:30, Fri & Sat til 3. Dinner Mon-Thur 5:30-9:30, Fri & Sat til 11, Late Supper til 12. Reser sugg. AE,DC,MC,V.* **681-3533.**

This sleek cafe with its high terrace overlooking South Craig's university/museum scene is what real dining is all about. There's a wonderful European feel under the low tan awning...a lazy, summer ambience in which you can forget time and place and while away an hour...an afternoon...an evening...with a glass of wine at sunset. At dusk when the candlelight casts shadows on the blue-clothed tables, this is one of the city's most romantic settings. And the cuisine and fluid service play their roles to perfection. The restaurant's interior is also beguiling, classic lines blended in restful shades of beige, soft light filtering through louvered blinds.

**When To Go:** Lunch. Try 1:30-2 after peak hours or a relaxing light dinner at 8 or 9. The terrace is open Mar-Oct in good weather.

**What To Order:** The menu offers American-style French cuisine i.e. Salmon en Papillote (cooked in parchment paper), Duck and Pheasant Ragout in Puff Pastry and gourmet versions of shrimp, chicken, fish, and steak ($16-$24). But there's also a delicious **Grilled Jamaican Spiced Chicken Breast** with black bean/rice timbale ($15) and a **Parmesan Fettucini with Mushrooms, Red Peppers & Artichokes** ($13). If budget allows, add hors d'ouevres or a fine soup ($5-$7.50). Lunch on the terrace is also delightful on a sunny day...and moderate for extraordinary sandwiches i.e. a delicious **Grilled Vegetable Sandwich with eggplant, squash,** peppers and melted mozzarella with pesto ($5.95) and wonderful salads ($4.75-$9.50) including Hearts of Palm, a great **Blackened Chicken Caesar**, **Grilled Shrimp Spinach** and a daily Soup/Salad Special at $7.95. Or you can get a perfect **Croque Madame,** the original fried French bistro sandwich with ham, turkey, Swiss and Dijon mustard. Here wine is a necessity...try a light Zinfandel or dry Chilian Chardonnay $4.50 a glass. The aromas in this restaurant are wonderful...freshly baked French bread...served with little crocks of sweet cream butter...the heady scent of fine coffee. Cappuccino and a delicate sorbet make a fine finale. P.S. Friday/Saturday nights you can catch great jazz, dinner til 11 plus an interesting late menu from $5.50-$7.50.

**Prices:** Lunch $6-$10, Dinner $13-$24.

**What To Wear:** Informal to elegantly casual by day or night.

**Recommended:** French Cuisine, Connoisseur Dining, Night of Romance, Rich Man's Guide, Outdoor Dining, Late Supper, Jazz Rooms.

**Charming Cafe, Creative Cuisine**

## Cafe Sam

*5242 Baum Boulevard, Oakland. Lunch Mon-Fri 11:30-3, Dinner Sun-Tues 5-10, Wed & Thur til 11, Fri & Sat til 12. Reser sugg. AE,MC,V.* **621-2000.**

This little restaurant is still the favorite of Pittsburgh's "smart set" including the city's rich and famous who flock here for gourmet cuisine in a casual setting. The awninged two-story brick house exudes a '30s atmosphere from the cozy bar in the snug foyer... complete with piano...to the glowing inner rooms, softened by flowers and candlelight. In short, a most relaxing atmosphere. Extraordinary offerings by owner/chef Andrew Zins at wonderful prices has insured a long, well-deserved run for Cafe Sam, surely in the city's top five. A blue-awninged rooftop patio adds to the charm.

**When To Go:** Any night for a relaxing experience.

**What To Order:** What a menu! Affordable gourmet is the surprise here. Steak, veal, fish, seafood are in the $12-$18 range with pasta and light entrees from $4.75-$9. This place is a mecca for lovers of inventive, light gourmet. It's a temptation to team one of the smaller orders of pasta i.e. **Angel Hair and Sun Dried Tomatoes** or **Fettucini and Creamed Spinach** alfredo-style (both $4.50) with a fine **Seafood Ceasar Salad** with lobster, snow crab and scallops ($6.75) or the **Hearts of Palm/Avocado Salad** ($4.25)...delightful light eating. Or you can match a classic **French Onion Soup** baked with three cheeses ($3.25) with Steak & Fried Eggs ($8.95) or a delicious **Wood-Grilled Chicken Salad** ($6.50).

Dinners range from $17.95 for Cowboy Cut T-Bone or Double Cut Lamb Chops to fresh fish, seafood and chicken (12-$14). We loved the **Roast Long Island Duck with orange-raspberry sauce** ($13.95) and found the **Wood Grilled Trout** in pecan butter flawless for only $12.95! These wood-grilled items are wonderful...their deep woodsy tastes enhancing the well-turned-out dishes. House favorites are also available at a very affordable lunch.

**This is the kind of restaurant that gourmets—budget or otherwise—would design for themselves**...imaginative cuisine that fits both the pocketbook and the trend to healthier eating without sacrificing taste. You can come back here often not just for special occasions. No wonder so many Pittsburghers have made Cafe Sam's their own.

**Prices:** Lunch $5-$8, Dinner $8-$18.

**What To Wear:** Some come informal, many dress up.

**Recommended:** Continental Cuisine, Connoisseur Dining, Romantic Dining, Vegetarian, Fabulous Buys, Outdoor Dining, Late Supper.

| | |
|---|---|
| **Antiques, Charm In Old N Side Home** | ## Cafe Victoria |

## Cafe Victoria

1

*Torrance House, 946 Western Avenue, North Side. Lunch Tues-Sat 11:30-3, Tea 3-6. Dinner Tues-Sat 6-9. Sunday Brunch 10-3, Tea 3-6. D,MC,V. Reser sugg.* **323-8881.**

This old 1875 home in historic Allegheny West is replete with antiques and turn-of-the century charm. Two floors of quaint Victorian rooms take you back to another era. The house, built by Francis Torrance, "the father of central heating" (founder of American Heating & Plumbing), has been creatively restored by latest owner Joedda Sampson and is filled with Victorian antiques—many of them for sale. Ask for seating in the front parlor, the warmest, most evocative room with a real Victorian feel—a ceiling of Bradbury wallpaper with gold stars, an antique fireplace, huge sideboards and fringed lamps casting romantic shadows for dinner by candlelight. The upstairs 'garret' is a perfect scene for an intimate dinner for two complete with dim red lights and a chaise lounge...a 'courtin' settee.'

There's also a charming, flower-bedecked courtyard winding to the side and back of the house, named the "Angel's Watch" for the famous Tiffany Ascension window in the United Methodist Church across the lane.

This is a must for antique buffs...you can roam through the rooms and, when you're finished, continue browsing amid more curios two doors down at Allegheny City Stalls open Tuesday through Sunday from 10-5.

**When To Go:** Lunch or Tea indoors or on the patio. Romantic candlelight dinner.

**What To Order:** While half of the fun is the atmosphere, the staff is striving for one-of-a-kind, personally prepared dishes—unique soups of the day to homemade desserts. A typical dinner menu features anything from carrot bisque soup to cold mussels & scallops and main dishes of pasta, chicken, steak and seafood. Give yourself lots of time to savour the atmosphere. Some nice touches are the **warm fragrant herb bread** and the **salads with exotic greens...including a good Caesar**...and the fine mussels appetizer. Costs vary from Farfalle Pasta with sun dried tomatoes for $12.95 to **Chicken Stuffed with Blue Cheese, Pear & Brandy Sautee $15.95** and New York Strip with Portabella Mushrooms & Blue Cheese $16.95. All entrees include soup and salad.

**Prices:** Lunch $3.50-$8. Dinner $12.95-$18.95.

**What To Wear:** Modified dress-up.

**Recommended:** American Cuisine, Romantic Dining, Sunday Brunch, Outdoor Dining, Party Rooms.

# Caffe Giovanni

**Stylish Italian Finds S Side Home**

## Caffe Giovanni

*2302 E Carson Street, South Side. Lunch Mon-Sat 11-3, Dinner Mon-Thur 4:30-10, Fri & Sat til 11. Sun 4:30-9. AE,DC,MC,V.* **481-6662.**

This former Shadyide favorite re-emerges in South Side in a more casual, rustic setting. It's new 110-seat, two-story quarters, featuring exposed brick and a Tuscan red & green decor, has a more cozy feel and a more casual atmosphere. But the restaurant's spanking white-tableclothed look and dedication to fine service is still intact. And John Vennare, one of the city's best chefs, is still serving mouth-watering North & South Italian cuisine in his own inimitable style. Now there's piano music with dinner...and watch for an outdoor deck on the second floor.

**When To Go:** Sunny lunch, romantic dinner.

**What To Order:** A menu with many selections makes interesting gastronomic reading, a plethora of painstakingly prepared specialty dishes: 10 appetizers, 2 soups, 4 salads, 16 pastas!, 7 veals, 5 chickens and 7 seafood. You'll be confused but it's sweet confusion. Many of the dishes are recipes from Vennare's family including the house's **"own sweet sausage,"** a good beginning as an appetizer grilled with red & green peppers & served with goat cheese $5.95. But then so are the **Sweet Roasted Peppers** with fontina and olives $5.95. The sausage makes another entrance with **Spaghettini** along with red/green peppers in a good, spicy sauce. But best pasta of all is a divine **Granchio, Spinaci e Pignoli — Angel Hair Pasta with crabmeat, spinach and pine nuts** in a delicate, beautifully blended cream sauce, an inspired dish worth every bite of $16.95. Veal is the test of Italian and Giovanni's is first rate—Romano, in port wine, with roasted peppers...or for a hearty change...with gnocchi in a veal sauce.

The chicken dishes, around $14, are also unusual, particularly the **Breast of Chicken in a creamy Galliano with peaches, grapes and pistachio nuts.** These are real adventures in eating. Affordable lunches...Antipasto with eight selections i.e. artichoke, caponata, olives, sausage, prosciutto & fontina...all for $7.50 guarantee noonday attendance. And for lunch or dinner is the great **Gorgonzola Salad** with crunchy walnuts (a Vennare signature) $4.50. Treat yourself!

**Prices:** Lunch $4.50-$7.95, Dinner $8.25-$20.

**What To Wear:** Dress up to the food, decor.

**Recommended:** Italian Cuisine, Connoisseur Dining, Late Supper.

**Romantic Dining, Heavenly Food**

## Cerulean Bistro

*1227 Monterey Street, North Side. Dinner Tues-Sat 5-11.*
*AE,D,DC,MC,V.* **321-4221**

We fell in love with this little restaurant at first sight...dining romantically by the fireplace. And luckily the food matched the mood. A charming renovation of an old Mexican War Street pub, it's small and intimate with sophisticated ease and an aura all its own—white-clothed, candlelit tables beckoning from the glass front windows, a long cherry-wood bar, deep cerulean, sky blue touches, some very private high-backed wooden booths...friendly service and warmth... an A-plus for atmosphere. This is the kind of restaurant that defines what the "Rich/Poor Man's" dining experience is all about...affordable cuisine in a charming atmosphere.

**When To Go:** Dinner or pre/post theatre.

**What To Order:** Creative chef Robert Johnston (Westin William Penn/ Nemacolin Inn) has some delicious offerings starting with unusual appetizers, soups, salads ($3.95-$10)...Chicken Sausage with sauteed peppers, licorice-laced Shrimp Sambuca, Sweet-Spicy Swordfish, a great house salad and delicious mushroom soup. They herald a menu with cuisine for all tastes and pocketbooks from Pasta Primavera at $6.95 to Venison Chops at $24.95. There's **Salmon Strudel in Philo Dough and a wonderful Almond Crusted Red Snapper in Frangelica Cream** ($16-$17) and some terrific offerings for $12-$13 i.e. **Roasted Cornish Hen** with Honey Fig Sauce, **Cippino Fish Stew** with rosemary & fennel and **Catfish with Black Bean Salsa.**

For a late night repast we recommend the wonderful **Creme de Champignon Soup—delicious wild mushrooms floating in a hearty cream base under a delicate pastry crust** ($4.25) with a fabulous **House Salad, a 'wild' taste sensation** (also $4.25) a beautiful medley of exotic greens studded with raisins in raspberry champagne vinegar...or a piquant lemon-honey dressing. You can mushroom all the way with Portabella Salad on mesculin greens with balsamic sweet pepper dressing ($5.95).

Or you can mix and match the above with any entree...you can't go wrong with the deft use of herbs and seasonings here. Two other favorites are the **Sesame Seared Salmon** with grilled radicchio, Belgium endive and plum tomatoes or the **Braised Veal Shank**, both $14.95. Desserts, as you can imagine, are also heavenly.

**Prices:** Entrees $6.95-$25.

**What To Wear:** Fit the mood...your romantic mode.

**Recommended:** Continental/American, Romantic Dining, Late Supper.

# Christopher's

## Christopher's

*1411 Grandview Avenue, Mt Washington. Mon-Thur 5-10, Fri & Sat til 11. Valet parking. Reser. AE,D,DC,MC,V.* **381-4500.**
Get out your imaginary top hat, white tie and tails and get set for a marvelous evening at this spectacular restaurant 1000 feet above the city. Your excitement begins with fabulous views of the city on your ride to Mt Washington via the Duquesne Incline or up McArdle Roadway. As the top of Grandview comes into view at twilight you can see the sparkling lights of this tall, glass-walled restaurant against the sky. The thrill continues with your ride in the glass elevator up ten flights to the roof top. Neither the view nor the restaurant will disappoint you.

Steel, glass, aluminum, coal—Pittsburgh trademarks—have been used in a dramatically lit, multi-level room with the glamour of a 30's Hollywood musical set. **The glass walls, tallest in the country, afford elegantly framed views of Pittsburgh at its best**—by night—and despite the ultra-sophisticated setting, a smooth unobtrusive staff will make you feel at home. This is the place to show visitors "New Pittsburgh." Explore city views from various levels, checking out the Pittsburgh artifacts mini-museum at the entrance, the 20-ton, 60-ft wall of coal in the dining room and the Sports Hall of Fame in the back lounge...a wonderful place to sit and enjoy the city after dark.

**When To Go:** Any night for an elegant outing, by dusk or dark.

**What To Order:** The menu's also 'top flight' and expensive, but with the help of the house we've worked out an affordable fling. Entrees can go as high as $35 but there are many choices in the $17-$22 range—**Chicken Solaro**—braised in Parmagiana/reggiano crumbs and Galliano liqueur ($17), **Pork Tenderloin** with green peppercorn sauce ($19), delicious pastas ($16-$18) i.e. **Linguini with Shrimp, Garlic and Sun-Dried Tomatoes**...all served with salad, vegetable and potato/rice. An adventuresome alternative is a unique dinner of house specialties. Begin with the delicious **Onion Soup** $4.50. Then share a marvelous **Greek Salad** ($4-$5)...and for an entree, the tasty **Snow Crab Cake with sun-dried tomato** ($8.95). With wine at $4.25 a glass, you can keep dinner for two at $50. Add a wonderful dessert—**Cherries Jubilee,** $12 for 2 or splurge on affordable Roget's Champagne ($17) to celebrate your night at the top.

**Prices:** Dinner $16-$35.

**What To Wear:** Be a superstar...shiny or subdued...match the setting.

**Recommended:** Continental Cuisine, Connoisseur Dining, Night of Romance, City Views, Rich Man's Guide, Pgh After Dark.

| Sizzling 'Short-Order' At Pgh Bar | **Clark Bar & Grill** | 1 |
|---|---|---|

*503 Martindale St, N Shore, across from Three Rivers Stadium Gate B. Mon-Fri 11-2am, Sat 12-2am. Sun Stadium events. Lots of free parking except game days. AE,CB,DC,MC,V. 231-5720.* ♿

We rarely enthuse about short order cooking...but the fare at this popular sports bar in the historic Clark Building is so super its story deserves to be told. This is a real slice of Pittsburgh...and a fan-a-mania scene...a throw away from the Stadium. It even has a mini sports museum. After games it's loud and jammed...though the crowd's convivial. (Excess celebrators are siphoned off to Zagnut's, a big backroom sports bar). The good-looking room has a long bar, warm wood, old-fashioned booths and a nostalgic black & white checked tile floor. A sports haunt and after-game favorite, Clark's has been discovered by theatre-goers too. The atmosphere's also great here late of an afternoon when business lunchers leave and you can enjoy the food and surroundings in quiet.

**When To Go:** Pre/Post Game/Theatre.

**What To Order:** This is short order at its best...from the tantalizing barbecue sauce to the big, delicious Clark Bar desserts. This is a mean menu! We loved the sauce on the ribs and chicken, $9.95 for a 1/2 rack or 1/2 chicken, $14 full rack, $15 combo ribs & chicken and $19.95 for a boomer rack...to share of course! They're delicious with cole slaw—as it's meant to be—and the house's spicy, shredded fries...we always say we won't eat 'em but we do. There's pasta from $9-$12 and, at the high end, steaks from $17-$20.

But the best bet are the **Barbecued Ribs and Chicken** and terrific sandwiches ($5-$6) with slaw, homemade chips, lettuce, tomato...a neat lunch or supper. There's a good Reuben and big burgers—try the **Southwest**...jack cheese & jalepeno peppers. Our two favorites are the **Grilled Chicken Sandwich** with Swiss cheese & bacon (or if you ask for it, with **Barbecue Sauce**...wonderful!) and the **Turkey Texas**...bacon & Swiss on thick buttered Texas toast. **Sometimes you just feel like a sandwich!** This is unforgettable barroom food.

The desserts are also awesome...particularly the **Clark Bar Dessert**...peanut butter cookie crust, chocolate mousse, crumbled Clark Bars, whipped cream, chocolate sauce! Beautiful.

**Prices:** $5-$20, most under $10.

**What To Wear:** Who cares!

**Recommended:** American Cuisine, Fabulous Buys, Late Supper.

## Craig Street Shops

**Craig Street Walk & Shop**

### Craig Street Shops

*South Craig between Forbes & Fifth. Hours: Mon-Sat 10- 5:30. Some shops open Thur til 8. Parking in lot behind Gallery Shops off Winthrop or in the Carnegie Museum lot.* [&]

This street of shops, in the heart of Oakland's museum-university complex, packs a lot of charm into a small, walkable area. Houses in the short blocks up from Carnegie Museum have been remodeled into galleries, boutiques, import shops...with intriguing new restaurants and sidewalk cafes adding a European air. The area sparkles at holiday time, the trees lining the street a glittering fairyland of lights. Our shopping tour begins at the **Museum Art Shop** in the Scaife Gallery with its beautiful gifts and objects d'art and fascinating children's gifts in a second shop in the Natural History Museum. Browsing continues up Craig at **Arabica Coffee, Calaban Book Shop** for rare books and **Classic Video** for a steller film collection. The building across the street with the delightful giant pencil (by Lubutz Architects) is Top Notch Art Supplies and farther up is the studio of famous Pittsburgh sculptor **Virgil Cantini.**

In the next block there's unusual browsing at **Macondo**— clothing, jewelry, folk art from around the world. Then on to the Gallery Shops...fine, one-of-a-kind ceramics and jewelry by top US artisans in **Made By Hand**, lovely woolens and wares of the **Irish Design Center,** unusual jewelry & clothes at **Casablanca** and the **Sunshine Boutique** next door in Craig Square Shops. Also in the Shops are cards and stationery at **Papyrus** and the unique gifts of **Watermelon Blues**.

Here you can stop for a relaxing break at **Kane's Courtyard** ...pastries & sandwiches in the bricked outdoor patio or in the indoor solarium. Or try a delicious sticky bun, ice cream or coffee from **Bunznudders.** Don't miss the small shops around the corner...**Bryn Mawr-Vassar** used book store on Winthrop and 20,000 volumes at **Townsend Antiquarian Booksellers** on Henry Street...favorite haunts of book lovers. Across the street is **Phantom of the Attic**, head-quarters for the city's comic book collectors.

**When To Go:** Wonderful walk for a Saturday or off-day afternoon. A fairy-tale street during holiday light-up.

**What To Wear:** Your leisure best.

**Where To Eat:** **Ali Baba**, *404 S Craig. Lunch: Mon-Fri 11:30-2:30, Dinner 7 days 4-10. Bring your own wine. AE,MC,V.* **682-2829.** Popular Mid-East fare, pleasant surroundings. Great a la carte items—falafil, tabooli, hummus, baba ghanooj, spinach pie, Greek Salad, baklava, Arabic coffee $2-$4.50.

# Craig Street Shops

Dinners—shish kebab, lamb shank, couscous & more, $5.75-$l0. Best buy.

**Arabica** *420 S Craig. Sun-Thur 7-12, Fri-Sat til 1.* **621-2233**. Popular sidewalk coffee house with exotic coffees, desserts, urban conversation; veggie salads. Inexp.

**Bunznudders,** *305 S Craig. Mon-Thur 7:30-10, Fri-Sat til 11. Sun 9-8.* **683-9993.**An extraordinary bakery/ice creamery with hot-from-the-oven cinnamon buns, yogurt, muffins, meat/veggie croissants, pink lemonade, outside tables. A real treat $1-$3.50.

**Cafe Azure**, *317 S Craig. Lunch Mon-Thur 11:30-2:30, Fri-Sat til 3. Dinner Mon-Thur 5:30-9:30, Fri-Sat til 11. Jazz/Light Fare 10:30-12. AE,D,DC,MC,V.* **681-3533.** Lovely terrace dining with towering Cathedral of Learning in the distance. Beautifully served French provencial, croissant sandwiches, quiche, desserts. $6-$20. (See Review)

**Duranti's**, *Park Plaza, 128 N Craig St. 7 days 11-8. Sun Brunch 11-2. AE,D,MC,V.* **682-1155.** Up Craig just across Fifth Avenue; no surprises but great traditional American food for good prices in spacious, pleasant surroundings. $6.95 Early Birds. $4-$16.

**Kane's Courtyard,** *Gallery Shops, 303 S Craig Street. Mon-Fri 7-5:30, Sat 10-5:30.* **683-9988.** Great sandwiches, salads, soups at little tables in the court-yard or inside in the 'greenhouse,' $2-$5. Take-out.

**Museum Cafe,** *Carnegie Museum, Forbes & Craig. Lunch Tues- Fri 11:30-2 (also Sat Oct-Apr). Sun Brunch 12-2. AE,MC,V.* **622- 3225.** Beautiful luncheon view of the fountain from glass-walled cafe. Nice sandwiches, salads, soups in $6-$8 range. Great Sun Brunch. (See Review)

**Star of India,** *412 S Craig. Lunch Mon-Sat 11:30-2:30, Dinner Sun-Thur 5-10, Fri-Sat til 10:30. No liquor.* AE,MC,V. **681-5700.** The pungent tang of curry wafts up the avenue from this eatery with Indian delicacies, delicious breads, tandoori, BBQ chicken, vegetarian delights. $8-$15. (See Review)

**Union Grill** *413 S Craig. Mon-Thur 11-11, Fri & Sat til 12. AE,D,DC,MC,V.* **681-8620.** Polished oakwood room with big portions of hearty food—grills, ribs, chicken, steaks, burgers, salads, dinners. $5-$14. (See Review)

**YumWok,** *400 S Craig. Mon-Sat 11-8.* **387-7777.** Unique Chinese cafeteria in pleasant setting–the real thing for good prices $3-$6.75. Dinner specials $3.55.

### Cozumel/Southwest Bistro

**Lively Mexican Food, Dancing**

### Cozumel

*5507 Walnut Street, Shadyside. Mon-Fri 11-2:30, 5-10, Sat 12-10. Sun 12-9. AE,D,DC,MC,V.* **621-5100.**
Two new restaurants have been launched by Bikki Kochhar, energetic creator of a slew of local favorites including the ever-popular Simply French. Cozumel is in a big, good-looking second-floor room (former site of Simply French which is scheduled to reopen in the North Hills). It has adapted well to the city's current interest in Latin food and music, providing a wonderful setting for Saturday night dancing to the sounds of the popular salsa dance band Guaracha. The deft dancers provide a wonderful floor show.

**What To Order:**

By day lunchers are drawn to the good prices on tasty Mexican dishes—fajitas, burritos, enchiladas, quesadillas, tacos from $4.50-$9.50. House specialties are the **Shrimp Fajitas** ($10.25) and **Tacos de Carne Azada**—grilled rib-eye tacos with fried beans and tomatillo sauce ($8.75). Economical quick lunches packing 'em in are **Huevos Rancheros**, ranch-style eggs with rice, fried beans and corn tortilla ($5) and **Speedy Gonzales**—a taco, an enchalada with rice/beans for $4.45.

**Southwest Spices Up New Cuisine**

### Southwest Bistro

*129 Sixth Ave, Downtown. Lunch Mon-Fri 11-2:30, Dinner Mon-Sat 4:30-11. Some Sun shows. AE,D,DC,MC,V.* **261-8866.**
Another handsome site is luring downtown lunchers/theatre-goers with a refreshingly different venue—contemporary Southwest cuisine. The restaurant has a pleasant, clean-lined decor with a Western motif.

**What To Order:**

This is interesting food with Mexican, Spanish and Native American influences in dishes of varying heat. Pittsburghers aren't used to this cuisine and, the house reports, start out conservatively getting bolder as they appreciate the range of tastes...grilled and roasted beef, chicken, fish with SW spices. Dinner entrees ($6.95-$15) include, on the milder side, **Smoked Roasted Chicken** with black beans and **Braised Lamb** with rosemary black bean sauce, both $9.95. Getting hotter are delicious **Roast Pork with Sweet Red Peppers**, chili & carmelized onions and **Red Pepper Pasta** with portabella mushroom & smoked tomatoes in cilantro. There's also **Blackened Fish** and **Grilled Garlic Prawns.** Smaller luncheon versions are available for $6-$7 along with a zesty chimichanga, BBQ Ribs, sandwiches, salads ($4-$8). This is a unique alternative for downtown dining.

**Unforgettable
4-Star Dining**

### D'Imperio's

*3412 William Penn Highway, Wilkins Twp. Lunch Mon-Fri
11:30-3, Dinner 7 days 5-11. Lounge til 2. Reser sugg.
AE,CB,D,DC,MC,V.* **823-4800.** [♿]

When your palate craves the very best...that memorable
meal that makes dining a joy...hie on out to D'Imperio's
(Monroeville Exit 14 off Parkway East, one mile on the right)
for some of **the very best cuisine in the Pittsburgh and
the W Pa area.** This rare restaurant with its three beautiful
dining rooms has more than great food. The definition of a
truly elegant restaurant is that it makes the diner feel comfortable. And that's the secret of D'Imperio's. Dining is raised
to an art in this gracious old-world atmosphere...beautiful
table settings, shining silver and a peerless staff all orches-
trated by owner Tony D'Imperio who personally sees to the
comfort of his guests. You'll love the warmth here. After
dinner you can linger for music and dancing in Joe's Jazz
Lounge.

**When To Go:** Romantic dinner, night on the town.

**What To Order:** The menu is laden with unforgettable dishes...tastes that
can spoil you. All of the N Italian classics are superbly
done—succulent osso buco, veal scaloppine, lamb, steak,
lobster, fish flown in daily, plus perfecto pastas...ravioli with
fresh tomato basil, pasta ribbons in light cream tomato,
spaghettini with pignoli and basil. And the wines—superb!
For lunch we love to pair a pasta with the house's **great**
Antipasto, an exquisite medley of marinated mushrooms,
pungent caponata (cold eggplant salad), tarragon shrimp,
tart sweet peppers and salmon mousse...each distinct taste
blending into a wondrous whole. It's divine with the **brus-
chetta—heavenly garlic cheese bread**...a glass of wine...
and thou. (And maybe the addition of the fabulous **Ciop-
pino**—Italian fish soup!) There are also lunch specials with
entree, appetizer and dessert at $11.50.
Our dinner favorite is the zesty **Penne Gorgonzola** ($14.95)
or the tender **Veal Scaloppine** $16.95. Daily specials—
salmon, swordfish, beef Wellington with soup, salad and
vegetable are a bargain $19.95.
The dessert cart, needless to say, is irresistible...especially
**Tiramisu,** a light froth of espresso, cognac and mascarpone
cheese. If you're serious about food don't miss D'Imperio's.

**Prices:** Lunch $6.95-$11.50, Dinner $14.95-$32.50...most within
$17-$20 range...more with wine but worth it.

**What To Wear:** The food deserves your best—business or pleasure.

**Recommended:** Continental Cuisine, Connoisseur Dining, Rich Man's
Dining, Jazz Rooms.

## Davio's

**Divine Dinner
By David**

### Davio's

*2100 Broadway Ave, Beechview. (Up W Liberty, rt onto Pauline,
left to Broadway. Lunch Mon-Fri 12-3, Dinner Mon-Sat 4-11.
Sun 4-9.* **No credit cards. No liquor.** *Reser.* **531-7422.** ♿
Pittsburgh's roving Chef David Ayn, our candidate for the
city's best, has found a home in Beechview after years of
culinary grazing. He has left trails of devoted fans...remem-
ber The Fallen Angel, La Tache, more recently La Piccola
Casa in Oakland. Now he's happily ensconsed in the kitchen
of his own little restaurant, seven tables in a very cozy room
...a sunny Italian trattoria with green wine glasses, peasant
bread on the sideboard...simple and delightful. And the food
ah...not so simple and truly delightful! In summer there are
tables outside and next door David has opened Palio's, a
rustic bar/restaurant with Tuscan dishes, roasts, pizza.

**When To Go:**  Connoisseur dinner, sunny lunch.

**What To Order:**  Ayn, who loves to cook, has a wonderful time with food. He
draws on a wealth of experience and seemingly endless
creativity. He's in his element here with lusty peasant food
a la Roma. Savour the best you can afford. Dinner begins
appropriately with bread and wine (be sure to bring your
own wine). Ayn, known for his delectable breads, has rolled
them into one **long savory Italian breadstick** (& big Tuscan loaves)...delicious dipped in his fagiolini white bean/
garlic spread...or into basil olive oil & grated parmigiano/
reggiano. Then comes the **salad...superb with big plops
of roasted peppers, cannellini beans, artichokes in a
perfect balsamic vinegar**...what herbs!...topped with tangy
gorgonzola....the best we've ever tasted! Then in big bowls
comes the pasta...delicious...you're  almost sated...save
room for your entree! The menu highlights gourmet dishes
'from the maestro's hand'—Veal Chops, Lobster Linguine
($25-$29). But there's a big selection of seafood, fish, veal,
chicken, pasta from $9.95 to $18 including Eggplant Parmigiana ($9.95) and Sausage with Peppers ($12.95).
Lunch is a wonderful bargain at $5-$10, the same bread,
salad and entrees like **Italian Egg Drop Soup** with chicken
$4.95, **Polenta with beans, escarole, hot sausage and
peppers,** $7.95. Save room for the chef's homemade des-
serts...warm, fresh Raspberry Pie...Russian Sable Truffle
Cake! For gourmets this is a real night of romance..a love
affair with some of the best food in the city.

**Prices:**  Lunch $5.95-$11, Dinner $9.95-$28.95.

**What To Wear:**  Casual, comfortable or dress-up.

**Recommended:**  Italian Cuisine, Connoisseur Dining, Night of Romance, Rich
Man's Guide, Executive Dining.

| Big, Beautiful Eating/Meeting Place | **Dingbat's City Tavern** |
|---|---|

**1**

*Lower Plaza, Oxford Centre, Downtown. Mon-Thur 11-11, Fri & Sat til 12. Bar til 2 Fri & Sat. Parking in Oxford Centre garage. AE,D,DC,MC,V.* **392-0350.** [♿]

This handsome restaurant, the hub of the Grant Street business crowd, is a spacious, friendly place. Designed for socializing, it's centered around a big brass and marble bar. Borrowing elements from the Frank Lloyd Wright prairie school of architecture, it has a brass, burnished look with mosaic tile floor, dark wood, deep green fabrics and beautiful stoneware table settings. There's also a sunken patio with umbrellaed tables where in fine weather you can enjoy the terraced greenery off Grant—one of the loveliest outdoor dining experiences in the city.

You can also order from a lobby take-out window and eat at tables with a wonderful view of the glass-roofed Oxford Atrium. This is a bright place to be when you feel like being part of the crowd.

**When To Go:** Lunch, Dinner, Before/After theatre. Join the five o'clock cocktail rush.

**What To Order:** There's a tantalizing menu, the same day/night with lots of entrees and a la carte specialties til the wee hours of the morning. It includes some unique, big salads from $3-$7, ribs, barbeque, chicken and char-broiled seafood/steak. There's a tempting array of sandwiches including **The Waterworks**—grilled turkey breast, melted Swiss, bacon, lettuce & tomato on grilled Italian bun ($5.95). Quiche, omelettes, all kinds of pizza, pastas and specialty drinks to suit your fancy round out a varied menu that has made Dingbat's a happy name in Pittsburgh. (The restaurant also participates in the Dining with Heart 400 Club.)

A good dinner choice is the **Angel Hair Pasta with Roast Chicken** in tomato sauce with Italian sausage, mushrooms and peppers ($7.95). Salad with pasta is only $1.50 extra. Or try the **Filet Steak Sandwich** with mushrooms, onions & provolone on a kaiser roll ($6.95) or the **Chicken Quesadilla**, a tortilla with grilled chicken, cheeses, guacamole & sour cream ($5.95). The speciality of the house is a **Giant Onion Ring Loaf**, $2.95 a half.

Don't resist temptation, succumb to the **Oreo Blackout Cake**, $2.95, or the delicious **Mud Pie**—coffee ice cream, almonds and chocolate topped with hot fudge $2.95.

**Prices:** Lunch/Dinner $5.75-$14.

**What To Wear:** Downtown casual. You'll see and be seen.

**Recommended:** American Cuisine, Outdoor Dining, Late Supper.

### Frick Cafe/La Feria

**Elegant Cafe In the Park**

### Frick Cafe

*Frick Art & Historical Center, 7227 Reynolds St, Point Breeze. Tues-Sat 11-5:30, Sun 12-3pm. AE,MC,V.* **371-0600.**
There's some lovely, esoteric food at this beautiful little cafe on the Frick grounds midway between the Art Museum and Clayton. You can lose yourself in the charming, glassed-in pavilion with a garden view of the 'park' and an awninged patio. Worth the visit alone is the cuisine of Chef Susie Treon (formerly of Laforet). Light and elegant, it features fresh ingredients with a California touch—delicate salads, gourmet sandwiches, delicious desserts. Noteworthy are a **Green Salad with Sun-Dried Tomatoes**, goat cheese, toasted walnuts & balsamic vinegar and a **Salad Nicoise** with potatoes, tomatoes and beans, both $7.95. Gourmet sandwiches ($5.95-$7.95) include Grilled Chicken with roasted peppers on focaccia, **Fontina with Mushrooms & Dijon mustard** on sourdough & **Smoked Salmon with herbed cream cheese** on walnut wheat bread plus muffins, Irish soda bread, cheese and fresh fruit plates. There's a scrumptious 2-5:30 tea with sandwiches, scones and English cream and jam and a special Sunday lunch. The desserts...including fabulous creme brulee...are wonderful! This is a real Sunday kind of place for any day of the week for lunch or afternoon tea..

**Peruvian Find In Upper Room**

### La Feria

*5527 Walnut, Shadyside. Mon-Sat 10-9, Sun Cappucino Bar 9-2. D,MC,V.* **682-4501.**
This little restaurant looks like no more than a pleasant lunchroom in the midst of colorful Latin wares above Pamela's restaurant. But ah the food soon dispels that impression. The creation of Drew & Pam of Pamela's and Louisa (from Peru) it's serving extraordinary cuisine with intriguing spices from Peru and South America. It's a small but potent menu with daily meat/vegetarian specials for $9.99 served with rice, two empanadas (filled turnovers) and sweet potato chips. There's delicious **Peruvian Quinua,** a couscous-like grain served over salad with a sweet vinegar dressing; **Escabeche de Pollo**, sauteed chicken breast marinated in spicy vinaigrette, a wonderful **Black Bean Salad** on a bed of spinach; and unusual sandwiches i.e. spicy "Ropa Vieja" (Shredded Beef Sandwich) and homemade soups including a **smoothly spiced pumpkin soup.** Authentic Peruvian desserts—Alsajores (caramel cookies) are served from time to time. And the prices are right...under $10. Discover it now before crowds beat their way to the door.

# Froggy's

**1**

**Spiffy Downtown 'Hangout'**

## Froggy's

*100 Market St at 1st Ave (across Blvd of Allies), Downtown. Mon-Thur 11:30-12, Fri & Sat til 1. Bar til 2. Sun—Steeler home games. Reser sugg. AE,DC,MC,V.* **471-FROG (3764).**

A popular downtown meeting place, Froggy's, from its spiffy brown coronet awnings to the last detail of service, is a setting in which to lose yourself and your troubles in an aura of bygone days. Enter by the Market Street door with its green, glass frogs above, into an F. Scott Fitzgerald barroom with a long oak bar, overhead fans and an open brick grill. Then on to the adjoining dining room with its round oak tables, claw-foot chairs, Casablanca fans and hanging plants. Beautiful reproductions of barroom mirrors interlaced with local sports photos cover the walls. Upstairs there's a **romantic third floor roof patio** for cooling drinks in summer under Cinzano-umbrellaed tables. This restaurant is a feast for the senses even before you taste a bite.

Originally the site of one of the city's oldest taverns, the renovated warehouse is the creation of Steve 'Froggy' Morris of Zelda's Greenhouse fame. His dream was to create "a palace of fun and food to pleasure nifty people from all over...with a decor so splendiferous it would knock your eye out." And Froggy's does just that.

**When To Go:** Lunch after 1. Better get reservations. Late supper after 8. Jazz pianist Tues-Thur & Sat.

**What To Order:** The short, sweet Steaks & Chops menu is available all day from $5.95 to $20 for filet mignon. And there's an excellent a la carte menu, specials and burgers from $5.25 to $12. For a budget meal we suggest the **Bullfrog Burger** $6, or the **Chef's Grumpy Duffy Salad**—a crisp, sharp, vinegary, antipasto-like salad with ham, cheese, peppers, olives, red cabbage, a good house dressing—**and onions** if you ask for them—$6.50. Either item comes in around $13 for 2. Good alternatives are the Cajun Chicken ($9.95) and the popular **Steak Salad** ($7.95).

A favorite haunt of the city's fourth estate, Froggy's drinkers mean business and these are the biggest drinks in town from the long bar—4-oz liquor for $4, a 12-oz wine for $3.75 and beer $2.25 & up.

**Prices:** Lunch/Dinner $5.95-$24.

**What To Wear:** Keep up the Fitzgerald illusion. Match the beautiful setting with sweaters, tweeds or after-theatre weeds.

**Recommended:** American Cuisine, Steak, Late Supper.

**Sumptuous Shops Real Delight**

## Galleria

*1500 Washington Road at Gilkeson, Mt. Lebanon. Shops Mon-Sat 10-9:30. Sun 12-5. Restaurants, cinemas later.* **561-4000.**  This sumptuous shopping center lifts your spirits with its beautiful Mediterranean design. Patterned after a 19th Cent Milan market-place, it's centered around a soaring 50-ft clock tower in a five-story atrium housing 58 specialty shops, five restaurants and six cinemas. The pale salmon walls, terra-cotta touches, teal green tile and shining marble floors make a beautiful background for some first-class shopping. It's a browser's feast for the eyes! The best architectural view of the atrium is from the balcony for a close-up of the tower, the tall palm trees, brass lion-head railings and the gleaming first level below. The subdued richness could teach Trump Tower a thing or two about upscale design.

Many come just to enjoy the beautiful high-fashion stores...these windows are gorgeous...**Harve Bernard, Polo/Ralph Lauren, Venetia, AnnTaylor, Cache, Mondi** and the exquisite creations of **Lillie Rubin** and **Laurel**. Many other shops are also quite affordable...The Gap/Gap Kids/Baby Gap, Talbot's and Talbot's Kids, Larrimor's, Pendleton Wools, Sachet Clothing, Ann Chapman, **Sincerely Yours** cards & **Christmas Store.** It's a pleasure to come just for a movie and a delicious, fresh-baked bun at **Cinnamon Jim's** on the balcony level...you'll find your way by the wonderful aroma...or at La Prima Espresso for coffee & desserts.

**Where To Eat:**

**Armstrong's** *Upper Level. Mon-Sat 11-11. Sun 12-8. No credit cards.* **341-9460.** Soups, salads, sandwiches, hoagies, plus entrees, pastas at very economical prices; patio dining. $4.25-$9.

**Augie's American Bistro**, *Balcony. Mon-Thur 11-10, Fri-Sat til 11. Sun 11-9.* AE,CB,D,DC,MC,V. **571-1157.** Euro-Amer pasta, pizza, light food; outdoor deck dining with greenery. $5-$14.

**Hotlicks** *2nd level. Mon-Thur 11:30-10, Fri-Sat til 12. Sun 12-10.* AE,DC,MC,V. **341-7427.** A Pgh original for mesquite ribs, chicken, burgers, vegetarian fare; patio. $3.75-$10. Kids 83c on Sun.

**Mark Pi's China Gate** *2nd level. Mon-Thur 11:30-10, Fri-Sat til 11. Sun 12-9.* AE,MC,V. **341-9582.** Exquisite decor, Szechuan, Hunan, Mandarin specialties. $4-$13.

**Ruby Tuesday** *1st level. Mon-Thur 11-10, Fri-Sat til 12.* AE,D,DC,MC,V. **343-6855.** Casual dining, diverse menu, children's menu. Mod.

**Happiest Hour, Best Bargain In Town**

## Gandy Dancer

1

*Station Sq Carson at Smithfield St. Bridge. Mon-Thur 11:30-1am, Fri & Sat til 2. Sun 2:30-10. AE,D,DC,MC,V.* **261-1717.** ⟨&⟩ Celebrities, office workers, Pittsburghers of all ages and backgrounds gravitate to this lively saloon off the elegant Grand Concourse restaurant. Site of the former baggage room of the restored P&LE Station, it gets its name from the itinerant railroad workers "gandy dancers" named for a legendary Irish boss "Gandy." And some of the old railroad spirit lives again in this bustling bar with wonderful food, fun and camaraderie. You can sit at the Oyster Bar for quick service, enjoy a booth in the back for less lively moments or join in the happy crowd at the piano from 4:30-1am Mon-Sat.

**When To Go:** Happy Hour Monday thru Friday 4:30-6:30. In addition to music there are free hors d'oeuvres.

**What To Order:** Prices are always right for delicious seafood, pasta, sandwiches, soups, finger foods. Everything's good and there are bargains galore...famous **Charley's Chowder** $3 a tub, $2.25 a bowl—a meal in itself with the house's deliciously-flavoured **pizza bread**, some of the best in town. From the steamer there's peel 'n eat shrimp, smoked salmon, oysters, mussels, clams ($5-$7.50), Seafood Panroasts (shrimp, oysters, scallops simmered in cream sauce), delicious **Seafood Provencales** on rice pilaf in tomato wine sauce ($7.50-$9) and new grills i.e. **Raspberry Chicken** ($10.50) to **Texas Barbeque Shrimp** ($13.75). Zingy appetizers include popcorn shrimp and Armadillo Eggs of cheese & jalapeno peppers. But the appetizing pastas ($7-$11) continue as house favorites, especially the **Linguine with Red/White Clam Sauce**.

Traditionally there are even bigger bargains through the week, $2 off regular prices for seafood specials: **Mondays—Mussels for $3.75, Wednesdays—Peel 'n Eat Shrimp for $5.25, Thursdays—Oysters & Clams on the Half Shell $4.50-$5.50 and Fridays—Big Fish Sandwich for $3.50.** Even without the specials you can eat here easily under $10. Given the quality of food it's no wonder this place is always humming.

While you're at the Square explore the big Bessemer converter and antique railrway cars in Museum Court...and check out the new outdoor **Garden Cafe** with Euro ethnic food outside the Dancer. This is a special Pittsburgh place.

**Prices:** Same all day menu $3.50-$14.50.

**What To Wear:** You'll see everything from jeans to button down suits.

**Recommended:** American Cuisine, Seafood, Fabulous Buys, Happy Hour, Late Supper, Pgh After Dark.

## Grand Concourse

**Elegant Early Bird At Pgh Showcase**

### Grand Concourse

*One Station Square, Carson Street at Smithfield Street Bridge. Lunch Mon-Fri 11:30-2:30. Dinner Mon-Thur 4:30-10, Fri & Sat til 11. Sun Brunch 10-2:30, Dinner 4:30-9. Parking—East Lot off Carson. Reser. AE,D,DC,MC,V. 261-1717.* 🚹

This Pittsburgh showcase is one of the most beautiful restaurants in the city...and the U.S. The splendidly restored old P&LE railroad station with its soaring stained glass ceiling and grand marble staircase has been transformed into a wide, palm-treed dining room with the elegant feel of a Grand Hotel. This is a marvelous setting for a special occasion or celebration. And if you're in a romantic mood, it's worth the wait for a seat in the River Room to watch the lights of the city reflected in the water at dusk. Nightly piano music by local favorite Reid Jaynes helps sustain the mood. And in an era of rising costs, the Concourse still offers the grandest early dinner of them all, **a veritable phoenix among early birds,** Mon thru Sat 4:30-6 and Sun 4:30-9.

**When To Go:** Take advantage of early prices. Seating before 5:45.

**What To Order:** Early dinner here includes a choice of 13 elegant entrees from $9.95-$16. For fish lovers there's Rainbow Trout, Boston Cod, Nantucket Bluefish, Flounder, Poached Salmon, Shrimp/Artichoke Pasta, and Garlic Shrimp. Other entrees include Veal Piccata, Grilled Ribeye Steak, Braised Lamb Shank, Shrimp Artichoke Pasta, Pork Tenderloin, Raspberry Chicken, Linguini Primavera, Petite Filet Mignon. Who could ask for anything more? Dinners come with appetizer, salad or soup, vegetable or starch, plus dessert and beverage. First timers—don't miss **Charley's Chowder, an unforgettable fish soup par excellence.** House wine, still an economical $2.50, brings your dinner to around $30 for 2...**making this fabulous restaurant accessible to more and more Pittsburgh families and visitors.** Regular dinners are relatively moderate for a plethora of fresh fish, meat, seafood and pasta made on the premises, from $13-$25. There are also luscious desserts i.e. **Peppered Strawberries** with Grand Marnier, Pernod and Cream $6.50 or you can share a **Dessert Assortment** of house favorites including Chocolate Silk Torte and Key Lime Pie for $7.75. Another delightful addition is the **Children's Menu** for 12 and under—burgers, chicken, grilled cheese with chips, fries and beverage $2-$3.25, a boon for family diners.

**Prices:** Lunch $7-$14, Dinner $13-$25—Early Birds $9.95-$16.

**What To Wear:** Your very best to match the elegant atmosphere.

**Recommended:** American Cuisine, Seafood, Connoisseur Dining, Night of Romance, City Views, Fabulous Buys, Brunch, Party Rooms.

**Big, Brassy & Beautiful**

## Houlihan's Old Place

1

*Freight House, Shops at Station Square. Sun-Thur 11-11, Fri-Sat til 12:30am, lounge til 2. AE,D,MC,V.* **232-0302.**
Big, bold, brassy and beautiful describes Houlihan's, the hub of Station Square. This lush restaurant-bar with a glorified pub atmosphere has a plethora of paraphernalia from the past—mostly from England—a cheery bar with a big brass espresso machine, lots of wood and front tables with a foggy view through frosted antique glass...a London-like illusion. There are comfortable, colorful dining rooms and a small DJ dance floor that comes alive at 8.
One of Gilbert/Robinson's charming chain—"convivial food and the largest collection of pub mirrors in the world"—this place can adapt itself to everything from a snack to a full-fledged affordable fling.

**When To Go:** Leisurely lunch around 2. Dinner, Late Supper.

**What To Order:** Just reading the menu here is an appetizing pastime. You can opt for a traditional dinner ($9-$13) but the excitement's in a la carte appetizers, snacks, new light low-cal dishes, hot new salads and delicious Cajun & Mexican items...all well below the $10 mark. Some of the best are the spicy **Buffalo Chicken Wings,** the Cajun Shrimp Dinner, Soup 'n Pasta Salad and Shrimp Linguine.
We especially enjoyed the award-winning **Fajitas** (fa-hee-tas), tortillas you fill yourself with char-grilled beef or chicken in a sizzling skillet with bell peppers, guacamole, cheese, sour cream ($10) and the **Appetizer Sampler**—your choice from six appetizers i.e. buffalo wings, zucchini sticks and potato skins. The **Baby Back Ribs** are also especially good here with fries and slaw at $11.99. Portions are generous, so if you mix & match your orders, you can eat well for under $20 for 2.

Specialty drinks and luscious desserts like **Hot Apple Strudel Pie**, **Cappuccino Cake** and **Kamikaze Chocolate/ Nut Brownie** with hot fudge & vanilla ice cream ($3.50) may lure you into a higher bracket but there's no better place for a food fling than Houlihan's!

**Prices:** Lunch $5.95-$7.95, Dinner $7.95-$15.

**What To Wear:** Go in style...your style. Anything goes.

**Recommended:** American Cuisine, Fabulous Buys, Late Supper, Pgh After Dark.

# Juno Trattoria

| | |
|---|---|
| **Wining, Dining Italian Style** | **Juno Trattoria** |

*One Oxford Centre, Downtown. Mon-Thur 11-10, Fri & Sat til 12. AE,D,DC,MC,V.* **392-0225.** ♿

Pittsburgh loves Italian—and one of the proofs is this very popular trattoria in the beautiful glass-walled space of Oxford Centre's third level. The winning Juno formula—casual atmosphere, typical Italian dishes, hand-rolled pasta, homemade bread & pastries—is thriving downtown and in Ross Park Mall. The marble tables and wood floors of the downtown site blend well with the ultra-modern Oxford setting for a bright, contemporary look. A winner of the National Pasta Assn's "best pasta in the city" award, Juno is the creation of Dominic Abbott and Joseph DeMartino, the forces behind Abate Italian/seafood restaurant in Fox Chapel and four popular Dingbat's restaurants—one of them on Oxford's first level.

**When To Go:** Anytime—lunch, supper.

**What To Order:** A voluminous menu offers a wide selection of appetizers, pizza, pasta, sandwiches, plus entrees from $8-$17 featuring chicken, beef, seafood and a slew of veals—a specialty here. There's Veal Piccata, Romano, Marsala, Melanzane and a Saltimbocca, some of the most expensive menu items, along with versions of filet mignon from $17-$18. The superb pastas are more economical and come in two sizes—"piccolo" ($4.95-$8) and "tutto" (dinner) serving ($8- $13). They lend themselves well to a la carte dining paired with one of the house's fine salads and dessert. You can match a salad with a piccolo **Angel Hair Lobster** or a delicious **Fettucine Chicken & Broccoli**.

And antipasto lovers can meal from the **Antipasta Cart** from 5 to 9 nightly ($4.95-$8.95)—delicious banana peppers, roasted califlower, prosciutto, polenta marinara, tomato & onion vinegarette, sweet peppers and sausage, marinated mushrooms, romaine salad, tiny 'anci de pepe' pastas, broccoli/chicken rapeni...great tastes, doubly wonderful with **Focaccia with cheese and sun-dried tomatoes** ($4.95) or the aromatic **Parmesan/provolone garlic bread** ($2.50). Then end with delightful Italian dessert—homemade cannoli, rum cake and lemon Italian ices. You can take home many of the restaurant's menu items from the tempting glass-cased take-out counter. P.S. "400 Club" light entrees are also featured.

**Prices:** Lunch $4.95-$13, Dinner $7.95-$19.

**What To Wear:** Downtown casual.

**Recommended:** Italian Cuisine, Gourmet To Go, Late Supper.

**Phillipine Fare
In Island Oasis**

## La Filipiniana

*5321 Butler Street, Lawrenceville. Dinner Wed-Sun 5-10.
AE,MC,V. Reser sugg.* **781-8724.**
Tucked away in Lawrenceville, this little restaurant is one of
the city's hidden secrets with a loyal following for its unique
cuisine and soothing atmosphere. You enter into a calming
Manila cream and bamboo room, an oasis in the city...with
rattan screens, island artifacts, beautiful hand-embroidered
tablecloths. And casting a sunny light over all is charming
owner/chef Teody Schipper who has re-created the magic of
her original restaurant in the Phillipines. The atmosphere is
so warm and homelike you'll feel you're dining with a friend.
Summers you can eat outdoors in the garden where herbs
and lemon grass are grown for La Filipiniana's unique
dishes. And there's also food for the mind at a Sunday
"Philosopher's Brunch." (See Brunch)

**When To Go:** Dinner 4-10, delightful outdoors in summer.

**What To Order:** Chef Teody uses her own herbs and spices to create unique
Filipino cuisine—a blend of Thai, Indian, Spanish and Western cooking. She has tempered this spicy cuisine into exotic
yet naturally-healthful low-salt, low-cholesterol dishes—cited
by Weight Watchers for its low-fat, high flavour. For starters
we recommend a refreshing mango juice cocktail. Then the
delicious **Sweet Pepper Salad** with papaya pickles and a
wonderful ginger and herb cucumber dressing...a taste all
its own...and crispy, pungent **Empanaditas** filled with
ground beef, raisins, peas and herbs and **Filipino Egg
Rolls** with a delicious Raisin Sauce. You'll love the
tastes here.
Entrees include house specialties **Trout Steamed in Banana Leaves** with fresh mushrooms and herbs, **Chicken
Adobo** marinated in palm vinegar and garlic and simmered
in a clay pot, and an ambrosia-like deliciously smooth
**Lemon Grass Shrimp Curry**...all $12-$13. Other entrees
include curries, vegetarian and beef dishes including a brac-
ing Murcon–rolled steak filled with sausage, herbs & spices,
a Filipino version of bracciole. Entrees come with plain or
vegetable rice and stir-fried vegetables. And no meal is
complete without piquant **Ginger & Lemon Grass Tea** and
subtle island desserts...yam and cassava cakes and flan.
For your first visit try the **Dinner Special,** Adobo Chicken,
egg rolls, soup, fried rice, stir-fry veggies & dessert, $11.95.

**Prices:** Dinner $9.95-$12.95. Bring your own wine.

**What To Wear:** Comfortable, informal.

**Recommended:** Filipino Cuisine, Fabulous Buys, Outdoor Dining, Party
Rooms.

# Le Pommier, The Apple Tree

---

**Quiet Charm At Country French**

## Le Pommier, The Apple Tree

*2104 E Carson Street, South Side. Dinner Mon-Thur 5:30-9, Fri & Sat til 10. Reser. AE,DC,MC,V.* **431-1901.** ♿

Le Pommier is reminiscent of the simple French country inns found outside great cities where a chef retreats to create dishes for gourmet patrons in a quiet, unhurried atmosphere. There's a delight in finding the same quiet charm and a sure, deft hand in the kitchen of this elegant little in-city restaurant where the attention of Owner Christine Dauber and French Chef Habib Ben Allal make each dish a fresh experience. The decor behind the blue, lace-curtained facade on Carson is deceivingly simple...candle-lit wooden tables, blue & white check tablecloths, the work of local artists on the brick walls—all conspire to create a cozy, comfortable setting. The small number of choices is pleasing to the connoisseur...you have confidence the day's menu was planned around the freshness of the morning's market.

**When To Go:**   Superfine Dinner.

**What To Order:**   This is cuisine for the serious diner so give yourself time to savour your meal. The fare changes seasonally—inimitable versions of "fish, birds, meat" ($19-$29) including haute cuisine i.e. Lobster Tail with Morel Mushrooms, Duck with Honey/Cider Vinegar and Couscous Royale—N African stew with lamb, chicken and vegetables. A delicious start is the Braised Fennel Salad with carrots, onions and Gruyere... wonderful with a Kir Royale—champagne and Chambord ($5) or a glass of fine house wine ($5.50-$10).
If budget allows, try the outstanding **Salmon Filet** with **Sorel Sauce, Baby Lamb Chops** or the **Vegetarian Couscous** in the $19-$23 range. The soups, typically French...deliciously creamy, savory...Scallop & Garlic Soup, Fish with Wine & Herbs, Leek & Potato...come in big bowls worth the $5-$7. For lighter eaters they can be paired with a unique salad...**Cold Smoked Salmon & Shrimp** with **Hearts of Palm, Avocado, Pineapple & Tomato**...great eating for $11...or a hot appetizer such as **Scallops & Oysters in Champagne Sauce** or Langoustines with Zucchini ($8-$10). Desserts are also smashing.
P.S. Another good way to discover the cuisine here is at monthly regional dinners, four courses for $25. (See Rich Man's Guide).

**What To Wear:**   Something casually fine.

**Prices:**   Dinner $19-$30.

**Recommended:**   French Cuisine, Connoisseur Dining, Executive Dining.

**Melt-In-Your Mouth Mexican —Hot Design**

## Mad Mex

*370 Atwood at Bates, Oakland. 7 days 11-1am. Brunch Sat & Sun 11-3..* **681-5656.** *2000 Smallman.* **261-6565.** *7905 McKnight Rd, Ross. 7 days 11-1.* **366-5656.** *AE,MC,V* &#9855;

A hot beat goes on at this lively bar/restaurant which has taken the town by storm. Get there early to avoid the seven o'clock lines for the best Cal-Mex food in town. This isn't an old standby menu but a fresh, inventive approach with exciting offerings. The brainchild of Tom Baron (Wheel Deliver) and Juno Yoon, Mad Mex has a hip cherokee red adobe exterior and some unique Southwestern touches— dark wood rafters, hanging Mason jar lights, back-lit petro- graphs in a unique wooden bar. To appreciate the decor you'll have to go on an off-hour or Sunday when the crowd thins. While this is an all-ages haunt be warned—the sound track gets decibels higher as the week and the hour progres- ses...it's a mad, mad music scene late weekend nights.

**When To Go:** Off hours for food; late nite for food & fun.

**What To Order:** The house salsa and black bean dip are heralds of the tastes to come. This is terrific, well-thought-out cuisine beginning with the appetizers...Chili with Sour Cream & Onions, Black Bean Soup and Quesadilla...grilled Mexican pizza, a 10" tortilla with scores of toppings i.e. chicken, steak and even tofu sour cream for non-dairy eaters for $3-$4. The food and drinks here have the right combination. The plates, beautifully presented with the "works", are satisfying economical meals from $5-$8. The kitchen rule seems to be 'if it tastes good together, try it' resulting in some singular offerings such as **Eggplant & White Bean Salad** served with rice & beans...and the **Grilled Shrimp & Baby Corn** with roasted peppers, zucchini, red onions. You can't go wrong with a dizzying array of Burritos & Enchiladas— meals in themselves with rice, beans, cheese 'on the inside' and sour cream, guacamole, salad on the side. Try the **Chicken or Vegetarian Enchilada**—the latter a mouth- watering melange of tomatoes, zucchini, roasted peppers, red onions, mushrooms ($7.50)...this is vegetarian heaven! And the **Mexican Wings** are hot and tangy with jalepenos, cumin. Also an ole for the beer list—a big selection from micro-breweries ($2.50-$3), Mexican, Belgian—up to $11 for 25oz...plus potent margaritas ($4-$4.50) If you love Mexican food you'll love this place.

**Prices:** Great! $4.95-$8.95.

**What To Wear:** Beat, informal.

**Recommended:** Mexican Cuisine, Vegetarian Fare, Fabulous Buys, Brunch, Late Supper.

**City First—Sophisticated Spanish**

### Mallorca

*2228 East Carson St, S Side. Mon-Thur 11:30-10:30, Fri-Sat til 11:30. Sun 12-10. Reser 5 or more. AE,D,DC,MC,V.* **488-1818.** Giving Pittsburgh it's first real taste of Spanish cuisine is Mallorca (pronounced my-or-ka). This unusual restaurant has laid its own distinctive personality and polish over the romantic decor of the old Brady Street Bridge Cafe, a handsome Victorian restoration with hanging ferns, etched glass and a dark green, mellow look. There's also a charming umbrellaed outdoor patio. Evenings and after-theatre the scene bustles...long lines in the hallway, the sweep of dark-clad waiters as they expertly maneuver through the tightly packed, white-clothed tables. Throughout there's a warm, casual atmosphere set by Portuguese owner Antonio Pereira and his staff, a chief reason why Mallorca has become a favorite local dining spot.

**When To Go:** Dinner/after-theatre or lunch on the patio.

**What To Order:** This is one place we recommend you begin with wine... whatever the cost...Tio Pepe sherry, sangria or a mellow Iberian or Portuegese wine ($4-$5). The menu includes a wide variety of seafood/meat dishes prepared in unusual Iberian ways. But be warned...the portions are more than generous. Many of the dishes' fame has spread...an interesting cold 'Gaspacho' and a **Sopa de Ajo**–house Garlic Soup–a pungent broth thick with chunks of bread and egg (both $3.95) and a plentiful, steaming **Paella Valenciana**, traditional Spanish "fish stew" with spicy sausage, chicken, shellfish, saffron rice served in a deep pot...milder than one expects...easily enough for 2 at $16. The gusty, broiled **Chorizo Sausage**...pork, garlic, spices...bursts with flavour ($6.95)...almost a meal in itself with excellent house sourdough and a salad of exotic greens.

Though on the high side the seafood dishes can't be beat—especially a delicious **Lobster laced with Crabmeat** ($20) and **Seafood in Spanish Brandy**, both huge portions shareable for a $4 plate charge. More economical are tasty **Veal Marsala** and **Pork Chops in Garlic Sauce** ($12-$13). Everything's served with a giant vegetable platter, saffron rice and crisp potato-chip-like Spanish fries. For dessert try the smooth, orange-flavored Flan with Spanish coffee. Your plate truly runneth over. P.S. Economical lunch has smaller versions of the same dishes.

**What To Wear:** Dramatic or casual fits the scene.

**Prices:** Lunch $6.50-$10.95, Dinner $12-$24.

**Recommended:** Spanish/Continental Cuisine, Seafood, Outdoor Dining, Late Supper.

# Mario's Southside Saloon

**Hearty Italian Food, Fun**

## Mario's Southside Saloon

**1**

*1514 East Carson Street, South Side. Mon-Sat 11-2am. AE,DC,MC,V. Reser.* **381-5610.** [♿]

Not a restaurant for the faint-hearted, Mario's, from its pasta hung windows to its second floor gallery, is a home for the convivially intrepid. If you love being part of a crowd and don't mind the din and noise (especially on the balcony) this is the place to go for wonderful Italian fare at relatively low prices. Seekers of quiet can take the narrow back stairs to the small third floor rooms which accommodate the over-flow. And the overflow seems constant at this popular neighborhood saloon/restaurant which draws Pittsburghers from all over.

**When To Go:** Lunch, Dinner, Late Supper—things are always humming here.

**What To Order:** Give yourself time to study a rambunctious menu jammed with unique daily specials and a variety of Italian dishes. The linguini, sauces, soups, dressings, pies are all made daily in Mario's kitchen. There's a full line-up of **pasta conveniently available by the whole or half order** ranging from $3 to $13 in a variety of sauces—marinara, garlic butter, pignola, red or white clam sauce, gorgonzola, Alfredo, carbonara, Florentine and top-of-the-line seafood and langostino.

One of the beauties of a half order—plenteous in itself—it leaves you room to sample some of the house specialties—the **Antipasto** or **great Fried Calamari** at $3.95 or unique French fries with cheese or gravy $2.95.

Sandwiches range from $2.95 for the fish Whale's Tale to $3.50 for the meatball-pepperoni-mushroom-cheese **'Too Full to Float Italian Boat'** and the **South Side Sicilian**—pepperoni, prosciutto and provolone with peppers and onions. And sooner or later you'll want to try a huge 36-oz **yard of beer** in a long, long glass flagon—around $6.25. Or you can try a $2.50 shot—you keep the glass. It's good to find a fun restaurant that takes its food seriously. You'll like this super Italian saloon.

P.S. Nothing succeeds like success. Owner Robert Passo-lano also owns **Blue Lou's** next door and **Nick's Fat City** across the street.

**Prices:** Good a la carte buys, $3 up. Serious dinners $8-$12.

**What To Wear:** No need to bother too much...unless you're expecting to meet company. Come as you are and enjoy.

**Recommended:** Italian Cuisine, Fabulous Buys, Late Supper.

# Max's Allegheny Tavern

**Oldtime German Food, Atmosphere**

## Max's Allegheny Tavern

*Corner of Middle/Suismon Sts, North Side. Mon-Thur 11-11, Fri-Sat til 12. Sun 11-8. No reser. AE,DC,MC,V.* **231-1899.**
Turn back the clock, put on your appetite for hearty German dishes and get in the mood for rollicking fun. This old time North Side saloon has real Tiffany lamps, a unique player piano with a mini-orchestra under glass, superb food—and nostalgia for the time when North Side was the city of Old Allegheny. In operation since 1899 the tavern is a wonderful place to show visitors the real old Pittsburgh.

**When To Go:** Timing's important at Max's. This Pittsburgh German 'gastehaus' is always crowded. We recommend **supper weekdays** at 6 or 6:30. Give your name at the door. This should give you an ideal wait of 20 minutes at the bar and time to savour the atmosphere. Order draft **lite or dark from a great selection of beers**...$2 a Mason jar full...or splurge on Beck's at $2.75. Scoop up some popcorn. Take in the original mahogany mirrored bar, the wooden tables, the old mosaic tile floor, the bright Tiffany lamps above the wooden booths. That wonderful music is coming from the player piano past the bar. Wander back, beer in hand, to examine what surely must be one of Pittsburgh's wonders—percussion, tambourine and accordion squeezing in and out behind the piano's glass front. Play a few selections of honky-tonk or old favorites at 25c a throw. If you like crowds, wait for a table in the main room—but the three other rooms carry over the barroom feel.

**What To Order:** Enjoy the menu, a replica of an 1898 *Allegheny Evening Record,* with sauerbraten and wursts, all from $6.50-$10.75. Our favorite and the biggest bargain in the house is the **Bratwurst Dinner**, a delicate veal and pork sausage for $5.75 including two side dishes...we love the delicious **Sweet & Sour Cabbage** and the perfectly seasoned **German Potato Salad**...or the delectable **Potato Dumplings** ($1.95 extra!) Homemade dark & light rye is served with generous crocks of apple butter. **This food is good!** To top off dinner there's Bavarian Cheesecake with strawberries or homemade **Apple Strudel** & ice cream ($3-$4). Dinner with beer, strudel, coffee, tax...and two piano plays... comes in at $22 for 2—a real bargain for hearty cuisine. P.S. In early evening walk off your hearty meal with a stroll around the atmospheric Old Allegheny neighborhood with its tall houses and narrow passageways.

**Prices:** Lunch/Dinner $4.25-$10.75.

**What To Wear:** Comfortable clothes of your choice.

**Recommended:** German Cuisine, Fabulous Buys, Late Supper.

| | |
|---|---|
| **Sensuous Steak, Superb Ambience** | **Morton's of Chicago**         **1** |

**Morton's of Chicago**

*CNG Tower, 625 Liberty Avenue, Downtown. Lunch Mon-Fri 11:30-2:30. Reser sugg. Dinner Mon-Sat 5:30-11. Sun 5-10. AE,CB,DC,MC,V. Valet parking.* **261-7141.** ♿

Another great steakhouse has come to Pittsburgh (rated by many as best in U.S.)—one of the famous Morton's chain. Entered via an elegant doorway in the CNG building, the warm club-like quarters have a burnished atmosphere...the color of brandy...dark, gleaming wood, soft lighting, beautiful flowers, banquettes, candlelit tables. Comfortable and relaxing, it's an ideal setting for executive unwinding and enjoyment of a superior steak. It's success proves there's always a market for a first-class steak...and restaurant.

**When To Go:** Dinner, more economical Lunch.

**What To Order:** This is great dining. Evocative of the elegant restaurants of old, it calls for a Manhattan, an Old-Fashioned or Scotch to start off your meal. A Morton tradition, the dinner cart rolls out to show off all the finest of ingredients—USDA prime, aged beef...helpful in choosing the size of your steak...fresh fish/seafood, top-cut chops and even potatoes & vegetables. Depending on your appetite and pocketbook you can have the steak of your desire—tender as butter, delicious in flavour, sizzling with seared-in juices, grilled at 800-1000 degrees. There are spectacular portions—a 24oz Porterhouse ($29.95), 14oz Double Filet Mignon Bernaise ($26.95), Ribeye ($20.95) Tenderloin Brochette ($19.95). Also offered are veal/lamb chops, chicken and fish ($16-$25). A la carte sides—salad ($4.75-$4.95) and baked potato, spinach, mushrooms, broccoli, and asparagus ($3.95)—can skyrocket your tab...but a 4-star house salad should suffice...or the **truly marvelous asparagus**... perfectly-done big spears, firm and tender.
Lunch, more economical, comes with its own sides—**NY Strip with Potato** ($17.95), the **Tenderloin with Fettucine**, or **Chicago Peppersteak with Rice Pilaf** ($12.95)...everything's beautifully presented. Salad ($3.95) is worth it. Desserts, around $4, also beckon. They're all special— Raspberries or Strawberries in Sabayon, NY Cheesecake, Pecan Pie, Chocolate Velvet Cake or a frothy **Souffle for 2—Chocolate, Grand Marnier or Lemon—**$9.25.
Don't miss this restaurant. It's one of Pittsburgh's best, terrific food in a shining ambience.

**Prices:** Lunch $7-$18, Dinner $16-$29.

**What To Wear:** This is elegant dining...jackets for men.

**Recommended:** American Cuisine, Steak, Connoisseur Dining, Rich Man's Dining, Downtowner, Executive Dining.

# Moscow Nights

**Robust Russian Food, Revelry**

## Moscow Nights

*1722 Murray Ave, Squirrel Hill. Mon-Thur 11-10, Fri & Sat til 11-12. AE.* **No liquor. 521-5005.**

We got a kick out of Moscow nights, a plain old-fashioned room with flecked wallpaper, heavy china and terrific cuisine. It's the creation of Chef/Owners Oleg and Victoria Glazov who mix cooking from their Russian/Israeli backgrounds with influences from their travels in the Mid-East and Turkey. On weekends live Russian/Israeli folk/pop enlivens the room, adding to the ethnic flavor. Russian cuisine is hard to find in Pittsburgh and this menu's a delightful combination of hearty home-cooking and exotic dishes. The atmosphere calls for vodka...but bring your own.

**When to Go:** Weekends - music begins at 8:30 Fri & Sat night.

**What To Order:** The food here is hearty, homemade, full of gusto and delicious surprises...from caviar and blintzes to Russian Beef Stew–Siberian style with great touches of dill. And most entrees are under $10! Don't miss the soups...savory Pehenny kreplach-style with tender little meat-filled dumplings in light broth. And oh the **Russian Borscht—not the usual thick beet soup but a melange of cabbage, beets, carrots, potatoes and tomatoes swimming with flavour.** Unique vegetarian salads include the Moscow—tasty potato, pea, and dill, the Odessa—pickled potatoes, carrots, red beans and the Azerbaijan—sauteed eggplant. There's herring, sprats and an **Assorted Fish Plate** with smoked whitefish, salmon & lox for $9.50 and lovely, economical plates of Black Caviar ($12.50) or Red ($7.50) served with hard-boiled eggs and dark Russian bread.

We can suggest all kinds of choices here. You can meal on the **Borsch or Pehennny Soup** ($2.50-$3) with a salad and some of the house's wonderful **Blintzes**—with Red Cavier $8.25...Black $14.95...or delicate, sweet **Cheese Blintzes** studded with raisins—**some of the best we've ever tasted,** only $3.95. And don't miss the **Chicken Kievski**...marvelously tender marinated chicken rolled into a drumstick, sauteed with sour cream to a crisp, succulent finish...with flavourful roasted potatoes & salad—a great meal for $9.95. You might also try the **Whole Baked Chicken with cherry, plum/nut stuffing**—only $20.95 for 2. You can dance it off! For dessert...rich creamy cakes & **Turkish Coffee**.

Moscow Nights is a great new experience. Don't miss it!

**Prices:** Mostly under $10....caviar to $14.95.

**What To Wear:** Be comfortable, informal. Food & fun's the thing.

**Recommended:** Russian/Israeli Cuisine, Vegetarian Fare, Fabulous Buys, Late Supper, After Dark.

**Serenity At
The Scaife**

## Museum Cafe

**1**

*Carnegie Museum of Art, Forbes & Craig, Oakland. Lunch
Tues-Fri 11:30-2 (Also Sat Oct-Apr). Sun Brunch 12-2 Jan-May,
Sept-Dec. AE,MC,V.* **622-3225.** *Museum* **622-3131.** ⑤
There are few places in Pittsburgh more satisfying than
the serene glass and gray granite of the Scaife addition...
perfectly blended into the older buildings of the famous
Carnegie Museum. The best approach is down the wide
stone steps off Forbes, past the fountain to the main glass
doors. New York may have its Metropolitan, Cleveland its
fabled galleries, but Pittsburgh has the perfect planes of
the Scaife by architect Edward Larabee...one of the most
beautiful public spaces in the city. Matching the perfect
setting is the lobby Cafe, a picturesque study in pink and
green, its marble tables overlooking the outdoor fountain...
a wonderful place to linger over lunch.

**When To Go:** Museum hours: Tues-Sat 10-5 (also Mon Jul-Aug) Sun 1-5.

**What To Order:** The Cafe offers a beauteous lunch in the glass-walled dining
area along Forbes. There's a good mix of light and hearty
foods, a changing menu of fish, chicken, pasta, sandwiches,
salads i.e. Chinese Chicken Salad, Vegetable Fajita, Lemon
Chicken, Turkey Devonshire...all in the $6-$8 range. (For
hungry kids there's a more basic cafeteria downstairs.)
Begin your tour by ascending the wide, cantilevered staircase along the sheer glass wall overlooking the Sculpture
Court. At the top to your left begins the Pittsburgh collection—the expansive white galleries a perfect background for
**Monet's Waterlilies, Rouault's Old King, Milton Avery's**
beautiful new **Dunes & Sea I,** and **Giacometti's famed
metal sculpture, the tall, solitary Walking Man.** And don't
miss Segal's **Tightrope Walker,** precariously balanced on
the high wire over the entrance by the Sculpture Court.
In the Museum of Natural History next door are more
marvels...the famous **Dinosaur Hall, Artic Exhibit, Walton
Egyptian Hall,** the new **Africa Hall** and **Heinz Architectural Center** off the Hall of Architecture's second floor gallery. And on the ground floor is the spectacular **Hillman
Hall of Minerals & Gems**...one of the most beautiful
exhibits in the world.
In good weather you can enjoy the outdoor sculpture and
the cooling waterfall. And don't miss delightful items for
children and adults in the two Museum shops.

**Cost:** Museum Admission $5 adults, $4 Sr Cit, $3 students. Mem-
bers free. Cafe Lunch $6-$8. Brunch $9.50.

**What To Wear:** Casual...or your Sunday best.

**Recommended:** American Cuisine, Experiences of the City, Sunday Brunch.

**New Eateries Boom With North Side**

## North Side

*Across the 6th, 7th Street Bridge from Downtown.*
New eateries are springing up all over "new" North Side to serve the influx of visitors and tourists. The most intriguing of Pittsburgh's neighborhoods, "Old Allegheny"—once a city in itself—has become a second cultural hub with the Carnegie Science Center, the WW II sub, Three Rivers Stadium and the bright new Andy Warhol Museum on Sandusky ... don't miss it...drawing thousands of visitors. On nearby cobble-stoned Landmark Square is the acclaimed Pittsburgh Children's Museum with the Aviary just a block away. North Side's streets and hills with their tall brooding buildings and charming gentrified homes of the Mexican War Streets and Allegheny West make for intriguing walks. And down along N Shore is Roberto Clemente Park with its sculpture court and marvelous camera views of the city across the river.

**Where To Eat:**

**All in Good Taste** *Warhol Museum, 117 Sandusky St. Sun, Wed 11-6, Thur-Sat 11-8. MC,V.* **237-8310.** Cafe/coffeehouse atmosphere, light gourmet, good prices; surprising menu i.e. grilled focaccia, grain salads, fruit plate. kids' cookies. $3-7.
**Billy's Bistro** *1720 Lowrie, Troy Hill. Sun-Thur 11:30-10, Fri-Sat til 11. AE,MC,V.* **231-9277.** Sandwiches to lobster (Mon only), ribs, NY strip. $2-$15. Piano Fri-Sun. Inexp-Mod.
**Cafe Victoria** *946 Western Ave. Lunch Tues-Sat 11:30-3, Dinner Tues-Sat 6-9. Sun Brunch 10-3, Tea Tues-Sun 3-6. AE,MC,V.* **323-8881.** Quaint old Victorian atmosphere amid antiques for sale. Unique. Mod-Exp. (See Review)
**Cerulean Bistro** *1227 Monterey St. Dinner Tues-Sat 5-11. AE,D,DC,MC,V.* **321-4221.** Candlelight dining, charming, intimate atmosphere, fine country Fr. Inexp-Exp. (Review)
**Clark Bar & Grill** *Clark Bldg, 503 Martindale, opp Gate B, Stadium circle. Mon-Sat 11-2am. Sun events. AE,D,MC,V.* **231-5720.** Great barroom food, atmosphere; chicken/ribs, grills, sandwiches, pasta; Pirate mini-museum. Inexp-Mod.
**James St Tavern** *422 Foreland/James. Mon-Thur 11-10, Fri-til 12, Sat 4-12. Bar til 2. AE,D,DC,MC,V.* **323-2222.** 2 blocks west of Alleg Ctr. Popular tourist/jazz spot. Cajun, seafood, grills, prime rib; cool jazz Wed-Sat nights. Mod.
**Maxwell's** *110 Federal. Mon-Thur 11:30-9, Fri & Sat til 11. AE,DC,MC,V.* **231-2366.** Bouncy room/bar with remnants of Pgh past, eclectic menu. Inexp-Mod.
**Max's Allegheny Tavern** *Middle/Suismon. Mon-Thur 11-11, Fri & Sat til 12. Sun til 8. AE,DC,MC,V.* **231-1899.** Great German food, atmosphere. Inexp-Mod. (See Review)
**Penn Brewery** *Troy Hill Rd. Mon-Sat 11-12. AE,MC,V.* **237-9402.** Great food/fun in old German beer hall. Wurst, sauerbraten; bands Wed-Sat. Inexp-Mod. (See Review)

**Sleek Skyscraper Visitor's Must**

## One Oxford Centre

1

*301 Grant Street, Downtown. Shops open weekdays 10-6, Mon & Thur til 9. Sat 10-5:30. Restaurants later. Garage on Cherry Way connects to second level.* **391-5300.** 🚿

This gleaming 46-story octagon tower, a major Renaissance II addition, has changed the character of Grant Street with its sleek, silver lines. A great place for visitors and shoppers, it's an exciting downtown urban space with lots of 'pedestrian pleasures.' Centered around a graceful, five-story Atrium with a green-treed, white-tabled indoor plaza, its beautiful glass and aluminum interior is a good place to rest and people-watch. Piano music in the main lobby Mon-Sat from 11-2 adds to the relaxing atmosphere. Smooth, steel escalators glide through the Atrium offering many-faceted views of the plaza and the glistening upper levels. **At holiday time the Centre is a glittering sight both indoors and out.**

Oxford shops and services make browsing and buying a delight here. Some shops and sights not to be missed are **Cache's** statue-like, glass-enclosed mannequins encircling the Atrium's third level...the two-story, glass walls of **Polo/Ralph Lauren**...the showcases of **Rodier-Paris'** French collection, **AnnTaylor, K Barchetti, Emphatics, Talbots** and the terrific all-white collection at the **White House**...all wonderful browsing. There's also precious-gem jewelry at Hardy & Hayes, American Indian art at the **Four Winds Gallery** and melt-in-your-mouth truffles at St Moritz Chocolatier.

**Where To Eat:** The Centre has three popular restaurants.

**Au Bon Pain** *Lower Level. Mon-Fri 6-6, Sat 8-5.* **566-9429.** Delicious light foods, salads, sandwiches, soups for eating in sunny atrium plaza. Inexp.

**Dingbat's City Tavern** *Lower Level. Mon-Thur 11-11, Fri-Sat 11:30-12. AE,D,DC,MC,V.* **392-0350.** A handsome restaurant/gathering place with a long bar, good food and an outdoor cafe on the Grant St side. Takeout window off lobby. (See Review)

**Juno Trattoria** *Third Level. Mon-Thur 11:30-10, Fri-Sat til 12. AE,D,DC,MC,V.* **392-0225.** Popular Italian restaurant with homemade pasta, pizza in beautiful, sleek setting on third floor. (See Review)

**What To Wear:** Be prepared for a very sophisticated setting.

**Recommended:** Shopping, Experiences of the City.

**Seafood Lover's Dream Buffet**

## Orchard Cafe

*Pittsburgh Vista Hotel, Liberty Center, 1000 Penn Avenue, Downtown. Mon-Thur 6:30am-10:30pm, Fri-Sat til 11. Sun Brunch 11:30-2:30. AE,D,DC,MC,V.* **227-4470.** ♿

This lovely room on the second level of the Vista Hotel is well named...the Monet-like watercolors and flowered chintz in hues of peach, pink and salmon create a country garden setting. Luminous light through the diaphanous curtains at the floor-to-ceiling windows casts a rosy glow over the spacious, comfortable room. Etched glass partitions add to the airiness while creating private dining nooks.

Part of the pleasure here is exploring the luxurious Vista Hotel beginning with the four-story atrium lobby with its transparent glass roof, Grecian marble floors and soft carpets...an aura of subdued elegance. Don't miss the wonderful chandeliers in the second floor ballroom.

**When To Go:** Anytime—breakfast, lunch or dinner but we recommend the Friday Sea Fest or the superb Sunday Brunch.

**What To Order:** The lunch menu features sandwiches, soups and salads in the $3-$6 range including a traditional Club, Shrimp Salad and Fruit Platter. **But the lavish Daily Buffets are the star of the show** with three hot dishes, meat, chicken, fish and sometimes pasta plus vegetable, salads, soup and a luscious array of desserts for $8.95. You can do the Soup 'n Salad Bar alone for $5.95.

The hotel is known for its fabulous **Friday Night Sea Fest,** a seafood lover's dream and best buy of the house. At these feasts (modeled after the famous buffet of the Chicago Drake Hotel) you can revel in delicacies such as **shrimp, gumbo, oysters, crab claws, seafood salads** and hot entrees i.e **mahi mahi, broiled New England scrod and flounder** for $19.95.

Other dinner house specialties include Prime Rib ($14.50), Fettuccine & Smoked Chicken Breast, a delicious dish ($10.95), Stir Fried Vegetables ($9.95) and Reef & Beef ($15.95) and Salmon or Mahi Mahi for $12.50. The Salad Bar—an additional $3.95 at night is worth it. You can finish with some very special desserts from the buffet.

**Prices:** Lunch/Dinner $5-$15.95.

**What To Wear:** It's informal but you'll be comfortable in your finest.

**Recommended:** American Cuisine/Seafood, Connoisseur Dining, Brunch.

**1**

## Pittsburgh's Crystal Palace

### PPG Place

*Off Market Square, Downtown. Shops, Food Court Mon-Fri 10-6, Sat 10-3. Wintergarden open Mon-Fri 6am-7pm, Sat & Sun 9-7. Garage entrances on 3rd & 4th Aves.* **434-3131.**
Already a Pittsburgh architectural landmark, the shimmering PPG Tower has become the visual center of downtown's Renaissance II...its glass spires creating a 'crystal palace' in the heart of the city. On a five-acre site adjacent to historic Market Square, the soaring 40-foot tower and the five smaller buildings exemplify the city's new goal of creating not just office buildings but pleasurable urban spaces. The vast, calm Plaza, reminiscent of the grand squares of Europe, is a wonderful place to watch the play of light and shadow on the glass buildings enclosing it on all four sides. And the airy Wintergarden, the light from its high webbed-glass roof pouring down on a profusion of greenery, has become a popular Pittsburgh people place. PPG Two, with an entrance off Market and Fourth, has shops with out-of-the-ordinary gifts—**Sincerely Yours** and fine leather goods from **Specialty Luggage.**

**Where To Eat:** You can stop for an economical lunch or shopping break at the International Food Court which seats 600 in Bldg Two's lower level. Here from the inviting cafe tables amid potted greenery you have a sweeping view of the two-level atrium. The Court has eight eateries with varied cuisine...Greek food from the Grecian Isles, soups, salads, sandwiches from Strawberry Saloon, super pizza from Somma, gourmet sandwiches & salads from Au Bon Pain and Burgers, Burgers & Chili from an eatery of the same name. In summer, **a pushcart serves lemonade to lunchers at outdoor tables off the Plaza.** There are also three sit-down restaurants:

**China Cafe** *Two PPG Place. Mon-Fri 10-6, Sat til 3. AE,DC,MC,V.* **281-7033.** Szechuan/Hunan specialties in garden atrium. $5-$10.

**River City Inn** *5 PPG, Mon-Sat 10-10. AE,DC,MC,V.* **391-1707.** Sandwiches, light fare $2.50-$4.75.

**Ruth's Chris Steak House** *Six PPG Place. Lunch Mon-Fri 11:30-3, Dinner Mon-Sat 5- 11. Sun 5-9. Reser sugg. AE,DC,MC,V.* **391-4800.** Home of serious steaks,' one of the nationally acclaimed chain. Lunch $6-$13, Dinner $16-$22. (See Review)

**What To Wear:** It's a business, shopping or sightseeing crowd.

**Recommended:** American Cuisine, Shopping/Experiences of City.

## Pasquarelli's

**Romantic Magic Atop the City**

### Pasquarelli's

*1204 Grandview, Mt Washington. Mon-Thur 5-10, Fri-Sat til 11. AE,D,MC,V.* **431-1660.**
We ask ourselves why we singled out this particular Mt Washington restaurant for review when there are so many from which to choose. (See Views of the City). It's definitely the wonderful ambience. This small two-tiered room with a great view from every table was the site of the original Tin Angel restaurant years ago before its move to larger quarters next door. Deja vu! It brings back memories of when the romantic, intimate Angel was the only restaurant atop the city. This room has the same perfect view of the Point...and at night...the added excitement of lights and revelers in Le Mont's glass-walled restaurant perched over the hillside a few doors down. We love the cozy feeling here, the tables' closeness to the view. A design of 'fairy' lights on the brick walls reflect in the windows at night, adding to an already spectacular view. This is magic!

**When To Go:** Romantic by night. Go at dusk to see city lights flick on.

**What To Order:** The kitchen is the purlieu of the Pasquarelli's...Gino, Mario and Joseph...who have served Italy's Abruzzi cuisine for 14 years in Upper St. Clair. This is good basic Italian food—fish, steaks, chicken, pasta (made daily) in a wide price range—$9.95 to $25 for rack of lamb. The steak is excellent as are the veals—the house speciallty—Romano, Marsala, piccato, scallopine, cutlet, chops, saltimbocca, and an interesting Veal Chop/Stuffed Quail combo ($16-$26). At the menu's high end are Beef Wellington, Surf 'n Turf and a Seafood Platter but there are several steak/seafoods $14-$18 including Baked Stuffed Shrimp for $15.95 and a good **Lemon Sole** ($13.95). We liked the interesting chicken selections...especially the **Chicken alla Marsala** and the **Grilled Chicken Parmigiana** $13-$14.
The homemade pasta ($10-$14) also makes an economical entree...**Ricotta/Cheese Manicotti** and **Fettuccini Alfredo** both $9.95...the latter with crabmeat for $13.95. You can also team an appetizer ($3-$6) with a pasta side ($5.50) and a salad ($3-$5).
But remember we're here to enjoy the view. You can linger with a homemade dessert or an after-dinner Italian coffee. And this is one place we insist on spirits...a glass of wine... chablis, zinfandel, champagne...$4 up...to celebrate the beauty of the city...lucky Pittsburghers!

**Prices:** $9.95-$25.

**What To Wear:** Casual elegance.

**Recommended:** Italian Cuisine, Night of Romance, Views of the City.

**Still the City's Italian Favorite**

## Pasta Piatto

*736 Bellefonte Street, Shadyside. Mon-Sat Lunch 11:30-3, Dinner Mon-Tues 4:30-I0, Wed-Thur til 10:30, Fri-Sat til 11. Sun 3-9. No reser. MC,V.* **621-5547.**

This restaurant, #1 in the city for fine N Italian cuisine, has grown into a fashionable, sophisticated room. The Piatto took the starch out of Pittsburgh dining more than a decade ago, serving up terrific food at economical prices in a white-tablecloth atmosphere. Other restaurants followed suit. Now ensconced in fashionable quarters on Bellefonte, the dining room expanding in tiers, the Piatto is still crowded, there are still lines at the door, still the same fine food and assiduous attention to detail by owner Linda Jeannette. But the menu has expanded tremendously, and in many cases so have the prices into a well-deserved but much higher bracket. It's thanks to the enterprising "Presto Pranzo"—early dinner specials—that the Piatto keeps its old budget fans happy. But this is still some of the best pasta in town!

**When To Go:** Lunch or Dinner. Try the economical "Presto Pranzo" Mon-Fri 4:30-5:45 and Sun 3-4:30.

**What To Order:** A huge menu...delightful reading...boasts a wondrous medley of seafood, veal, salads and all kinds of pasta including tortellini from a shiny machine from Italy. Lunches are $3.75-$9 and dinners $9-$20 with many dishes in the $14-$18 range. We have lots of favorites here—one more delicious than the other—the **heaping Antipasto** ($12.95) with shrimp, scallops, mozzarella, zucchini, eggplant, artichoke hearts...more than enough for dinner...creamy **Fettuccini alla Carbonara** with bacon, cheese and butter, **Ravioli with Melanzane** eggplant filling, **Linguini heaped with clams in the shell**—a wonderful dish, all in the $9-$13 range. Dinners are served with a perfect green salad and crusty house bread. Worth the extra is another perennial favorite, the **Gorgonzola Salad**—crisp, crisp romaine with walnuts and gorgonzola dressing—a salad lover's dream for $5.75. There are also heavenly desserts—zabalone, tiramisu and house special **Pasta Delight**—vanilla cream, fresh fruit, whipped cream and toasted pecans $3-$5.

P.S. **Smart eaters can enjoy the restaurant's fine food** at the "Presto Pranzo" Early Bird with choice of entrees i.e. Angel Hair with Shrimp in Champagne Sauce, Crabmeat Ravioli and Veal Scallopini...served with appetizer, salad, pasta or vegetable...**a tremendous buy for under $9.95.**

**Prices:** Lunch $3.75-$9, Dinner $9-$20.

**What To Wear:** Fashionably informal.

**Recommended:** Italian Cuisine, Connoisseur Dining, Late Supper.

# Penn Brewery

| | |
|---|---|
| **Wunderbar!**<br>**Fun At Oldtime**<br>**Beer Hall** | **Penn Brewery**<br>*Troy Hill Road, North Side. Across 16th St Bridge. Mon-Sat*<br>*11-12am. Sun 2-10. AE,MC,V.* **237-9402.** &#x267F;<br>We loved this touch of old Heidelburg in Pittsburgh, a German beer hall in a wonderful setting—the atmospheric old Eberhardt & Ober Brewery on Troy Hill, an old German section of the city. You pass through the gate into a stone courtyard—shades of Frankenstein—the brewery's brooding walls high above. Inside a German pub has been recreated complete with wooden beams, high windows, smooth tables and benches made by owner Tom Pastorius...the only draw-back—the benches are backless! But while you're eating you can watch Penn Pilsner's oldtime beer-making in gleam-ing copper vessels behind a glass wall. (This is the first 'tied house'—brewery attached to a restaurant—in Pennsylvania since Prohibition...brewing pure German beer without addi-tives.) There's a new Rathskeller and in summer the Pub spills out into an outdoor beer garden. Zany German & jazz bands add to the fun. |
| **When To Go:** | Definitely for live bands Tues-Sun 7:30-11:30. Watch for the Boilmarker Five and German bands. Young/old love 'em! |
| **What To Order:** | Wonderful wursts, sauerbraten, smoked pork chops, roast pork, soups, chicken and an interesting salad plate...served with your own loaf of dark sourdough rye & butter...and authentic versions of sauerkraut, spaetzle (tiny German dumplings), apple sauce, sweet & sour red cabbage and of course—German potato salad. We suggest you prepare your palate with **freshly brewed beer**—wonderful tasting Penn Pilsner ($1.75) with a **salty, soft pretzel** hot from the oven & horseradish mustard. The Fruit/Cheese Plate ($5.95) is also a good beginning. Our entree choice is the **Wurst Plate ($7) with two big juicy German sausages**—a firm pale pork and a big brown link bursting with flavour. They're served with potato salad & sauerkraut but we like them with the **mealy, buttered spaetzle and tangy red cabbage.** Also good are the **Sauerbraten** (marinated beef roast) $10, **Smoked Pork Chop** $9 and **Potato Pancakes** $2. And who can resist old-fashioned bread pudding, apple strudel, Linzer torte or Black Forest cheesecake ($2-$2.75.) |
| **Prices:** | Are right! Lunch under $5, Dinner under $10. 2/$25 with beer/dessert. |
| **What To Wear:** | It's a mixed crowd, young & old, preppy, peppy, grand-pappy—all having a wonderful time. Come as you are...welcome! |
| **Recommended:** | German Cuisine, Fabulous Buys, Outdoor Dining, Late Sup-per, Pgh After Dark. |

## Poli's

**Seafood in Sleek New Setting**

*2607 Murray Ave, Squirrel Hill. Tues-Sat 11:30-11, Sun Brunch 11-2, Dinner 2-9:30. AE,CB,DC,MC,V.* **521-6400.** [♿]
A handsome new look has made dining at this favorite seafood house a double pleasure. From a small lunchroom started by Joseph Poli of Lucca, Italy in 1921, Poli's has grown into a sprawling 400-seat restaurant under the tutelage of the Poli family. Its no-nonsense decor has given way to a surprisingly handsome, sophisticated design... shiny brass lobsters at the doorway, muted sand/brown tones, colorful striped ceiling drapes, tapestry chairs. Don't miss the new bar with its sleek gray tile floor and intriguing cubes and angles. The changes cast a welcome hush over the once noisy rooms but regular fans need not fear...the ambience is still comfortable and it's the same stellar fare that has made Poli's a name for seafood in Pittsburgh.

**When To Go:** Lunch/Dinner/Late Supper. Early Bird Tues-Fri 3-5:30.

**What To Order:** What else but seafood flown in fresh daily. It's all good, from the North Carolina **She Crab Chowder** ($2.50-$3.50) rich with cream and sherry to the delicious **Jumbo Seafood** Platter—lobster tail, broiled shrimp, seafood coquille, fish fillet, stuffed oysters Rockefeller, crabmeat in shell which may be enough for 2 ($24, sans lobster $16.75.) There's a big choice of shellfish, scallops, crab cakes and sole, trout, swordfish, haddock, scrod, salmon cooked to order ($13-$25) plus terrific Tristan lobster tails at market price. Our favorites are the **Seafood Coquille**—scallops, king crab and shrimp in a "velvety cream sauce" ($13.25) and the **Rainbow Trout**, pan-fried or broiled, $12.95 (stuffed with crabmeat $16.95. Is your appetite ready!
Entrees are served with two sides—salad, potato/pasta or vegetable. There's also veal, steak, chops and pasta with or without seafood ($10.50-$21). An interesting note...you can get a half-order of pasta...which may be enough with the good house salad...for half price. **Another good way to eat here is at the Early Bird with terrific seafood items for $8.50-$12.95. A daily hot-line 594-4473 tells you if your favorite's in the night's line-up.**
Poli's also has a great late-night menu including Monte Cristo, hot turkey and fish sandwiches ($4-$5.50) and **Turkey** and **Crabmeat Devonshires** ($8-$9.50) also served for lunch and dinner.

**Prices:** $9.50-$24 & up (market price)

**What To Wear:** Informal or dress-up, cool & comfortable.

**Recommended:** Seafood, Early Bird, Late Supper.

# The Primadonna

**Provincial Eatery Makes Waves**

## The Primadonna

*801 Broadway, West Park—McKees Rocks. Mon-Sat 4-11. AE,D,CB,DC,MC,V.* **331-1001.**

Say hello to a provincial primadonna...a bountiful Italian restaurant sending gastronomic waves around the Pittsburgh area. As many rebound from effete gourmet cuisine to hearty home cooking this neighborhood restaurant took front and center. It's definitely Italian and folks from all over are heartened to see many McKees Rocks natives as regulars—who should best know good Italian!—cheek by jowl so to speak with the visitors. As usual with local successes, this is a family affair, in this case the Costanzo family—Joe as official greeter, Pino as chef, cooking some of Mama's recipes in the kitchen, and their ancestors...keeping an eye on things from their oval frames on the walls. The back room with its portraits and flowered wallpaper, resembles an old-fashioned diningroom in an Italian home. The warm family feeling extends to the service. This and good prices for big servings have led to long waits for a Primadonna table.

**When to Go:** No reservations so try to make it early or later than 6-7 but you'll probably have to wait anyway...in anteroom or bar.

**What To Order:** This is good, plain cooking...but the best of its kind. There are too many good things to be an accident. It's a big menu, from pastas beginning at $9.95 to NY Strip at $18.95...with most of the dishes in the $11-$15 range. There are scores of pastas, some of the more interesting—**Spaghetti El Duce** with scallops, pepperoni & artichoke hearts and the **Veal Sicilian Pasta** with hot peppers, mushrooms & onions. There are also some wonderful staples like tender **Homemade Gnocchi** with meatballs just like Mom used to make ($8.50) and delicious homemade soups...**Beef Barley** and **Wedding Soup**...their aromas bringing back memories of the family kitchen. Hot, crusty garlic bread is served with every meal and we heartily recommend the **Antipasto,** very fresh Italian meats and cheeses over crisp greens with a **zingy-sweet Italian dressing**...enough for 2 with a meal. (Also terrific are the **Marinated Scallops** $5.50). Portions are generous, dinners come with a salad, pasta/baked potato and vegetable. Desserts are $3-$4.50 and wine by the half carafe $8-$9. This is the kind of place you'll want to come back to and try out house versions of linguine, ravioli, veal, seafood, spaghetti.

**Prices:** Dinner $9.95-$18.95.

**What To Wear:** You can be comfortable.

**Recommended:** Italian Cuisine, Fabulous Buys, Late Supper.

**Zesty Fare At Balcony Cafe**

## River Cafe

*Second Level, Station Square. Sun-Thur 11:30-10, Fri-Sat til 11. Sun 12-9. AE,CB,D,DC,MC,V.* **765-2795.** ♿

There's real dining going on high on the balcony at Station Square at this graceful, pretty Cafe overlooking the Shops. Patrons have been pleasantly surprised at the inventive cuisine, the fine service and the San Francisco decor. Stretched out along the second level, the rooms are bright and airy with ceiling fans and beautiful stained glass panels (on loan from the Pittsburgh History & Landmarks Foundation). Unusual dishes, the creations of Chef Steve Cortez, have made the Cafe a popular spot and a warm informality belies the traditional settings thanks to ever-present owner Richard Bozzo.

**When To Go:** Romantic lunch, dinner.

**What To Order:** This is a good place to take a group of enthusiastic eaters. "You've got to taste this" is a typical comment as patrons swap samples of unusual dishes from a wide array of fish, poultry, seafood, steak and pastas. Among delicious new tastes are **Chicken Breast with Apples, Brie & Port Wine**; **Pork Valdostano**—with prosciutto and fontina in rosemary butter, **Mountain Trout in Amaretto Cream Sauce** stuffed with Scallops & Vegetables, **Iron City Steak** chargrilled in a marinade of Iron City beer...all in the $14.95-$18 bracket. There are also great pastas for $14-$15.

But our favorite, hands down, is wonderful **Scallops in Sambuca Cream** over Linguini...a sweet, deliciously different pasta. Another good dish...but with a lot of heat...is the zesty **Linguini with Chicken, Hot Sausage & Hot Peppers** ($13.95). You can also get a half order of pasta...a good dinner with the house salad and dessert. And for light eaters *and* light pocket books...there's a special menu ($5.25-$8) with a wide selection of appetizers, salads, sandwiches...a popular fried ham/cheese **Monte Cristo**...plus interesting gourmet white pizza and a **Louisiana Pizza with Andouille Sausage**....also on the lunch and late night menu.

Nice extra touches are the crusty warm bread, tender salad greens...a delicious creamy raspberry dressing...an enticing dessert cart and for vegetable lovers—special dishes i.e. sauteed carrots and Anna potatoes. So many goodies!

**Prices:** Lunch $4.95-$8, Dinner $12.95-$19.

**What To Wear:** Informal to dress-up at night.

**Recommended:** American Cuisine, Late Supper.

# REVIEWS

## Ruth's Chris Steak House

**The Ritual of the Great Steak Dinner**

### Ruth's Chris Steak House

*PPG Place, Downtown. Lunch Mon-Fri 11:30-3. Dinner Mon-Sat 5-11. Sun 5-9. Free evening parking PPG garage, enter Third or Fourth Ave. Reser sugg. AE,DC,MC,V.* **391-4800.** 🦽

Pittsburgh steak lovers are still doing obeisance to the ritual of the perfect steak as practiced by this famous chain. One of 42 Ruth Chris' across the country, the stylish, comfortable restaurant is named for Ruth Fertel who purchased the Chris Steak House in New Orleans in 1965 and began franchising in '77. Pittsburgh's was brought here in '87 by Jack Offenbach of Samurai and Tequila Junction fame. The setting–lots of warm cherry wood, glass and subtle lighting– is a fitting background for the ritual of the perfectly cooked steak and the painstaking dedication required to achieve it. First you take only 'top of the top' U.S. prime (about 2% of all beef). Age in dry refrigeration (never freeze!) for 60 days to lock in flavour. Carefully hand cut just enough for each day's dining. Cook to order in a specially built, high temperature broiler that sears in juices at 1800 degrees. Place the steak...sizzling in butter...on a ceramic plate heated to 450 degrees. Then serve with a flourish. Disciples say this meat just can't be beat!

**When To Go:** A weekend or Sunday dinner seems only fitting.

**What To Order:** These tasty, butter-soft morsels range from $18 for a **petite 8-oz filet** to $21 for a **12 to 14-oz filet or 16-oz ribeye.** The **porterhouse is $44 for 2** or $88 for four for a massive cut. So far, so good—but the steak you see is what you get for your money. Potatoes, vegetables, salads—and in some cases even sauces!—are all extra. For instance an Italian salad $3-$4, a baked potato $3.50, and delicious creamed spinach $3.75, can add $10 or more to your check. Actually the steaks are so big and good, a salad or potato alone suffices. And since one good thing leads to another, how about rounding off your perfect dinner with **Blueberry Cheesecake, Apple or Pecan Pie** or **Bread Pudding with 80-proof Whiskey Sauce** ($3-$4). If you're a steak lover you'll eventually come here to do homage anyway. (For non-beef eaters there's chicken, lamb, pork, veal chops from $16-$23 and fresh fish and Maine lobster flown in daily.) You can sneak a peek at this restaurant at lunch—a better bargain—with **NY Steak Sandwich** or a **Petite Filet** $12.95, steakburger $6, and a great **Steak Salad** for $8.95.

**Prices:** Lunch: $6-$13, Dinner $16-$22.

**What To Wear:** Strictly downtown attire.

**Recommended:** American Cuisine, Steak, Connoisseur Dining, Executive Dining, Rich Man's Dining, Late Supper.

**Favorite Downtown Italian Find**

## Scoglio

**1**

*Balcony, Fifth Ave Place, 5th/Stanwix. Mon-Thur 11:30-10, Fri til 11. Sat 5-11. Reser sugg. AE,D,DC,MC,V.* **391-1226. Scoglio Uptown** *Law/& Finance Bldg, 429 4th Ave, Mon-Fri 11:30-9, Sat 5-9.* **263-0545.** ♿

As we write this review Scoglio, one of downtown's dining secrets... a little upper room off Liberty...is moving to a larger, airy space in Fifth Avenue Place. Fans will undoubtedly miss the intimacy of the original little room, reached by a hard-to-find canopied doorway...up steep carpeted stairs to a simple yet elegant setting. We're hoping the ambience won't change. The restaurant is so popular with downtowners there's already a second **Scoglio Uptown** in the Law & Finance Building which has kept the Scoglio trademarks. The new space...accessible from Lazarus' walkway...is larger with room for 190. But owners Chef Gary (formerly of Bravo! Franco) and Debbie Komorski promise to keep the same serenity in the spiffy new black, gray and white decor...candles, flowers at the white-clothed tables... plus dinner music from a new baby grand piano. They also hope to keep the line on reasonable prices for fine cuisine that have resulted in SRO at Scoglio since it opened.

**When To Go:** Lunch, Pre-Theatre.

**What to Order:** There's a fine North Italian hand in the kitchen producing simple, stylish dishes to match the decor—veal, chicken, and chops...the latter up to $24.95. But regulars are in love with the terrific pasta ($8.95-$13)—cappellini to linguini, penne to farfelle paired with seven sauces...one more scrumptious than the other...tomato basil cream, marinara, tomato/caper, salmon cream, with scallops, Abruzzese— with escarole, tomato and basil. Our favorite is the **Scoglio Pasta**—a seafood sauce for which the house was named— with shrimp, scallops, clams in basil olive oil. There's also terrific **Fried Zucchini** ($4.25) and a great **Caesar Salad** for $3. These prices are right! All entrees are served with salad and a vegetable or pasta marinara. Lunch features many of the same dishes plus Caesar, spinach and seafood salads. (There's a minimum lunch charge of $4.95!). Again, Italian desserts and pastries can't be beat for a sweet finish. ($2.75-$4).

**Prices:** Lunch $6.95-$8.95. Dinner $8.95-$15 (up to $24.95 for chops.)

**What To Wear:** Business duds to romantic by night.

**Recommended:** Italian Cuisine, Connoisseur Dining, Fabulous Buys, Late Supper.

**Shadyside Shopping Spree**

## Shadyside Walk & Shop

*Walnut Street between Ivy and Aiken. 77C bus stops at Walnut & Ivy. 71B,C,D two blocks away on Fifth Avenue.*

Shadyside, the city's finest specialty shopping area, has taken on new upscale sleekness. But the creative character of the street remains, an intriguing mix of elegance and offbeat charm—with just a little of Rodeo Drive thrown in. When East Enders talk about the 'Avenue' they usually mean Walnut Street—the place to see and be seen in the latest casual attire. There are some beautiful stores here...small one-of-a-kind speciality shops and sophisticated chains...making for delightful window shopping. The area also abounds in famous eateries and night spots.

**When To Go:** Day off or Saturday afternoon for meeting, greeting people. Stores open Wednesday til 9.

Reserve a whole day, for there's beauty aplenty in this three-block area with its charming use of space including upstairs rooms and awninged byways. Nationally famous chains—**AnnTaylor, e.b. Pepper, Victoria's Secret, Laura Ashley, Benetton** have brought new polish to the street along with the unique **Pamar** and **Maxalto** specialty clothing designs. They join the **William Penn Hat & Gown Shop,** Divine Knits, Basic Image, Kountz & Rider and men's **Stylegate** creating a fashion mecca in a very small area. More down-to-earth shopping at **Express, The Gap,** and the campy lure of **Banana Republic** add to the avenue's cachet. There are also several kids' fashion shops.

Along with the modern wares of **Pier One** are old-fashioned **Shadyside Variety Store,** a tradition for odds & ends and kiddie delights, Rollier's super hardware store, **Kards Unlimited** teeming with the unusual, **Annex Cookery** for avant garde kitchen wares, **Toadflax** for flowers & hard-to-get gourmet goods, **Marjie Allon** fine stationery and **Eureka** for rare cards/gifts. Don't miss **Urban Renewal's** singular housewares and half-price lower-level bargains. There's more shopping under the skylit roof of the **Theatre Mall** and **Glasswares** and delightful children's **Pinocchio Bookstore** in the little Shadyside Village mall on Aiken.

Jewelry lovers—don't miss the beautiful turquoise and silver at the native Indian **Four Winds Gallery** on Walnut and the gorgeous Turkish collection at **Ephesus** on Filbert.

Save time for browsing in the small malls with some of the city's best gourmet take-out. Stop for a refreshing yogurt at TCBY on Walnut or a quick sandwich/coffee at the Pita Garden, Arabica or Pgh Deli on Copeland. A few blocks away Ellsworth Avenue is blooming with the old Shadyside village atmosphere—antique shops, art galleries and some quaint specialty shops including **Eons** vintage clothing.

# Shadyside Walk & Shop

**Where To Eat:** **Cappy's** *5431 Walnut. Mon-Fri 11-2am, Sat-Sun 10-2am. AE,D,DC,MC,V.* **621-1188.** Mod, dim little bar/eatery with creative sandwiches, great BBQ-grilled chicken. $3.50-$6.

**Cozumel**, *5507 Walnut. Mon-Fri 11-2:30, 5-10, Sat 12-10. Sun 12-9. AE,D,DC,MC,V.* **621-5100.** Spacious, real Mexican; Sat night Latin dance scene. $4-$10. (See Review)

**Doc's Place/Grille** *5442 Walnut. Mon-Fri 4-2am, Sat 12-2. AE,DC,MC,V.* **681-3713.** Casual lounging, snacks in lively saloon. Grills to entrees, bright rooftop patio. Inex-Mod.

**Elbow Room** *5744 Ellsworth. Mon-Sat 11-2am. Sun 11-12. D,MC,V.* **441-5222.** Good mix of food, folks keeps three rooms, bar, patio crowded. Sandwiches to dinners. $2-$12.

**Hotlicks** *Theatre Mall. Mon-Thur 11:30-10, Fri-Sat til 12. Sun 4:30-9. AE,DC,MC,V.* **683-2583.** Hdq for great mesquite ribs, grills, chicken, burgers, salads, sandwiches $3-$15.

**La Feria** *5527 Walnut (above Pamela's). Mon-Sat 10-9. Cappucino bar Sun 9-2. D,MC,V.* **682-4501.** Unique S Amer/ Peruvian sandwiches, plates. $2.50-$6.99. (See Review)

**Max & Erma's** *5533 Walnut. Mon-Thur 11:30-11, Fri-Sat til 12. Sun til 10, Br 11:30-2:30. AE,D,DC,MC,V.* **681-5775.** Huge 2nd-fl room with warm, brassy nooks; eclectic menu— burgers to light entrees, make-your-own sundaes. $2-$10.

**Pamela's** *5527 Walnut. Mon-Sat 8-4, Sun 9-2. No CC.* **683-1003.** Breakfast, lunch, city's best hotcakes $2-$3.50.

**Pasta Piatto** *736 Bellefonte. Lunch Mon-Sat 11:30-3. Dinner Mon-Tues 4:30-10, Wed-Thur til 10:30, Fri-Sat til 11. Sun 3-9. MC,V.* **621-5547.** Top flight N Italian dining. $5-$20. (See Review)

**Shadyside Balcony** *Theatre Mall. Mon, Wed, Thur 11:30-12am, Tues til 11, Fri-Sat til 1. Sun Br 11-3. AE,D,DC,MC,V.* **687-0110.** Glass-wall view of avenue; innovative menu, nightly jazz ($5-$16). (See Review)

**Sushi Too** *5432 Walnut. Mon-Fri 11:30-3, 5-10:30, Fri-Sat til 11:30. Sun 1-9. AE,DC,MC,V.* **687-8744.** Sushi, traditional Japanese in charming decor. $4.50-$18.95. (See Review)

**Szechuan Gourmet**, *709 Bellefonte, Mon-Thur 11:30-10, Fri-Sat til 11, Sun 4:30-10. AE,D,DC,MC,V.* **683-1763..** Excellent Chinese, off-avenue setting. $7.95 up.

**Thai Place** *809 Bellefonte. Mon 4:30-10, Tues-Thur 11:30-10, Fri til 11, Sat 12-11. Sun 12-9:30. AE,D,DC,MC,V.* **687-8586.** Nationally rated Thai in pleasant surroundings; sidewalk tables in summer. $5-$15. (See Oriental)

# REVIEWS

## Shadyside Balcony

**Jazz Beat Goes On at Balcony**

### Shadyside Balcony

*Theatre Mall, 5520 Walnut Street, Shadyside. Mon, Wed, Thur 11:30-12am, Tues til 11, Fri-Sat til 1. Sun Brunch 11-3. Parking on/off Walnut Street. AE,D,DC,MC,V.* **687-0110.**

A Shadyside success story, the Balcony is as popular as ever with its great food and entertainment on the second level of the Theatre Mall. It sets the beat for Walnut Street, picking up the old Shadyside jazz tradition six nights a week. Its big open space, broken by the mall's main stairwell, allows many uses—quieter dining by the glass wall overlooking Walnut Street with a bird's eye view of the avenue... a livelier setting in the back cafe area where you can enjoy music with your meal...or a visit to the long, winding bar with plenty of room for stand-up conversation and crowds spilling down the staircase. The Balcony's music and ambience attracts a wide range of sophisticated partyers.

**When To Go:** Don't miss the music—Mon, Wed & Thur 9-12, Tues 7-11, and Fri & Sat 9-1am. Sunday Jazz Brunch 11-3.

**What To Order:** The excellent food and service continues...thanks to the hands-on management of young owners Muzz Meyers and Bob Feldman. This is one of the city's most innovative a la carte menus with deliciously simple, healthful dishes. Our favorites include the **Roasted Vegetable Salad**—greens, cheddar, herbs, walnuts and a hint of brown sugar—and six delectable **Gourmet Pizzas** i.e. **Spinach & Feta Pizza**—marinated tomatoes, mozzarella, provolone on crispy slightly sweetened dough—a zesty combination! Both are in the $8-$9 range. There's a delightful choice of beautifully crafted soups, salads & unusual sandwiches including the **Flame-Grilled Salmon BLT** with alfalfa sprouts, tomato & bacon. There's also a great **Foccacia Platter—marinated artichokes, roasted bell peppers, brie, tarragon, mushrooms, tomato-basil,** $8.95, and **Smoked Salmon Strudel in Philo** with toasted walnuts & gorgonzola...only $4.95. Dinners have kept their great quality with aromatic grilled versions of tuna, pork, shrimp, tenderloin $12-$16. A longtime favorite, **Cashew Chicken**, is still on the menu at $14. Note to lobster lovers: Mon & Tues are Lobster Nights—all you can eat $26.50 or 1 lobster $19, 2 for $22. Chocolate addicts get their just desserts here too with one of the city's best—**Balcony Hot Fudge** in your own little pitcher to pour over French vanilla ice cream...heaven for $2.95.

**Prices:** Lunch $5.50-$9, Dinner $6-$16.

**What To Wear:** Fashionable casual—Shadyside style.

**Recommended:** American Cuisine, Vegetarian Fare, Fabulous Buys, Late Supper, Pgh After Dark.

**Curry On
South Craig St**

# Star of India

1

*412 S Craig Street, Oakland. Lunch Mon-Sat 11:30-2:30, Dinner Sun-Thur 5-10, Fri & Sat til 10:30. Sun Buffet 12-3. AE,D,DC, MC,V.* **681-5700.**
One of the city's finest Indian restaurants, this serene, pleasant room sends tantalizing aromas up and down Craig Street...the subtle, exotic fragrances of Indian cuisine. The pleasant decor with its Far Eastern touches is a good setting for relaxing dining and introduction to some of the favorite dishes from many Indian states—Machan, Biryani, Delhi/Darbar, Bay of Bengal, Punjab, Bahare Murg—exotic Far Eastern names matched to an array of tempting dishes.

**When To Go:** Buffet—Sun 12-3, Mon & Wed 11:30-2:30.

**What To Order:** There are nearly 60 dishes here, most in the $8-$10 range. To find your favorites we suggest the **Noon Buffet** Sunday, Monday or Wednesday, a tasty and filling table including chicken tandoori, a second meat dish, three vegetable dishes i.e. pea/spinach paneer or tarka daal (lentils and garlic) plus raita (delicious thin homemade yogurt cooled with cucumbers), rice, salad, nan (a tender pita-like bread) and dessert—a bargain at $6.95. Another good idea is the **Thali**, a vegetarian or non-vegetarian assortment. We love the **Vegetarian version, a good full meal for $12.95— crispy Indian bread, peppery wafer-thin fried papadam...** **Dal** (a spicy lentil soup) and an unforgettable, herbed **Matar Paneer**...a delicate blend of green peas and cubed home-made cottage cheese. Even the dessert, **Gulab Jamun,** a bland-tasting fried cheese ball in light honey syrup is habit forming.
The meat Thali ($14.95) includes lamb or beef curry and moist, tender kiln-baked Tandoori Chicken, a favorite dish here. There's also a **Mix-Grill Tandoori** with shish kabob, lamb kabob, yogurt-marinated chicken and Shrimp & Chicken with rice & chutney—a bargain $9.95. For eggplant lovers is the herb-spiced **Bhartha** ($7.95) good with a tasty, crisp-crusted Pakora or Somasa appetizer.
Indian cooking—a medley of fragrant, unfamiliar spices subtly insinuates itself into your favorite cuisines. Don't miss the breads and the tea—two of Indian cuisine's finest offer-ings...the tea...scented and spicy with cardamone, cloves and the bread...moist **Onion Nan,** a gourmet version of un-leavened bread and soft, savory **Poori**...and of course the papadam, an Indian staple.

**Prices:** Lunch $7-$9, Dinner $8-$11.

**What To Wear:** Casually comfortable.

**Recommended:** Indian Cuisine, Vegetarian Fare, Brunch.

# REVIEWS

## South Side

**South Side Saturday Night!**

### South Side

*East Carson Street from Birmingham Bridge to 10th St, 5 minutes from Downtown,*

The historic "Birmingham" neighborhood continues to boom as more and more restaurants, art galleries and small shops open in the 20-block stretch within minutes of major city areas. South Siders are determined to keep their ethnic character amid the new sophistication, creating an interesting mix of urban charm and neighborhood nostalgia. The architecture alone is worth a visit...from the gentrified row houses in the 'flats' toward the river to East Carson's tall, Victorian buildings with their ornamental ironwork, some of the best examples in the U.S. This is prime territory for browsers and collectors—some 32 galleries, antique and craft shops in storefronts harking back to the '30s/'40s.

But if you really want to see South Side changes, visit on a Saturday night. Throngs of people crowd the sidewalks sampling new eateries, mod shops and jazz clubs. To an old-timer it's an unbelievable sight! Joining the **Rex Movie Theater** is **City Theatre's** new home, a restored church at 13th & Bingham. The eccentric **Beehive Coffee Shop** near 12th is still buzzing and more coffee shops, restaurants and shops have opened. South Side is fast becoming Pittsburgh's new Greenwich Village! Browsing on Carson don't miss **Down to Earth's** beautiful crafts at 1022, **South Bank Gallery** at 1300, **Groovy's** pop memorabilia at 1304 and **Perlora's** unique avant garde furnishings at 2220.

Of interest to architectural buffs are the restored Italianate **Antique Gallery** at 1713 and the 110-year-old **Cast Iron Building** at 1737—one of the area's largest intact cast iron facades. At 12th & Bingham off Carson are the rounded arches of the historic Romanesque **South Side Market House** in Bedford Sq. New riverside housing is in the offing and South Side's "restaurant renaissance" continues.

**Where To Eat:**

**Abruzzi's** *52 S 10th. Mon-Thur 11:30-10, Fri-Sat til 11. Sun 4-9. AE,MC,V.* **431-4511.** Fine Italian in warm, stylish town house. Traditional dishes with a flair. Mod. (See Review)

**Antonini** *2700 Jane St. Mon-Thur 11-12, Fri til 1. Sat 5-1. Sun 5-12. AE,D,DC,MC,V.* **381-9901.** Comfortable, family Italian, lovely patio; calamari, pasta, eggplant. Mod-Exp.

**Beehive Coffee House** *14th/Carson. Mon-Thur 7-12am, Fri- Sat til 4 am, Sun 9-11.* **488-4483.** Coffee/tea dessertery, off-the-wall decor, chess/charm, fabulous brews, sweets.

**Blue Lou's** *1510 E Carson. Tues-Sat 11-1:30am. AE,DC, MC,V.* **381-7675.** Barbecued ribs, chicken with lively juke box, waiters sliding down a firehouse pole. Inexp fun.

**Cafe Allegro** *51 S 12th. Dinner Mon-Thur 5-10, Fri-Sat til 11. Sun 4:30-9:30. Reser. MC,V.* **481-7788.** Charming with excellent Riviera cuisine, espresso bar. Mod. (See Review)

**Caffe Giovanni** *2302 E Carson. Lunch Mon-Sat 11-3, Dinner Mon-Thur 4:30-10, Fri-Sat til 11. Sun 4:30-9. AE,DC,MC,V.* **481- 6662.** Fine Italian cuisine in rustic surroundings. Great pasta, seafood, veal, chicken. Mod-Exp. (See Review)

**Chinese on Carson** *1506 E Carson. Mon-Thur 11-10, Fri-Sat til 11. Sun 4-10. AE,DC,MC,V.* **431-1717.** Good-looking 2nd fl room with beautiful ambience. Mod.

**City Grill** *2019 E Carson. Mon 11-10, Tues-Thur til 10:30, Fri-Sat til 11. Sun 4:30-10. AE,MC.V.* **481-6868.** Sizzling hardwood grills—steaks, ribs, chicken, fish. Mod.

**1889 Cafe** *2017 E Carson. Mon-Thur 11-10, Fri til 11. Sat 8:30am-11pm. Sun 8:30-4.* **431-9290.** Casual, seafood, pasta; great pancakes Sat-Sun breakfast 8:30-2. Inexp.

**Hunan Gourmet** *1209 E Carson. Mon-Thur 11:30-10, Fri-Sat til 11. Sun 2:30-9:30. AE,DC,MC,V.* **488-8100.** Superior Hunan/Mandarin, pleasant setting. Daily Dim-Sum. Inex-Mod.

**Le Pommier** *2104 E Carson. Dinner Mon-Thur 5:30-9, Fri-Sat til 10. AE,DC,MC,V.* **431-1901**. Simple, elegant country French. A thoroughbred! Mod-Exp. (See Review)

**Mallorca** *2228 E Carson. Mon-Thur 11:30-10:30, Fri-Sat til 11:30. Sun 12-10. AE,D,DC,MC,V.* **488-1818.** Excellent Spanish/Portugese seafood; lots of elan. Mod-Exp. (Review)

**Margaritaville** *2200 E Carson. Mon-Fri 11:30-2am, Sat-Sun 12-2am. AE,DC,MC,V.* **431-2200.** South of border menu—enchiladas, burritos, mean margaritas, music. Inex-Mod.

**Mario's** *1514 E Carson. Mon-Sat 11-2am. AE,DC,MC,V.* **381-5610.** Real Italian,casual,convivial. Inexp-Mod.(Review)

**Paparazzi** *21st & Carson. 7 days 11-11, Bar til 2. AE,CB,D, DC,MC,V.* **488-0800.** Casual Italian in burnished, two-level glass-front; jazz/blues Thur-Sun. Mod.

**Pgh Steak Co** *1924 E Carson. Mon-Thur 11-12am, Fri-Sat til 1. Sun 4-11. AE,DC,MC,V.* **381-5505.** Steak, grills, sandwiches, pasta. After-theatre favorite. Mod.

**17th St Cafe** *75 S 17th. Lunch Mon-Fri 11:30-2:30.Dinner Mon-Thur 5-10, Fri-Sat til 11. Sun 5-10. AE,DC,MC,V.* **431-9988.** Casual bar/cafe, good Italian. Mod.

# The Shops at Station Square

**Pgh's Ghiradelli Square**

## The Shops at Station Square

*Smithfield & Carson Streets, South Side. Mon-Sat 10-9. Sunday 12-5. Restaurant hours vary. Ten-minute stroll across Smithfield St Bridge or hop the subway to the Square.* **261-9911.** 🔾 Travel around the world in 65 shops...from Ireland to Japan and everywhere in between...all under the high-raftered roof of the restored P&LE Freight House and airy Commerce Court. A triumph of restoration, Pittsburgh's riverfront 'Ghiradelli Square' is a delightful shopping experience and a favorite visitor/tourist stop. And with more than 10 eateries ...good food **and** good taste abounds! Save time to visit the outdoor Bessemer Court and Transporation Museum.

**When To Go:** Any day, Sat til 9, Sun 12-5. Most restaurants open 7 days.

**What To See:** Give yourself at least half a day to explore the Shops... beginning with the Freight House world of Pittsburgh memorabilia, modish fashions and frills, imported coffee and cheeses, books and brass. Browse in beautiful **Michael's Gems and Glass, World's Treasures, Pgh Center for Arts Gift Shop**, **Heart to Heart** for unique gifts and be sure to see the Cat's Meow Village houses at **Parker's** on the balcony. Enjoy the fashions—wools, laces at **St Brendan's Crossing,** unusual art to wear **at Langbrok's,** classics by **Carroll Reed,** Chaz's shoes...and young mods at Casual Corner and The Limited...don't miss the handmade designs at **Chandree of Beverly Hills.** There are also art galleries and a well-stocked **B Dalton Books,** fine men's fashions at **Heinz Healey's** and sporting gifts at **Accent on Sports.** You'll love the children's clothing at **Eenie, Meenie, Miney, Moe**, toys at S W Randall's and the cartoon items at one of the rare **Stay Tooned Disney Outlets.**
Before you move on explore the balcony where you can take home a book or souvenir from the unique **Pgh History & Landmarks Shop.**Take a breather at a small table at **Coffee Express** or stop for ice cream/yogurt at **Likety Split.** Then on to Commerce Court—one of Pittsburgh's best interiors with its high, airy skylit atrium...an exhilarating upward view by the fountain. Here you'll find more beautiful browsing...Italian fashions at **Antonio da Pescara, Etienne Aigner** and the wonderful wares of **Flying Colors.**
Outside, the kids will love exploring Bessemer Court with its 10-ton Bessemer converter and railroad engine and the antique autos of the Transportation Museum open 7 days 12-8. You can explore the eight Railcar Shops with handmade items from quilts to leather (11-6, Sun 12-5) **Weekends in good weather the whole family can take a horse-drawn surrey ride through Station Square.**

**What To Wear:** Your casual best.

# The Shops at Station Square

**Where To Eat:**

**Bobby Rubino's** *Commerce Ct. 7 days. Mon-Thur 11-10:30, Fri-Sat til 12:30, Sun til 9. AE,MC,V.* **642-RIBS.** Handsome, big bar and barbecue—ribs $8-$17, chicken $6.95; burgers, colossal onion ring. Inexp-Mod.

**Chauncy's** *Commerce Court. 7 nights 4:30-2am. Dinner Tues- Sat 6-10. Happy Hour Mon-Fri 5-7. AE,MC,V.* **232-0601.** Spacious nightclub/dancing for sophisticated young, good buffet/dinner. Mod.

**Cheese Cellar** *Mon-Thur 11:30-1, Fri-Sat til 2. Sun Brunch 10:30-1:30, Dinner til 11. AE,DC,MC,V.* **471-3355.** Intimate Euro rathskeller, outdoor cafe in summer; delicious fondue, cheese & sausage boards, sandwiches, salads. $5-$11.

**Houlihan's Old Place** *Sun-Thur 11-11, Fri-Sat til 12:30am. AE,D,MC,V.* **232-0302.** Marvelous 'up' atmosphere, antique paraphernalia, good food, fun. DJ dancing. (See Review)

**Italian Oven** *7 days 11-10. MC,V.* **261-2111.** Wood fire oven pizza, pasta, sandwiches, family atmosphere. Inexp.

**Jimbo's Hot Dog Company** *Mon-Sat 11-9:30, Fri-Sat til 11. Sun 11-6.* **765-1543.** Hot dogs, kolbassi, chili, 140 beers from around the world, tables on the mallway. $1-$2.50.

**Jellyrolls** *7 days 5-2. AE,D,DC,MC,V.* **391-7464.** Piano, sing-a-long bar fun; sandwiches & nachos. Inexp.

**Kiku's of Japan** *Lunch Mon-Fri 11:30-2, Dinner Mon-Thur 5-10:30, Fri-Sat til 11:30. Sun 12-10. AE,DC,MC,V.* **765-3200.** Authentic Japanese; beautifully served sushi, tempura, a la carte specialties. $7.50-$35.

**River Cafe** *Sun-Thur 11:30-10, Fri-Sat til 11. Sun 12-9. AE,CB,D,DC,MC,V.* **765-2795.** Bar, lofty cafe on 2nd level, airy ambience, seafood, pasta, steak. $5-$19. (See Review)

**Roy Rogers** *Mon-Fri 7-9, Sat 9-9, Sun 10-6.* **765-2555.** Family restaurant, roast beef, burgers, chicken. Inexp.

**Sesame Inn** *Mon-Thur 11-10, Fri-Sat til 11. Sun 12-9. AE,MC,V.* **281-8282.** Szechuan/Hunan sesame specialties, serene surroundings. Lunch $5-$8, Dinner $8 up.

**Tequila Junction** *Mon-Thur 11:30-11, Fri-Sat til 12. Sun 12-10. AE,DC,MC,V.* **261-3265.** Real Mexican atmosphere, cuisine. Wonderful place to relax. (See Review)

(See also **Grand Concourse, Gandy Dancer,** outdoor **Garden Cafe** across the Square).

**Sights,
Smells, Taste
of Strip**

## Strip District

*Penn Avenue and Smallman Street from 17th to 28th.*
Pittsburgh's bustling wholesale food market is an invigorating adventure into one of the city's most colorful areas. This is the real Pittsburgh melting pot, the center for foodstuffs from all over the world. Beginning at 2 a.m. the Strip swarms with activity as trucks unload produce, cheeses, meats from Italy, Greece, the Orient and farms far and near as the city sleeps. Night revelers are catching a bite at Primanti's, Pittsburgh's famous late-night eatery, as workers break for lunch and the city's chefs seek out the day's freshest fare.

But Saturday morning the Strip belongs to retail buyers— serious cooks and discerning gourmets in search of fresh provender and hard-to-find ingredients at bargain prices. You can plunge into the Strip's exciting sights, smells, and tastes at Penn & 20th—the pungent cheeses, Italian meats, hot sausage, salami, Greek olives at **Pennsylvania Macaroni Company**, 2010 Penn, Barker Meats at 1812 Penn, **Parma Sausage** at 1734...and 10 blocks down on Smallman the **Pittsburgh Cheese Terminal.** Along with fresh produce and cheeses, **Sunseri's** at 1906 has delicious Italian breads—pepperoni, Tuscan rounds, focaccia and pepper/garlic/onion loaves brushed with olive oil. And at 1806 are **Julien's** delicate French pastries...tortes, truffles, mousses, croissants. There are fascinating displays of fish— a rainbow of liquid colors—at **Benkovitz Seafoods**, 23rd & Smallman and **Wholey's**, 1711 Penn. And everywhere is sidewalk produce—tomatoes, corn, lettuce, watermelon fresh from the farm. Your food basket runneth over!

Other wonders are Chinese pea pods and paper lanterns at **Sambok's**, 17th & Penn, hand-fired work from the kiln at **Penn Avenue Pottery**, 1905 Penn, baskets & wicker furniture on the lower level of **Alioto's Produce**, 2101 Penn. Complete your tour with a stop at Society for Art in Crafts, 2100 Smallman.

Further down Smallman, 100-year-old **St Stanislaus Church,** its horizontal stripes reminiscent of a Florentine basilica, looms over the cobblestone square. Its stained glass windows are worth the tour...ask at the church. Great times to sample the Strip are at the Oktoberfest or in spring when flower sales and little sidewalk cafes bloom. Open all year are **La Prima Espresso**, 21st St, and **USA Gourmet**, 2115 Penn, where you can take your treat to tables under trees in the backyard. There's another side of the Strip—**it's the city's latest boom town for tourist/night life...**with **Metropol, Rosebud** and the exciting **Boardwalk, On the Water** at 15th & Smallman (See Review). The area will soon have another tourist attraction, the block-long **Regional**

**History Center** at Smallman between 12th/13th. And plans for apartments in the old Armstrong Cork Bldg are still afoot.

**Where To Eat:** Some eateries keep market hours—open early am, closed afternoons.

**Benkovitz Seafoods** *23rd & Smallman. Mon-Thur 9-5, Fri til 5:30. Sat 8-5. MC,V.* **263-3016.** Great fish/seafood sandwich, soup; counter, snacking by big lobster pool. $3-$8.

**Brandy's** *2323 Penn. Mon-Thur 11:15-2am, Fri-Sat til 2:30. Sun 3-11. AE,DC,MC,V.* **566-1000.** Classy, good business lunch. Brandyburgers to full dinners; early breakfast. $3-$18.

**De Luca's** *2015 Penn. Mon-Fri 6am-3:30, Sat 6-3. Sun 7-3. No credit.* **566-2195.** Simple fare, 'best' breakfast. $2-$6.

**Italian Oven** *1700 Penn. Mon-Thur 11-10, Fri-Sat til 11. Sun 12-10. AE,D,MC,V.* **765-2440.** One of famous chain with pizza, pasta, salads, desserts in bright surroundings. $3-$9.

**Mad Mex** *20th/Smallman. AE,MC,V.* **261-6565.** An offshoot of popular Oakland restaurant. Terrific Mexican. (Dec '94)

**Paski's** *2533 Penn. Lunch Mon-Fri 11-2, Dinner Mon-Thur 5-10, Fri-Sat til 12. AE,D,DC,MC,V.* **566-2782.** Great food bargains; homey homemade, ribs on Fri. $4-$15.

**Primanti's** *46 18th St between Penn & Smallman. Mon-Sat 24 hrs. Sun til 5am. No credit cards.* **263-2142.** Local legend in tune with market hours. Workers, truckers, night owls come from all over for famous sandwiches. $3-$4.

**Roland's** *1904 Penn. Mon-Thur 11:30-10, Fri til 12, Sat 7am-12am. Sun 11-10. AE,DC MC,V.* **261-3401.** Convivial bar/restaurant with seafood grill. $5-$25.

**Rosebud** *1600 Smallman. Tues-Sat 11:30-2am. Sun 8pm-2am. Food til 10. Bar til 2. AE,D,DC,MC.* **261-2221.** Mod cafe with light meals, salads, sandwiches, coffees/desserts and entertainment every night. $4-$14. (After Dark)

**Spaghetti Warehouse** *2601 Smallman. Mon-Thur 11:30-10, Fri-Sat til 11. Sun 12-10. AE,CB,DC,MC,V.* **261-6511.** Big portions of Italian staples. Family prices to $10.

**Whiskey Dick's** *1600 Smallman. Mon-Sat 11-2am. AE,D, DC,MC,V.* **471-9555.** Casual fun place; hardwood grills, sandwiches, outdoor deck, big drinks. Inexp.

**Wholey's** *1711 Penn. Mon-Thur 8-5:30, Fri til 6, Sat til 5. No credit cards.* **391-3737.** Bustling, big fish market; sandwiches, shrimp in a basket, deviled crab, soup. $2.95 up.

(See **Boardwalk** Review for **Crewsers's, Buster's Crab**)

## Sushi Too

| | |
|---|---|
| **The Colors, Tastes of Japan** | **Sushi Too**<br>*5432 Walnut Street, Shadyside. Mon-Fri 11:30-3, 5-10:30, Sat 11:30-11:30. Sun 1-9. AE,D,MC,V.* **687-8744.** <br>The plain glass block front belies the charming interior of this Japanese restaurant. The entranceway surprises... delights...a mirrored rock garden—gray pebbles, cedar chips, bronze cranes, a big white Japanese drum. Children love it! Inside is a small room bright with the colors of Japan...bold calligraphy over a sushi bar, bandanaed chefs, rice paper sohji screens, colorful prints and even Japanese music...a gay, heartwarming scene. In the back is a plainer room. And upstairs...off a tatami mat corridor...is a series of private dining rooms with sliding doors, low tables and cushioned chairs...for parties of six to 60 by reservation. a perfect setting for traditional Japanese dining. |
| **When To Go:** | Bright dining—day or night. |
| **What to Order:** | Be venturesome. Try the sushi...for the cautious...much of it is cooked. The colorful placemats are a big help, telling you "everything you wanted to know about sushi but were afraid to ask" with bright color photos of sushi (rice-wrapped fish) and sashimi (elegantly-arranged sliced chilled seafood). The Japanese bring their aesthetics to the table...these plates are beautiful! There are also tips on dipping into your soy & horseradish sauces, cleansing your palate with ginger between courses and the correct way to eat sushi—with your fingers. Start with the popular California roll—a special sticky sushi rice, cucumber, avocado and shrimp wrapped in seaweed...sure to please. Your server—or if you're at the bar—the sushi chef, will help you find your favorites. But this is not just a sushi restaurant. There are oodles of noodles—udon & soba with shrimp, chicken, vegetables; plus pork & bean curd, steamed dumplings (shuma) and Donburi—chicken and shrimp meals in a box—and beef/shrimp Teriyaki in sweet/sour sauce. But our favorite is the **Tempura—meltingly light shrimp and vegetables** fried in hot oil. They're served with clear miso soup and a salad with a piquant ginger dressing ($8.95-$16). Another favorite is the **Chef's Smoked Salmon Salad** with ginger ($6.50). This is a colorful setting for discovering your first tastes of Japan—a delicious cuisine, perfect for the growing number of vegetarians in our midst. |
| **Prices:** | $4.95-$16. |
| **What To Wear:** | Informal, casual. |
| **Recommended:** | Japanese Cuisine, Vegetarian Fare, Late Supper, Party Rooms. |

**The Greek Experience**

## Suzie's

1

*130 Sixth Street, Downtown. Mon 11-3, Tues-Fri 11-8, Sat 11-8 show nights.* **No credit cards.** *No liquor.* **261-6443.** *Also 1704 Shady, Squirrel Hill. Mon-Thur 11:30-10, Fri & Sat til 11, Sun 4-9. D,MC,V.* **422-8066.** ♿

If you knew Suzie's like we do you wouldn't miss an opportunity to visit this little downtown Greek restaurant or its popular branch in Squirrel Hill—both with wonderful homemade food at great prices.

Greek cuisine is one of our favorites—a nostalgic reminder of an idyllic trip to the Aegean islands—wonderful memories of sitting at small cafes on sunny wharves, watching the sun set over the waters, sampling the local wine, the delicious moussaka, Greek salads—tangy olives, feta cheese, sliced tomatoes in a row—and then the thin filo pastries, moist with nuts & honey, washed down with strong Greek coffee. Bringing back all of these memories is the food at Suzie's—and as in Greece—the price is right. And in typical Greek fashion, Suzie's Downtown spills out into a busy sidewalk cafe in summer.

**When To Go:** As both restaurants are busy at regular lunch and dinner hours—try late afternoon or after-theatre.

**What To Order:** All of our favorite Greek dishes are here—cooked by the restaurant's owners Suzie Moraitis Grant and her husband Marc. You can get a sample taste of the various specialties with the **Appetizer Plate** ($10) which includes tarama—delicious Greek caviar of whipped pink fish roe, olive oil and lemon juice...fit for the gods—along with tzantziki—a cool mixture of cucumber, garlic, sour cream, grape leaves and hummus. For an entree there's a fine **Moussaka**—an eggplant-ground beef casserole with Bechamel sauce ($8.50) or the **Spanakopita...spinach-cheese pie in filo dough** ($7.50)—both served with rice, vegetable, a mini-Greek salad and delicious homemade bread.

Our dessert favorites are big bowls of creamy **Rice Pudding** with whipped cream ($2.25) or the delectable **Ekmek**—sponge cake soaked in honey with custard and whipped cream—one of the city's best, $2.50. With Greek coffee at $2 you can bring in dinner at around $20 for 2.

You owe it to yourself to try the food at Suzie's and...if you have but one trip to make in your life...make it the Greek islands for their unearthly beauty and inimitable cuisine.

**Prices:** Lunch $3.75-$6, Dinner $7.50-$12.50.

**What To Wear:** Informal, casual.

**Recommended:** Greek Cuisine, Fabulous Buys, Outdoor Dining, Late Supper.

## Tambellini's

| | |
|---|---|
| **Pittsburgh Name For Seafood** | **Tambellini's**<br>*860 Saw Mill Run Blvd, Rt 51 just other side of Liberty Tunnels. Mon-Sat 11-11. AE,DC,MC,V.* **481-1118.** <br>Tambellini's has been a name synonymous with good food & seafood in Pittsburgh for nearly 40 years with Tambellini restaurants all over town. But this is the granddaddy of them all. Many diners remember the original—a small, crowded room on Mt Washington from which grew Louis Tambellini's dream—this big, opulent restaurant, dedicated to good dining and large enough to accommodate all of the Tambellini fans. There's room for 800 in six rooms! This is the city's largest restaurant and true to its fame it's always crowded. |
| **When To Go:** | To really savour the seafood we suggest a relaxing late lunch from 2-4. |
| **What To Order:** | Lunch is a wonderful way to sample delicious house specialties at bargain prices—many from $6-$8 in the generous portions for which this restaurant is noted. There's everything from linguini with mussels for $7.50 to stone and soft crabs in season for $12. Luncheon menus include **Shrimp or Scallops Louie in garlic sauce with toasted bread crumbs—a dish created by the owner,** Louisiana Redfish Cajun Style, Virginia Spots, Lemon Sole, Broiled Scrod...all served with a wide choice of potatoes, vegetable or salad. And featured all the time is the delicious **Baked Stuffed Imperial Crab** for $17.50.<br>Scores of entrees are available anytime for lunch or dinner, a vast array of seafood, fish, steaks, chops and pasta for $14-$20. And each night there's a **Seafood Special** with potato, tossed salad, dessert and coffee for $11.75—a price that can't be beat.<br>For a special dinner try the gargantuan **Seafood Platter—lobster, crab cakes, shrimp, oysters, sole, scallops, a complete dinner for $23.50**—a wonderful buy in itself and even better when shared by two ($2 plate charge). There's also a smaller Platter for $15.95. Top off your meal with a half litre of house wine—red or white for $7—and enjoy your seafood feast.<br>Don't forget this restaurant's also open for after-theatre dining...full meals, sandwiches, snacks...weeknights til 11 weekends til 12, a boon for Pittsburgh late diners. |
| **Prices:** | Lunch $5.50-$8.50, Dinner $12.50-$17.50. |
| **What To Wear:** | Plain or fancy, eating is the serious business here. |
| **Recommended:** | American Cuisine, Seafood, Connoisseur Dining, Rich Man's Guide, Executive Dining, Late Supper. |

# Tequila Junction

**South of the Border in Pittsburgh, PA**

## Tequila Junction

*Second Level, Freight House, Shops at Station Square. Mon-Thur 11:30-11, Fri & Sat til 12. Sun 12-10. No reser. AE,D,DC,MC,V.* **261-3265.** 🚻

If you miss the warmth and romance of Mexican dining, a nice slow visit to Tequila Junction will bring back mellow memories. In an area where pastiche often triumphs, this restaurant has food and atmosphere authentic enough to please the most avid Mexican-Amer food buff. Relaxed is the best approach to the Junction so take a right at the door and make the small wooden bar your first stop to savour the stucco walls, red-tiled floors, blue & white counters...and the smell of salsa again.

For the strong, there's a Gold Shooter of Jose Cuervo Tequila, $3 & up, with the traditional lemon and salt and Mexican beer for $3.75. But the Junction is most famous for its **oversized Margaritas in giant cocktail goblets** (also $3.75) in regular, strawberry and nine other flavors—guaranteed to have you seeing through rose-colored glasses. As the drink is large and the night long, we suggest you sip and carry it to your table to last through the meal—but not before sampling the bar's **homemade tortilla chips with the house's piquant salsa...the best dip in town.** When you're sufficiently mellowed it's time to enter the gracious dining room with its candlelit tables, high backed Mexican chairs and veranda overlooking the Shops.

**When To Go:** Off-hours to savour the atmosphere. Lunch at 2. Dinner after 6 weekdays to avoid weekend lines of fellow sojourners.

**What To Order:** The "Tequila Gaceta" newspaper-menu will put your budget worries at ease. **Prices have barely budged here in years.** Highest item is Shrimp Sonora—a tortilla with sauteed shrimp & melted jack. ($9.50.) Combinations of Tacos, Burritos and Enchiladas with rice & frijoles start at $4.50. We recommend the **Chimichanga**—a deep-fried burrito with frijoles and beef or chicken—topped with guacamole, sour cream, tomatoes, served with rice...a good dinner at $7.50. Or you can **share an order** of three of the house's best—a **Ground Beef Taco, Chicken & Cheese Enchilada** and a **Shredded Beef Burrito** with delicious house sauce $3-$4. If you liked the dip at the bar you'll love the house's **Chili con Queso**—melted cheese with chilies, tomatoes, onions & chips for $2.95. Watch for it on other entrees.

**Prices:** Lunch/Dinner $6-$10.

**What To Wear:** Leisurely smile...clothes to match.

**Recommended:** Tex-Mex Cuisine, Vegetarian Fare, Fabulous Buys, Late Supper.

# The Terrace Room

**Elegant Dining At Grand Hotel**

## The Terrace Room

*The Westin William Penn, Mellon Square, Downtown. Open 7 days 6:30am-11, Sat til 12. Sun Brunch 11-2. Reser sugg. AE,DC,MC,V.* **553-5235.** ♿

Dining at this grand hotel is always an exciting occasion... more so since the renovation of the ornate Terrace Room off the lobby. A Pittsburgh landmark, the room has been restored to its 1916 splendor, the beautiful Italianate molded ceiling, crystal chandeliers, huge mirrors, walnut paneling and rose damask walls bringing back wonderful memories from a lavish era in Pittsburgh's past.

The service is excellent—and pleasant—the beef is unexcelled and the warm, comfortable surroundings make this restaurant ideal for a happy celebration...an anniversary, holiday dinner or reunion of old friends.

**When To Go:** Sunday Dinner or Saturday night for dining (5:30-11) and dancing from 8 to midnight.

**What To Order:** Dinner dancing in the "T" has become a tradition for many Pittsburghers who come to enjoy the fine cuisine and the music of the Nick Lomakin Trio. Come early any night to enjoy a cocktail ($4.25) or wine ($3.75) and the piano in the beautiful Palm Court Lobby, a wonderful prelude to dinner. A new menu returns the food to its original Renaissance theme, using the finest local Italian foodstuffs.

Entrees, served with soup or salad, include a wide range of tastes—an ever-popular Filet Mignon and NY Strip, Veal Ravioli with Lobster Claw Sauce, a house rendition of Paella plus homemade pastas—Pecorino Romano Tortellini, Spinach and Egg Linguine with Marinated Shrimp.

But we recommend you try the house specialty, **'the finest prime rib in Pittsburgh,'** a juicy 12-oz Crown Cut served with baked potato and vegetable...a hearty dinner for $18. Included is the Terrace Room Salad with crumbled gorgonzola or hot soup of the day from Ray's Kettle. And for dessert...the renowned **William Penn Cheesecake with fresh strawberries** ($3.95), one of the best anywhere. Also delicious are the warm Cobblers, Chocolate Mud Cake and Lemon Curd with Raspberries $2-$4. Dinner with house wine and dessert comes to around $60 for 2 for an elegant urban repast.

**Prices:** Breakfast $5-$12, Lunch $6-$13, Dinner $8.25-$22.50.

**What To Wear:** Enjoy your finery in beautiful surroundings.

**Recommended:** Continental Cuisine, Night of Romance, Steak, Rich Man's Guide, Executive Dining, Brunch, Pgh After Dark.

## Tessaro's

### Sizzling Food From The Hardwood Grill

*4601 Liberty Avenue, Bloomfield. Mon-Sat 11-12. AE,D, DC,MC,V.* **682-6809.**

Long before we visited this eatery, rumors of its fabulous hardwood grills wafted back to us. Ribs, big thick pork chops, sizzling steak at great prices. First impressions of just another neighborhood bar were quickly smothered in the heavenly aromas at the door and helped us through the first long wait for a table. And we found—'tis true, 'tis true! This is real good eatin', some of the best in town.. A hungry man/woman's mecca, Tessaro's is a warm, friendly place with eight tables opposite a very busy bar. Owner Kelly Harrington, a big, mild 'black Irishman' greets you at the door and somehow keeps the long lines moving...no reservations. From the denizens of the booths happily packing away food—many from the shirt & tie crowd—it's obvious something extraordinary is going on here. It's a Pittsburgh resurgence of real down home cookin'.

**When To Go:** Lines subside some during weekdays—Mon for Mexican, Thur for ribs. it's a busy place late night weekends.

**What To Order:** We were lucky enough to taste the ribs first, a Thursday special...and they were **delicious...zesty and tender with big flavour seared in by the intense, hardwood flame** $9.50-$10.50. After the ribs we were hardly able to sample our big **Grilled Chicken Sandwich** ($5-$6)...best we've ever had...with heaps of Mom's potato salad and homemade cole slaw. Fit for a queen! On our next visit the burgers ($4.75-$5.95) came up to their big reputation...the crust charred, tender pink inside...with melted cheese & mushrooms oozing out over the edge...wow! Then we had to sample the entrees ($12-$16)...for our readers of course... and were happy to find that salmon and swordfish were perfect from the grill and the fried potatoes were out of sight. So...what was left but to go back Monday for Mexican. It turned out to be the biggest surprise...a delectable homemade recipe, the **Big Bear,** a deliciously melting union of chicken/beef, cheese, sour cream, salsa, guacamole, tomato—grilled inside a tortilla...crisp around the edges. This was the best. They had to haul away the plate. What can we say...good eatin' is good eatin'. Someone waiting for a table told us, "I discovered this place last Friday and I've already been back three times." Now all that remains is to sample the big steak, the huge chops, the chili...

**Prices:** $2.50 for soup to $16 for filet mignon.

**What To Wear:** Something loose and comfortable.

**Recommended:** American Cuisine, Steak, Fabulous Buys, Late Supper.

# REVIEWS

## Tramp's Grand Old Saloon

**Old Pgh Site Has '90s Charm**

### Tramp's Grand Old Saloon

*212 Blvd of the Allies (between Market & Wood), Downtown. Hours: Mon-Thur 11:30-10, Fri til 11, Sat 5-11. Bar til 2. Reser sugg. AE,DC,MC,V.* **261-1990.**

This is one of downtown's most charming restaurants with small rooms, brick walls, a Greenwich Village atmosphere and lots of private nooks for romantic rendezvous. Owners Ed & Bill Zelesko have renovated an old 1860 building (the stained glass transom gives the location as '80 Second St) which traces its history back to one of Pittsburgh's oldest bar-bordellos. Loaded with atmosphere, Tramp's has candle-lit tables, a skylight room on the site of a former garden, a venerable old bar and a 200-year-old clock which sometimes chimes on the hour. A second floor rooftop patio, ensconced amid downtown buildings, is like dining in the midst of Gotham. And for food and service Tramp's is in the tradition of the small, good New York restaurants.

**When To Go:** Lunch 11:30-5, Late Supper Fri & Sat til 11.

**What To Order:** Dinners range from $11-$19 for some great steak entrees— Mixed Grill with Filet Mignon, Brasciole, NY Strip, Louisiana Steak and the **famous Pittsburgh Steak**...seared on the outside...rare inside. There's also a great, crunchy **Walnut Breaded Flounder**, Stuffed Shrimp, Seafood and Cajun platters...all served with vegetable rice pilaf or a twice-baked potato and a garden salad. But we also found good chicken dishes, **Maryland Crab Cakes** and a **Pasta Medley** in the $11-$13 range.

Other pasta dishes and the "Entertaining Entrees" can be had for much less–$8-$9. Named after former ladies of the house are the Adeline—Chicken Breast on a bed of Rice Pilaf, Stella— Pasta with Crabmeat, Shrimp in cream sauce and Rosa—Baked Rigatoni with Meatballs. For lunch try **Steak Salad** with vegetables & pasta and **Angel Hair** in tomato sauce ($6-$8) with house wine $3.75...about $25 for 2. The Beefburger, Virginia Ham and fish sandwiches ($6-$7) are also available day or night as are soups, salads and desserts.

Before you leave, climb the long, narrow front staircase to Dolly's Boudoir, a comfortable second floor room and bar. Next door is Madame's Room complete with fireplace, antiques and adjoining patio. Both are popular spots for private parties.

**Prices:** Lunch $5-$9. Dinner $9-$17.

**What To Wear:** Lovely atmosphere lends itself to dress-up for evening tryst, informal for lunch.

**Recommended:** American Cuisine, Steak, Party Rooms, Late Supper.

| | |
|---|---|
| **Great Food At At Oakland "Cheers"** | **Union Grill**<br>*413 S Craig Street, Oakland. Mon-Thur 11-11, Fri & Sat til 12. AE,D,DC,MC,V.* **681-8620.** ♿<br>A favorite Craig Street haunt (formerly Great Scot) this is a polished oakwood room with 'honest American food'—big portions of no-frills grills, sandwiches and hearty entrees. Retaining its old, friendly "Cheers" barroom atmosphere, the handsome room is as comfortable as ever. The carpet has taken on a burgundy hue but the long bar, wooden booths and tables from the glassfront area to the raised back level are much the same. A genial "hang-out" for Craig Street denizens, museum/concert go-ers and late nighters, it's as crowded as ever. |
| **When to Go:** | Lunch/Dinner/Late Supper. |
| **What To Order:** | The menu however *has* changed—to more economical, no-nonsense, American cooking—grills, sandwiches, salads and nightly entrees all under $15. Burgers still star here in various versions $6-$7 as do soups i.e. roasted corn chowder...vegetarian black bean chili...and the salads excel. There's everything from a big house salad $1.75 to a traditional Caesar with Chicken at $6.25 and Grilled Vegetable Salad, a Tostoda Chicken, Shrimp Pasta and Fruit with yogurt...all in $5-$6 range.<br>But the good news is the "meat and potatoes" entrees— Meatloaf, Bratwurst, Penne Pasta, Tomato Fettuccine, Pita Pizza all around $6-$7, served with the house salad and focaccia. We heartily recommend the **Union Meatloaf with roasted garlic potatoes** ($6.50) or **the tasty Grilled Bratwurst** ($6.75) with the garlic potatoes and onion marmalade ...lots of food at good prices.<br>Burgers here are as good as ever...big and mealy. They, along with a big variety of sandwiches—NY Steak, Grilled Salmon, Grilled Vegetarian, Smoked BLT—come with your choice of potatoes, onion rings or a unique black bean and corn salad. **There are lots of Southwest touches here** by a chef from the Coyote Cafe in Sante Fe.<br>There are also nightly specials, full dinners i.e. ribs, chicken, salmon, mahi-mahi, steak from $11 to $15. Desserts, also hearty and relatively economical ($2.50-$2.75), include Turtle Pie, Carmel Cheesecake and a very chocolatey Suicide Cake. While the kitchen here is still changing, the plethora of offerings under $10 are welcomed by the area's many singles and seniors who dine out nightly. |
| **What To Wear:** | Casual to nightime dress-up. |
| **Prices:** | $5-$15. |
| **Recommended:** | American Cuisine, Late Night. |

# Gourmet's Glossary

**almondine**—garnished with blanched almonds sauteed in butter.

**aperitif**—a short alcoholic beverage, usually taken as an appetite stimulant; may refer to any pre-dinner drink.

**Barsac**—sauteed in butter & Sauternes, sprinkled with cheese & bread crumbs.

**beef Wellington**—marinated filet, topped with mushrooms and baked in a puff pastry crust, garnished with bordelaise— a red wine and marrow sauce.

**Bearnaise**—Hollandaise sauce with tarragon, shallots, other seasonings & wine.

**bechamel**—a white cream sauce seasoned with cloves and nutmeg.

**bisque**—a rich cream soup usually from fish or shellfish; a rich frozen dessert.

**Bourguignon, a la**—a red wine sauce with mushrooms & onion.

**Chateaubriand**—thick slice from center cut of beef filet, grilled, usually sliced at tableside and served with Chateaubriand sauce (wine, shallots & butter) or Bearnaise, a creamy wine sauce.

**cherries jubilee**—stone cherries simmered in syrup, flamed in brandy or liqueur.

**coquille St. Jacques**—scallops.

**crepes Suzette**—thin pancakes flamed in a sauce of Curacao & orange juice.

**en crute**—in a pastry shell.

**English trifle**—mixture of cake soaked in Madeira or liqueur with rum custard, whipped cream & fruit jam.

**escargot**—snails, usually served in the shell.

**flambe**—flamed with brandy or liqueur.

**foie gras**—specially fattened goose or duck liver.

**Hollandaise**—thick sauce made with eggs, butter, lemon juice or vinegar.

**Madeira**—a brown sauce of meat stock and Madeira wine.

**medallions**—small round or oval pieces of meat, often called tournedos when beef.

**mousse**—a molded, usually cold dish, either a dessert with rich cream ingredients or a gelatin based meat, fish or vegetable mold.

**osso buco**—veal shank simmered in spiced white wine, treasured for bone marrow.

**peach Melba**—a dessert of half peach with vanilla ice cream, topped with raspberry sauce & whipped cream.

**persillade**—chopped parsley topping often mixed with garlic & bread crumbs.

**piccata**—veal sauteed in lemon, butter, mushrooms and white wine.

**provencale, a la**—spicy, generally with garlic and tomato.

**saltimbocca**—veal cutlets stuffed with ham, sage & Mozzarella cheese, sauteed in white wine sauce.

**scallopini**—thinly sliced meat, usually veal, or fish, flattened and fried in butter or oil.

**siciliana**—broiled steak, baked with coating of oregano & garlic seasoned bread crumbs.

**sorbet**—a light fruit ice generally less sweet than sherbet, served between courses to refresh the palate.

**souffle**—a high, light dessert or savory dish, pureed and thickened with egg yolks and beaten egg whites.

**torte**—usually dessert, rich layers of cake made with crumbs, eggs, nuts, topped with whipped cream and fruit.

**truffles**—underground fungus used for flavoring and as a garnish.

What makes a fabulous meal? A combination of good food, wine, beautiful surroundings, elegant service...and most especially...the company. Here are some fabulous feasts for those special occasions when money's no object...showcasing the extraordinary talents of local chefs and the variety of fine cuisines available in the Gr Pittsburgh area.

## 4-Star In-Town Dining

### Baum Vivant

*5102 Baum Blvd, Oakland. Dinner Mon-Thur 5:30-10, Fri & Sat til 11. AE,CB,D,DC,MC,V.* **682-2620.**
This is a little jewel of a restaurant with a band-box look and a sophisticated New York ambience–to be expected from owner Toni Pais, former maitre d' of La Normande. He has created a fine Portuguese/Italian menu—haute-cuisine dishes with individual touches...bass with fennel and eggplant, fresh fish, beef with foie gras, steak with chestnuts, delicious house soups. Every meal includes a creamy complimentary pate and the house signature herbed cream cheese with your crusty bread. Our feast here is a special Lobster Flambe.

### Suggested Feast:

**Appetizer:** Duck Confit Macau, wrapped in a mo shoo shell with plum wine sauce $7.95 and complimentary Chicken Liver Pate.
**Salad:** Baby Californian lettuce with passion fruit vinaigrette.
**Intermezzo:** Orange juice with campari, rum and raspberry schnapps.
**Entree:** Lobster Flambe with Tarrogon Creme Fraiche with fresh vegetables and a starch, $25.95.
**Dessert:** Roasted Hazelnut Tart with hazelnut butter from Piedmont, Italy and mascarpone cheese, $4.50.
**After Dinner Drink:** Algarvinha Almond liqueur. Complimentary.
**Wine:** House champagne Devin de Marqui, $4.50 glass with your duck; and a white burgundy Meursault le Pilets 1/2 bottle $32.
**The Tab:** Appetizer $7.95; Entree $25.95; Dessert $4.50 Wine $41. Total for 2: $118 for a splendid in-town adventure in dining.

## Romantic French Dining—On The Terrace

### Cafe Azure

*317 S Craig Street, Oakland. Lunch Mon-Thur 11:30-2:30, Fri-Sat til 3. Dinner Mon-Thur 5:30-9:30, Fri-Sat til 11. Reser. AE,D,DC,MC,V.* **681-3533.**
Attention to every detail of cuisine, ambience and service have combined to make a winner of this sophisticated Oakland cafe with a suave contemporary decor. Chef Amy Henry's fine French cuisine highlights inspired appetizers i.e. Vegetable Ragout and inventive fish, fowl and pasta entrees $6-$12 for lunch and $12-$24 for dinner. In good weather add to your delight by dining on the blue-awninged patio, one of the city's best ambiences. For our feast the house has chosen a Lamb Dinner.

### Suggested Feast:

**Appetizer:** Oriental Crab Cake with tamari garlic butter, $7.
**Salad:** Warm Asparagus with grilled new potatoes, beets and hard-cooked eggs with a creamy Parmesan tomato-chive vinaigrette, $6.75.
**Entree:** Lamb Loin filled with goat cheese, spinach, pine nuts and a fresh tomato-thyme demi-sauce, $23.
**Dessert:** Baum Torte, alternating layers of almond pastry and pistachios finished with a butter cream, glazed with chocolate and served on a bed of creme Anglaise, $6.
**Wine:** Beringer Private Reserve Cabernet Sauvignon 1986, $60.
**The Tab:** Appetizer $7, Salad $6.75, Entree $23, Dessert $6, Wine $60 for a total of $145.50 for a delightful dinner.

*"A man hath no better thing under the sun than to eat, and to drink, and to be merry."* Ecclesiastes 8:15

## Adventures in An Italian Trattoria

### Davio's

*2100 Broadway Ave, Beechview. (Up W Liberty, rt onto Pauline at Rohrich Cadillac, left to Broadway).* **No credit cards.** *No liquor.* **531-7422.**
Pittsburgh's chef-extraordinary David Ayn now holds forth in his own restaurant, a warm, cozy trattoria with seven white-clothed tables, bread loaves on the sideboard and the real feel of Italy. Everything's beautifully done...the bread's delicious...the salad's superb... the pasta's perfecto. The price can be modest for familiar Italian dishes—chops, fish, sausage, pasta (Lunch $6-$11, Dinner $10-$18). But for a special dinner you can order dishes "dal mano del maestro...from the hand of the maestro...charred filet mignon, pan fried sole with curried crab meat, veal scaloppine, poached salmon with crabmeat and capers from $24-$29. For our feast Chef Ayn has chosen two of his favorite signature dishes.

### Suggested Feast:

**Peasant Bread/Olio Santo** The chef's savory Italian breadsticks dipped in fagiolini Tuscan white/bean garlic spread or basil olive oil & grated parmigiano/reggiano.
**Antipasti:** Portabella mushrooms in olive oil and garlic, $7.95 for 2.
**Salad:** The delicious house salad with roasted peppers, cannellini beans, artichokes in balsamic vinegar, topped with gorgonzola, included with dinner.
**Pasta:** Cavatappi, corkscrew pasta, in marinara sauce (with the veal).
**Entrees:** Grilled Double Veal Chop served with roasted peppers and zucchini, $27.95 and Linguine alla Pescatora—tossed with lobster tail, shrimp and scallops in a seasoned tomato blushed garlic oil, $28.95.
**Dessert:** Fresh Raspberry Pie, $5.95 and Russian Sable, a dense chocolate truffle cake, $4.95.
**Wine:** Bring your own–Chef's suggestion–a white Tuscan Terra di Tufo Vernaccia, $29.
**The Tab:** Antipasto $7.95, Entrees: $56.90, Desserts: $11.90, Wine, $29. Total: $105.85 for an Italian feast for 2. .

## Steak Dinner Extraordinaire

### The Colony

*Greentree & Cochran Roads, South Hills. Mon-Thur 5:30-10:30, Fri-Sat til 11. Sun 9-4. Reser sugg.* **561-2060.**
A warm restaurant with an informal atmosphere around an open brick grill, this is where many Pittsburgh executives go to enjoy what is indubitably one of–if not the best–steaks in town *(Travel/ Holiday* & local awards). And now there's nightly entertainment and music in the lounge til 12. The menu boasts grilled swordfish, lemon sole, lamb chops, lobster, veal ($20-$26), but it's the steak you'll want. P.S. You can now take home some of the house's famous steak sauce.

### Suggested Feast:

**Appetizer:** House specialty Shrimp Scampi in garlic sauce, $7.50, a wonderful prelude to dinner.
**Entree:** Sirloin Steak (13-14 oz) sizzling from the charcoal grill, basted with special 'Colony Sauce,' $26, served with a salad and baked potato/pasta, vegetables and sour cream, chives & bacon toppings.
**Dessert:** Fresh fruit or selection from the pastry tray, included with dinner.
**The Wine:** A Robert Mondavi Cabernet Sauvignon $28.
**The Tab:** Appetizer $7.50, Steak $26, Wine $28. Total: $95 for a relaxing feast.

## Dinner In The Country

### Chestnut Ridge Inn

*Rt 22, Blairsville. Dinner Mon-Thur 5-10, Fri & Sat til 11. Sun Brunch 11-2, Dinner til 9.* **459-7191.**

This big inn with a sweeping view of the Chestnut Ridge golf course, is known for its superb dining and superior service. The upstairs restaurant is an elegant setting...plush blue carpeting, crystal chandeliers and a beautiful stained glass ceiling window. Lunches and late supper in the downstairs restaurant are a moderate $3-$10 but upstairs dinner entrees climb from $14-$23 for delicacies i.e. Medallions of Beef stuffed with Swiss Cheese and Lobster, fresh fish and a new lamb dish with dried prunes, exotic spices & brandy—all served with relish tray and potato/vegetable. For our feast the house presents a Salmon Banquet.

### Suggested Feast:

**Relish Tray:** All of the Inn's dinners are preceded by a beautiful tray of crisp vegetables with black Italian olives.
**Appetizer:** Scalloped Mousse Florentine, Clam Sauce Nouvelle, $6.95.
**Soup:** Italian Wedding Soup, $1.50.
**Salad:** Tossed fresh garden greens vinaigrette, $2.95.
**Sorbet:** Lemon-lime to clear the palate.
**Entree:** Baby Salmon Filet stuffed with a duxelles (pureed mushroom) and crabmeat, baked in a puff pastry and served with dill Hollandaise, $19.95 accompanied by a vegetable, potato or rice and house-baked French bread.
**Dessert:** Special Coffee Espresso, $1.50.
**Wine:** A good dry white Calif Pinot Chardonnay Les Charmes, $13.50.
**The Tab:** Appetizer $6.95, Soup $1.50, Salad $2.95, Entree $19.95, Dessert Coffee $1.50, Wine $13.50. Total for 2: $79 plus tax and gratuity for a beautiful dinner in the country.

## The High Life—Feasting Atop Mt Washington

### Christopher's

*1411 Grandview Ave, Mt Washington. Mon-Thur 5-10, Fri & Sat til 11.* **381-4500.**

One of the best dining experiences in the city is at this restaurant high atop Mt Washington with spectacular views in all directions from its sheer glass walls. An outside elevator whisks diners to the glamorous multi-level rooftop room with dramatic lighting, a top-hat/white-tie feel and innovative use of glass, aluminum and coal—a sophisticated showcase for Pittsburgh products. Everything about this restaurant says Pittsburgh is some-place special. Dinner can be done for less—entrees range from $15-$32, several in the $19-$22 range—but for our feast Owner Christopher Passodelis and the house has put together a menu to match the spectacular decor. Allow at least four hours for your meal.

### Suggested Feast:

**Appetizer:** An exciting beginning—Caspian Sea Caviar (market price) and a bottle of Taittinger champagne ($208).
**Salad:** Smoked Duck Salad, $5.95.
**Entrees:** Creole Bouillbaise, an array of fresh shellfish and crustaceans served in a sea broth with tomato and saffron wine, $25, or Lamb Chops with Apricot and Mustard, $30.
**Dessert:** Cafe Leigoia—coffee ice cream in a cookie shell with coffee liqueur, garnished with banana slices—and Chocolate Macademia & Praline Tarts, $4.50 each.
**Finishing Touch:** Glass of Louis XIII cognac, $95 for 2.
**The Tab:** Appetizer around $165, Salad $5.95, Entree $27, Dessert $4.50, Wine $303. Total: $542.90 for 2 plus tax and gratuity for your night at the top!

---

*"Make no small plans. They have no power to stir men's souls."*

## Roman Banquet in Hills of Pittsburgh - CCCLVI for Two

### D'Imperio's

3412 William Penn Hwy, Wilkins Twp. Lunch Mon-Fri 11:30-3, Dinner Mon-Sun 5-11. Reser. **823-4800.**
A mecca for serious diners, D'Imperio's has earned a reputation as one of the best restaurants in Western Pa for the grace of its Continental cuisine and service. Its famous $35 six-course meal, available upon request, includes entrees i.e. Trout stuffed with Escargot, Baked Shrimp with Roquefort, Beef Wellington, veal, steak—with hot/cold appetizers, soup, salad, fresh fruit and delicious desserts. (A $25 four-course version is available to budget diners.) Owner Tony D'Imperio drew on some of the restaurant's best dishes for a fabulous 'once in a lifetime' Roman banquet, a feast fit for a Pittsburgh king!

### Italian Feast:

**Aperitif:** Punt e Mes, an aperitif of herbs & spices served on ice, $3.50
**Appetizer:** Grilled Swordfish with Coconut, $6.95
**Pasta:** Spinach Spaghettini with Pesto Genovese, $3.95.

**Entree:** Red Snapper in thin pastry with spinach, minced oysters and Galliano, asparagus with Hollandaise, $18.75.
**Salad:** Hearts of Endive & Escarole Vinaigrette, $3.
**Intermezzo:** A sorbet of grapefruit ice generously drenched with Polish Wyborowa (vodka), $5.
**After Dinner:** A final touch—Ghiottini, crunchy almond cookies, espresso, $3.
**Wines:** With Appetizer/Pasta: Vernaccia di San Gimignano, a crisp dry old Italian white wine (Michaelangelo's favorite) from the 13th C, $38; with Entree: California Chardonnay from Farniente Winery, $65; with Dessert: 1/2 bottle Trockenbeerenauslese, a German dessert wine from selected late harvest berries, $90. Then a glass of King Louis XIII, the world's most exclusive cognac, 1oz $75 for 2, ($1000 a bottle). Is it any wonder the old Romans reclined on couches while dining!
**The Tab:** Food: $88.30 for 2 plus $268 for wine for a total of $356 for 2 for your wonderful epicurean feast plus tax & gratuity. As the Romans do!

## Candlelight Dining in Elizabethan Castle

### Hyeholde

Coraopolis Heights Rd, Moon. 10 min from Airport. Lunch Mon-Fri 11:30-2. Dinner Mon-Sat 5-10.Reser. **264-3116.**
A legend in and out of the city, this lovely, castle-like restaurant is on two acres of beautiful wooded grounds. Every Pittsburgher should dine at least once in the warm Elizabethan mansion with its big fireplaces, flagstone floors and hanging tapestries. The cuisine (awarded by Distinguished Restaurants of N Amer), features a wide range of steak, beef, fish for dinner starting at $17. More casual lunches are $7-$13. Chosen for our feast are two top Hyeholde dinners.

*Suggested Feast:*
**Appetizer:** The house's famous Sherry Bisque from a 'secret recipe', $3.
**Salad:** Field greens with lemon, chives, and extra-vigin olive oil, $4.
**Entree:** Grilled Beef Filet with blue cheese & red wine in wild mushroom sauce, Roesti Potatoes, $28, and Roast Lamb with artichoke potato puree and truffle sauce, $29
**Dessert:** Creme Brulee, $5.50 with Cappucino, $3.
**Wine:** Clos Du Bois Merlot, $35.
**The Tab:** Appetizer $3, Salad $4, Entrees $57.50, Dessert/Cappucino $8.50. Wine $35. Total: $123.50 for a romantic night for two.

## Intimate Edwardian Elegance

### The Harvest

*Pittsburgh Vista Hotel, Liberty Center at Penn Avenue, Downtown. Lunch Mon-Fri 11:45-2:30, Dinner Mon-Sat 5:30-10:30. AE,D,DC,MC,V.* **227-4480.**

This warm, intimate room has an Edwardian flavour—glass, brass, a genial, comfortable bar and paintings of the harvest bounty. The classic cuisine, which has earned a 4-Star Mobil rating, changes with each season, offering the freshest of ingredients in creative, elegant entrees ...fish, steak, duck, chicken, veal, fresh fruits and vegetables. Lunch ranges from $9-$14, dinner $14-$26 with special pre-theatre dinners on performance nights, an opportune time to sample the food and matchless service of the European-trained staff. Chef extraordinaire Willi Nuenlist has included several of his favorites in this Swordfish Feast.

### Suggested Feast:

**Aperitif:** A refreshing beginning, a sparkling glass of Shramsberg Cremant Demie Sec '88, $9.75 glass.
**Cold Appetizer:** Seared Peppered Filet of Beef with Haricot Vert (green bean) Salad and shaved Romano cheese, $7.50.
**Hot Appetizer:** Warm Goat Cheese in Phyllo Crust with Summer Salad and tomato vinaigrette, $7.25.
**Soup:** Gold Oak Mushroom Consomme with an herb croissant, $4.50.
**Entree:** Broiled Fresh Swordfish with Roasted Vegetables, Sauce Choron, $17.
**Dessert:** Terrine of Fresh Berries with two-fruit sherbet, $4.95.
**Wine:** '92 Grgich Hills Fume Blanc, $28.
**The Tab:** Aperitif $9.75, Appetizers $14.75, Soup $4.50, Entree $17, Dessert $4.95, Wine $28. Total: $129.90 for 2 plus tax. gratuity for an extraordinary fish feast.

## Sizzling Night on the Town

### Morton's of Chicago

*CNG Tower, 625 Liberty Avenue, Downtown. Lunch Mon-Fri 11:30-2:30, Dinner Mon-Sat 5:30-11. Sun 5-10. Valet parking. AE,CB,DC,MC,V.* **261-7141.**

Of the famous Chicago chain, this burnished, club-like room is a splendid setting for superior steak. The lights are dim, the atmosphere relaxing, the service impeccable and the overall feeling one of great comfort. These are perfect prime steaks, sizzling with seared-in juices—filet mignon, porterhouse, NY strip, ribeye, tenderloin. Entrees from $16-$30 also include veal, chicken, lamb, fish and lobster. For our feast General Manager Chuck Simeone and Chef Alan Blumenfeld have chosen the house specialty, Porterhouse Steak.

### Suggested Feast:

**Appetizer:** Smoked Pacific Salmon, sliced thin, with capers, onions and toast points, $8.95.
**Salad:** Morton's Signature iceberg and Romaine topped with blue cheese dressing, $4.75.
**Entree:** Porterhouse Steak, combination of NY and the filet, 24 oz cut, $29.95.
**Vegetables:** Baked Idaho Potato, $3.95 and fresh steamed asparagus with Hollandaise, $6.50.
**Dessert:** Chocolate, Grand Marnier or Lemon Souffle—$9.25 for 2.
**Wines:** With appetizer: Jordan J sparkling wine from Alexander Valley $65; with entree: '90 Spottswoode, Napa Valley, $95. After-dinner, a glass of '85 Dowsport, $12.50 ea.
**The Tab:** Appetizer $8.95, Salad $4.75, Entree $29.95, Vegetable/Potato $10.45, Dessert $9.25 for 2. Wines: $185. Total: $302.45 for a sizzling night on the town.

*"A man's reach should exceed his grasp...
Else what's a heaven for! " - Browning*

## "Dinner in the Diner" — Railroad Car Romance

### Prima Classe—DiSalvo's Station

*325 McKinley Avenue. Latrobe. Railroad car dining by reser only Fri-Sat 5-11. (Regular restaurant Tues-Fri 11-11, Sat 4-11, Sun 10-9.) AE,CB,D,DC,MC,V.* **539-0500.**
It's "prima classe"—first class all the way—in this unique turn-of-the-century railroad dining car. Restored to its original 1909 elegance, the shiny red car sits resplendent in the center of DiSalvo's colorful restaurant, a former railway depot. It's the pride of owner Guy DiSalvo and son, Joseph of DiSalvo's restaurant in Jeannette, who opened the Station in 1990. The railroad car gleams inside and out... nothing has been spared on appointments...pristine, sparkling crystal, crisp table linens, silver service. And there's a "Prima Classe" menu to match bringing back memories of the heyday of elegant railroad car dining. It's well worth the hour's drive from downtown Pittsburgh...especially for railroad buffs. Here's a house veal specialty for your unique excursion.

***Suggested Feast:***
**Appetizer:** Chargrilled shrimp in a pesto cream sauce, $9.95.

**Soup:** Scrippelle 'M Busse, crepes in chicken broth, $2.95.
**Pasta:** Linguine Putanesca with olive oil, banana peppers, tomatoes, green and black olives, $4.95.
**Salad:** Fresh homemade mozzarella, tomatoes and red onions in a vinaigrette, $5.25.
**Entree:** Veal Chops Costoletta, stuffed with proscuitto and provolone, sauteed in a white wine sauce, $17.95.
**Dessert:** Flambee a la Prime Classe, sauteed strawberries with Chambord liqueur and cognac over ice cream, $6.
**Conclusion:** Espresso or cappuccino, $2.50.
**Wines:** With appetizer, soup & pasta: Signorello Napa Valley Chardonnay, $45; With entree: a red Brunello di Montal cino, $36. (Optional–for bubbly beginning or after-dinner–Ferrari Brut Champagne, Trentino, Italy, $65.)
**The Tab:** Appetizer $9.95, Soup $2.95, Pasta $4.95, Salad $5.25, Entree 17.95, Dessert $6, Espresso $2.50... $99.10 for 2 plus Wines $81. Total $180 plus tax & gratuity—$200 with Champagne for a novel feast.

## Before the Symphony—Dine As Mozart Did

Pgh Symphony season subscribers can now partake of dinner two hours before performances in the damask-walled, crystal-chandeliered **Mozart Room**. A doorman awaits at the Hoezel entrance to Heinz Hall (to the right of the main 6th Street entrance) to check your coats, which you need not retrieve til after the performance. Then on to dinner with choice of four entrees— poultry, beef, seafood, veal/lamb ($18-$22) complete with vegetable, salad, sorbet and pre-dinner hors d'oeuvres...drinks and dessert cart extra. Only one seating and 15 tables for dinner so be sure to reserve. Then you step directly into the Heinz Hall lobby, returning to exit from the restaurant entrance. A most convenient way to dine and beat pre-performance traffic...wonderful in cold weather. Reservations only. Call **392-4879.**

## Plush Dinner for Two — Sweeping View

### Piccolo Mondo

*Foster Plaza Bldg 7, Greentree, off Holiday Inn Drive. Lunch Mon-Fri 11:30-3:30, Dinner 4-10, Fri & Sat 4-11. Reser sugg six or more. AE,D,DC, MC,V.* **922-0920.**

One of the city's most beautiful restaurants, this chandeliered, carpeted room, warmed with multi-hues of mauve, burgundy and blue, is the elegant home of Rico Lorenzini of North Hill's Rico's. He returns, with sons David and Rico, to the South Hills where he began his culinary career. This spacious hilltop room with a sweeping view of Greentree's woodlands, is noted for its splendid cuisine, continental service and relaxing atmosphere. Dining here, a gastronomic celebration, is surprisingly reasonable... lunch for $8-$10 and dinner from $14-$32 & up. The menu encompasses lobster, steak, pasta, fish, all served with a North Italian flair. One of the house specialties is veal, our feast for a special occasion.

#### Suggested Feast:
**Appetizer:** "Half & Half", two homemade pasta dishes—Rotolo Milanese with pink marinara, and Stuffed Agnolotti in white cream sauce, $7.25.
**Salad:** Boston bibb house salad included with dinner.
**Entree:** Thick veal chop grilled then roasted to your liking, topped with wild mushrooms, bordelaise sauce with a sprinkle of Parmigiano cheese, $23.
**Dessert:** Tiramisu, an Italian delicacy with mascarpone, served with a blend of chocolate/espresso coffee, $4.
**Wine:** Villa Cafaggio Chianti Classico, $33.
**The Tab:** Appetizer for 2 $14.50, Entrees $23, Desserts $4, Wine $33. Total: $101.50 for 2 plus tax and gratuity for a wonderful night.

## Romantic Everyman's Feast—$75 for 2

### Redwood

*87 Castner Street, Donora, 45 minutes from Pgh on Route 51. By reser only. AE,D,MC,V.* **379-6540.**

Every man can be a rich man for a night and enjoy a delectable dinner at this small restaurant which has received laurels from *Travel, Holiday* and *Fortune* magazines for its cuisine and unique personal service. Dinner is surprisingly affordable at this intimate eight-table 'living room,' with consummate attention to detail. Alabaster lamps, cut roses on the tables, beautiful settings create a romantic atmosphere for an unforgetable evening. Entrees–rack of lamb, shrimp stuffed with crabmeat, veal Francaise, filet au poivre ($16-$23)–arrive with many extra touches. Before or after dinner you can relax with cocktails in the flagstone courtyard of the grape arbor behind the restaurant.

#### Suggested Feast:
**Appetizer:** Dinner begins with three delicious hors d'oeuvres—Cheese & Pate, Hot Crab Coquille and Shrimp Feurtine...all for $15 a couple.
**Entree:** House specialty Beef Braccialette, medallions of filet mignon simmered in a rosemary butter sauce, $21.50. Included are a salad with tarragon from the restaurant's herb garden, stuffed baked potato, freshly baked rolls and Parmesan cheese bread.
**Dessert:** Your choice of Chocolate Chambord Torte, Bananas Foster or L'Orange Grand Marnier Jubilee from $2.50-$3.50.
**Wine:** There are more than 75 wines in the cellar but one of the house's best is a light, dry rose, only $10.50 a bottle.
**The Tab:** Appetizer $15 for 2, Entree $21.50, Dessert $3.50, Wine: $10.50. Total: $75.50 for 2 plus tax and gratuity for an unforgettable everyman's feast.

## Gracious Dining In Hilltop House

### Rico's

*Park Place off Babcock Blvd, N Hills. Lunch Mon-Sat 11:45-2:30, Dinner Mon-Thur 4-10:30, Fri-Sat til 11:30. Reser for eight or more. AE,CB,D, DC,MC,V.* **931-1989.**

A country manor retreat...a house high on a hilltop...is the unique setting for this restaurant with a sterling reputation for fine N Italian cuisine and quality fish, steak, seafood. There are six rooms for warm, intimate dining. And not all of the entrees here are in the Rich Man's bracket. You can lunch for $6.95-$10 and sup for $11.50-$32.50 with the filip of fine service. But for our dream dinner, Rico's has put together a fine Italian feast—a Veal and Seafood Platter with the best of wines. And as the ingredients are always at hand, it can be served with very little notice.

### Suggested Feast:

**Appetizer:** Lump Crabmeat Hoelzel, $9.95, a white Girard Chenin Blanc, $19.

**Salad:** Hearts of palm with house Italian dressing, Roquefort, $3.95.
**Pasta:** 1/2 order of Farfalle–bow-tie pasta with Beluga caviar in a pink cream sauce–and I/2 order of Angel Hair in a light cream sauce topped with roasted pignola nuts, $12.50 for 2. With a 1979 Mersault white wine, $69.
**Entree:** A Veal and Seafood assortment for 2—three different types of veal, fresh fish and seafood served with a sauteed Spinach Aglio con Olio—garlic with oil, $29.95. Continue with the Mersault or a soft red Barbarossa, $49.
**Dessert:** Sauteed Strawberries a la Don flambeed with Grand Marnier over French vanilla ice cream, $6.50 person. With a 150-year old Cuvee Grand Marnier, 1-1/2-oz glass, $16 each.
**The Tab:** Appetizer $9.95, Salad $3.95, Pasta $12.50 for 2, Entree $29.95, Dessert $6.50, a total of $113.20 with Wines $169, a total of $282.20 for 2, plus tax & gratuity.

## Your Carriage Awaits...
### Duesenbergs. Ragtops, Flashing Neon

Stretch out...settle back...relax...your carriage will glide to the door of your destination for that very special night on the town.

You can rent anything from a Lincoln stretch limo to luxury sedans, vans or busses...for getting VIPs to and from the Airport, a night on the town, weddings, proms or any special event. A plethora of local limo companies includes **Carey Pgh Allegheny Limousines, Carriage Limousine, Pittsburgh Limo** and **A Limousine.**

If you want to be noticed you can lease one of **American Tiffany Limo's** party cars including a 10-passenger white

Phantom, a replica of a 1937 Duesenberg with a cranberry cloth roof, solid walnut running boards, high-tech stereo, CD, electronic computerized bar, balloon roof and neon lights inside and out. **678-1930.**

Or travel in style in the ultimate in ragtops, **Vintage Limo's** 1936 White open-air touring car with oak floors and panels, a carved oak dash, brass trimmings, stereo, three bars, air-conditioning and a top that folds back to open the roof to the sky. Ideal for groups up to 14. $100 an hour includes chauffeur. Reserve far ahead with John Damratoski. **793-2132.**

## A Steak Lovers Feast — for Serious Eaters

### Ruth's Chris Steak House

*6 PPG Place, Downtown. Lunch Mon-Fri 11:30-3. Dinner Mon-Sat 5-11, Sun 5-9. Free evening indoor parking. Reser sugg. AE,DC,MC,V.* **391-4800.**
This burnished restaurant in PPG Plaza is an impressive steak house—the 19th of the famous Ruth's Chris chain. A warm, comfortable room with lots of rich cherry wood and glass, it's a gracious setting for a very special sizzling steak. It also has excellent grilled chicken, veal and lamb chops plus seafood, fresh Maine lobster, beautifully done vegetables and potatoes prepared seven different ways. Lunch ranges from $6-$13, dinners $16-$33.

*Suggested Feast:*
**Appetizer:** Mushrooms stuffed with Crabmeat or Shrimp Remoulade—a spicy, garlicky beginning for your steak lover's feast, each $6.95.
**Salad:** To clear your palate, the special house Italian Salad—a bed of fresh greens with tomatoes, artichoke hearts, chopped eggs, onions, celery, olives, topped with Parmesan, anchovies, $4.
**Entree:** Feast on an aged US Prime NY Strip, cut and broiled to your specifications and served in sizzling butter, $22. (For a non-beef entree, Chicken California—a marinated, herb-seasoned grilled double breast $15, or 2-5 lb Maine Lobster at market price.)
**Vegetable:** The house special, Creamed Spinach, $3.75.
**Dessert:** Finish with a warm, fragrant Bread Pudding with Whiskey Sauce, $3, or Pecan Pie a la Mode, $4.25.
**Wine:** Duckhorn Merlot, a light-bodied, full-tasting California red, $60 bottle.
**The Tab:** Appetizer $6.95, Salad $4, Entree $22, Vegetable $3.75, Dessert $3, Wine $60. Total: $140 for 2 plus beverage, tax, gratuity for a super steak dinner.

## Stellar Seafood Banquet For Two

### Tambellini's

*860 Saw Mill Run Blvd, Rt 51, just beyond Liberty Tunnels. Mon-Fri 11:30-10:30, Sat 11:30-11. AE,DC, MC,V.* **481-1118.**
Pittsburgh's premiere name in seafood, this big, elegant restaurant grew from the first small Tambellini's on Mt Washington. Now the city's largest, it's still serving stellar seafood and Italian cuisine in five rooms that seat 800...and there's been no compromise with quality. This is the place for that special seafood feast when eating well in convivial surroundings is the main object. Let yourself go on the specialties here—Lobster, Shrimp or Scallops Louie, Scrod, Louisiana Redfish, Crab Imperial and a host of fresh seasonal items flown in daily—plus delicious pastas and antipastos. This is a seafood lover's paradise. For our feast Chef Andrew Tambellini has chosen a Seafood banquet.

*Suggested Feast:*
**Appetizer:** Antipasto for 2—a big, zesty array of Italian meats, peppers, olives, cheeses, $8.50.
**Entree:** Assorted Seafood Platter a la Louie—lemon sole, lobster tail, sea scallops, jumbo shrimp, baked fresh oysters, small deviled crab—broiled in garlic butter with seasoned bread crumbs, originated by Louis Tambellini himself, $23.50.
**Pasta:** Angel Hair with cream sauce & pignola nuts, $7.50 for 2.
**Dessert:** A cool finish–spumoni $2.50, or rich Black Forest Cheesecake, $2.75.
**Wine:** Santa Margherita Pinot Grigio, a white Italian wine, $26.
**The Tab:** Appetizer $8.50 for 2, Entrees $23.50, Pasta $7.50 for 2, Dessert $5.25 for 2. Wine $26. Total: $99.50 for 2 for a seafood night to remember.

## Fireworks at the Angel

### Tin Angel

*1204 Grandview Avenue, Mt Washington. Mon-Sat 5:30-10. AE,DC,MC,V. Reser.* **381-1919.**

The first restaurant atop Mt Washington, now an elegant two-tiered room, the Angel is still one of the most glamorous and romantic spots in town. With its sweeping view of the city, it's a wondrous place from which to view July 4th fireworks at the Point. The verbal menu, with entrees from $23.75 to $42.50, includes filet, NY strip, medallions of beef, sole almondine, Black Forest filet (President Clinton's choice on his visit here), S African lobster, veal Romano and combination Surf 'n Turf chosen for our special dinner here.

***Suggested Feast:***

**Entree:** Your Steak & Lobster comes complete with appetizer, vegetable, delicious rice pilaf, dessert, $36.50.
**Appetizer:** Your meal begins with a Fresh Fruit Cocktail followed by an unforgettable hors d'oeuvres platter– grape leaves, huge olives and exotic marinated items—best appetizer in town!
**Dessert:** Tin Angel Parfait or the Walnut Ball with hot fudge sauce. Then refreshing pineapple with creme de menthe to finish in a mellow mood as you watch the city lights.
**Wine:** Rutherford Hill Chardonnay or a red Robert Mondavi Pinot Noir, both $27.
**The Tab:** Surf 'n Turf $36.50, Wine $27. Total: $100 for 2 plus tax and gratuity for a heavenly night atop the town.

## What a Weekend At World Class Spa!

An hour from Pittsburgh is **Nemacolin**, rated one of the top five spas in the country. Featured on TV's "Life Styles of the Rich & Famous," the scenic mountain resort is located in Farmington, Rt 40 E in the Laurel Mountains. The 550-acre resort/conference center has beautiful grounds, three lakes, a 200-seat amphitheatre, 18-hole PGA golf course, a stable and its own private airstrip.

You can take off pounds in this posh setting and enjoy regular cuisine at the four-star Golden Trout Restaurant or healthy spa fare at Allures restaurant. (The resort also has a 10,000-bottle wine cellar.)

Housed in a separate building, the spa boasts a Jr Olympic-size pool, sauna, steam room, whirlpool, exercise equipment and treatment facilities.

**Woodlands Discovery Package:** two days, one night including meals and six spa treatments—custom facial, body polish, Swedish massage, manicure, pedicure, make-up application (women) and reflexology (men), aroma therapy, scalp treatment and hair styling.
**The Tab:** $607 per person/double occupancy including gratuities and access to all resort facilities.
**Mini Spa Retreat:** Overnight plus choice of two treatments i.e. facial, massage, hydrating manicure, pedicure. $197.50 double .occupancy.
**Morning of Beauty:** Lunch plus a 1/2 hour massage, a facial, manicure, shampoo & style for $129; Lunch & facial only, around $60.
**Contact:** Spa Director Tammy Pahel— **1-800-422-2736** or **412-329-6772.**

*"Among the great whom heaven has made to shine....
How few have learned the art of arts—to dine."*
*— Oliver Wendell Holmes*

## Nostalgic Night At the Terrace Room

### The Terrace Room

*Westin William Penn, Downtown. 7 days. Breakfast 6:30-11, Lunch 11-2, Dinner 5-11. AE,DC,MC,V.* **553-5235.**
The hotel's beautiful grand lobby sets the stage for a feast in this elegantly restored Edwardian dining room—a page from a Pgh's more lavish past. The crystal chandeliers and ornate ceilings make a perfect setting for Continental dining from $12-$24 for Veal, Rib Chops, New York Steak, Filet Mignon, Swordfish and menu items in keeping with the room's original Italian Renaissance theme, and of course the restaurant's specialty—the best prime rib in the city. Stay on for dancing Saturday til midnite.

Our dinner here is a beautifully designed Roast Loin of Veal.
***Suggested Feast:***
**Appetizer:** Stuffed Mushroom Caps with asiago cheese, $6.95.
**Soup:** Seafood Gumbo with spicy andouille sausage, $4.25.
**Entree:** Medallion of Veal Oscar, $22.95.
**Dessert:** Pizzele Cone with seasonal fruit and Marsala Zabaglione, $3.50, or famous Wm Penn Cheesecake, with/without strawberry sauce, $3.95.
**Wine:** Chateau Greysac Medoc, $28.
**The Tab:** Appetizer $6.95, Soup $4.25, Entree $22.95, Dessert $3.95, Wine $28. Total: Just $104 for 2 (plus tax/gratuity) for a nostalgic night on the town.

## Fine Dine and Wine

### Wooden Angel

*Sharon Road & Leopard Lane, Bridgewater, Beaver Valley (45 min from Pgh, 20 min from Airport). Tues-Fri 11:30–11. Sat 5-11. AE,CB,D,DC,MC,V. Reser.* **774-7880.**
The fame of this restaurant's owner, Alex Sebastian, has spread near and far for his wine wizardry and passion for American vintages. People drive for miles to savour the restaurant's cuisine and explore its huge cellars of American wines—more than 500 from all over the US–California, New York, Washington State, Oregon. The restaurant's wine list, lauded in '87 as one of the Top 10 in the World by *Wine Spectator Magazine,* has also garnered several *Holiday* and *Mobil* awards. Your host will graciously take you on a tour of the cellars after your dinner in this warm restaurant with lots of brick and rough-hewn wood. Lunch is a reasonable $5-$12 with dinners $15-$30 for steak, lobster, lamb and fish. For our Rich Man's Feast, Sebastian has matched fine American wines to American cuisine, rare

food and rare vintages at a fixe prix of $225 for 4, $56 a person.

***Fine Wine Feast:***
**Appetizer:** Fresh Maryland Crab Cake with orange butter sauce, $7.85. **Wine:** Chardonnay.
**Pasta:** Smoked Chicken Ravioli with a blue cheese cream sauce, applewood smoked bacon and sun-dried tomatoes. **Wine:** Zinfandel.
**Fish:** Sun Pueblo Salmon with cilantro butter sauce. **Wine:** Sauvignon Blanc.
**Sorbet:** Grapefruit Sorbet.
**Entree:** Organic Veal Tenderloin, medallions of veal with blackberry ketchup and wild mushrooms. **Wine:** Pinot Noire.
**Salad:** Tomatoes with fresh Mozzarella, fresh basil and balsamic vinegar.
**Cheese & Fruit**
**Dessert:** Amaretto Cake with fresh assorted berries. **Wine:** Santino "Lisa Marie."
**The Tab:** $225 for dinner for 4 incl tax & gratuity—for a sparkling night of wining/dining.

## Gourmet Wining/Dining Clubs...Special Dinners

"Where there is no wine there is no love."
*– Euripides*

### La Chaine de Rotisseurs

For the serious gourmet—enthusiasts, chefs, food professionals—this chapter of the international, Paris-based society meets every three months at prominent restaurants. The object—to enjoy good food, wine and fellowship. There are 30-40 members—by invitation—with a $175 membership fee, and dinners at about $125 a person. Black tie is required at club dinners. If you're interested call Pete Hanowich. **486-3946.**

### Les Amis du Vin

The Pittsburgh chapter of this internartional society has received the Chapter of the Year award for its ambitious activities. About 500 members—wine lovers all—meet twice monthly for tastings, dinners and wine classes at the Pittsburgh Vista Hotel and various city locations. Tastings run about $20-$40 an event. Dinners, with a selection of fine wines, range from $75-$125. Wine lovers can apply to Ray Szymanski, **655-2852.**

### Les Dames du Vin

The only women's wine tasting group outside California, Les Dames' 25-30 members meet twice monthly at members' homes or restaurants to sample the fruit of the vine. They share the cost of wine and purchase their own dinners— or a hostess provides cheese & crackers. Membership in this 12-year-old group is a modest $5. Male guests are invited to four annual events including a Wine Dinner, Bastille Day tasting and a Belgium Beer tasting. The occasional male guest at regular meetings must come bearing champagne. Distaff tasters can call Sharryn Donn Campbell at **661-4180.**

### Le Pommier Wine Tastings/Dinners

Le Pommier has weekly wine tastings Friday nights from 5:30-7:30 at their Wine Bar...three wines plus hors d'oeuvres for $15 a person. This fine country French restaurant at 2104 E Carson Street, South Side, also holds occasional dinners highlighting French provincial and French influenced cuisines i.e. Cajun, Moroccan. They're fun and affordable—around $25 a person including tax plus wine. For information call **431-1901.**

### March of Dimes Gourmet Gala

Local celebrites and business leaders join renowned chefs to create their own recipes for charity at an annual gala the first week of June at the Pittsburgh Hilton. $150 person. **391-3193.**

### Children's Hospital/ Post-Gazette Gourmet Dinner

Famous chefs come to town each fall for one of the biggest dinners of the year, the Children's Hospital/Pgh Post-Gazette Gourmet Dinner, traditionally at Le Mont Restaurant on Mt Washington. Donations are around $500 a couple for a worthy cause. **263-1421.**

### Taste of the Nation

Every spring more than 40 Pittsburgh chefs showcase their best for the benefit of the Greater Pittsburgh Food Bank at the Pittsburgh Vista Hotel. Only $40 a person for some first-class cuisine. **672-4949.**

*"A man's reach should exceed his grasp else what's a heaven for."*
*– Browning*

# PGH AFTER DARK

Welcome to Pittsburgh's exciting new night life...from Happy Hours at dusk to the wee hours of the morning in 24-Hour Pittsburgh. New night life in the South Side, the Strip and Mt Washington is adding excitement to Pittsburgh After Dark. For many 'Burghers the day begins at sundown!

# Happy Hours

*If you want to take a short ride in the fast lane you can move around to the city's weekday Happy Hours ...a lively hub of the local social scene where you can unwind, relax and find people driving on the same track. You may find a niche you visit ritually or speed up to make a variety of stops between 5-7 Monday thru Friday. And, with the emphasis on Happy Hour food, in the doing you can snack your way to dinner on a selection of buffets for a happy, hungry hour.*
**Drinks: *Inexp–under $3. Mod–under $4. Exp–$4 & up.***

## DOWNTOWN AREA

### Carlton
*One Mellon Bank Center, Downtown.*
**Food:** Varies—wing-dings, eggrolls, sometimes turkey, roast beef.
**Crowd:** Bankers—suit & tie.
**Atmosphere:** Professional.
**Drinks:** Mod-Exp.

### Chauncy's
*Commerce Court, Station Square.*
**Food:** Hot & cold buffet, wing-dings, veggies, stuffed mushrooms. Super Friday buffet—ham, beef, multi-salads.
**Crowd:** Yuppie mania. You'll have to fight your way in.
**Atmosphere:** Crowded fun.
**Drinks:** Mod.

### Consigliere
*425 Cherry Way, Downtown (across from Kaufmann's garage).*
**Food:** Varies.
**Crowd:** Lots of lawyers, especially on Friday.
**Atmosphere:** Convivial.
**Drinks:** Mod.

### DelFrate's
*971 Liberty, across from Vista, Downtown.*
**Food:** Finger foods, wings, nachos...all you can eat.
**Crowd:** Business 30s-40.
**Atmosphere:** Relaxed.
**Drinks:** Inexp-Mod.

### Dingbat's City-Tavern
*Oxford Centre, Downtown.*
**Food:** 1/2 off appetizer, draft; nightly & 8pm free buffet on Fridays.
**Crowd:** Yuppies—young, loud & lively.
**Atmosphere:** Great! Outdoor patio.
**Drinks:** Inexp.

### Donzi's
*Boardwalk, On the Water, 1501 Smallman, Strip.*
**Food:** (Fri only) Free Buffet at Rush Hour Cocktail Party. Cover $1 til 9.
**Crowd:** Swish, strictly downtown.
**Atmosphere:** An exciting place right on the river, sometimes a mob scene.
**Drinks:** Mod-Exp.

### Fat City
*1601 E Carson St, South Side.*
**Food:** Reduced rate on food 10-12 Tues-Thur plus Fri-Sat Hungry Hour 12-1am. Varied inc $2 pizza, 15c chicken wings Wed...ladies free.
**Crowd:** Fun and friendly, all ages.
**Atmosphere:** Rollickin'.
**Music:** Live bands, reggae/R & R.
**Drinks:** Inexp.

### Froggy's
*100 Market St, Downtown.*
**Food:** Munchies, nachos/cheese.
**Crowd:** Seasoned—reporters/sports writers.
**Atmosphere:** Intellectually stimulating.
**Drinks:** Mod—for largest shot in town.

### Gandy Dancer
*Landmark Bldg, Station Square.*
**Food:** Varies—hot wings, nachos/cheese, hot potato cubes, veggie salad. Good eatin'!
**Crowd:** A great mix. Everyone fits in.
**Atmosphere:** Crowded, relaxed fun.
**Music:** Piano.
**Drinks:** Inexp.

**3**

# Happy Hours

### Grandview Saloon
*1212 Grandview, Mt Washington.*
**Food:** Drink bargains, chips & dip.
**Atmosphere:** The place to be. Wall-to-wall yuppies spilling onto outdoor decks with great city view.
**Music:** High decibel rock/pop.
**Drinks:** Mod-Exp.

### Holiday Inn, University
*100 Lytton Ave, Oakland.*
**Food:** Terrific! $1 buys a medley of hot/cold items changing nightly—Mexican, Italian, wings, ribs & Fri Night Shrimp Fest. A real meal!
**Atmosphere:** Lively, business & professionals.
**Music:** Background.
**Drinks:** Mod-Exp.

### Houlihan's
*Freight House, Station Square.*
**Food:** Mon-Fri 5:30-7:30, Sun 9-11. 1/2 off on appetizers i.e. fried calamari, tortilla chips/veggies with spinach/mushroom dip. Thur-Fri free buffet i.e. wings, ribs.
**Crowd:** Young professionals.
**Atmosphere:** Very laid back.
**Music:** DJ rock/oldies.
**Drinks:** Inexp.

### Kason's
*Bank Tower, 31 Fourth, Downtown.*
**Food:** Munchies, 1/2 off on hors d'oeuvres Mon-Thur.
**Crowd:** Fun young professionals.
**Atmosphere:** Lively, DJ dancing.
**Drinks:** Mod-Exp.

### Mad Mex
*370 Atwood, Oakland.*
**Food:** $1 off drinks/lite menu daily 4-6. (Also 1/2 price on food 7 nites 11-1am.)
**Crowd:** Mix—yuppies, locals.
**Atmosphere:** Friendly, open.
**Drinks:** Inexp-Mod.

### Margaritaville
*2200 E Carson, S Side*
**Food:** 50c off drinks and $1 off outstanding appetizers.

---

### Wine Lovers Take Note

Pommier's Wine Bar is drawing a connoisseur crowd Fridays 5:30-7:30 to taste three wines each week and partake of hors d'oeuvres, $15 a person. A good change of pace. Noted for its Country French cuisine, the restaurant is located at 2104 E Carson St, S Side. **431-1901.**

---

**Crowd:** Mixed.
**Atmosphere:** Happy, friendly.
**Drinks:** Mod.

### Max & Erma's
*630 Stanwix St, Downtown.*
**Food:** Egg rolls, munchies.
**Crowd:** Interesting corporate types, brokers, computer buffs.
**Atmosphere:** Spirited, friendly.
**Drinks:** Inexp.

### Motions
*Pittsburgh Vista Hotel, Downtown.*
**Food:** Buffet Mon-Fri, drink specials.
**Crowd:** Young downtown professionals.
**Atmosphere:** Sophisticated, lively.
**Drinks:** Exp.

### Ruddy Duck
*Ramada, Bigelow Blvd, Downtown.*
**Food:** Hot hors d'oeuvres never run out.
**Crowd:** Sophisticated professionals.
**Atmosphere:** Classy, quiet, laid back.
**Drinks:** Mod.

### Seventh St Grille
*137 7th St, Downtown.*
**Food:** Fri Prime rib! Back Bar Beer Club - drink all 42 beers & get your name engraved on a wall plaque.
**Crowd:** Mostly downtown business...but little of everything.
**Atmosphere:** Loud, busy, casual.
**Drinks:** Mod.

# Happy Hours

## Sophie's
*1600 Smallman, Strip.*
**Food:** Mon-Thur bargains on drinks. Fri free appetizers plus grilled hot dogs/hamburgers—25c for charity.
**Crowd:** Casual, blue/white collar.
**Atmosphere:** Neighborhood saloon.
**Drinks:** Inexp.

## Shootz Cafe
*2305 Carson St, South Side.*
**Food:** Tex-Mex buffet plus drink specials & billiards at half price.
**Crowd:** Mixed.
**Atmosphere:** Lively sports bar.
**Drinks:** Inexp.

## Top of the Triangle
*USX Tower, Grant St, Downtown.*
**Food:** Cheese, veggies, hot item; discounts on appetizers.
**Crowd:** Downtown business.
**Atmosphere:** A cut above the rest, dazzling view of city from 62nd floor.
**Drinks:** Mod-Exp.

## Waterfall Terrace
*Sheraton Station Square.*
**Food:** Hot & cold hors d'oeuvres.
**Crowd:** Sophisticated.
**Atmosphere:** Beautiful riverfront views.
**Drinks:** Mod.

## Whiskey Dick's
*1600 Smallman St, Strip.*
**Food:** Mon-Fri 9-7 drink specials. Free Friday Buffet i.e. hamburgers/hot dogs for donation for charity. 50c off drinks.
**Crowd:** Blue collar, some suits, loud & raucous.
**Atmosphere:** Relaxing, convivial.
**Drinks:** Inexp.

---

## Shopper's Happy Hour
Shoppers Alert! There's a Happy Hour on the 11th floor...**Kaufmann's Department Store,** Downtown in Edgar's Dining Room—Mon-Fri 4-6. Big values—$1 off food, drinks.

---

SUBURBS

## Cahoots
*Marriott Hotel, Greentree.*
**Food:** Great! Mon $1.99 steak dinner; Tues, tacos; Wed, Italian; Thur, subs; Fri drink specials plus Buffalo Wings & Shrimp...all for $1!
**Crowd:** Professional, sales, corp types.
**Atmosphere:** Classy, upscale, laid back.
**Drinks:** Inexp.

## Cheat'n Heart Saloon
*Holiday Inn, Mosside Blvd, Monroeville.*
**Food:** Great buffet spread hot & cold.
**Crowd:** Exec set, 30 something & plus.
**Atmosphere:** Jumpin' up crowd. DJ Friday.
**Drinks:** Mod.

## Colony Lounge
*Greentree/Cochran Rds, Scott Twp.*
**Food:** 1/2 off on appetizers, mixed drinks.
**Crowd:** Business/professional.
**Atmosphere:** Congenial, low-key.
**Drinks:** Exp.

## Dingbat's
*Waterworks, Fox Chapel, Robinson, Ross. (Also 9-11 Mon-Fri at Ross.).*
**Food:** Varies—hoagies, wings, pizza.
**Crowd:** Young professionals & all ages.
**Atmosphere:** Friendly, good noise level.
**Drinks:** Mod.

## Getaway Cafe
*Sussex Ave/McNeilly Rd, South Hills.*
**Food:** Drink/beer specials.
**Crowd:** Mixed group.
**Atmosphere:** Friendly, casual.
**Drinks:** Inexp.

## Longnecker's
*Holiday Inn, Greentree.*
**Food:** Plentiful munchies.
**Crowd:** Young, corporate, prosperous.
**Atmosphere:** Airy, lots of greenery.
**Drinks:** Mod.

3

# Late Supper

### Houlihan's
*300 Mall Boulevard, Monroeville.*
**Food:** Reduced drinks plus appetizers $2.50—shrimp, potato skins, nachos, onion rings, calamari. Also late Happy Hour Sat 10-12.
**Crowd:** Business & shoppers—21 & up.
**Atmosphere:** Comfortable & relaxed.
**Drinks:** Inexp.

### Jergel's
*3385 Babcock Blvd, North Hills.*
**Food:** Free hors d'oeuvres—wings, chili, chicken, shrimp.
**Crowd:** Mixed–local plus after-work stop.
**Atmosphere:** Friendly, lively.
**Music:** Hottest hits piped in.
**Drinks:** Inexp.

### TGI Friday's
*240 Mall Boulevard, Monroeville.*
**Food:** 1/2 off hot/cold appetizers.
**Crowd:** Local business crowd—25-35.
**Atmosphere:** Casual, informal.
**Drinks:** Mod.

## LATE SUPPER
(See also Oriental/Asian restaurants)

### Abruzzi's
*52 S 10th Street, S Side. Fri-Sat til 11. AE,MC,V.* **431-4511.**
Charming townhouse, warm atmosphere; great pasta, Italian specialties, appetizers. ($4-$20). Drinks: Mod. (Review)

### Antonini
*2700 Jane St, S Side. Sun-Thur til 12, Fri-Sat til 1. AE,D,DC,MC,V.* **381-9901.**
Family Italian, lovely patio; calamari, chicken, pasta. ($10-$27). Drinks: Exp.

### Aussie's
*4617 Liberty Ave, Bloomfield. Sun-Thur til 11, Fri-Sat til 12am. AE,DC,MC,V.* **681-2290.**
Atmospheric Australian bar, everything from lobster to wings. "Aussie Burgers" with pineapple & BBQ sauce ($3-$20). Australian beer on tap. Drinks: Mod.

### Baum Vivant
*5102 Baum Blvd, Oakland. Fri-Sat til 11. Reser. AE,D,CB,DC,MC,V.* **682- 2620.**
Elegant, intimate room; top-flight Portugese/Italian—seafood, steak, chops ($17-$27). Drinks: Exp. (See Review.)

### Billy's Bistro
*1720 Lowrie, N Side. Fri-Sat til 11. AE, MC,V.* **231-9277.**
Lobster, ribs, steak, sandwiches ($2-$15) in lively bar. Drinks: Inexp-Mod.

### Boardwalk, On the Water
*1505 Smallman. Enter thru parking lot at 15th St. AE,MC,V.* **281-1600.**
Two restaurants, patio on floating boardwalk. **Crewsers** 7 days til 12. **281-3680.** Spacious, romantic river view; grills, fish/steak, sandwiches. Mod. **Buster's Crab** 2nd level. Mon-Sat til 12. **281-3683.** Seafood/raw bar. Mod. Food/fun **Patio Deck.**

### Bobby Rubino's
*Commerce Court, Station Sq. Fri-Sat til 12:30. AE,MC,V.* **642-RIBS.**
Popular handsome room, long bar; ribs, burgers, snacks ($4-$16). Drinks: Mod.

### Brandy's
*2323 Penn, Strip. Mon-Thur til 11-12, Fri-Sat til 2, Sun til 11. AE,D,DC,MC,V.* **566-1000.**
Romantic hanging gardens, skylight roof. Entrees ($12-$16) plus burgers, dessert, breakfast ($3.50-$6). Drinks: Mod.

### Bravo! Franco
*613 Penn, Downtown. Fri-Sat til 11 for shows. Reser AE,DC,MC,V.* **642-6677.**
Ideal before/after theatre dining in spiffy decor. Late dinner—osso buco, fish, seafood, great appetizers, desserts. ($5-$20). Drinks: Exp. (See Review)

### Cafe Allegro
*51 S 12th St, S Side. Fri-Sat til 11. MC,V.* **481-7788.**
Charming rooms with inventive Italian/French 'Riviera' cuisine. One of city's best. ($8-$23). Dinner, appetizers. Drinks: Mod. (See Review)

## Late Supper

### Cafe Azure
*317 S Craig, Oakland. Fri-Sat til 11, Late supper til 12. AE,DC,MC,V.* **681-3533.**
Super supper club, live jazz with your gourmet French, full dinner, late bites. ($5.50-$24). Drinks: Exp. (See Review)

### Caffe Giovanni
*2302 E Carson, S Side. Fri-Sat til 11. AE,DC,MC,V.* **481-6662.**
1st class Italian dining/service; cozy rooms. Dinner, appetizers, desserts ($8-$20). Drinks. Mod-Exp. (See Review)

### Cafe Sam
*5242 Baum Blvd, Oakland. Wed-Thur til 11, Fri-Sat til 12. Reser sugg. AE,MC,V.* **621-2000.**
Chic late dining from inventive gourmet kitchen. Amer-Cont dinners, snacks. Roof patio. ($5-$18). Drinks: Mod. (Review)

### Cappy's
*5431 Walnut. 7 nites til 2am. AE,D,DC, MC,V.* **621-1188.**
Small bar/restaurant, great grilled chicken, super sandwiches. ($3-$6). Drinks:Mod.

### Cheese Cellar
*Shops Station Sq. Mon-Thur til 1, Fri-Sat til 2. Sun til 11. AE,DC,MC,V.* **471-3355.**
Intimate booths, lively bar. Dinners, delicious fondues, cheese/sausage boards, luscious desserts ($5-$11). Drinks: Mod.

### City Grill
*2019 E Carson, S Side. Fri-Sat til 11. AE,MC,V.* **481-6868.**
Crowds come for great hardwood grills, snacks in urbane setting. After-theatre favorite. ($4.50-$13). Drinks: Mod.

### Cerulean Bistro
*1227 Monterey, N Side. Tues-Sat til 11. AE,D,DC,MC,V.* **321-4221.**
Romantic little 'white tablecloth' restaurant, candlelight, long cherrywood bar, great food. ($7-$25). Drinks: Mod. (See Review)

### Clark Bar & Grill
*503 Martindale St, across from Gate B, Stadium Circle. Mon-Sat til 2am. AE,CB, DC,MC,V.* **231-5720.**
Lively bar in old Clark Candy bldg; sports atmosphere, great grills/ribs, sandwiches. ($5-$16). Big sports bar Zagnut's in back room. Drinks: Mod. (See Review)

### Del's
*4428 Liberty, Bloomfield. Mon-Thur til 11, Fri-Sat til 12am. AE,D,MC,V.* **683-1448.**
Homey, Italian dinners, salads, seafood, appetizers ($3-$15). Drinks: Inexp.

### Dingbat's City Tavern
*Oxford Ctr, Downtown. Mon-Thur til 11, Fri-Sat til 12. AE,D,DC,MC,V.* **392-0350.**
Burnished room, convivial bar, good day/night menu; char-broiled seafood, steak, pizza, sandwiches. ($5.75-$14). Drinks: Mod. (See Review)

### Doc's Place/Grille
*5442 Walnut, Shadyside. Mon-Sat til 2. AE,D,MC,V.* **681-3713.**
Grills, sandwiches, appetizers, lively rooftop patio above the avenue. ($4-$15). Live music Fri. Drinks: Mod.

### Dunning McNair's Ale House
*1105 S Braddock, Regent Sq. Fri-Sat til 11:30. AE,MC,V.* **243-3900.**
Informal bar/restaurant across from Regent Sq Theatre with eclectic menu— dinners, snacks ($2-$13). Drinks: Mod.

### Elbow Room
*5744 Ellsworth, Shadyside. Mon-Sat til 2, Sun til 12. D,MC,V.* **441-5222.**
Popular Shadyside bar/eatery with good dinners, burgers, sandwiches, patio. ($2-$12). Drinks: Inexp-Mod.

### Frenchy's
*136 Sixth St, Downtown. Mon-Sat til 12. AE,MC,V.* **261-6476.**
Full dinners plus sandwiches, salads, cold buffet ($3.50-$20). Fast, casual, pre-theatre meals. Drinks: Mod.

**3**

# Late Supper

## Froggy's
*100 Market & 1st, Downtown. Mon-Thur til 12, Fri-Sat til 1. AE,DC,MC,V.* **471-3764.** Popular, lively downtown bar; big drinks, great grills/burgers/sandwiches ($6-$24). Drinks: Mod. (See Review)

## Gandy Dancer
*Station Square. Mon-Thur til 1am, Fri-Sat til 2. AE,D,DC,MC,V.* **261-1717.** Fun atmosphere, great buys on seafood, pasta ($3-$14). Drinks: Mod (See Review)

## Gullifty's
*1922 Murray, Sq Hill. Sun-Thur til 12, Fri-Sat til 1. AE,D,DC,MC,V.* **521-8222.** Big menu, informal, deli atmosphere. Meals, sandwiches, famed desserts ($3-$13). Drinks: Inexp.

## Harris Grill
*5747 Ellsworth Avenue, Shadyside. 7 days til 2. AE,MC,V.* **363-0833.** Popular 'taverna'; good Greek specialties –gyros, moussaka, salad–and good conversation, outdoor patio. ($3-$10.) Imported beer. Drinks: Inexp-Mod.

## Hotlicks
*Theatre Mall, 5520 Walnut, Shadyside. Fri-Sat til 12. AE,DC,MC,V.* **683- 2583.** Popular hang-out, great mesquite ribs, fish, burgers, chicken, sandwiches. ($3-$15). Drinks: Inexp-Mod. .

## Houlihan's
*Station Sq. Sun-Thur til 11, Fri-Sat til 12:30, Bar til 2. AE,D,MC,V.* **232-0302.** Lively, colorful pub paraphernalia. Entrees, snacks, DJ Dancing nightly ($8-$15). Drinks: Mod-Exp. (See Review)

## Jake's Above the Square
*430 Market, Downtown. Mon-Thur til 11, Fri-Sat til 12. AE,DC,MC,V.* **338-0900.** Elegant 2nd floor room with great view of Square, upscale N Ital/Amer entrees, appetizers ($8-$33). Drinks: Mod-Exp.

## James St Tavern
*422 Foreland/James, N Side. Fri-Sat til 12. AE,D,DC,MC,V.* **323-2222.** Cajun, seafood, char-grilled chicken, prime rib; dinners/appetizers ($7-$20). Great jazz Wed/Sat nights. Drinks: Mod. (See Jazz Rooms)

## Juno Trattoria
*One Oxford Ctr, Downtown. Fri & Sat til 12. AE,D,DC,MC,V.* **392-0225.** Handsome balcony room, great pasta, focaccia, pizza, antipasta, chicken, seafood. ($5-$19). Drinks: Mod-Exp. (Review)

## Khalil's
*4757 Baum Blvd, Oakland. Tues-Sun til 11. AE,DC,MC,V.* **683-4757.** Mid-East dinners/appetizers; grape leaves to shish kabob ($3-$11). Drinks: Inexp-Mod.

## Mad Mex
*370 Atwood, Oakland. Sun-Wed til 11, Thur-Sat til 1am.* **681-5656.** *2000 Smallman, Strip* **261-6565.** *7905 McKnight Rd. 7 days 11-1.* **366-5656.** *AE,MC,V.* Lively in-place for young/music fans. Terrific Cal-Mex, unique beers, margaritas. ($5-$9). 1/2 price on food 11-1am nightly. Drinks: Inexp-Mod. (See Review)

## Mallorca
*2228 E Carson, S Side. Fri-Sat til 11:30. AE,D,DC,MC,V.* **488-1818.** Sophisticated Spanish/Continental with a flair. Full menu—paella, seafood, chorizo sausage ($5-$24). Drinks: Mod. (Review)

## Margaritaville
*2200 E Carson, S Side. 7 nights til 2. AE,DC,MC,V.* **431-2200.** Jumpin' place with Mex-Amer cuisine, platters/munchies ($2.50-$10), 12 kinds of margaritas. Drinks: Mod.

## Mario's South Side Saloon
*1514 E Carson, S Side. Mon-Sat til 2. AE,DC,MC,V.* **381-5610.** Lively Italian eatery with excellent pasta, meats, seafood ($3-$12). Crowded fun. Drinks: Inexp.

## Late Supper

### Max & Erma's
*630 Stanwix, Downtown. Fri-Sun til 11.*
**471-1140.** *5533 Walnut, Shadyside:*
*Mon-Thur til 11, Fri-Sat til 12.* **681-5775.**
*AE,D,DC,MC,V.*
Up atmosphere for pasta, sandwiches,
appetizers. ($2.50-$13.) Drinks: Mod.

### Max's Allegheny Tavern
*537 Suisman St, N Side. Mon-Thur til 11,*
*Fri-Sat til 12. AE,DC,MC,V.* **231-1899.**
Old-time atmosphere, German wursts,
beer, sandwiches. ($4-$12). DJ/live music
Fri-Sat Rathskeller. Drinks: Mod. Review

### Morton's of Chicago
*CNG Tower, 625 Liberty, Downtown. Mon-*
*Sat til 11. AE,CB,DC,MC,V.* **261-7141.**
Upscale dining at super steakhouse of
Chicago chain. Also chicken, lobster
($16-$30). Drinks: Exp. (See Review)

### Moscow Nights
*1722 Murray Ave, Sq Hill. Fri-Sat til 11-*
*12. No liquor. AE.* **521-5005.**
Late supper, dancing to Russian, Israeli
folk/pop. Delicious blintzes, smoked fish,
caviar. ($5-$15). (See Review)

### The 1902 Landmark Tavern
*24 Market St, Downtown. Mon-Sat til 12.*
*AE,DC,MC,V.* **471-1902.**
Restored old tavern with big bar, tile
walls, ceiling fans. Dinners, sandwiches,
raw bar ($5-$21). Drinks: Mod.

### Paparazzi
*21st & Carson. 7 nights til 12, Bar til 2.*
*AE,MC,V.* **488-0800.**
Casual Italian in glass front two-level
($8-13). Live entertainment Wed-Sun
Drinks: Mod. (See Pgh After Dark).

### Park House
*403 E Ohio, N Side. 7 days til 2. AE,DC,*
*MC,V.* **231-0551.**
Popular, convivial bar with good light fare.
($2-$8). Drinks: Mod.

### Pasquarelli's
*1204 Grandview, Mt Washington. Fri-Sat*
*til 11. AE,D,MC,V.* **431-1660.**

Small, intimate room, great view, excellent Italian. ($9.95- $25). Drinks: Mod.

### Pasta Piatto
*736 Bellefonte, Shadyside. Fri-Sat til 11.*
*MC,V.* **621-5547.**
Pgh's favorite Italian, wonderful homemade pastas, desserts, appetizers ($5-
$20). Drinks: Mod. (See Review)

### Penn Brewery
*Troy Hill Rd, N Side. Mon-Sat til 12am.*
*AE,MC,V.* **237-9402.**
Wonderful German beer, cuisine, full
menu til closing ($4-$10). Live music
Wed-Sat. Drinks: Inexp-Mod. (Review)

### Per Favore
*Royal York, 3955 Bigelow, Oakland. Fri-*
*Sat til 11. Reser. AE,DC,MC,V.* **681-9147.**
Elegant Italian, gracious decor; dinner,
appetizers, pasta, gourmet pizzas,
snacks ($5-$22). Drinks: Mod.

### Pgh Steak Co
*1924 E Carson St, S Side. Mon-Thur til*
*12am, Fri-Sat til 1. Sun til 11. AE,DC,*
*MC,V.* **381-5505.**
After-theatre favorite; stylish room with
steaks, grills. ($5-$28). Drinks: Mod.

### Pietro's Italian Chophouse
*Hyatt Regency Pgh. 7 nights til 11. AE,*
*DC,MC,V.* **471-1234.**
Fine Italian dinners, appetizers, sand-
wiches in glass-walled room; patio over
looking city ($5-$22). Drinks: Mod-Exp.

### Poli's
*2607 Murray Ave, Sq Hill. Tues-Sat til 11.*
*AE,CB,DC,MC,V.* **521-6400.**
Famous seafood plus great late menu—
appetizers, salads, sandwiches ($4-
$8.50). Drinks: Mod. (See Review)

### River Cafe
*Station Sq. Fri-Sat til 11. AE,CB,D,DC,*
*MC,V.* **765-2795.**
Colorful decor, inventive entrees, appetiz-
ers, sandwiches. ($5-$19). Drinks:Mod.
(See Review)

**3**

# Late Supper

### Ruth's Chris Steak House
*6 PPG Place, Downtown. Mon-Sat til 11.*
*Reser sugg. AE,DC,MC,V.* **391-4800.**
Polished setting; premiere steaks/seafood
($16-$22). Drinks: Exp. (See Review)

### Samreny's
*4808 Baum Blvd, Oakland. Sat til 11:30.*
*MC,V.* **682-1212.**
Lebanese favorites in homey atmosphere,
cozy bar. Dinners, appetizers ($3-$14)
Drinks: Mod.

### 17th St Cafe
*75 S 17th St, S Side. Fri-Sat til 11. AE,*
*DC,MC,V.* **431-9988.**
Casual bar/dining room; pasta, chicken,
veal, sandwiches ($5-$21). Drinks: Mod.

### Seventh St Grille
*Century Bldg, 130 7th St. 7 nights til 2am.*
*AE,CB,D,DC,MC,V.* **338-0303.**
Handsome bi-level, handy for lunchers/
theatre crowd; entrees, sandwiches.
($5-$15). Drinks: Mod.

### Scoglio
*5th Ave Place, 5th/Stanwix, Downtown.*
*Fri-Sat til 11. AE,D,DC,MC,V. Reser*
*sugg.* **391-1226.**
Downtown favorite; Italian specialties,
pasta; great prices. Drinks: Mod. (Review)

### Shadyside Balcony
*5520 Walnut St, Shadyside. Mon, Wed,*
*Thur till 12am, Tues til 11, Fri-Sat til 1.*
*AE,D,DC,MC,V.* **687-0110.**
Stellar food, music 7 nights of the week.
Drinks: Mod. (See Reviews, Jazz Rooms).

### Suzie's
*1704 Shady, Sq Hill. Fri-Sat til 11. D,MC,*
*V. No liquor.* **422-8066.**
Great Greek food in simple room; dinners/
appetizers ($4-$13). (See Review)

### Sweet Basil's
*5882 Forbes, Sq Hill. Fri-Sat til 11. MC,V.*
**421-9958.**
Popular, informal, with charming, clean-
cut look, back-to-basic dinners, snacks.
($3-$14). Drinks: Inexp-Mod.

### Tambellini's
*860 Saw Mill Run, Rt 51. Mon-Sat til 11.*
*AE,DC,MC,V.* **471-1118.**
Famous Pittsburgh name for great seafood, pasta. Dinners, a la carte ($8-
$17.50). Drinks: Mod.

### Tequila Junction
*Station Sq. Mon-Thur til 11, Fri-Sat til 12.*
*AE,DC,MC,V.* **261-3265.**
Romantic setting, full Mex-Amer menu
($6-$10). Tiled bar with big margaritas.
Drinks: Mod. (See Review)

### Tessaro's
*4601 Liberty, Bloomfield. Mon-Sat til 12.*
*AE,D,DC,MC,V.* **682-6809.**
Cozy neighborhood bar, great dinners/
sandwiches; hardwood grill ($5-$14).
Drinks: Inexp-Mod. (See Review)

### Tramp's
212 Blvd of Allies, Downtown. Fri-Sat til
11, Bar til 2. AE,DC,MC,V. **261-1990.**
Oldtime bar-bordello, brick walls, candlelit tables. Dinners/snacks ($6-$17).
Drinks: Mod. (See Review)

### Union Grill
*413 S Craig. Mon-Thur til 11, Fri- Sat til*
*12. AE,D,DC,MC,V.* **681-8620.**
Popular polished room with grilled ribs,
chicken, steaks, burgers, salads. Drinks:
Mod. $5-$14. (See Review)

### Waterfall Terrace
*Sheraton, Station Sq. 7 days til 12am.*
*AE,DC,MC,V.* **261-2000.**
Dinner, appetizers ($4-$23) in pretty cafe
along riverfront. Drinks in adjoining
**Atrium Lounge.** Mod.

### Whiskey Dick's
*1600 Smallman St, Strip. Mon-Sat*
*11-2am. AE,D,DC,MC,V.* **471-9555.**
Fun late-bite stop indoors or on the deck.
Hardwood grilled burgers, chicken, ribs,
sandwiches, salads ($3-$12); big drinks &
lots of merriment. Acoustic Tues/Thur.
Drinks: Inexp-Mod.

# PIANO BARS

## Christopher's Lounge
*1411 Grandview, Mt Washington. Wed-Sat til 2. AE,D,DC,MC,V.* **381-4500.**
Exciting nightime views of the city in glamorous glass-walled lounge of famous restaurant to the piano music of Bobby Negri Wed-Sat 7-11. Appetizers & Desserts. ($5-$9). Drinks: Exp.

## Froggy's
*100 Market St at First, Downtown. Tues-Thur til 2. AE,DC,MC,V.* **471-3764.**
Lively bar, jazz piano Tues-Thur, some Sat til closing, full menu til 11. Great grills, sandwiches ($4-$18), 'biggest drinks in town' 3-1/2 oz–$3.50. Drinks: Mod.

## Gallagher's Pub
*2 Market Place, Downtown. Mon-Sat til 1:30. AE,DC,MC,V.* **261-5554.**
Sing-a-long fans love this warm Irish saloon with Joe Salamon's piano from 9 Wed, Fri, Sat. Lively sentimental crowd. Irish beer. No food eves. Drinks: Mod.

## Gandy Dancer
*Landmarks Bldg, Station Sq. Mon-Thur til 11, Fri-Sat til 1. AE,DC,MC,V.* **261-1717.**
Rollicking crowds & nightly fun in famous bar off Grand Concourse with piano til 1. Full menu Mon-Thur til 11, Fri-Sat til 1. Great prices on seafood, pasta $3-$10. Drinks: Mod.

## Jellyroll's
*Station Sq. 7 days 5-2am. AE,D,DC, MC, V.* **391-7464.**
Friendly piano sing-a-long, "dueling pianos." Karaoke Happy Hour Tues/Fri 5-7, Free Buffet Fri. Nachos/sandwiches $2.65-$5. Drinks: Inexp.

## More
*Bayard & Craig, Oakland. Wed-Fri til 12, Sat til 1. AE,DC,MC,V.* **621-2700.**
Classy "neighborhood bar" with piano Wed-Sat from 7 til closing. Regulars occasionally break into song—some solo. Drinks: Mod-Exp.

## Pgh Jazz Society Jams

### Foster's, Holiday Inn, Univ.
*100 Lytton Ave. Fri-Sat 9:30-1:30. Sun 7-11. AE,DC,MC,V.* **682-6200.**
Comfortable, couched lounge off diningroom with top local jazz bands Fri-Sat and Pgh Jazz Society bands Sundays 7-11. You can join the Society at the door & get 20% off drinks, 10% off food. Sandwiches/appetizers $5-$8. Drinks: Mod-Exp.

## Palm Court Lobby
*Westin William Penn, Downtown. 7 nights 5:30-8. AE,DC,MC,V.* **281-7100.**
Jazzman Joe Negri on the grand piano in the chandeliered lobby early evening til 8 nightly. Dim Sum—Chinese appetizers ($4.25-$8.50) til 11. (Also piano at afternoon tea 2:30-4:30.) Elegant ambience. Drinks: Exp.

## Shiloh Inn
*123 Shiloh Street, Mt Washington. Mon-Sat til 2. AE,DC,MC,V.* **431-4000.**
Convivial crowd at charming bar atop the Mount with piano music nightly 9-1:30. Dinner ($10-$18) Fri-Sat til 11:30 in antique drawing rooms. City's best pousse cafe—15 layers of liqueur poured in 4 minutes by colorful owner-barkeeper. Drinks: Mod.

## Top of Triangle
*USX Bldg, 600 Grant. Fri-Sat til 11, Lounge til 2. AE,D,DC,MC,V.* **471-4100.**
Piano music, dancing at the bar Fri/Sat 6-11 in elegant 62nd fl restaurant with stunning city view. ($16-$24), appetizers for less. Drinks: Mod-Exp.

## Jazz Rooms

### JAZZ ROOMS

#### Cafe Azure
*317 S Craig St, Oakland.Fri-Sat til 11. AE, DC, MC,V.* **681-3533.**
Top jazz talent Fri & Sat from 8-11. French cuisine, full dinner, late bites. ($5.50-$24). Drinks: Mod-Exp.

#### Crawford Grill
*2141 Wylie Avenue, Hill District. Fri 5:30-9:30. No credit cards.* **471-1565.**
Jazz Fri 5:30-9:30. Dinners, sandwiches, snacks ($3.75-$10.50). Drinks: Inexp.

#### James St Pub
*422 Foreland & James, N Side. Wed/Fri/Sat til 2. AE,DC,MC.V.* **323-2222.**
Casual upstairs/downstairs; live jazz Fri-Sat 9-1. Wed Banjo Club Sing-A-Long. Dinner/snacks til 12 wknds. ($13-$16). Good crowd. Drinks: Mod.

#### Paparazzi's
*21st/Carson, S Side. 7 nites til 12, Bar til 2. AE,CB,D,DC,MC,V.* **488-0800.**
Burnished 2-story glass-front. Jazz Thur-Sat. Sun 'Barbara Sings Blues' 9:30-2. Casual Italian. ($8-$16). Drinks: Mod.

#### Ramsey's
*7310 Frankstown Ave, Homewood. Thur til 2am. MC,V.* **371- 3445.**
It's an all ages House Party Thur night from 5pm on. Bridge, backgammon, board games of all kinds to jazz...sometimes live.

---

### Jazz in the Afternoon
Saturday afternoon jam sessions are becoming popular around the city. You can catch them at:
**Frankie's**, 1822 S Braddock, Swissvale 4:30-8:30. **351-8000.**
**Blues Cafe**, 19th/Carson, S Side at 3:30. **431-7080.**
**Too Sweet Lounge**, Frankstown & N Lang, Homewood. **731-5707.**
Local musicians have a standing invitation to sit in from 6-10.

---

### Mellow Sunday Sit-In

#### Jazz at Hill House
*Kaufmann Auditorium, 1835 Centre, Hill District.* **392-4400.**
It's a mellow sit-in every Sunday at this Hill District community house. Starting at 5:30pm, local and visiting jazz greats sit in for mellow sessions. Many bring their own food to enjoy with the sounds. Free parking in Hill House lot or lot across the street. You can buy set-ups at door.

---

Some bring their own table. Sandwiches ($3-$5.50), Ribs $13.95. Drinks: Inexp-Mod.

#### Shadyside Balcony
*5520 Walnut, Shadyside. Mon-Sat til 2. Sun Jazz Brunch 11-3. AE,DC,V.* **687-0110.**
Where it's at on the local jazz scene—six nights a week in this lively cafe/restaurant with the best jazz/fusion bands in town. Listen while dining or join the crowd at very busy bar. Late bites with cuisine as creative as music—quiche, cashew chicken, chili, pizza $5 up. Drinks: Mod.

#### Too Sweet Lounge
*7107 Frankstown Ave, Homewood.* **731-5707.**
All star jazz jam session 6-10 Saturdays. Light dining, wings. Drinks: Inexp.

### TOP 40s/OLDIES

#### Cahoots
*Marriott Hotel, Greentree. 7 nites til 2. AE,DC,MC,V.* **922-8400.**
Plush lounge with stylish 25-40 crowd. Live bands, two shows Fri-Sat, $3 cover. Karaoke sing-a-long Thur 9-12. Dinner/snacks til 12am at hotel restaurants. Drinks: Mod-Exp.

## Houlihan's
*Freight House, Station Sq & Monroeville Mall. Mon-Thur til 11, Fri-Sat til 12:30, Bar til 2. AE,DC,MC,V.* **232-0302.**
DJ nightly in small, cozy lounge off the bar. Dinner/snacks $5-$13. Drinks: Mod.

## Motions
*Pittsburgh Vista Hotel, Liberty Center. 7 days til 2am. AE,DC,MC,V.* **281-8164.**
Intimate, sophisticated lounge with top 40s listening/dancing, DJ Fri-Sat, occasional live entertainment. Great late menu til 12, $4-$8. Drinks: Mod-Exp.

# ROCK/R & B

## Anthony's Southside
*1306 E Carson St, S Side. Mon-Sat til 2. No credit cards.* **431-8960.**
Rock/R & B nitely. No cover. Drinks: Mod.

## Birmingham Inn
*1707 E Carson St, S Side. Mon-Sat 12-2am. DC,MC,V.* **431-9214.**
Rythmn & Blues Wed-Fri 3pm-2am. Light food. $1-$4. Young, mixed crowd. Drinks: Inexp-Mod.

## Bloomfield Bridge Tavern
*4412 Liberty Ave, Bloomfield. Mon-Sat 11am-1:30am. AE,D,MC,V.* **682-8611.**
Local bands, alternative rock, R & B, new wave Thur 9-12, Fri-Sat 10-1am. Ethnic food til midnite—perogies, haluski, Polish Platter Sampling $6. 100 imported beers. Blue/white collar crowd. Drinks: Inex-Mod.

## Blues Cafe
*19th/E Carson, S Side. Wed-Sat til 2. Sat 3:30-7:30. AE,D,MC,V.* **431-7080.**
Live blues/Jazz Wed-Sat. $2 cover Fri, Sat & Sat 3:30pm jazz session. Burgers/snacks around $5.25. Drinks: Mod.

## Cafe Carousel
*759 E Railroad, Verona. Mon-Thur 5-11, Fri-Sat til 12. bar til 2. AE,MC,V.* **828-6919.**
Acoustic/blues Fri-Sat from 9pm. No cover. Hardwood grills—lamb/ribs $10-$12. Variety beer, liqueurs. Mod-Exp.

## The Decade
*223 Atwood Street, Oakland. Sun-Sat til 2. No credit cards.* **682-1211.**
Legend in its own time—now 20 yrs old, popular singles spot with hottest rock action in town, live bands nightly. Cover $1-$4, natl bands $5-$6. Drinks: Inexp.

## Electric Banana
*3887 Bigelow Blvd, Oakland. Tues-Sat 8-2.* **682-8296.**
On cutting edge of rock—alternative, new age, new wave, psychedelic, thrash metal, original Pgh music, occasional star attraction. Tues-Sat 8-2, cover $3 up; All Ages show Sun 7:30-11, cover $7 & up. Pizza, burgers. Drinks: Inexp-Mod.

## Excuses Bar/Grill
*2526 E Carson St, S Side. Thur-Sat til 2. D,DC,MC,V.* **431-9847.**
Good age mix on hand for live blues/R&B/rock Thur-Sat til 2. Great wings! Cover $2-$4. Drinks: Inexp.

## Frankie's
*1822 S Braddock Ave, Swissvale. 7 days til 2 am. AE,MC,V.* **351-8000.**
R&B/reggae/rock wknds, Sat afternoon jazz 4-8. Pasta, seafood, overstuffed sandwiches; good age mix. Drinks: Mod.

## Getaway Cafe
*3049 Sussex Ave, McNeilly Rd, S Hills. 7 days 11am-2am. D,MC,V.* **343-1333.**
Sandwiches/appetizers til 2 $4.75-$8. (All-you-can eat for $13 Wed-Sat til 9pm). Drinks: Mod.

## Graffiti
*4615 Baum Boulevard, Oakland. Wed-Sat 4-2. AE,D,DC,MC,V.* **682-4210.**
Unique 2nd floor loft showcasing headliners...some of the hottest acts playing Pgh. Hard rock to country, comedy, Irish singers, reggae, open stage. Balconied dance hall, lounge, restaurant (advance reserv only). Annual Pgh Rock Challenge. Finger foods under $5 til 12. Cover varies. Drinks: Mod.

## Rock/R&B

### Pittsburgh Music Shows

Local music shows to watch for are the **Graffiti Rock Challenge**, an annual event co-sponsored by WDVE highlighting local, national stars, and the **In Pittsburgh Music Awards**—local musicians from rock to classical.

### Jergel's

*3385 Babcock Blvd, N Hills. Mon-Sat til 2am. AE,D,MC,V.* **364-9902.**
Rock, rhythm & blues, country Wed-Sat from 9:30-1:30 in lively, upbeat bar/restaurant. Dinner, late night menu Mon-Sat til 12am ($3-$21). Drinks: Mod.

### Kangaroo's Outback

*4550 McKnight Rd, Ross. 7 days 11am-2am. AE,D,DC,MC,V.* **931-3370.**
Jumpin' crowd for Australian fun, 'home of the velcro wall.' Inflatable Sumo wrestling Wed; R & R Fri & Sat, Reggae Sun, Retro Disco Thur with great food specials. Cover Fri-Sat $3-$4. Full menu, snacks, wings, ribs $4-$13. Drinks: Inexp-Mod.

### Loop Lounge

*8 Brilliant Ave, Aspinwall. 7 days til 2. No credit cards.* **781-0355.**
Lively center for 20-30's crowd. Live blues/rock Fri-Sat. Wings/draft special Mon. Weekend cover $2, guest artists, $5. Drinks: Inexp.

### Margaritaville

*2200 E Carson, S Side. Mon-Thur 11:30-11, Fri & Sat til 12. Sun 5-12. AE,D,DC, MC,V.* **431-2200.**
Top 40's, jazz, R & B Mon-Sat til 2am. Young/mixed group. Mexican fajitas, ribs. $6-$13. Famous big-sized $3.50 margaritas. Drinks: Inexp-Mod.

### Misty Harbour

*19th/River Rd, Sharpsburg. Tues-Sun til 1, Bar til 2. AE,D,MC,V.* **781-4222.**
Live R & B/reggae Fri-Sat; Sun Jazz, DJ weeknights on boat/barge on the Allegheny. Dancing, romantic river view. Seafood sandwiches til 11. $5-$17. Occasional cover. Drinks: Inexp-Mod.

### Moondogs

*378 Freeport Rd, Blawnox. Mon-Sat 9:30-2. No credit cards.* **828-2040.**
Live blues, R & R, reggae, country. Wed-Sat. Open stage Tues 10-2. All ages, snacks. Cover $1-$5. Drinks: Inexp.

### Nick's Fat City

*1601 E Carson, S Side. Tues-Sat 10-2am. AE,DC,MC,V.* **481-6881.**
Local R & B, old rock groups, alternative, reggae Tues-Sat. No cover. Pizza—30 toppings, $2 late Thur-Sat. Drinks: Mod.

### Silky's Crow's Nest

*17th/River Rd, Sharpsburg. Mon-Thur til 11-12, Fri-Sat til 2. AE,D,DC,MC,V.* **782-3701.**
DJ Dancing Sat nite, mostly blues, occasional live bands at romantic riverside room, three outdoor decks. Sandwiches/dinner Fri-Sat til 11. Drinks: Inexp-Mod.

### Someplace Else

*Rt 51/Streets Run Rd, Baldwin. 6 mi from Liberty Tunnels.* **884-8660.**
Popular S Hills spot. Jam night Tues with free beer 9-10. Rhythm & Blues Fri-Sat. Weekend cover $5. Drinks: Mod.

### Thirsty's

*301 N Craig St, Oakland. Mon-Sun til 2am. No credit cards.* **687-0114.**
Area, out-of-town rock/blues bands Fri-Sat. Local/student crowd. Sandwiches/burgers $4-$5. Drinks: Inexp.

### Zelda's Greenhouse

*117 Bouquet St, Oakland. Mon-Sat til 2. No credit cards.* **681-3971.**
Popular young singles spot goes on forever! High voltage music, sing-a-longs amid hanging greenery. Cover Wed, Thurs & Sat. Drink discounts Tues-Fri. Snacks. Drinks: Inexp.

## COUNTRY/WESTERN

*(To find out who's playing where call WDSY Wknd Country Line 333-9583.)*

### Cheat 'N Heart Saloon
*Holiday Inn, Mosside Blvd. 7 nights til 2. AE,CB,D,DC,MC,V.* **372-1022**
DJ Country Dancing every nite but Tues. Line dancing lessons Sun 7-9. Sandwiches/appetizers $6-$7. Drinks: Mod.

### Crystal Lounge
*1216 Woods Run Ave, N Side. Sat til 2am. No credit cards.* **766-9255.**
Urban cowboy band Sat til 2am on big, big dance floor. Fri rock. Bring your dancin' shoes! Drinks: Inexp.

### D J Mike's Cafe
*4968 Library Road, Rt 88 Bethel. Tues-Sat 9-2. No credit cards.* **833-1585.**
Live music Fri-Sat, $2 cover. Tues/Thur Country DJ; Wed Open Stage. Sandwiches/cheese plates. Drinks: Inexp.

### Nightscape
*Holiday Inn, RIDC Pk, Blawnox off Rt 28. 7 days til 12-1. AE,DC,MC,V.* **963-0600.**
Casual country music/dancing Sun from 8-12; live jazz Sat. Sandwiches/snacks til 11. No cover. Drinks: Inexp-Mod.

### Rockin' Rodeo
*1165 McKinney Lane, Parkway Center Mall. Fri-Sat. AE,MC,V.* **921-3388.**
Get on your dancin' boots for live bands Fri-Sat, cover $3 after 8. Line dancing Wed-Sun, free lesssons 6:30pm. Wed—cover after 10, $2. Sun Family Nite 4-11 (no drinks), $5. Sandwiches/light menu, Steak Stampede Fri-Sat $3. Drinks: Inexp.

---

### Russian/Israeli Dancing
Dancing to Russian & Israeli pop and folk tunes 8:30 Fri & Sat at **Moscow Nights,** 1722 Murray Ave, Squirrel Hill...with flavourful food. BYOB. D,MC,V. (See Review). **521-5005.**

---

### The Latin Beat
The Latin American dance craze has a strong following in Pittsburgh with serious aficionados following the top Latin dance band Guaracha for hot salsa from floor to floor...Thurdays at **Rosebud** in the Strip and Saturday nights at **Cozumel**, 5507 Walnut St, Shadyside. Many of the dancers are real pros...so deft they're better than a floor show! You can learn the new dance steps at regular teach-ins.

---

**3**

### Ruth & Herb's
*Rochester Road, Ross Twp. No credit cards.* **366-8770.**
Live country Sat only. Sandwiches. Drinks: Inexp.

## MOSTLY DANCING

### Chauncy's
*Commerce Court, Station Square, 7 nights 8-2. AE,MC,V.* **232-0601.**
An over-25 Yuppie haunt with a classy, spacious ballroom atmosphere, crowded every night. Tues—Oldies; Mon/Wed/Thur/Sun Top 40s; Fri-Sat Disco 9-12. Dinner 6-9:30, $10-$16. Drinks: Mod-Exp.

### Cloud 9
*21st/Smallman, Strip Dist. Tues-Sun 11am-2am. AE,MC,V.* **281-8277.**
DJ dancing every nite—house/rock/disco; big, handsome rooms. Snacks/grills $2-$8 Cover after 10, $2. Drinks: Inexp.

### Cozumel
*5507 Walnut, Shadyside. Sat night 9-2. AE,D,DC,MC,V.* **621-5100.**
There's a great beat here Sat nights when deft Latin-Amer dancers take the floor from 9 to 2am. Mexican fajitas, burritos, tamales. $4.25-$9. Drinks: Mod.

# Dining/Dancing

### Metropol
*1600 Smallman, Strip District. Wed-Sat 9-2. AE,MC,V.* **261-2221.**
Pittsburgh's hottest, an exciting high-tech club with nightly DJ, live bands, top recording artists; room for 1000 revelers. Industrial decor—exposed pylons, gusts of steam, catwalks linking multi-levels, Strobes create high intensity atmosphere for dancing or watching from balconies. You'll see everything from jeans to stretch limos. Cover Wed-Thur $2, Fri-Sat $3 til 11, $5 after 11. Sun Metro Mix 9pm $2. Free buffet at Fri Happy Hour & sometimes thru week. **Rosebud** next door for more serious revelers. Drinks: Mod.

### Upstage
*3609 Forbes Avenue, Oakland. Mon, Thur thru Sat. No credit cards.* **681-9777.**
Young crowd for DJ alternative/progressive dance music Mon, Fri & Sat. Thur Retro 70's/80's. No food. Cover $2. Drinks. Inexp $1-$1.25.

### Windjammers
*10 Washington Ave, Oakmont. Thur-Sat til 2. AE,D,MC,V.* **828-4441.**
Spirited young crowd for DJ dancing to top 40's in booming room overlooking water. Thur reggae, Sun afternoon Deck Party. Drinks: Mod.

---

### Ballroom Dancing

Pittsburgh's ballroom dance fans can indulge their hobby at several local sites–Thur nights at the Coraopolis Convention Center, Fri at the Pallisades in McKeesport and Sat at the American Legion on McKnight Road. And there's an afternoon Tea Dance Mon from 12-4 at the Airport Holiday Inn. The US Amateur Ballroom Dancers hold their annual Crystal Ball in Feb. **767-2327.**

---

### Dancing in the Dark

### Fox Chapel Yacht Club
*1366 Old Freeport Rd, Fox Chapel. AE,MC,V.* **963-8881.**
Dancing to live music under the stars Fri-Sat on a romantic outdoor deck/bar along the Allegheny. No cover. Drinks: Mod.

---

## DINING/DANCING

### Costanza's
*240 Fourth Ave, Downtown. Mon-Sat til 2. AE,DC,MC,V. Reser.* **232-0706.**
Night club dining/dancing Fri-Sat 9-1 to DJ/live 40s bands. Dinner til 11 ($7-$10) Italian, burgers—til 2. Drinks: Inexp-Mod.

### Harley Hotel
*Off Rodi Road, Penn Hills. Mon-Thur til 1. AE,DC,MC,V.* **244-1600.**
Elegant evening–dining in romantic Three Rivers room til 11 with live band dancing in the lounge Fri-Sat 9-1. Dinner/appetizers $7-$20. Drinks: Exp.

### Joe's Jazz Lounge
*D'Imperio's, 3412 Wm Penn Hwy, Wlkins. Mon-Sat til 2. Reser sugg. AE,CB,D,DC, MC,V.* **823-4800.**
Follow delectable dinner at one of city's finest with mellow music in the romantic lounge. Dancing to live combo Wed-Fri. Dining in restaurant or intimate Lounge. $16-$29, great appetizers $4-8. Drinks: Mod-Exp.

### The Living Room
*1778 N Highland Rd, Upper St Clair. Mon-Sat til 2. AE,D,DC,MC,V.* **835-9772.**
Informal supper club with mellow music, dancing, live bands Wed, Fri, Sat 9:30-1:30. Class act. Italian specialties $13-$23. Drinks: Mod.

## Dinner Theatre

**3**

### Longnecker's
*Holiday Inn, Greentree. Fri-Sat nights 9-2. AE,DC,MC,V.* **922-8100.**
Dinner & DJ dancing Fri/Sat in big beautiful glass-walled room; casual atmosphere Dinner/snacks. $4.75-$15.Drinks: Mod.

### Terrace Room
*Westin William Penn, Mellon Sq, Downtown. Sat til 12. AE,DC,MC,V.* **553- 5235.**
An "oldie" Sat night tradition—dinner in nostalgic Terrace Room, dancing to strains of Nick Lomakin Trio. $8.25-$22.50. Drinks: Mod-Exp. (See Review)

### Top of the Triangle
*USX Tower, 600 Grant. Mon-Thur til 11, Fri-Sat til 12. AE,D,DC,MC,V.* **471-4100.**
Dancing, requests to pianist/vocalist in glamorous 62nd fl lounge; breathtaking view. Late supper Sat til 11. Drinks: Exp

## DINNER THEATRE

### Conley Inn
*3550 Wm Penn Hwy, Monrv. AE,DC,D,* MC,V. **824-6000, 1-800-426-6539.**
Hawaiian buffet and "Hawaii in Pgh" show (16 yrs in Pgh) 8 & 9:30–$35. Dancing, audience participation after the show 10:30-11. Also lunch shows 1 & 2:30–$24. Late supper Sat til 11. Drinks: Exp.

### Holiday Inn
*4859 McKnight Road, Ross Twp. Thur-Sat. AE,DC,MC,V.* **366-5200.**
Musical revues Apr-Jun and Sept-Nov. Thurs/Sat Package—dinner at 6, show at 8, $25-$30. Show only, $13. Drinks: Mod.

### Club Wet

*Sandcastle Water Pk, W Homestead,, Rt 837 bet Hi Level/Glenwood bridges (Jun-Labor Day. Wed- Sat after 6)* MC,V. **462-6666.** *Hotline* **462-1072.**
Romantic, spirited DJ outdoor dancing along Mon, Wed, Fri-Sat 9-1am. Grills, burgers at patio tables $3-$5. Cover Wed $1, Fri-Sat $3. Drinks Inexp.

### Fun on the Boardwalk

**Boardwalk, On the Water**
1501 Smallman, Strip. Parking lot at 15th St. AE,MC,V. **281-1600.**
Exciting nightlife on Pgh's rivers on this 420-ft floating boardwalk on the Allegheny. (See Review).

**Donzi's**
*Wed-Fri 8-2am, Sat 5-2am. AE,MC,V.* **281-1586**
Sleek, ultra-modern nightclub with dancing to DJ's, live bands Wed-Fri 8-2am & Sat 5-2am. Cover $2-$5. Drinks: Mod-Exp.

**Patio Deck**
*May-Sep.* **281-3680.**
Riverside fun on big Boardwalk deck. Two bars, docking, dancing under the stars. Bands add to summer fun–Tues DJ Splash Party, Wed live bands, Thur Oldies, Sun Rock from 9pm. Steel Bands Sat/Sun aft. Great river view. Drinks/Food. Mod. Seafood, snacks on **Patio Deck** and inside at **Crewsers, Buster's Crab.**

### Linden Hall
*Dawson, Pa, 45 mi south of Pgh. Rt 51 S at Perryopolis sign, follow signs to Linden Hall 5-6 mi on right. AE,MC,V.* **461-2424.**
Dinner at Sara B's restaurant on beautiful estate with sweeping view of the Laurel Mountains $6-$16. Then on to 7:30 curtain at nearby Theatre in Loft ($11.75) Sat Mar-Oct.

### Radisson Hotel
*101 Mall Blvd, Monroeville. AE,D,DC,MC, V.* **373-7300.**
Big, beautiful Luau Buffet at 6:45, Four different Polynesian shows/"Pgh Follies" at 8pm, $31.95. Matinee $22.

# Variety/Showcase

## VARIETY/SHOWCASE

### Artery
*5847 Ellsworth, Shadyside. Tues-Sun til 1. AE,MC,V.* **362-9111.**
Dinner/snacks eclectic entertainment in restaurant/gallery; hip music, art, dancing, performance. 'Art Happy Hour' Tues-Fri 5-7. ($4-$17). Drinks: Inexp.

### Blarney Stone
*30 Grant Avenue, Etna, Rts 8/28. AE,DC, MC,V.* **781-1666.**
City's unofficial Irish center; souvenirs, imports, Irish folk/balladeers, sing-a-long, entertainment Fri-Sat from 9. Cover guest artists $2-$3, concerts $15-$22. Dinner Theatre Sept-Dec Fri-Sat $31.95, Sun Aft $28.95. Sandwiches til 11. Drinks: Mod.

### Grandview Saloon
*1212 Grandview, near Duquesne Incline, Mt Washington. Sun-Thur til 12, Fri-Sat til 1, Bar til 2. AE,DC,MC,V.* **431-1400.**
After-sundown fun, great view from five levels, outdoor decks. Bar/music, lively young upscale crowd. Burgers, light dining. ($5-$18). Drinks: Mod.

### Hemingway's
*3911 Forbes, Oakland. 7 days 11-2. AE, DC,MC,V.* **621-4100.**
Tues Poetry Readings 8:30-10:30 in back room of popular college haunt with all ages; interactive tv trivia nightly, full menu wknds til 12. ($5-$12). Drinks: Inexp-Mod.

---

### Dinner, Show at the Square

Five Station Square eateries offer dinner/theatre packages to  long-running "Nunsense"/"Forever Plaid" at the **Station Sq Playhouse** near Bessemer Court. Dinner (2 hrs before showtime) Fri 8:30, Sat 8, Sun 2:30. River Cafe, Sheraton, Gr Concourse, Cheese Cellar, Tequila Junction. $30-$35 inc tax/tip. Show only $18 at TIX, Heinz Healey, St Sq. **279-3881.**

---

### Munchin' at the Movies

#### Shadyside Cinema Grill
The city gets its first full-scale movie/restaurant at Ellsworth Plaza where you can eat while you watch current films. Two  screens, room for up to 275 viewers at small tables for sandwiches, pizza, dessert, drinks. Shows  7:30, 9:30, three on week-ends. $2.50-$3.50. Food $4-$10.

#### Beehive Oakland
You can also eat as you watch a film from little tables in the back of this bustling coffee shop/movie house, 3807 Forbes, Oakland. Art films, mainstream, old classics, often til midnite on wknds, some afternoons. $4-$6.25; Also poetry readings Thur 8pm, Sun play readings. Vegetarian snacks, desserts. $1-$3. **687-9428.**

---

### Liberty Belle
*2204 E Carson, S Side. Fri-Sat til 2. No credit cards.* **431-0850.**
Home of Frankie Capri, the king of kitsch, a zany one-man-band crowd participation act Fridays. Patrons put on animal hats, dance around and let it all hang out, $2 cover. Live bands Sat. Drinks: Inexp-Mod.

### Luciano's
*1023 Forbes Ave, across from Duq U. Mon-Wed 10-10, Thur til 2am, Fri-Sat 5-1am. Sun 9-2am.  MC,V.* **281-6877.**
Student bistro/cafe with local theatre/rock bands Fri-Sat at 7:30. Italian meals, sandwiches. $2-$8.50. Drinks: Inexp.

### Mullaney's Harp/Fiddle Irish Pub
*24th/Penn, Strip. Tues-Thur til 12am, Fri-Sat til 2. Sun 4-12am. AE,D,MC,V.* **642-6622.**
Live Irish/Celtic musicians/singers Wed-Sat; Ceili dancing Tues, local talent Sun. Irish beer, specialties--smoked salmon, shepherd's pie $5-$11. Patio deck. Cover Fri-Sat $2. Drinks: Inexp-Mod.

## Variety/Sports Bars

**3**

### Penn Brewery
*Troy Hill Rd, N Side (acrs 16th St Bridge.)*
*Mon-Sat til 12. AE,MC,V.* **237-9402.**
German beer hall—wood tables/benches,
view of beer-making. Food, fun, live
music Tues-Thur 7-10, Fri-Sat til 11:30.
German bands, Dixieland. Hearty food
$7-$12. Drinks. Inexp-Mod. (See Review)

### Rosebud
*1650 Smallman. 7 nights til 2am. AE,D,*
*DC,MC,V.* **261-2221.**
Large, inviting space next to Metropol
with state-of-art stage facilities for top
acoustic band, performing artists. Free
flow environment for coffee to full menu
$3-$10. Cover enter. Drinks: Mod.

## SPORTS BARS

### Champs
*5832 Forward, Sq Hill. 7 days 3pm-2am.*
*12pm Steeler games. Food til 12am,*
*Fri-Sat til 12:30. AE,MC,V.* **422-6414.**
Small, lively bar, wall-to-wall photos,
haunt of sports figures/fans. 9 TVs, food
$4-$7. Drinks: Inexp-Mod.

### Comedy Anyone?

**Funny Bone Station Square**
*Mon-Sat. AE,MC,V.* **281-3130.**
National/local talent at area's #1
comedy club. Tues Open Stage 8:30,
$5 cover; Wed-Thur 8:30, $6-$7; Fri
8:30 & 10:30, $9-$10; Sat 7:15, 9:30,
11:30, $9-$10. Sun 8pm $6. Two bev
min. Snacks $3. Drinks: Mod-Exp.

**Funny Bone East**
*Hollywood Grill, Rts 48/22, Monrv.*
*Thur-Sun. MC,V. Reser.* **856-7888.**
Thur 8:30, Fri-Sat 8:30 & 10:30, Cover
$5-$9. 2 bev min. Sandwiches, salads
$1.50-$6 Drinks: Mod-Exp.

**Comedy Club, Marriott**
*Greentree Marriott, Fri-Sat. AE,CB,D,*
*DC,MC,V. Reser.* **635-0708.**
Fri-Sat 8:30/10:30 $7.50-$8; Snacks/
sandwiches $2.50-$10. Drinks: I-Mod.

### Banjo Sing-A-Long
It's a rollickin' good time 8 pm Weds
as members of the **Pgh Banjo Club**
get together at James St Tavern, 422
Foreland, N S. You're invited to come
along, sing along or just tap your toes.
4-string players can sit in. **364-4739.**

### Karaoke
So you want to be a singing sensation
but just need that big break. Why not
try Karaoke (ka-ri-o-kee). A Japanese
import, it offers pub patrons a chance
to take the mike and belt out their favorite tunes to recorded music for over
800 songs. Every day of the week at:
*7 nights:* **Jelly Rolls** (Stat Sq). *Wed:*
**Getaway Bar** (S Hills), **Brass Rail**
(Bill Green's Shop Ctr) & **Too Sweet
Lounge** (Homewood). *Thur:* **Greentree Marriott.** *Fri:* **Del Frate's** (Downtown). *Sat:* **Yesterday's** (S Baldwin
Plaza). *Sun:* **Ryans Pub** (Pt Breeze).

### Silky's
*1731 Murray Ave, Sq Hill. Mon-Sat til 2.*
*Sun til 12. MC,V.* **421-9222.**
Catch every sports game on TV at this
lively neighborhood bar; munchies,
burgers, full dinners ($3-$11). Get there
before game time. Drinks: Inexp-Mod.

### Shootz Cafe/Billiards
*2305 E Carson, S Side. Mon/Fri 11:30-*
*2am. Sat-Sun 1pm-2am. Food 5-10pm.*
*AE,D,MC,V.***488-3820.**
Popular, lively billiard hall, 18 tables, 6
TVs, two bars, large diningroom. Dinner/
snacks $5-$20. Drinks: Inexp.

### Zagnut's
*503 Martingdale (Clark Candy Bldg), N*
*Side. Open 3 hrs before Stadium events*
*til 2 am. AE,DC,MC,V.* **231-5720.**
Big, convivial area for after-game crowds.
Basketball, baseball, video games, DJ
dancing wknds. Burgers, fish sandwiches,
up to $6.50. Drinks: Inexp-Mod.

### All Night Long

**Fast Food:** All Denny's, most Eat 'n Parks, King's, Wendy's–Baum Blvd. **Convenience Stores:** 7-Elevens, Co-Go's, A-Plus Mini Mkts, Gulf stores. **Supermarkets:** Giant Eagles in Sq Hill, Penn Hills, Monroeville, Parkway Centr, McKnight Rd, McKnight/Peebles; Village Sq, Caste Village, Va Manor, Waterworks, Fox Chapel. **Pharmacies:** Thrift Drug—Miracle Mile, Monroeville. **372-5288. Animal Emergencies:** After Hours Animal Hosp **344-6888.** Animal Emergency Service **885-3375.**

### OPEN ALL NIGHT

**Del-Kid**
5536 Steubenville Pike, Robinson. Mon-Sat 24hrs. **787-9945.**
24hr breakfst; super omelettes. $1.50-$13.

**King's Family Restaurants**
*7 days 24 hrs—Bridgeville, Cranberry, Fox Chapel, Penn Hills, Steubenville Pike Versailles, Upper St Clair, Plum, Moon. (Monrv–wknds only).*
Hearty food, one of best breakfasts in city all night long. $3-$5.

**Norwin Diner**
*Rt 30 7 mi past McKeesport. 7 days 24 hours. MC, V.* **863-2941.**
Famed nostalgic diner/restaurant with great chicken, homemade pie $2-$7.

**Primanti's**
*46 18th St nr Penn/Smallman. Mon-Sat 24 hours, Sun until 5am.* **263-2142.**
Legend for food in wee hours–for Strip workers/college revelers while city sleeps. Breakfast, famous sandwiches with fries/slaw *inside.* $2.75-$3.50. Drinks: Inexp.

**Ritter's Diner**
*5221 Baum Blvd, Bloomfield. 7 days-24 hours. No credit cards.* **682-4852.**
City favorite at 3 o'clock in morning. Breakfast, spaghetti to NY strip. $2-$10.

**South Shore Diner**
*17th/Carson. 7 days 24 hours.* **431-9292.**
Typical diner–breakfast, burgers $2-$5.

**White Tower**
*7 days, 24 hours. Chestnut/16th, N Side.*
Only one left now...the familiar black/white turrets a friendly beacon to night people, cops, cabbies. Breakfast 95c, burgers 40c, stool-to-stool conversation til dawn.

### FOOD IN EARLY AM

**Brandy's**
*Penn/24th St, Strip Dist. Mon-Thur 11-12, Fri-Sat til 2am, Sun 3-11.* **566-1000.**
Romantic greenery, atmosphere. Snacks, burgers, dessert concoctions. $3.75-$7.

**Beehive Coffee Shop**
*14th/Carson, S Side. Mon-Fri 8:30-1, Sat-Sun 9-3. No cred cards.* **488-4483.**
Zany art, interesting denizens, non-stop coffee/desserts all weekend long.

**Dick's Diner**
*Rt 22, Murrysvlle. Sun-Thur open 6:30am, Fri-Sat from 6am. No credit cds.* **327-4566.**
Late nite institution. Great prices, hot beef sandwiches, homemade pies $1-$7.

**Lindos**
*947 Western Ave, North Side. Mon-Fri 6am-3pm, Sat-Sun 7am-3.* **231-0110.**
Small, homey diner; big breakfasts for early workers, night owls $2-$3; homemade soup 95c, gyros, platters $3.75.

**Mike's Lunch**
*200 Brownsville Rd, Mt Oliver. Mon-Sat 6am-3:30am.*
Breakfast around the clock with strawberry whipped cream pancakes, French toast, burgers, homemade soups. $3-$5.

**Original Hot Dog Shop**
*Forbes & Bouquet. Sun-Thur til 4:30am. Fri-Sat til 6.* 621-7388.
Native Pittsburgers have been known to travel home for famous "foot long hot dog", now 7-1/2" but still best in town–$1.98 with everything. Burgers, ribs, pizza, imported beers. $3-$10.50.

4

Here are "Pittsburgh Originals," dishes indigenous to the city, some famous throughout the world. Pittsburgh is also noted for its unique ethnic cuisine. Here's where to find it and enjoy it year 'round at local food fests. Phil Isaly, grandson of the stores' founder, poses with a famous Klondike at an old-time Isaly's on Perry Highway.

# Pittsburgh Originals

## A COSMOPOLITAN CITY

*Visitors to Pittsburgh are entranced with the variety of its ethnic foods. One of the city's strengths has always been the richness of its cultural traditions—it has one of the highest percentages of ethnic groups in the U.S. The old-country recipes of the families who came here to make iron and steel have been proudly passed on from generation to generation. And through the years new populations of Mid-Eastern and Asian peoples have added their own special cuisines. This has given the city's food infinite variety...a variety that Pittsburghers take for granted but that makes visitors and business travelers sit up and take notice. Yesterday's ethnic town is today's cosmopolitan city...ready to make visitors welcome with a taste of their own cuisines—a bit of home away from home. In turn Pittsburgh has invented a number of dishes on its own and exported them to other cities. Here are some of the foods that Pittsburgh made famous—and the ethnic dishes that made it strong.*

## FOODS THAT STARTED HERE

### The Big Mac

The world's most famous burger "The Big Mac" was concocted in Pittsburgh in 1968 by McDonald's franchise owner Jim Delligatti. Made up of two beef patties, shredded lettuce, cheese, pickles, onions and a special sauce on a three layered, sesame-seed bun, the big burger has sold into the millions.

### Chiodo's Mystery Sandwich

This sandwich is made at one of the 'Burgh's most famous bars, Joe Chiodo's in Homestead. It's a basic mixture of steak, pepperoni, kielbasa, sauerkraut, Amer/provolone, tomato sauce (and whatever mystery ingredient happens to be on hand) all served on an Italian bun. The bar is another Pittsburgh tradition.

### Corned Beef on the Heel

There's a claim this sandwich originated in Pittsburgh using the ends or heels of the bread generally discarded. You cut the heel off a loaf of Kosher rye, slice it horizontally like a bun, pile it with corned beef for a crusty bread/meat combination. It was served this way at the old **S & B** (Blvd of Allies & Craft) famed for its corned beef sandwiches. You can still ask for it "on the heel" at **Richest Deli,** 6th Ave, Downtown (serving it since '36) and **Rhoda's** and **Catz N Kids**, Sq Hill.

### Clark Bar

One of the most popular candy bars in the U.S. was made on the North Side for over 100 years, and is still being made in O'Hara Twp (since '86). The big Clark Bar sign on the roof of the old plant near the Stadium advertises the crunchy peanut, chocolate, taffy creation in its familiar orange-red wrapper. It was the product of David Lytle Clark who opened his first candy factory in 1880 on East Ohio Street and started the Clark Company in 1887. Some people remember sending in the wrappers for free Clark chewing gum.

### Crabmeat Hoelzel

This is a popular Pittsburgh appetizer—Maryland crabmeat with oil, tarragon/cider vinegar and black pepper served in a terrapin dish. Created at the Duquesne Club in the late 40s, it was named for club member John P (Jack) Hoelzel, president of the former Pgh Screw & Bolt Co. It's still on the Duquesne Club menu, other menus around town and is served all over the country.

## Pittsburgh Originals

### Devonshire Sandwich

This open-face sandwich—originally chicken (now usually turkey) with a blanket of cheddar cheese sauce and crisp bacon was invented here by Frank Blandi, owner of Le Mont restaurant and the old Park Schenley. He concocted it in 1936 at his first restaurant, the Stratford, at the corner of Centre & Millvale in Oakland...across from Devonshire Street ...and that's how the sandwich got its name! There are many recipes for the Devonshire but here's the real thing from Blandi himself: For the sauce, start with a roux of flour and butter, add hot milk, a little sharp cheddar, a tbl of chicken base (or 2 to 3 bouillon cubes) and a splash of Worcestershire. Layer the breast of chicken, crisp bacon, then the sauce over toast. Top with paprika & grated Parmesan, dot with a little butter and oven brown (about 15 min) for a crispy top. A popular Pittsburgh menu item, the Devonshire has spread to other cities. It was a staple at the old Oakland Park Schenley.

### Heinz Ketchup

A world-famous name in food, H J Heinz Company makes its Pittsburgh home on Progress St at North Side's 16th St Bridge. Founded in 1869 in Sharpsburg by H. J. (Henry) Heinz and famous for its 57 varities, it now has more than 3000 products in 150 countries. Pittsburgh still uses more Heinz ketchup than any other U.S. city and though the bottling's done elsewhere, ketchup is still being made & packaged at the N Side plant for single-serve packets...along with Heinz baby food and private label soups. Famous for pickles, gravy and relish, Heinz's newest success is the Weight Watchers label.

### Iron City Beer

A Pittsburgh trademark. "Pumpin' Iron" has been a favorite Pittsburgh pastime since 1861. The city's home brews, Iron City & IC Light, are on tap almost every-where. Pittsburgh Brewing Company can claim the world's first snap-top can, the first canned draft, twist-off bottle tops, first

### The Isaly's Story

#### Chipped Ham

By far one of Pittsburgh's most famous foods, this spicy lunch meat made its debut in 1933 on the slicing machines of Isaly's, a locally-based family chain of dairy stores (1929-1972). Generally made from press-ed chopped ham sliced wafer-thin, it can be found at almost any local deli counter. You're not a real Pitts-burgher until you bite into soft mounds of chipped ham on white bread or bun...with plain mustard or mayonnaise. It's so missed by former natives that Pittsburgh clubs around the country often truck or fly it in to their celebrations. No longer family-owned, Isalys has about nine stores in the Pittsburgh area, all of them still selling Isaly's ice-cream, chipped ham and

#### ...Klondikes

This is another Isaly's specialty—a vanilla ice-cream bar dipped in pure chocolate and packaged in a familiar silver wrapper. Invented in '29 by Sam Isaly, Klondikes were made with vanilla ice cream. (If you got one with a pink center you got a free Klondike.) They're now sold nation-ally in vanilla or chocolate, plain or crispy, singly or by the dozen. Used to be a nickel...now 75c.

#### and Skyscraper Cones

Isaly's unique 9-inch skyscraper ice cream cones were part of every old Pittsburgher's childhood. Phil Isaly, grandson of founder Henry Isaly, still has 12 of the original steel sky-scraper scoops. Remember White House (vanilla with big red maraschino cherries) and the old rainbow flavour—a medley of orange, lime, raspberry and lemon still available, 99c, 2 scoops $1.30.

**4**

## Pittsburgh Originals

### The Pittsburgh Steak

This NY strip, delicately charred on the outside, blood-rare on the inside (cooked less than a minute) was named for Pittsburgh by a NY chef. The smoke created when the cold steak hit the sizzling skillet reminded him of his hometown in its old mill days. You can get the 'Pittsburgh rare' at **Tramps**, Downtown, **Tessaro's** in Bloomfield and the **Pgh Steak Co,** South Side. You'll see this steak on menus in other cities.

beer cooler (Hop 'n Gator in 1970) and the first holiday beer, Olde Frothingslosh–"the pale, stale ale with the foam on the bottom." Pgh beer fans can get memorabilia at the gift shop (Liberty & Sassafras) at the far end of the Brewery, 3340 Liberty Avenue, Lawrenceville.

### Lemon Blennd

This popular lemon drink, one of the first fruit concentrates, was created about 50 years ago at old Reymer's Confectionaries, Downtown/E Liberty. It's now sold all over the U.S. Philip Reymer opened his first store at Wood & old Water St in 1846. Lemon Blennd came along in 1932.

### Maurice Salad

This salad was created by the Variety Club kitchen in the William Penn Hotel for band leader Phil Spitalny. Hotel officials say it was originally called the Spitalny Salad and then the Phil Salad—neither of which caught on—and ended up named for Phil's band leader brother Maurice. It's had a long run—it's been on the hotel's Terrace Room menu since 1945. The salad consists of julienne turkey, Swiss cheese and ham over iceberg and bibb lettuce already mixed with a spicy mayonnaise, red peppers & relish. It's served on a plate (rather than a bowl) with tomato wedges and black olives. Variations can be found on many Pittsburgh menus.

### Original Hot Dogs

Pittsburgh's famous "foot-long hot dog" was a staple at the old Original Famous Sandwich Shop at Larimer & Station Sts in East Liberty, started by "Big Sam" in 1928. Now you can get a 7" dog at the 'new' Original Hot Dog Shops, the "Big O" at Forbes/Bouquet in Oakland—opened in 1960 by Syd Simon who worked 15 years at the old Famous. Roasted in its skin for flavour, the big dog is 75% beef, 25% pork. Former Pittsburghers have been known to make a trip home just to taste an Original again! (The "Big O" also does a prodigious business in French fries...40,000 lbs—18 ton—of Idahoes are trucked in, peeled & sliced each week.

### Penn Pilsner

This local beer is now being made at Penn Brewery (in North Side's old Eberhardt & Ober Brewery on Troy Hill), the first 'tied house'...a restaurant attached to a brewery...in Pennsylvania since Prohibition. It's pure German beer without additives, made by a German breumeister. While you eat at the re-created German pub you can watch the brewing process in shiny copper kettles through a glass wall.

### Oyster House Fish Sandwich

This jumbo sandwich, breaded cod on a plain bun, is the city's most famous. To get the real thing you have to go to the 120-yr-old Original Oyster House, an historic Market Sq landmark (1870), stand at the bar and have a beer—or a buttermilk—with your sandwich & enjoy the "sawdust atmosphere." Real Pittsburgh!

### Pecan Ball

Another creation by Pittsburgh restaurateur Frank Blandi...a dessert everyone loves...a scoop of vanilla ice cream rolled in syrupy pecans. In the original recipe a butter rum sauce was poured over the pecans. The Pecan Ball was another staple at the old Park Schenley and the fondly remembered Pgh Playhouse Restaurant.

## Ethnic Foods

## Primanti's Sandwiches

This sandwich has been reviewed in *Newsweek, Penthouse* and Calvin Trillin's book *Third Helpings*. It's claim to fame—French fries and cole slaw are right in the basic sandwich...beef patty and cheese on thick Italian bread. Night owls & Strip workers can get them 24 hours a day at Primanti's 18th Street, Strip, and into the wee hours at 3803 Forbes in Oakland.

## Sarah's

The fame of Sarah Evosevich's home-made Yugoslavian meals still lingers though the restaurant closed in '92. For over 50 years Sarah cooked in her 1850 South Side 'townhouse'...dishes like Serbian Chorba–vegetable barley soup, Podvarak–turkey with sauerkraut, homemade bread and apple strudel. Pittsburghers and visiting VIPs have warm memories of her ethnic meals. The story of *"Sarah: Her Life, Her Restaurant, Her Recipes"* is now available at the Pgh History & Landmarks store in Station Sq. .

## William Penn Cheesecake

From one of the most regal kitchens in the city came one of Pittsburgh's most famous desserts, William Penn Cheese-cake—a rich, rich recipe, usually topped with strawberry sauce...and still a favorite on the hotel's menu. It dates back to 1921 to two German chefs, brothers Oscar and Hans Joerg, who worked at the William Penn shortly after it opened in 1916. At one time it was exported worldwide.

---

## White Tower Hamburgers

Pittsburgh was once famous for the White Tower's old-time flat-grilled burgers, wrapped in the wonderful aroma of grease and frying onions, served with sour pickles. Originally a nickel...they last sold for 99c. White Tower burger stands were once beacons all over Pittsburgh. Of the original 14 only one remains...at the 16th Street Bridge on the North Side.

---

## Pittsburgh Ethnics— Where to Get 'Em

### Bagels

The best are at **Bageland** in Squirrel Hill which sells to many city restaurants. They come in 17 varieties from raisin to onion, blueberry to baby bagels. Close seconds are the nine **Bruegger's Bagels** outlets and **Schwartz's**, Oakland and the Strip.

### Breads

Pittsburgh breads can be summed up in two names: **Breadworks,** a favorite restaurant supplier with wonderful breads of all kinds and **Susan Bakes & Cooks** for some of city's best French, brown breads & baked goods. For Italian, **Mancini's** is the big name with **Sunseri's** in the Strip now baking creative pepporini, onion and garlic breads. Good bakeries abound here—among them **Prantl's** in Shady-side, **Jenny Lee's** all over town & **Rosenblum's** and **Pastries Unlimited** in Squirrel Hill. Some great restaurant breads are the Italian bread sticks at **Davio's**, cinnamon swirls at **Bundz-nudder's** and melt-in-your-mouth pecan sticky buns at **Cinnamon Jim's** in the Galleria.

### British

You can get authentic British "high tea" with pasties (meat pies) at **Cathy's Windsor Tearoom** in Sewickley. Formal tea is served in the **William Penn Lobby** and other local rooms. (See Teas). The best modern tea sandwiches are at Kaufmann's **Tic-Toc Coffee Shop,** great with their unique coffee ice cream soda. P.S. Yorkshire pudding is served with prime rib at the Westin William Penn. And **Aussie's,** a Bloomfield pub, has authentic Australian food and atmosphere.

### Caribbean

Interest in Caribbean food is growing in this area. Catering to island tastes are **Royal West Indian**, Broad St, E Liberty with Jamacian hard dough bread, plan-

**4**

## Ethnic Foods

### Wednesday Greek Lunches

Everyone's welcome at Wed lunches 11-1:30 every other week at **Holy Trinity Greek Orthodox Church,** 302 W North Street, N Side for Greek-style chicken. baked fish, cheese/spinach pies, baklava & loukumades (honey balls). **321-9282.**

tains, rice & peas, snapper & curries....
**Negril Caribbean** Penn Ave, Wilkinsburg; and **Jamacia,** a little Cajun/Creole spot 5th Ave, Uptown. You can get New Orleans cuisine at **James St Tavern**, N Side, the **Mardi Gras** in North Hills and **Buckingham, LTD**, Swissvale, specializing in "Cajun, Creole & Gourmet." **Foster's, University Holiday Inn,** Oakland, has some mean Bayou Gumbo.

### Fish/Seafood
Biggest name for fresh fish in Pittsburgh is wholesaler **Wholey's** on Penn Avenue, Strip...sharing the limelight with **Benkovitz** nearby on Smallman where fans swear by the shrimp/lobster bisques. The **Fresh Fish House** in Sq Hill has some great fresh/cooked fish. Famous local seafood restaurants are **Tambellini's** on Rt 51 near the Liberty Tunnels, and **Poli's,** Sq Hill, and newer **Rodi Grille** in Penn Hills. The **Pgh Vista** has a stellar seafood buffet and **Grand Concourse** features fresh fish, wonderful Charley's Chowder & great 'raw bargains' at adjoining **Gandy Dancer Saloon.**

### French
Pittsburgh has seen the passing of some great French restaurants...world-class La Normande which introduced many to Gallic dining here, it's successor Jacqueline's, and the extraordinary Laforet. The economical Simply French plans to reopen in N Hills. But French cuisine can still be had at **La Pommier** (Country Fr) ) on the S Side and **Cafe Azure** in Oakland. **La Charcuterie** in Ellsworth Plaza,

a gourmet shop run by former Laforet chefs Candy & Michael Uricchio, is still making gastronomic rarities i.e. truffles, fois gras and hard-to-get herbs available to local French connoisseurs.

### German
You can enjoy German food and fun at scores of local Octoberfests. The North Side, once "Old Allegheny" with a big German community, has two fine German restaurants—**Max's Allegheny Tavern,** an old eatery with some of the best wursts, beers & atmosphere and **Penn Brewery** up on Troy Hill Road with great German food, Penn Pilsner beer and sometimes a German band in an authentic beer hall and outdoor biergarten. There's also **Otto's Hofbrau House** in Dormont, **Candle Keller** in McMurray and **Kleiner Deutschmann** in Springdale. Also known for big beer selections are **Hampton Inn** in Allison Park, **Park House** on the North Side & **Chiodo's** in Homestead. (Most eateries make their own wursts or send to Milwaukee!)

### Greek
You can get all of the makings for Greek/ Syrian cuisine at **Stamoolis Bros,** Penn Ave in the Strip. **Salim's,** Centre Ave, Oakland, has Greek/Lebanese foodstuffs & take-out. Best local Greek eateries are **Suzie's**, Downtown/Sq Hill, **Harris Grill**, Shadyside and **Klay's** on Banksville Rd, S Hills. For gyros it's **Salonika**, 6th St, Downtown. You can get Greek food at church/community festivals throughout the year and at Wed lunch at N Side's Holy Trinity Greek Church.

### Farmer's Markets
Pittsburgh ethnic specialties—kielbasa, homemade breads/pies—and to-go dishes i.e. sauerkraut/hot dogs can be found at local Farmers' Markets June thru November on the N Side, S Side, Highland Pk, Carrick, Wilkinsburg.

## Ethnic Foods

### Croatian Sunday Picnics

Every Sunday from Memorial to Labor Day you can get janjetina (slowly roasted lamb), prasetina (suckling pig), barbecued lamb and pork at the **Croatian Center** picnics at Schnitzen Park Road in Ross. Everyone welcome. Polka band.

### Hamburgers

Currently vying for best hamburger title are **Tessaro's** hardwood grill in Bloomfield, the **Pgh Steak Co.** & **Clark's Bar & Grill**. Oakland's **CJ Barney's** also has a big burger reputation. Some swear by **Burger King's** flame-broiled fast burgers and others love **Dave's Lunch's,** 237 3rd Ave, Downtown, which makes a mean grilled burger with onions and hot peppers.

### Indian

Center for Pittsburgh's sizeable Indian population is the **Bombay Emporium** on Craft Ave, Oakland for foodstuffs & delicate spices. You can also get saffron, coriander, cumin, hard-to-get items at **India Foods,** 4141 Old Wm Penn Hwy, Monroeville. It's near the Sri Venkateswara Hindu Temple in Penn Hills which serves Indian food Sundays and at festivals. Newly opened on S Craig Street is **Kapoor's Indian Imports..** Pittsburgh's growing list of Indian restaurants includes **Darbar** and **Star of India**, North Oakland; **India Garden** & **Delhi Grill**, both on Atwood, South Oakland and **A Taste of India** in Bloomfield. Many Oriental eateries also serve Indian items. (See Oriental)

### Irish Food

The city's unofficial Irish headquarters is Tom O'Donoghue's **Blarney Stone** in Etna with Irish food, Irish coffee, Irish entertainment and an Irish pastry chef. You can also sing-a-long at **Gallagher's Pub** in Market Sq and enjoy Irish entertainers at the **Harp & Fiddle**, Penn Ave in the Strip. Green beer flows throughout the city at St Patrick's Day celebrations after the big parade. For music/dancing there's the annual **Irish Centre Feis** in Squirrel Hill.

### Italian Hot Sausage

Pittsburgh is also the "home of Italian." Some of the best hot sausage in the area is at **Merante's,** Bates/McKee in Oakland...southern style, pungent with spices and at **Parma Sausage** and **Sunseri's** in the Strip. Specializing in hot sausage sandwiches are **Primanti's,** Strip/Oakland and **Frankie's** at 3535 Butler Street. P.S. You can get wonderful Italian cheeses in the Strip at **Pgh Cheese Terminal** and **Pennsylvania Macaroni Company.** Sunseri's has some of the best provolone in the city.

### Italian Groceries

Best of show are **Merante Groceria** on Bates, **Pennsylvania Macaroni** & **Sunseri** in the Strip. Also good are **Donatelli & Son** (since '32) and **Groceria Italiano** both in Bloomfield, **Labriola's,** Penn Hills and Aspinwall, **DeLallo's** in Pleasant Hills...and **The Uncommon Market** in Upper St Clair. And it's hard to beat the Italian pastries at **Moio's** in Monroeville. Pittsburgh has more Italian restaurants than other kind...many of them the city's finest—**D'Imperio's** in Wilkins Twp, **Pasta Piatto**, Shadyside; **Bravo! Franco** and **Scoglio's** Downtown; **Franco's** in Fox Chapel Mall and **Davio's** in Beechview.

### Polish Eats

Everyday is Polish Day at the **Bloomfield Bridge Tavern,** 4412 Liberty Ave. You can get kielbasa, pierogi, haluski, golabki (pigs in a blanket—stuffed cabbage), kluski (noodles & cottage cheese) and 100 imported beers—11am-1am or til the food runs out! $5.95. AE,D,DC,MC, V. **682-8611.**

**4**

## Ethnic Foods

### The Perogi Parade

You don't have to be Polish—or even Slavic—to enjoy Pittsburgh pierogi. You can get them homemade by ladies of local ethnic churches (see below) or at **Clara's Pittsburgh Pierogies** at 2717 Library Road, Castle Shannon (882-3555) in a plain concrete building with some of the best pierogi in town ...and a drive-thru window! Pierogi (also known as pirogi, perogi, pirohi, pirohy), tender triangles of dough with various fillings, are an East European staple. They can be purchased, along with haluski (fried noodles & sweet cabbage) and other Slavic dishes at the following churches:

**Byzantine Church of Resurrection** 455 Center Rd, Monroeville. 3rd Fri Jun-Aug. Order Mon-Wed. Perogi—potato, lekvar (prune), cottage cheese, sauerkraut, $3 doz. **372-9415.**

**Holy Ghost Byzantine** 225 Olivia, McKees Rocks. Fri 8-4:30. Advance orders. Potato/sauerkraut/cottage cheese, $3.25-$3.75 doz (25c cheaper with own container). **331-5155.**

**Holy Trinity Ukrainian** 731 Washington Ave, Carnegie. Thur-Fri 8-12 except Jul. Potato/sauerkraut/cottage cheese/prune. Easter Bread. $3-$3.50 dz. **279-4652.**

**Nativity of BVM Byzantine** 4027 Beechwood Blvd, Sq Hill. Ev other Fri 8-5. Ev Fri in Lent. potato/cheese/kraut, cottage cheese, lekvar $3.50 doz; haluski $3 qt. Order Thur. **521-9918.**

**St Elias Byzantine** 4200 Homestead/ Duquesne Rd, Munhall. Fri 10:30-1. Potato/cheese, cottage cheese/sweet cabbage, lekvar. $3.50 doz. **461-1712.**

**St George Ukrainian** 3455 California Ave, Brighton Heights. Thur-Fri 10am-5. Cheese/potato/sauerkraut, $2.50-$2.75 doz; sauteed onions 25c. **766-8800.**

**St Gregory's Russian Orthodox** 214 E 15th St, Homestead. Fri 9:30-4. No perogi but delicious haluski & fish sandwiches $3—Fr Shuga fries the fish himself. **462-8256.**

**St John Baptist Cathedral** 913 Dickson, Munhall. Fri 10-4. Sept to mid-May. Potato/cottage cheese/sauerkraut/ lekvar, $3 doz; also haluski, bean/lentil soup, cheregi (donut-like cakes). **461-6882.**

**St John Baptist Ukrainian,** 109 S 7th St, S Side. Thur-Fri 11-3:30. Perogis—potato/cottage cheese, kraut, 1/2 & 1/2. $3.50 dz. **351-4407.**

**St John Baptist Ukrainian,** 204 Olivia, McKees Rocks.Thur 3-6, Fri 9-3. Potato/sauerkraut/cottage cheese $2.50-$3 doz. Haluski, hulupka. **331-5605.**

**St Mary's RC Church** Lower Lyceum, 45th St, Lawrenceville. Tues/Fri 9-2. Sauerkraut & bacon, cheese and potato/cheddar. $3.50 doz. **682-9307.**

**St Nicholas Orthodox** 6th/Marne, Monongahela. 1st/3rd Fri, every Fri in Lent 11-2. Advance orders. Potato & sauerkraut/lekvar, $2.50-$3. **258-5072.**

**St Vladimir Ukrainian Orthodox,** 1810 Sidney, S Side. Thur Oct-Jun. Potato/ kraut/cheese. $3-$3.25 dz. **431-9758.**

### Kielbasa

You haven't lived ethnic until you've tasted this spicy Slavic sausage a.k.a. kielbassa, kolbassi, kolbassa, kolbasi, kohlbasa depending on your ethnic origin. A big Pittsburgh item, the best can be found at the **Mission Market**, other South Side markets and at many Strip outlets including **Stamoolis. The McGinnis Sisters** in South Hills/Monroeville also have good homemade kielbasa. **Primanti's** and the **Bloomfield Bridge Tavern** have it all the time.

## Ethnic Foods

## Kosher/Jewish Food

Murray Avenue in Squirrel Hill is the city's center for Kosher & Jewish foods. You can get kosher meat & deli at **Kosher Mart, Prime Kosher Food of Pittsburgh** and **Bear** Jewish/Russian **Grocery**. For restaurants there's **King David** Kosher/Chinese & **Yakov's** Kosher/vegetarian. Sq Hill's **Pastries Unlimited,** one of best bakeries in the city, is strictly Kosher. Up the street is another great Jewish bakery **Rosenbloom's.** Jewish-style delis **Catz N Kids** and **Rhoda's** have everything—latke (potato pancakes), matzo balls, chicken soup, noodle kugel, pickled herring. **Adler's Deli/Catering** has the best lox in the city & **Marvin's Meats** on Forward Ave can't be beat! Best Reubens are at **Rhoda's** & the **Richest Deli** & **Sammy's** downtown...also terrific hot corned beef. All these good foods come out at Sq Hill's June **Jewish Food Fest.**

## Latin/South American

It's Reyna Foods 2023 Penn Ave in the Strip for hard-to-find ingredients for Mexican, Cuban, Puerto Rican and Latin American menus—plus fiesta pinatas. **Mejico** brand tortilla chips (in red, white, blue and yellow corn) are made right here in Etna. A Latin-American rage is sweeping the city with **Mad Mex** wowing them in Oakland, food and Latin-Amer dancing at **Cozumel** and Peruvian dishes at **La Feria** in Shadyside. Upscale **Mallorca**, South Side, has the real thing—Spanish/Portugese cuisine. Other good Tex-Mex eateries are **Tequila Junction** in Station Sq, **Sante Fe** in Upper St Clair, **Margaritaville,** S Side; **Jose & Toni's,** Mt Lebanon; **Fajita Grill**, Pleasant Hills and **Chili's** & **Chi Chi's** all over.

## Strip District

Pittsburgh's United Nations of food is the Strip wholesale marketplace where you can find foodstuffs for every cuisine. (See Strip Review).

## Mid-Eastern

There's a big selection of Mid-Eastern foodstuffs at **Cahine's** in Squirrel Hill, **Salim's** on Craig St and **Pita Land** in Brookline. The city abounds with Mid-East eateries, fine cuisine at **Ali Baba, Sanremy's, Khalil's** in Oakland, **Amel's**, Dormont & **Klay's** on Banksville Rd. You can get gyros at **Open Flame** in Sq Hill and **Salonika Gyros** 6th St, Downtown.

**4**

## Oriental/Asian

Asian food is one of the city's most popular cuisines. Biggest food outlet is **New Sam Bok** 1735 Penn Ave, Strip, for hard-to-get exotic Chinese/Japanese/Korean items i.e. cuttlefish, banana leaves, burdock root, dried mushrooms. Also in the Strip is the **Asian Mart**, 2112 Penn, with Asian/African goods and the **Lotus Noodle Co** on Smallman. There's also a big selection at **Young's Oriental Grocery,** Forward Ave, Sq Hill. **Kim-Do**, 5th Ave, Oakland, has Chinese/Viet/Thai and African foodstuffs. **Tokyo Japanese Food Store,** Ellsworth Plaza, Shadyside, has the city's best sushi, exotic fish, and a wide selection of foodstuffs. You can get the makings for seven Asian cuisines including Japanese, Thai, Korean, Phillipine at **East Oriental Food Store,** Wm Penn Hwy, Monroeville.

## Pizza

Two of city's best pizzas are at **Mineo's** and **Aiello's** a few doors apart on Squirrel Hill's Murray Avenue. Many swear by **Pizzeria Uno** in Monroeville, **Pizza Perfectta** in Shadyside, and **Shadyside Balcony's** gourmet versions. Local **Pizza Huts** and **Pizza Outlets** also have scores of fans..

## Soul Food

Headquarters for Pittsburgh soul food is **The Southern Platter** with down-home, sit-down dinners...and the **Rendezvous Lounge**, both in Homewood. Also popular are **Ramsey's II** in Penn Hills and **King James** and **Damon's** Southern Style in Wilkinsburg, There's great cookin' at **Vera**

## Ethnic Foods/Festivals

**& Rick's & Eddie's Restaurant** (made famous in August Wilson's "Two Trains Running"), both on Wylie Ave in the Hill District. **Wilson's**, N Side, is a tradition for tangy ribs with big flavour...a close second is **House of Sauce**, Centre Ave, Oakland, & **Mr P & P Ribbs**, 5th Ave, Uptown with wonderful greens, corn bread & biscuits. Watch for soul cookin' at the annual **Hill House Jazz Fest** and the **Black Expo** at the ExpoMart.

### Sweet Potato Pie

Tops are **Leonard & Dorothy Washington's** homemade pies at Hoagie Castle, Homewood & Hamilton, (they also come from all over for the steak hoagies here). Food stores carry other sweet potato pies seasonally and at Thanksgiving including Steve's at Giant Eagle.

### Steak

Steak certainly isn't indigenous to Pittsburgh but you can get one of the best in the country here. There are two stellar steak houses Downtown—**Ruth's Chris** and **Morton's**, both famous chains. **The Colony** in Greentree is long known for its flame-broiled product and the **Tin Angel** atop Mt Washington has one of city's best. You can get the famous "Pgh Steak," charred on the outside, raw inside at **Tessaro's** a small neighborhood eatery in Bloomfield, at **Tramp's**, Downtown and **Pgh Steak Co**, S Side. Other local steak houses of renown are the **Winchester Room**, N Versailles, and the **Lone Star Steak House** in Monroeville. Many swear by their neighborhood butcher but famous citywide are Marvin's Meats, Wholey's and McGinnis Sisters.

### Vegetarian

While the city has no vegetarian restaurant per se there are scores of great veggie dishes at the **East End Co-op Cafe, The Shadyside Balcony, Cafe Allegro, Cafe Sam, Southwest Bistro, Mad Mex, La Feria** and other Mexican, Latin, Mid-East, Indian, Chinese and Asian restaurants. (See Oriental)

## ETHNIC FOOD FESTIVALS

### SPRING

**Ambridge Nationality Days** 3rd wknd May. 26 ethnic food booths, dancing. **266-3040.**

**Hill House Jazz Fest**, Hill Dist. May. Soul food, music. **392-4400.**

**Pa Maple Festival** Meyersdale. 5 days in Apr. Freshly tapped maple syrup, hot cakes, sausage. **1-814-634-0213.**

**St Nicholas Greek Cathedral Fest** 419 S Dithridge, Oakland. 1st full wk May. Spanakopeta, mousaka, rice pilaf, lamb, pastries; bouzouki music. **682-3866.**

**Strip District Festivals** May Springfest & Octoberfest. Fresh fare from Strip food merchants. Hot sausage, perogis, gyros, music. **788-9322.**

**Black Expo**, ExpoMart. Arts, booths, soul food. May. **391-3594.**

**Polka Parties** Seven Springs. Memorial wknd, July 4 & Oct. **1-800-452-2223.**

**Latin American Fest** Univ Pgh. Variety Latin/Caribbean food—tacos to Brazilian seijoda (pork, beans, rice). **648-7392.**

**May Market** Pgh Civic Garden Ctr, Fifth/Shady. Flower market, country fair delicacies–mushroom sandwiches, strawberries in fondant, funnel cake. **441-4442.**

### SUMMER

**Jewish Food Fest** Temple Sinai, Squirrel Hill. Early Jun. 3-day fest with all the Jewish specialties. **421-9715.**

**Monessen Heritage Festival** 3rd wk Jun. One of biggest, 19 nationalities, food, music. **684-3200.**

---

### Pittsburgh Food Festival

Ethnic foods are featured year-round at scores of area festivals. You can sample them all at the annual **Pittsburgh Folk Festival** Memorial Day weekend at the ExpoMart when thousands join more than 20 ethnic groups for continuous music/dancing, food booths. **373-0123.**

## Ethnic Foods/Festivals

**Holy Dormition Greek Fest** Oakmont. Last wknd Jun. Mousaka, pastitso, spanakopeta (spinach pie), stuffed grape leaves; dancing. **828-4144.**

**Armstrong Heritage Days** Ford City. 5 days, near July 4. 36 ethnic foods...Ukrainian Polish, Italian, German, Oriental. **548-3226.**

**Intl Food/Art Fest** Weirton, W Va. July 4th wknd. 40 food booths, art, music, entertainment. **1-304-748-7212.**

**South Side Summer Spectacular** Wk in Jul. Ethnic food booths—hot sausage, kielbasa, entertainment. **481-0651.**

**Slovene Fest** Lawrence Co. 2nd wknd July. Kolbasi, perogi, apple dumplings, 20 polka bands. **336-5180.**

**Bavarian Fun Fest** Conneaut. Last wknd Jul/1st wknd Aug. Wursts, halupki, gyros, music, dancing. **1-800-828-9619.**

**Fayette Co Italian Fest** Uniontown. 2nd wknd Aug. One of area's biggest; homemade pasta, calzone, stromboli. **438-1876.**

**Slavic Fest** Herminie. 3rd Sun Aug. Barbecued lamb, kolbasi, haluski, Serbian cevapcici (spicy rolled meat). Polka, kolo, tambura dancing. **373-0888**

**Dankfest** Harmony. Late Aug. German sausage, strudel, homemade ice cream, root beer...plus hay rides. **452-7341.**

**McKeesport Intl Village** last wk Aug. One of oldest fests; 17 ethnic groups— Croatian, Serbian, Irish, African; music, dancing. **675-5033.**

### FALL

**Allegheny Rib Cook-Off** Labor Day wknd. BBQ rib-makers from all over compete with locals. **678-1727.**

**Apple 'n Arts Fest** Shield's Farm, Delmont. 3rd wknd Oct. Apple cider, apple butter, baked goods. **468-4422.**

**German-Amer Octoberfest** Station Sq. 3rd wk Sept. Potato pancakes, wienerschnitzel, strudel, music. **561-3354.**

**Covered Bridge Fest** Greene/Wash Co. 3rd wknd Sept. Ethnic home/country food at 8 covered bridges. **746-2333.**

**Holy Trinity Greek Church Fest** 302 W North, N Side. Sept. All the Greek specialties. **321-9282.**

**Mars Apple Festival** 2nd Sat Oct. Homemade apple butter, cider, dumplings, pies. Music/entertainment. **625-3571.**

**Octoberfest** Penn Brewery, Troy Hill Rd. Last 2 wknds Sept. Old time German food, bands, beer. **237-9402.**

**Ohiopyle Buckwheat Festival** 2nd wknd Oct. Buckwheat cakes/sausage, apple sauce, baked goods. **329-8591.**

**Old Economy Village Fest** Ambridge. Erntefest (Oct). Sauerkraut, dumplings, wursts. Crafts, tours. **266-1803.**

**Penn's Colony Fest** Prospect. Wknds in Sept. "Pioneer" food—apple fritters, smoked ham, homemade jams/jellies. Crafts, entertainment. **487-6922.**

**Scottdale Coke/Heritage Fest** 3rd wknd Sept. 30 ethnic booths, Greek/Ital/Slavic food, music. **887-5700.**

**Sri Venkateswara Hindu Temple Fests** Penn Hills. Homemade Indian delicacies every Sun and at Jan Thanksgiving Fest & Oct Festival of Lights. **373-3380.**

**Three Rvs Indian Pow-Wow** Dorseyville. Last wknd Sept. Buffalo meat, maize; dances/demos. **782-4457.**

**Ukrainian Renaissance Fair** Univ of Pgh. Last wknd Sept. Pyrohy, borscht kolbassa/sauerkraut, nalysnyky (crepes). Music/dancing. **624-6150.**

### WINTER

**Chinese New Year Banquet** Jan-Feb, Sat nearest Chinese New Year. Exotic dishes, various provinces; dancing/music. **833-2339.**

**Pitt Nationality Room Open House** Costumed nationalities serve their foods at Dec holiday open house. **624-6000**

**Polishfest** Soldier's Hall. 2nd Sun Nov. Polish foods, polka bands. **486-3819.**

**St Patrick's Day Celeb** Blarney Stone, Etna. Thru Mar. Area's biggest. Irish food, music, entertainment. **781-1666.**

**4**

# 10 TERRIFIC DAY TRIPS

Escape the city. Relax the body...refresh the mind...mend the spirit with these 10 terrific day trips...most only an hour away. All include wonderful new places to stop and dine.

## AUTUMN LEAVES AT LIGONIER

### Ligonier

*Rt 30 E of Pgh. Ligonier Chamber of Commerce*—**238-4200.**
The best time to enjoy Laurel Mountain's colorful autumn foliage is early Oct—Ft Ligonier Days are 2nd wknd. (Ligonier Highland Games, another wonderful fest, is 2nd Sat Sept.) Ligonier, a small town, executive retreat, is built around a charming square, "The Diamond," complete with gazebo, ice cream parlor, antique, arts and crafts shops. There's good shopping in and around town including a discount clothing outlet further up 30 E.
**Fort Ligonier (238-9701)** Rt 30 & 711 on edge of town. History buffs/kids love this 1758 British fort, largest recreated stockade fort in US with French/Indian War relics. Apr-Oct Mon-Sat 10-4:30, Sun 12-4:30. Adm. $5. **Compass Inn**, Laughlintown, 3 mi east of Ligonier **(238-4983)**. A restored log 1799 stagecoach stop, now a museum. **Tours:** Fascinating 90-min tour by costumed guides includes old stagecoach/conestoga wagons. (Great during Living Hist Weekends Jun-Aug). Tues-Sat 11-4, Sun 12-4. Closed Mon/Hol. Adults $4. On the way home don't miss beautiful **Rolling Rock Farms,** Rt 381 east of Ligonier. For Pgh continue on Rt 381 to Rt 31 N to Donegal & Turnpike.
**DINING:**
**Ligonier Country Inn** Laughlintown (238-3651). Charming with bar/fireplace. Mod. Across the street is famous **Pie Shoppe** freshly baked goodies, sandwiches. **Colonial Inn,** Rt 30, 2 miles W of Ligonier (238-6604) stately, white house in scenic lake setting. Antiques, brass chandeliers, stone fireplace. Mod-Exp. **DiSalvo's Train Station** (539-0500) Latrobe off Rt 30 W, 15-20 minutes away–great dining in splendidly restored train depot. Mod-Exp. **Blue Angel,** at Latrobe Airport with close-up view of planes. Inexp-Mod. **Mountain View Inn** (834-5300) Off Rt 30W bet Latrobe &

## THE CIRCLE TOUR

### Ft Necessity...Ohiopyle... Fallingwater, Seven Springs

Our photographer Herb Ferguson has shared with us his out-of-town visitors' Circle Tour, a special day-long trip to major countryside sites.
Take I-279 S to I-79 S to Washington, Pa to 40 E to **Century Inn**, Scenery Hill, for lunch at charming old stagecoach stop (See next page).
Continue on Rt 40 E through Brownsville for a stop at **Nemacolin Castle** by the Monongahela. (Daily Easter-Labor Day 11-4:30, wknds yr round.) Adm $5. **785-6882.** Continue on Rt 40 E thru Uniontown, past Chalk Hill & General Braddock's grave to **Ft Necessity Natl Battlefield** ...the fort's small but the French/Indian War Museum is interesting. 7 days 8:30-5. $2 adm. **329-5512.**
Continue on 40 E to Farmington, 381 N to **Ohiopyle** for swift-running rapids amid huge boulders. Then on to **Fallingwater,** Frank Lloyd Wright's famous Kaufmann house in Mill Run. (Daily Tues-Sun Apr-mid Nov, wknds yr round.) Reser required. **329-8501.** Completing the circle take 381N/711 N to **Seven Springs** resort for dinner. **(1-800-452-2223).** Then home via 711 N to Donegal Turnpike entrance. Approx 200 miles, 6-8 hours.
(For a shorter trip skip Nemacolin and Scenery Hill. Take 51 S to Uniontown to Rt 40 E to Ft Necessity, Ohiopyle, Fallingwater and Seven Springs.)

Greensburg for a beautiful view. Mod. On your return note the Beaux Arts Westmoreland Courthouse.
**DIRECTIONS:** Turnpike E, Irwin Exit, to Rt 30 E. Or scenic route Turnpike E to Donegal, 711 N to Ligonier. 50 mi, 1 hr from Downtown Pittsburgh.

**5**

## OLD STAGECOACH STOP AT SCENERY HILL

### Century Inn

*Rt 40, south of Pgh, 12 mi east of Washington, Pa. (Apr-Nov).* **945-6600.**
You can spend a peaceful afternoon amid beautiful "scenery" at **Century Inn,** a 1794 stagecoach stop—the oldest continuously operating tavern on historic National Pike (now Rt 40). General Lafayette & President Jackson stopped here. The handsome old fieldstone building is decorated with Early American antiques and mementos including a flag from the Whiskey Rebellion. There are six upstairs guest rooms for overnight stays. Take a walk down the street for hours of delightful browsing in charming antique, arts/craft shops in old Victorian houses. Don't miss the Always Christmas store–Heartstrings upstairs–the Tea Shoppe, old country store. Open: 7 days. (Closed Dec-mid Mar).

**DINING:**
You'll savour the atmosphere at **Century Inn**—five diningrooms, antiques, candlelit tables with a Colonial costumed staff. You can sup in the parlour with a magnificent old highboy, in the original kitchen with a huge walk-in fireplace or on the veranda overlooking the valley. Hours: Lunch 7 days 12-2:30, Dinner Mon-Thur 4:30-7:30, Fri-Sat til 8:30, Sun 3:30-6:30. Closed Dec to mid-March. Reser sugg. No credit cards. **(945-6600).**

**SIDE TRIPS:**
**Nemacolin Castle,** 22-room mansion, only 20 min away. (Rt 40 E to Brownsville, over bridge, right 1st stop light, right next block) Tours: Apr to mid-Oct Sat-Sun 10-4:30. Jun-Aug Tues-Fri 11-4:30. Also Christmas Candlelight Tours. Adm. $5. **(785-6882).**

**DIRECTIONS:**
I-279 S to I-79 S, Houston exit to 519 S, 10 miles, left to Rt 40 E, 5 mi on left. 40 miles, 1 hr from Downtown Pgh.

## QUAINT SHOPS NEAR AMISH COUNTRY

### New Wilmington, Pa

*Lawrence County, 60 miles north of Pgh.* *Merchants Assn—***946-2898.**
Delightful sightseeing and a near-the-city glimpse of the Pennsylvania Dutch—*Western* Pa Dutch—without traveling to Lancaster. You'll see their neat white farmhouses dotting the countryside and their buggies driving by. Great browsing in quaint shops in an old schoolhouse and in individual homes—quilts, candles, Amish furniture, hex signs, artwork, ceramics. Don't miss the unique teddy-bears at **Berlin's Antiques/Glassware** and Gibb McGill's Amish paintings at the **Nest Egg** on Market St. The **Cheesehouse** (946-8409) a mile W at 208 & 18, has 50 cheeses incl fresh mozzarella & provolone made next door plus maple syrup, jelly, apple butter and Amish chests, rockers, crafts. 7 days 10-6.

**DINING:**
Dine/tea at charming, shuttered **Tavern on the Square,** 101 N Market (946-2020). Country fare–chicken & biscuits, famed sticky rolls–amid antiques, massive stone fireplace. Guest Lodge across the street. Closed Tues. Lunch Mon-Sat 11:30-2, Tea 2:15-4:15, Dinner 5-8. Sun 12-6:30. Mod.

**SIDE TRIPS:**
On the way don't miss **Volant,** picturesque village of shops, five restaurants on Rt 208 four miles away. Enjoy Old Mill waterwheels, candles, weaving, an old-fashioned General Store & Miniature Shop, Freight Car Shops with quilting, wonderful chocolates—great at Yuletime—and a rare store with musical-motif gifts. Mon-Sat 10-5, Sun 12-5. Closed holidays except Memorial/Labor Day.

**DIRECTIONS:**
Take I-279 N to I-79 N, London Exit to Rt 208 W. 60 mi, 1 hr from Downtown Pgh.

## FOLKWAY CRAFTS
## IN THE COUNTRY

### Penn Alps/Spruce Forest Village

*Rt 40, Grantsville, MD. Mon-Sat 10-5 Memorial Day wknd thru last Sat Oct (Artisan shops closed Sun and Nov-May).* The largest display of indigenous handicrafts in the Alleghenies is at the **Penn Alps Craft Shop (1-301-895-5985)**. Daily 9-9. Sun 9-3. Excellent, one-of-a-kind finely-stitched quilts, wood-turnings, hand-thrown pottery, hickory rockers. Nearby is the **Spruce Forest Artisan Village (1-301-785-3332)** Mon-Sat 10-5 Memorial Day wknd thru last Sat Oct. Closed Sun & Nov-May. Original log cabins and historic structures where spinners, weavers, potters, stained glass workers, wood sculptors, bird carvers display their talents, wares. **Summerfest/Quilt Show** 2nd Thur-Sat in July–more than 70 quilters, craftsmen; demos by blacksmith, caner, tinsmith, cooper, basket-maker, rug braider, wool-dyer plus story-telling and folk music on dulcimer.
**DINING:**
Five charming rooms at the **Penn Alps Restaurant**, a restored 1818 stagecoach stop. Delicious home-cooked sauerkraut, sausage, apple sauce, apple butter, homemade breads. Mon-Thur 7-7, Fri & Sat til 8, Sun 7-3. (Year round except Dec 24-25 & Jan 1).
**SIDE TRIPS:**
Nearby **Springs Pa,** 4 mi N of Grantsville, MD Rt 669 **(1-814-662-4150). Museum** plus **Springs Folk Festival** (1st Fri-Sat Oct) with mountain folk arts/crafts, great fall foliage. Don't miss **Yoder's Country Market**, Rt 669, Grantsville (1-800-321-6148). Fresh, natural foods you haven't seen in years. Mon-Sat 8-6 year round.
**DIRECTIONS:**
Rt 51 to Uniontown, Rt 40 E to Grantsville, 1/2 mi. Or I-279 S to I-79 S to Morgantown to 68 E, exit 19 Grantsville, follow signs. 85 miles, 2 hrs from Downtown Pittsburgh.

## LOVELY DAY AT
## LINDEN HALL

### Linden Hall

*Dawson, Pa. 5 mi east of Perryopolis.* **461-2424.**
A uniquely designed mountaintop mansion with a sweeping view of the Laurel Highlands. The creation of this beautiful 1913 estate by coal baron widow Sarah Cochran, beloved by the people of Dawson, is a fascinating story. The spacious home, surprisingly light and airy, has 35 rooms, a great hall, gorgeous $3.5 million **Tiffany windows**—ranked in top 11 in the country–and a hand-carved **Aeolian pipe/player organ**–only three in the world. Grounds, trails, lake, 72-room hotel, golf course, tennis, swimming pool, restaurant/dinner theatre. **Tours:** Daily 1 hour tours Mar-Oct Sat-Sun 1-5. Adm $7, $5 Srs/under 12 free.
**DINING:**
Linden Hall's **Sara B's** 7 days 8-9. Breakfast/lunch dinner $4-$16. Inexp-Mod. Sat night Loft Theatre Mar-Oct.
**SIDE TRIPS:**
The unique **Family Store** (736-2301) 101 S Liberty, has been there 'forever'... since 1896...with clothing, household goods, "a little bit of everything." You try on clothes in owner's livingroom. Mon-Sat 9-4, Wed 9-12.
**DIRECTIONS:**
Rt 51 S, left at Perryopolis sign, follow signs to Linden Hall, 5-6 mi on right. 55 mi, 1-1/4 hrs from Downtown Pgh.

5

---

### New Grove City Outlet

You can take a day's outing to the new **Grove City Factory Shops** on Leesburg/Grove City Road. Scores of outlets, food court are open Mon-Sat 9-9 and Sun 11-6. Total of 100 outlets will include AnnTaylor, Bugle Boy, Springmaid, Adolfo II, Royal Doulton, Publishers Warehouse. **(748-4770). Directions:** I-79 to Rt 208, Grove City Exit 31. 60 miles, 1-1/2 hr from Pgh.

## FABULOUS RETREAT IN MOUNTAIN GREENERY

### Nemacolin Woodlands Resort

*Rt 40, Farmington, Pa.* **800-422-2736, 412-329-8555.**
You can drive—or fly into the private air-strip—for a mini-getaway at this elegant Tudor estate in Laurel Highlands. Center-ed around a luxurious 98-room hotel, it's replete with antiques, fireplaces, fine paintings and a gift shop for souvenirs. You can enjoy a one-day treatment at the world-famous **Spa**, horseback riding, ten-nis, miniature golf, cycling, croquet, forest trails for hiking and relaxing carriage rides through lush wooded grounds. One-day/weekend Spa specials. Overnight/week-end rates. (See Rich Man's Guide).
**DINING:**
Five charming restaurants, casual to elegant. Main diningrooms—**Golden Trout** 4-Star Mobil awardee (Exp. Reser 329-6958) and **Allures** (Mod-Exp) plus Cafe Woodlands on Sun Porch, Caddy Shack and Gazebo on the green. (Mod).
**DIRECTIONS:** Rt 51 S to Uniontown, Rt 40 E to Farmington. 75 mi, 1-1/2 hrs from Downtown Pgh.

## SHOPPING SPREE IN BEAUTIFUL COUNTRY

### Georgian Place Outlet Center

Somerset, Pa. **1-814-445-3325.**
A pleasant shopping trip for 30-70% off at national manufacturers' outlets i.e. Jones NY, Cardin, Harve Bernard. Apr-Dec Mon-Sat 10-8, Sun/Hol 1-6. Jan 2-Mar 31 Mon-Sat 10-6. Also nearby **Pine Haven Village Shoppes (1-814-443-3379).** May-Dec Mon-Fri 10-5. Jan-Apr Tues-Fri 10-5, Sat 10-6. Sun holiday season.
**DINING:**
Daily 3-course "High Tea" ($8.50) or cocktails at **"The Mansion"** splendid Inn at Georgian Place. (1-814-443-1043). **Tours** daily 1:30, $3. Overnight rooms. Or quaint **Oakhurst Tea Room** on Rt 31,

Somerset (1-814-443-2897). A homey smorgasbord. Tues-Sat 11-10, Sun 11-8. Inexp-Mod.
**SIDE TRIPS:**
**Somerset Historical Center** 601 N be-comes Rt 985, 4 mi on left. **(1-814-445-6077).** Depicts life of early rural settlers. Tues-Sat 9-5, Sun 12-5. Closed Mon/holidays. Adm: $3.50.
**DIRECTIONS:**
Turnpike E, Somerset exit, left onto Rt 601. Outlet on right. Approx 75 mi, 90 min from Downtown Pgh.

## RELAXING ON THE RIVER AT SPEERS

### Speers, Pa

A relaxing, refreshing day by the riverside ...sunshine on the water, intriguing little shops and good dining. Visit Riverside Shops in Lower Speers **(483-2290)** small rustic two-story mall with quaint, unusual goods and a country store. Don't miss **Sheila's** delightful miniatures of Charles-ton, New England, Cape May houses at **Le Collection** (483-5330) and **Fields of Heather** flowers. Down the street **With Lasting Impressions**, a Victorian home, has five rooms of hand-crafted arts and flowers. Shops Tues-Sat 11-9, Sun 12-8. Closed earlier in winter.
**DINING:**
You can dine across the street at the **Back Porch**, a refined Colonial setting with excellent fare—amid antiques by candlelight or on the sun porch. Tues-Thur 11:30-10, Fri til 11, Sat 5-11, Sun 4-9. Reser sugg. Mod-Exp. 483-4500. Nearby **Speers St Grille**, a yellow Victorian house, has informal fare and a river view from outdoor deck. Tues-Sun 11:30-10. 483-1911. Or eat out on the water at **Snooters** with wide river vistas from the big outdoor deck. 7 days 11:30-10, bar til 2. 483-6000
**DIRECTIONS:** Rt I-279 to I-79S. Look for I-70 E, Exit 17 to Speers. 30 mi, 35 min from Downtown Pgh.

## WHIRLWIND TRIP TO WHEELING!

### Wheeling, W Va

**General Info—1-800-828-3097. Oglebay Park. 1-800-624-6988.** *On city's outskirts off Rt 70* 1500-acre spread of woods and gardens and **Wilson Lodge**, a rustic, rambling timber/stone inn with restaurant, gift shop and overnight rooms. Great year round, spectacular at holiday season Festival of Lights. Tour beautiful white **Mansion Museum's** period rooms (9:30-5 daily year round, Adm $4.25) and **Glass Museum** with glass-blowing demos. Down the road are **Stratford Spring Craft Shops** open daily 9-5. **Dining: Wilson Lodge Restaurant** big informal room. 7 days 6:30-10. (Closed 2-5). Inex-Mod

**Downtown Wheeling:**
**Old Town Historic District/Center Mkt,** 21st/22nd/Main Sts, N Wheeling. 3-block area shops, antiques, eateries incl **Coleman's Fish, Dad's Sweet Tooth** bakery, **Louie's hotdogs**. Eight min away is Stifel Fine Arts Ctr, lovely **Mansion** at 1330 National Rd with fine modern art/sculpture Mon-Sat 9-5, Sun 12:30-5). **Independence Hall Mus,** 1518 Market (7 days 10-4, free) has intriguing historic/antique doll exhibits—worth a visit. **Victorian Wheeling Homes Tour (304-232-6400)** includes four unique styles of Victorian architecture. Tues-Sun 10am & 1pm.

**Wheeling Downs**
5 Penn/Stone St **(1-800-445-9475)** plush entertainment center with year-round greyhound racing (Mon, Wed, Thur-Sat 7:30pm and Wed, Sat, Sun at 1pm). **Dining:** Big choice of seating/eating. 3rd level terrace dining with TV viewing of payoffs/replays; elegant Lounge–light menu under splendid brass ceiling or on balcony overlooking finish line; Peoria Lounge with private booths, TVs. Grandstand level–Paddock Rm, food stands. **SIDE TRIPS: Valley Voyager Boat Ride** on Ohio. **(1-800-237-1867)** daily by reser. $6.75 1-1/2 hr sightseeing. 2-3 hr breakfast, lunch, dinner cruises ($14-$27). Or watch famous performers at **Capitol Music Hall** 1015 Main **(1-800-624-5456). DIRECTIONS:** Rt I-279 S to Rt I-79 S to I-70 W to Downtown Wheeling. **Park:** Oglebay Exit. Wheeling Downs: Wheeling Island Exit. 60 miles, 1 hr from Downtown Pgh.

## ROMANTIC INTERLUDE AT SOUTHERN INN

### Tara Country Inn

*3665 Valley View, Clark, Pa.* **962-3535.** We've been getting raves from visitors at this Mobil 4-Star inn with world-class dining/lodging. Step into a romantic past in a tree-shaded "Gone With the Wind" Greek Revival 1854 mansion–27 guest rooms with Civil War/movie themes including Rhett's Room, Fiddle Dee Dee and Belle's Boudoir. Overnight or drop-by guest, you–and the kids–will be treated royally. (Stay-overs get champagne reception, breakfast in bed.) Gift Shop daily 3-5. **Tours:** Daily 10-3 on hour, $5. **Overnight:** $180-$430 night per couple inc dinner, breakfast, afternoon tea. **DINING:**
Elegant, atmospheric Southern fare in **Ashley's Gourmet** Mon-Sat 11:30-2:30, Dinner Sun-Thur 6-7:30, Fri-Sat til 8:30. Exp. **Stonewall's Tavern** (Sun 12-7, Mon-Thur Lunch 11-3, Dinner 5-8, Fri-Sat til 9. Mod. **Old South Armory Family Restaurant** (groups only) with a collection of Civil War firearms. **Afternoon Tea** in Library or Sun Porch, daily 4-5 $5.95. Reser. 2 weeks ahead for Tea.
**SIDE TRIPS:** Worth a stop in nearby Sharon are Reyer's Famous Shoes, The Winner for unique discount clothing/gifts; Daffin's Candy, and Kraynack's Floral Shop for unusual holiday displays. Amish country is only a half-hour away.
**DIRECTIONS:**
Rt I-279 N to I-79 N to 80 W, Exit 1 N to Rt 18 N, 7 miles to Rt 258, Tara on right. 90 mi, 1-1/2 hr from Downtown Pgh.

**5**

# 50 THINGS TO DO

Pittsburgh is a warm, wonderful town with places to go, things to see...and unexpected beauty. And sometimes the best things in town are free! Here's a list of some of the city's best old and new attractions. Check the *I Love Pittsburgh Pull-Out Guide* and the *Pgh Pleasures Events Calendar* to keep busy year 'round in America's best city!

# Romantic & Unusual Things To Do

1. Spend an afternoon at North Side's sleek new **Andy Warhol Museum**...finish the day in their little gourmet cafe.

2. **Take a walking tour** of Downtown Pittsburgh's architecture & Renaissance II buildings using the *"I Love Pittsburgh! Sightseeing Guide."*

3. Visit the Strip's exciting **Boardwalk, On the Water**. Join summer revelers, boat dockers, have dinner/drinks on Patio Deck...enjoy river lights...music at night. Return for sparkling holiday decorations.

4. **Take an incline** to Mt Washington...view the city from unique observation pods...watch the sun go down. Have cocktails on Grandview Saloon's outdoor decks, romantic dinner with a view at one of the Mount's fine restaurants.

5. Have fun on the Boardwalk at **Sandcastle on the Mon** waterpark...go down the giant slides, linger for music, dancing...eats...walk along the shore for great night river views.

6. **View moon, planets** thru big 31" refractor telescope at Allegheny Observatory's once-a-year September open house.

7. Lunch/tea at **Carnegie's Museum Cafe**...tour beautiful Hall of Minerals/Gems, see Pittsburgh collection...visit outdoor Sculpture Court.

8. Spend a day at fascinating **Carnegie Science Center** on the North Shore...don't miss thrilling Omnimax theatre...tour the **USS Requin submarine** moored on the Ohio.

9. Take the romantic **Valentine's Day** Candlelight Tour of the beautiful flowers at Phipps Conservatory.

10. Enjoy food with your movie at tables in the rear of the **Oakland Beehive** theatre or new **Shadyside Cinema Grill.**

11. Join the Saturday night crowds in **South Side**, Pittsburgh's new village... tour the shops...hear some jazz sounds

...pick a restaurant...have dessert at zany **Beehive Coffee Shop**.

12. Ride the new Steel Phantom, world's fastest roller coaster at **Kennywood Park**...try bungee jumping!

13. Enjoy a concert under the stars on a summer's night at vast **Star Lake Amphitheatre.** Order a box lunch ahead or picnic from food booths there.

14. Have lunch/tea...antiquing at charming **Cafe Victoria** on the North Side...visit antique shops next door.

15. Enjoy peaceful river vistas from 300-ft barge-restaurant **Misty Harbour** in Sharpsburg...dance under the stars at **Fox Chapel Yacht Club.**

16. Become a member of **The Carnegie** ...attend openings, Silent Auction...visit behind-the-scenes at Member's Night.

17. Take your own tour of the **Mexican War Streets** or join the annual Sept House Tour. Visit unique **Chatham Village** housing atop Mt Washington.

18. Have **afternoon tea** at elegant Westin William Penn Hotel...or romantic cocktails in Palm Court lobby lounge.

19. Visit a quaint Pittsburgh neighborhood...catch a window street view at Bloomfield's charming **El Dolce Cafe**... visit Liberty Avenue's intriguing old stores.

20. Meet a friend at **Station Square ...** browse...eat at one of great restaurants, visit outdoor museum, Railcar Shops... take a buggy ride through the Square.

21. **Tour Pitt Nationality Rooms**...roam through the cavernous Commons on ground floor. Discover the beautiful stained glass windows in Heinz Chapel. (See Sightseeing Guide)

22. Spend a Saturday morning shopping at the produce market in the **Strip District.** Explore the fascinating stores, lunch at one of the little outdoor cafes/eateries.

**6**

## Romantic & Unusual Things To Do

23. **Ride the Subway** back & forth to Station Square stopping to enjoy the art at Wood Street & Gateway Stations.

24. **Take a Gray Line Tour** and learn something about the city. Watch for Pgh History & Landmarks' intriguing neighborhood tours and community house tours.

25. Have weekend **Dim-Sum** (Chinese Brunch) or get eight friends together for a duck banquet at an Asian eatery.

26. **Walk the beautiful Trillium Trail** in bloom late April, May on Squaw Run Road, Fox Chapel.

27. Take part in inspiring Christmas "**Messiah Sing-A-Long**" at Heinz Hall heralding the opening of the holiday season.

28. Spend a whole day at **Oxford Centre**...enjoy the architecture, atmosphere, delightful browsing in sleek shops. Finish on the patio at Dingbat's.

29. **Browse at Craig Street Shops**... lunch outdoors at Kane's Courtyard or on Cafe Azure's lovely terrace.

30. Make a lunchtime visit to **Trinity Cathedral's** 200-year-old burial ground on Sixth Ave in the heart of town.

31. Enjoy the real thing—**formal British tea** at Cathy's Windsor Tea Room in Sewickley. Browse in unique local shops.

32. Get a **riverside view of Pittsburgh** from the North Shore. Walk down to Allegheny Landing through the colorful outdoor Sculpture Court. Take a camera for Downtown building shots.

33. Watch the **fun-filled buggy races** in Schenley Park at CMU's Spring Carnival ...catch the **Vintage Grand Prix** auto races in Schenley Park in July.

34. Don't miss the flowers/food at the city's most delightful fete—annual **May Market** at Pgh Civic Garden Center.

35. Check out the fun—reggae night...or any night at unique **Graffiti**...catch the mod dancing scene at **Metropol** or unique entertainers at **Rosebud.**

36. Don't miss the **thrilling Grand Prix Formula I speedboat races** at Three Rivers Regatta. Linger thru dusk, walk past the hundreds of boats docked at the Point..their colored lights flickering in the waters—a romantic night in Pittsburgh.

37. Spend a day in **Shadyside**...browse at avenue shops...have dinner/jazz at the **Balcony**...watch the wonderful Latin dancers at **Cozumel** Saturday nights.

38. Take a child to the **underground Twilight Zoo** or the delightful **Children's Zoo**...ride the little railroad. Watch for holiday Zoo Lights.

39. Take out a **gourmet picnic** (See Gourmet to Go)...eat it by fireside or at Roberto Clemente Park along the river.

40. Watch the **Pittsburgh Marathon** at a neighborhood celebration in Oakland, Shadyside, South Side or North Side. Enjoy the outdoor cafes, cheering crowds & camaraderie.

41. Watch a child enjoy the intriguing hands-on exhibits at the **Pgh Children's Museum's** on the North Side...watch for the May **Children's Festival.**

42. Enjoy Pittsburgh's rich ethnic fetes... dance, sing, eat ethnic at the May **Pittsburgh Folk Festival**...watch for Greek church food fests...summer neighborhood fairs all over the city.

43. Do **afternoon cocktails for two** on Froggy's hideaway roof patio or Tramp's "Gotham-city" deck in the midst of downtown rooftops.

44. Spend Sunday evening with the **Pittsburgh Jazz Preservation Society** at Oakland's Holiday Inn...or enjoy Hill House's **Sun Afternoon Jazz Sessions.**

45. Enjoy bagpipes, sheep herding, beautiful scenery at **Highland Fling** in Ligonier...plan a weekend camping party in a log cabin at Lynn Run State Park.

# Romantic & Unusual Things To Do

46. Tour remarkable **Old Economy Village** in Ambridge...try to catch their annual Kuntsfest...or time your visit with Ambridge Nationality Days.

47. Watch the stirring **Royal Regiment's Fife & Drum Corps** parade at Point State Park on summer Sunday afternoons.

48. Spend a day at **Hartwood.** Picnic on beautiful grounds...tour the Tudor Mansion...in summer stay for music, theatre-on-the green.

49. Watch the **July 4th fireworks**...something special in Pittsburgh...a marvel from close range at Pgh Symphony's concert at the Point...from on high in Mt Washington for a panoramic view...or from a Gateway Clipper cruise midst colorful reflections in the waters.

50. Take a **riverwalk** along the shores (See Riverfront Restaurants) or a **Gateway Clipper** boat tour...the best way to understand Pittsburgh's history, geography.

**...and some for good measure**

51. Sit in on **Pgh Banjo Club's** jam/sing-a-long Wednesdays at the North Side's James St Tavern.

52. Meet new people...attend opening night performance/party at **Pgh Public Theater.**

53. Join Irish revels at the **Feis/Dance Competition** at Irish Center in Sq Hill.

54. Go on a shopping spree at **Station Square**...eat outdoors at flower-bedecked Grand Concourse **Garden Cafe** or at **Cheese Cellar** sidewalk cafe.

55. Don't miss the arts and crafts at fall **Fair in the Park** at Mellon Park.

56. **Go strawberry pickin'** in June at Simmons, Trax, Schramm Farms in nearby countryside.

57. Listen to the strains of Sousa at American Wind Orchestra's stirring **"Marches" concert** by the riverside.

58. Take your own **tour of North Side's streets**...up the steep hills for unique city vistas. Have dinner at Max's Allegheny Tavern or join in music/fun at Penn Brewery on Troy Hill Road.

59. Start off the holiday season amid artful wares of **Pgh Center for Arts Annual Christmas Sale**. Visit the giant decorated Christmas trees at Carnegie Museum's Hall of Sculpture.

60. Meet a friend for **Light-Up Night**... see PPG luminaria, Oxford Centre lights, USX holiday decorations at close range...discover festive Pittsburgh!

61. Take a romantic **Midnight Cruise** from 10 to 1am on the Gateway Clipper Friday nights during summer.

62. See the hidden gardens in the Victorian homes in Allegheny West at annual August **Garden Tour...**or attend their Oct **Haunted House Tour.**

63. Do the beautiful **Victorian Christmas Tour** at Clayton Mansion in Point Breeze.

64. Take in the August **Shadyside Arts/ Jazz Festival** for shopping, fun...or the unique **Mt Washington Festival** high above the city.

65. Join in the fun at the **Buggy Races** at CMU's Spring Carnival

66. Be sure to catch July's **Squirrel Hill Happening** for best shopping in town.

67. Take a small group on a wonderful, personal **tour of hidden Pgh**...Ed Ackerman's Pgh Sightseeing/Expedition.

(For a complete day-by-day listing of 850 events and activities in the Greater Pittsburgh area see our annual *"Pittsburgh Pleasures Events Calendar"* with 13 beautiful color photographs of the city.)

6

# CITY VIEWS

A city of rolling hills and rivers, Pittsburgh is famous for its spectacular views...from the top of Mt Washington...from Downtown...from new riverfront vantage points. Here are the best places to view the city... wonderful by day...breathtaking by night...perfect entertainment for both natives and visitors.

## FROM MOUNT WASHINGTON

### Christopher's
*1411 Grandview. Dinner Mon-Thur 5-10, Fri-Sat til 11. Reser. AE,DC,MC,V.* **381-4500.**
Exciting three-sided view of city from glass walls of glamorous rooftop restaurant. Dancing Fri in Lounge. $15-$32. Drinks: Exp. Visitor must! (See Review)

### Cliffside
*1208 Grandview. Dinner/Lounge. Mon-Thur 5-10, Fri-Sat til 11. AE,DC,MC,V.* **431-6996.**
Spectacular view in sleek, modern decor. Inventive American menu, appetizers. $4-$20. Drinks: Mod.

### Georgetowne Inn
*1230 Grandview. Lunch, Dinner, Late Snacks Mon-Thur 11-12, Fri-Sat til 1. Sun 4-10. AE,D,DC,MC,V.* **481-4424.**
Great view, best bet on limited budget. Entrees include seafood $13-$26; late snacks, desserts. $3-$7. Drinks: Mod.

### Grandview Saloon
*1212 Grandview, next to Duquesne Incline. Sun-Thur 11-12, Fri-Sat til 1. Bar til 2. AE,V.* **431-1400.**
Spectacular view in the Mount's first casual eatery with two outdoor decks—young/family place. Light dining, sandwiches $5-$17. (See Outdoor Dining)

### LeMont
*1114 Grandview. Dinner Mon-Fri 5-10:30, Sat til 11:30, Sun 4-9:30. Lounge til closing. Reser. AE,D,DC,MC,V.* **431- 3100.**
Superb view of Golden Triangle from banquettes. Continental dining in posh surroundings. $11-35. Drinks: Mod-Exp.

### Pasquarelli's
*1204 Grandview, Mt Washingtn. Mon-Thur 5-10, Fri-Sat til 11. MC,V.* **431-1660.**
Small, intimate room with beautiful view. Italian specialties—veal, seafood, poultry, steak, pasta, good tiramisu. Daily dinner specials. $10 to $26 for Surf 'n Turf.

### Tin Angel
*1200 Grandview. Dinner Mon-Sat 5:30-10. Reser. AE,DC,MC,V.* **381-1919.**
Top-of-town favorite for beautiful view, intimate ambience, music...'most romantic place in town.' Dinners $21-$43. Drinks: Exp. (See Rich Man's Dining)

## FROM DOWNTOWN

### Top of the Triangle
*USX Tower, 600 Grant. Lunch Mon-Fri 11:30-3, Sat 12-3. Dinner Mon-Thur 5:30-10, Fri-Sat til 11. Sun 4-9. Parking free in bldg after 4:30. Reser sugg. AE,D,DC,MC,V.* **471-4100.**
Breathtaking view from 62nd floor with city at your feet—great tourist spot. Amer menu $16 up. Piano bar, DJ dancing. Mon-Sat til 2. Drinks: Mod-Exp.

## FROM THE RIVERFRONT

### Carnegie Science Center Cafe
*N Shore, next to Three Rivers Stadium. Half hour before Center opens Mon-Thur 10-5, Fri-Sat til 9, Sun til 6.* **237-3400.**
Three rivers' view of the Point from exciting Science Center's glass-walled restaurant seating 200, outdoor terrace. Lunch/Dinner. Mod. **237-3400.**

### River Room, Grand Concourse
*Landmarks Bldg, Station Sq. Mon-Thur 11:30-10, Fri-Sat til 11. Sun Brunch 10-2:30, Dinner 4:30-9. AE,DC,MC,V.* **261-1717.**
It's worth the wait for a seat in the River Room for splendid sunset views in city's most elegant restaurant with seafood, steak. Lunch $7-$10, Dinner $17-$30; Great break on daily Early Bird dinners $10-$16. (See Review)

### Waterfall Terrace
*Sheraton Hotel, Station Sq. 7 days 6am-midnite. AE,D,DC,MC,V.* **261-2000.**
Indoor cafe with close-up views of downtown buildings across the river. Dinners, light fare, sandwiches, late supper, $3-$25. Sun Brunch 10-3 in **Reflections** diningroom with sunny river view $10.95.

**7**

# THE DOWNTOWNER

Here's a quick guide to Downtown restaurants for the convenience of visitors...tourists...shoppers. Eateries are listed geographically by Convention Center/Vista...Penn/Liberty Cultural District...Gateway/Market... 4th Avenue/Midtown...Grant/Uptown.

## CONVENTION CENTER/ VISTA/STRIP

### Boardwalk, On the Water
*1501 Smallman. Floating barge out on Allegheny. Parking lot entrance 15th St.* **Crewsers (281-3680)** big, 250-seat informal restaurant with nautical theme, great river views; sandwiches to dinners. Inexp-Mod. **Buster's Crab (281-3683)** seafood/raw bar on 2nd level. Delightful open air **Patio Deck** for eating/drinking, bands Thur/Sun. Inexp-Mod. **Donzi's (281-1586)** European disco. Mod.

### British Bicycle Club
*923 Penn. Downtown. Mon-Fri 11-8:30. AE,DC,MC,V.* **391-9623.**
Good grills, sandwiches, fish & chips in lively pub atmosphere. Mod.

### Brandy's
*2323 Penn, Strip. Mon-Thur 11am-12, Fri-Sat til 2am, Sun 3-11. AE,DC,MC,V.* **566-1000.**
First class dining amid romantic greenery. Amer cuisine, patio. Mod. (See Review)

### DelFrate's
*971 Liberty. Mon & Sat 11-10, Tues-Fri 11-9. AE,DC,MC,V.* **391-2294.**
Authentic Italian, veal, pasta in warm surroundings. Bar til 2. Inexp-Mod.

### Liang's Hunan
*Vista/Liberty Center, Penn & Liberty. Sun-Thur 11:30-10, Fri-Sat til 11. AE,DC, MC, V.* **471-1688.**
Outstanding Hunan, Szechuan; splendid decor. Smoked duck, pheasant, venison. Dim Sum Sat/Sun 11:30-3. Mod-Exp.

### Mahoney's
*949 Liberty. Mon-Fri 11-8. AE,D,DC,MC, V.* **471-4243.**
Good sandwiches, steak, chicken, seafood in handsome eatery. Inexp.

### Spaghetti Warehouse
*2601 Smallman, Strip. Mon-Thur 11-10, Fri-Sat til 11. Sun 12-10. AE,CB,D,DC, MC,V.* **261-6511.**

Family prices in big, lively restaurant; popular Italian dishes, spaghetti with 11 sauces, lasagna. Inexp-Mod.

### Vista—Pittsburgh
*Liberty Center, 1000 Penn. AE,D,DC,MC, V.* **281-3700.**
Deluxe buffet, Euro-Amer, seafood in beautiful **Orchard Cafe.** Mon-Thur 6:30-10:30, Fri-Sat til 11. Mod-Exp. (See Review). Amer Regional/Continental in Edwardian **Harvest** Mon-Fri 11:45-2 & 5-9:30, Sat til 10:30. Exp. Lunch, late bites, music in **Motions** 7 days 4-11. Mod.

## PENN/LIBERTY CULTURAL DISTRICT

### Bravo! Franco
*613 Penn. Mon-Sat Lunch 11:30-4, Dinner 5-11. AE,DC,MC,V.* **642-6677.**
Sophisticated before/after-theatre favorite across from Heinz Hall. Cont. Mod-Exp.

### Carmassi's
*711 Penn. Mon 11:30-9, Tues-Fri til 10:30, Sat 4:30-10:30. Open Sun 4:30 show nights. AE,D,DC,MC,V.* **281-6644**
Modern two-level with Italian seafood, pasta, veal; swordfish, crab- cakes. Mod.

### Frenchy's
*136 6th St. Mon-Sat 11-12.AE,MC,V.* **261-6476.**
One of area's oldest, popular room specializing in seafood, pasta. Inexp-Mod.

### The Overture
*212 6th St. Lunch Mon-Fri 11:30- 3, Dinner Mon-Thur 5-10, Fri-Sat til 11. Open Sun from 4:30 show nights. AE,D, DC, MC,V.* **391-0500.**
Multi-level with theatrical decor, Broadway sound track, piano. Italian-Amer steak, seafood, veal, pasta. Mod-Exp.

### Richest Restaurant
*140 6th St. Mon-Sat 9-9. AE,D,DC,MC,V.* **471-7799.**
NY deli/bar, institution since 1936. Kosher corned beef, blintzes. Inexp.

**8**

# THE DOWNTOWNER
## Gateway/Point/Market Sq

### Seventh St Grille
*Century Bldg, 130 7th St. Mon-Fri 11-2am Sat-Sun 12-2. AE,CB,D,DC,MC,V.* **338-0303.**
Popular lunch/theatre spot with steak, prime-rib, seafood grills, chicken, pasta, sandwiches. Mod.

### Suzie's
*130 6th St. Mon 11-3, Tues-Fri 11-8, show nights Sat 4-8. No credit cards.* **261-6443.**
Authentic little Greek cafe, sidewalk tables in summer. Inexp. (See Review)

### Tambellini's
*139 7th St. Mon-Sat 11:30-11. AE,MC,V.* **391-1091.**
Busy room with good Italian fare–veal, pasta, fried zucchini. Mod-Exp.

### GATEWAY/POINT/MARKET SQ

### Avenue of the Cafes
*Fifth Ave Place, 5th/Stanwix. Mon-Sat 10-6, Mon & Thur til 7:30.* **456-7800.**
Popular eateries in arcade food court with with balcony view of splendid lobby— **Sbarro's** Italian, **Steak Escape**, **Arthur Treacher's Fish**, **Au Bon Pain**. Inexp.

### Froggy's
*100 Market. Mon-Thur 11:30-11, Fri-Sat til 12. AE,DC,MC,V.* **471-3764.**
Charming, old style bar/diningroom with good beef, big drinks, atmosphere. Mod. (See Review)

### Gallagher's
*2 Market Place. Mon-Fri Lunch only 11-2:30, Sat 12-3. Bar til 2. AE,DC,MC,V.* **261-5554.**
Friendly Irish pub with good sandwiches, stew, Irish coffee, sing-a-longs. Inexp.

### Hana's
*#1 Graeme, Market Square. Lunch Mon-Fri 11:30-3, Dinner 4:30-10. AE,DC, MC, V.* **471-9988.**
Japanese/Oriental 2nd fl room with sushi, tempura, shrimp flambee. Inexp-Mod.

### Hilton Hotel
*Gateway Ctr. AE,D,DC,MC,V.* **391-4600.**
Bright **Promenade Cafe** on park, patio. Mon-Sat 6:30-5, Sun 7-5. Mod. Formal dinner, steaks in **Sterlings** 7 days 5-11:30. Mod-Exp.

### Jake's Above the Square
*430 Market. Mon-Thur 11:30-11, Fri-Sat til 11-12.. Sun 4-10. AE,D,DC,MC,V.* **338-0900.**
Upscale cuisine with North Italian/Amer regional—great fish, superior wine list. Dinner piano. Valet parking. Exp.

### Jamie's on the Square
*435 Market. Mon-Sat 11-11. AE,D,DC, MC,V.* **471-1722.**
Popular for casual business lunch. Huge steak salad, Amer cuisine. Mod.

### Max & Erma's
*630 Stanwix St. Mon-Thur 11-10, Fri-Sat til 11. AE,D,DC,MC,V.* **471-1140.**
Bright room with eclectic menu, popular downtown happy hour. Inexp-Mod.

### Mick McGuire's
*22 Graeme, Mkt Square. Mon-Sat 8-12. Sun 10:30-7. AE,DC,MC,V.* **642-7526.**
Cozy Irish pub with juicy burgers, stew. Acoustic music Fri eve. Inexp.

### 1902 Landmark Tavern
*24 Market Sq. Mon-Sat Lunch 11:30-4, Dinner 5-11. AE,D,DC,MC,V.* **471-1902.**
Quaint, restored tavern, marble floors, raw bar, oldtime atmosphere. Inexp-Mod.

### Original Oyster House
*20 Market Place. Mon-Sat 9-11. No credit cards.* **566-7925.**
Historic old saloon with fabulous fish sandwich, oysters, clams. Inexp.

### PPG Food Court
*#2 PPG Place. Mon-Fri 10-6, Sat 10-3.*
Varied eateries in Atrium's grand lower level inc Grecian Isles, Somma's Pizza, Au Bon Pain, 4th Ave Franks, Little China, Mexican Hat Dance, Strawberry Saloon and Burger, Burger & Chili. Inexp.

## Ruth's Chris Steak House
*6 PPG Place. Lunch Mon-Fri 11:30-3. Dinner Mon-Thur 5-10:30, Fri-Sat til 11. Sun 5-9. AE,DC,MC,V.* **391-4800.**
Burnished steak house of famous chain; #1 prime steaks, accessories. Exp. (See Review)

## Scoglio
*Fifth Ave Place. Mon-Thur 11:30-10, Fri til 11. Sat 5-11. AE,D,DC,MC,V.* **391-1226.**
Serene decor, extraordinary N Ital cuisine –chicken, pasta, veal. Mod. (Review)

## Southwest Bistro
*129 Sixth Street. Lunch Mon-Fri 11-2:30, Dinner Mon-Sat 4:30-11. Sun for shows. AE,D,DC,MC,V.* **261-8866.**
Innovative foods with SW spices–grills, roasts, blackened fish plus popular lunch favorites. Inexp-Mod.

## Tramp's
*212 Blvd of Allies. Mon-Thur 11:30-10:30, Fri-Sat til 11:30. AE,DC,MC,V.* **261-1990.**
Charming restored old bordello/bar with lots of atmosphere, good late supper menu. Inexp-Mod. (See Review)

### MIDTOWN 4TH/WOOD

## First Side Grill
*100 Wood at 1st. Mon-Fri 11:30-1:30am, Sat 5-1:30. AE,CB,DC,MC,V.* **471-9222.**
An offshoot of Piccolo, Piccolo; upscale pizza, quesidillas, shish-kabob, burgers, dinners $2-$14.95.

## Kason's
*Bank Tower, Lower Level, 311 Fourth. Mon-Wed 11:30-11, Thur-Fri til 1. Sat 12-7. AE,D,DC,MC,V.* **391-1122.**
A Pgh institution. Popular lunch, Happy Hour spot. Pre-Pirate/Penguin game 2 for 1 specials. Inexp.

## Mandarin Gourmet
*YWCA Lobby, 305 Wood. Mon-Sat 11-9. AE,D,DC,MC,V.* **261-6151.**
Popular lunch spot; specialties–lobster, General Tso's chicken. Inexp.

## Morton's of Chicago
*CNG Tower, 625 Liberty. Lunch Mon-Fri 11:30-2:30, Dinner Mon-Sat 5:30-11. Sun 5-10. AE,CB,DC,MC,V.* **261-7141.**
Burnished club-like famous chain; prime steaks, other entrees. Exp. (See Review)

## Piccolo, Piccolo
*1 Wood. Lunch Mon-Fri 11:30-3, Dinner Mon-Thur 5-10, Fri-Sat til 11. AE,CB,D, DC,MC,V.* **261-7234.**
Popular trattoria with extraordinary antipasto buffet, pastas; sidewalk tables in summer. Mod.

## Smithfield Cafe
*637 Smithfield St. Mon-Fri 6-9, Sat 7-3. AE,D,DC,MC,V.* **281-5452.**
Oldtime favorite for pasta, salads, seafood, sandwiches, burgers. Daily specials. DJ Fri from 6pm. Inexp.

## Warner Center Food Court
*332 Fifth. Mon-Sat Lunch 11-3.* **281-9000.**
Bevy of Balcony eateries–Warner Cafe, Grand Deli, Pasta Al Dente, Chicken Filet, Grand Wok, Steak Escape. Inexp.

### GRANT STREET/UPTOWN

## Apollo
*429 Forbes. Breakfast/Lunch Mon-Fri 7-3. No credit cards.* **471-3033.**
Upscale fast-food with homemade soups & salads, chargrilled sandwiches. Inexp.

## The Carlton
*1 Mellon Bank Ctr, Grant. Lunch Mon-Fri 11:30-2:30, Dinner Mon-Thur 5-10, Fri-Sat til 11. AE,D,DC,MC,V.* **391-4099.**
Business favorite, handsome room with prime beef, chops, fresh fish, seafood. Mod-Exp.

## Chinatown Inn
*522 3rd. Lunch Mon-Fri 11-2:30, Dinner Mon-Sat til 10. Sun 2-10. AE,D,DC,MC,V.* **261-1292.**
Chinese specialties in serene surroundings. Inexp-Mod.

**8**

## Grant/Uptown

### Common Plea
*310 Ross. Lunch Mon-Fri 11:30- 2:30, Dinner Mon-Sat 5-10. AE,DC,MC,V.* **281-5140.**
Lawyers' favorite upstairs room with 'courtly' atmosphere, great appetizers, seafood. Mod-Exp.

### Consigliere
*428 Cherry Way across from Kaufmann's pkg lot, Mon-Fri 11:30-9, Sat 5-9. AE,D, DC,MC,V.* **281-0003.**
Relaxing lawyer's haunt, good chicken, veal, steak, seafood, Italian desserts. Lunch Soup/Salad Special $6.95. Mod.

### Dingbat's
*One Oxford Ctr. Lunch Mon-Sat 11:30-2, Dinner 5-12am.AE,D,DC,MC,V.* **392-0350.**
Popular, handsome restaurant, summer patio, big bar, eclectic menu—dinners, sandwiches, salads. Inexp-Mod. (Review)

### Juno Trattoria
*One Oxford Ctr, 3rd L. Mon-Thur 11:30-11, Fri-Sat til 12. AE,D,DC,MC,V.* **392-0225.**
Authentic Italian specialties in sleek balcony setting; great homemade bread, pasta, pizza. Inexp-Mod. (See Review)

### Kaufmann's Dept Store
*5th/Smithfield. Store charge only.* **232-2682.**
Best coffee shop food in town at 1st fl **Tic-Toc** 11-7. Inexp. Also **Michael's, Edgar's, Forbes** 11th floor dining rooms Mon-Sat 11-4, Mon & Thur til 8. Happy Hour Tues, Wed & Fri 4-7. Inexp-Mod.

### Me Lyng
*Lawyer's Bldg, 428 Forbes. Mon-Sat 11-9. AE,MC.V.* **642-2922.**
Popular variety of Chinese, Vietnamese dishes inc Hunan, Cantonese. Inexp-Mod.

### Pietro's Italian Chophouse
*Hyatt Regency Pittsburgh. 7 days 6:30-11. AE,DC,MC,V.* **288-9326.**
Modern, spacious, two-level room with fine dining on N Italian cuisine, sumptuous Sun Brunch; pleasant outdoor patio overlooking city. Mod-Exp.

### Ruddy Duck
*Bigelow/6th Mon-Thur 6:30am-1, Fri til 10, Sat-Sun 7-12. AE,D,DC,MC,V.* **281-3825.**
Warm, brassy room, breakfast to supper; good duck, sandwiches. Mod.

### Sammy's Famous Corned Beef
*Manor Complex, 564 Forbes* **261-7033.**
*Also 217 9th/Liberty; 420 Smithfield. Mon-Thur 7-10, Fri til 11.*
Popular downtown deli; big Kosher beef dogs, corned beef, pastrami, roast beef, chicken soup, beer, outdoor tables. Inexp.

### Scoglio Uptown
*Law & Finance Bldg, 429 4th Ave. Lunch Mon-Fri 11:30-2, Dinner Tues-Fri 4-9, Sat 5-9. AE,D,DC,MC,V.* **263-0545.**
An uptown replica of popular restaurant with fine N Italian cuisine, great pasta, veal. Lawyers' haunt. Inexp-Mod. (See Review)

### Top of The Triangle
*USX Bldg. Lunch Mon-Fri 11:30-3, Sat 12-3. Dinner Mon-Thur 5:30-10, Fri-Sat till 11. Sun 4-9. AE,D,DC,MC,V.* **471- 4100.**
Fine Amer/Cont dining with spectacular view from 62nd floor. Dancing, bar til 2. Great visitor site. Mod-Exp.

### Westin William Penn
*Mellon Square. AE,D,DC,MC.V. 7 days 6-11.* **281-7100.**
Breakfast/lunch/dinner, Continental cuisine in elegant **Terrace Room** off grand lobby. 7 days 6-11. Mod-Exp. Breakfast/lunch in **Garden Deli**, mezzanine, Mon-Fri 7-2. Inexp. Tea, cocktails, piano in relaxing **Palm Court Lobby** 7 days 11-11. Mod. (See Review)

**Station Square** (See Reviews)
**Mt Washington** (See City Views)

# RIVERFRONT DINING/FUN

Pittsburgh now boasts an amazing number...72 riverfront and outdoor eateries...thanks to the city's Riverside Renaissance! Whether you choose to eat with a river view or at one of the city's charming new patios and sidewalk cafes...it's a good way to mingle with other city dwellers and enjoy the greatest of urban pleasures—dining al fresco.

# Riverfront Restaurants

### Allegheny River Boat Club
*314 Arch St, Verona. Mon-Fri 3pm- 2am. Sat-Sun 12-2am.AE,DC,MC,V.* **828-7775.** Casual pub—soup/sandwiches $2-$6, picnic packs to go. Courtyard for large parties for clean-up fee.
**Docking:** Free for patrons.

### Back Porch
*114 Speers St, Lower Speers near Belle Vernon Bridge (Exit 17 off I-70). Lunch Tues-Fri 11:30-4. Dinner Tues-Sat 5-10, Sun 4-9. AE,D,MC,V.* **483-4500.** Charming 1806 Colonial home tucked away in tiny riverside community near waterfront. Amer cuisine, dining on garden veranda. Lunch $4-$8, Dinner $13-$19. More casual dining downstairs at English-pub **Side Door.**
**Docking:** Public launch ramp/trailer parking across street.

### Fox Chapel Yacht Club
*1366 Old Freeport Rd, Fox Chapel. Lunch Mon-Sat 11-3. Dinner Mon-Thur 5-9 (summer til 10) Fri-Sat til 11. Sun Brunch 10-2, Dinner 5-9. AE,MC,V.* **963-8881.** Fine dining on Allegheny shore with a view of some of Pittsburgh's most impressive pleasure craft. The name may sound exclusive but the restaurant's open to the public. American cuisine. Lunch/

### Terrace Dining At Science Center
Carnegie Science Center's **River View Cafe** has an outdoor terrace fronting the Allegheny on North Shore with a great view of the Point. A family restaurant seating 200, it's open Mon-Fri 8:30-5, Sat & Sun til 6 and later on game nights with a Pre-Pirate Game Cart—burgers, dogs, chips, beer, soft drinks. Daily specials—hot items, salads, gourmet desserts—around $4. Box lunches $3.75 for eating on the terrace. No credit cards. **237-3417.**

### Captain's Dinner
Dine under the stars on the decks of the **Gateway Clipper** at the Captain's Dinner or on 265-ft **Majestic,** sailing most days 7-10, May-Dec. The $31.95 tab includes buffet, dancing, beautiful city view—a moving feast. **355-7980.**

Dinner $4.95-$29. Live music Fri-Sat in diningroom and romantic summer dancing to live bands on outdoor deck/bar. Shorts, casual dress acceptable if coming off river. Drinks: Mod.
**Docking:** Members only, free for dining patrons. Reserv.

### Marina One
*Mile Post 32.5 on the Mon, RD #3, Riverway East, Monongahela. Sun-Thur 11-10, Fri & Sat til 11. AE,MC,V.* **258-2300.** Big deck, space to dock and swim; everything from sandwiches to crab legs and lobster $5-$22. DJ Dancing Thur-Sat.
**Docking:** Guest docking available.

### Misty Harbour
*14th & River Rd, Sharpsburg. Tues-Sun 11-11. Bar til 2. Sun Br 10-3. AE,D, MC,V.* **781-4222.** A blue-canopied ramp leads you aboard this charming 240-ft tug & barge for great indoor/outdoor dining with a peaceful river view. Good big shrimp, seafood, meats, sandwiches. ($7.95-$16.95). DJ/live bands Fri-Sun nights.
**Docking:** Limited slots available.

### Silky's Crow's Nest
*19th/River Rd, Sharpsburg. AE,MC,V. Mon-Thur 11-12, Fri-Sat til 2. Sun 12-9.* **782-3701.** Casual eating/meeting place. Elegant, glass-walled, multi-level room seats 150 with great river view. Dinners—pasta, steak, seafood $6-$15. Grand piano, entertainment. Also dinner, sandwiches,

## Riverfront Restaurants

### Floating Boardwalk on the Water

#### Boardwalk, On the Water
*Strip District. Parking at 15th/Smallman under bridge.* **471-2226.**
Lots of wonderful vistas in exciting new riverfront complex. On a 420-ft floating barge 30 ft from Allegheny shore are:
**Crewsers**—Big seafood house, nautical theme, sliding glass doors onto river; romantic views; snacks/dinner. 7 days 11-12. Bars til 2. Mod. **281-3680.**

**Buster's Crab**—Baltimore-style raw bar with topside view, patio. Mon-Sat 5-12. (Summr Sat-Sun 12-12).Mod. **281-3683.**
**Patio/Deck**—2 bars, restaurant service under the stars. Summer bands Thur Sun at 9pm, Sat/Sun afternoons.
**Donzi's**—Euro-style disco. Wed-Thur 8-2am, Sat 5-2am. Sun in summer. Cover varies. Mod-Exp. **281-1586.**
**Docking:** 60 slips free to patrons. (Downtown Yacht Club next door.)

late snacks in **Boaters Bar** on lower level with outside decks.
**Docking:** Docking free for patrons.

#### Snooters
*119 River Rd, Lower Speers, near Belle Vernon Bridge. (Exit 17 off I-70) 7 days 11:30-10, Bar til 1-2am. AE,DC,MC,V.* **483-6000.**
One of the most popular eating spots on the Mon (formerly Smitty's) with nautical theme and a big, awninged outdoor deck. Seafood, pasta, chicken, sandwiches all day, food to go for boaters. Party room. Lunch/Dinner $5-$15.
**Docking:** Nearby public ramp/trailer parking. Docking free to patrons at Boat World Marina if space available.

#### Speers St Grille
*Lower Speers, near Belle Vernon Bridge. (Exit 17 off of I-70). Tues-Sun 11:30-10. MC,V.* **483-1911.**
Old Victorian home next door to the **Back Porch.** Cool lemonade and homemade ice cream on small patio with river view. Casual restaurant with ribs, chicken, sandwiches, munchies. $4.50-$9.
**Docking:** Public ramp/trailer parking.

#### *Riverside Shops*
*Boaters, diners can take advantage of a collection of unique specialty shops– antiques, crafts, boutiques with a Victorian motif–in Lower Speers.* **483-4668.** *(See 10 Terrific Trips)*

9

### Pgh's Spectacular Water Park

#### Sandcastle on the Mon
*W Homestead, Rt 387 between Homestead & Glenwood Bridges. (Parkway: Squirrel Hill/Hmstd Exit, across Hi-Level Bridge, right to 387, follow blue signs.) June-Labor Day. 7 days 11-6, Fri-Sat til 7. Eve Wed-Sat 6-1am. MC,V.* **462-6666.**
Everybody loves Pittsburgh's fabulous waterpark along the Mon. The 30-acre water wonderland has 15 major slides (some of tallest in world—85 ft) 3 kiddie slides, a 1400-ft "lazy river" for floaters,

2 pools, volleyball, mini-golf course, go-cart track and a charming, old-fashioned 1000-ft Boardwalk...second only to Atlantic City's. At night the fun goes on—two dance floors, huge hot tubs along the river and nostalgic piano fests and sing-a-longs up on the Boardwalk. Young, old love it! Picnic food— pizza, burgers, hot dogs, sauerkraut $3-$5. Adm $12.95. Eve: Wed-Thur $1, Fri-Sat $4.
**Docking:** 50 slips, patrons free with admission price.

## Marinas

### Washington's Landing

*Herr's Island. 2 miles upriver from Golden Triangle. 7 days 8-8.* **741-1077.**
This amazing 42-acre riverfront development on Herr's Island has a full service marina with fuel, ship's store, laundry facilities and members' club/lounge. The project also includes a public park with river overlook, a tennis complex, jogging/biking trails and a nautical store and specialty shops in the Town Center. Three Rivers Rowing Association also headquarters here.
**Slips:** 160 dry stack and 150 wet slips; guest docking. Overnight $25.

### RIVER VIEWS

#### River's Edge
*16 Alleg River Blvd, Verona. Lunch Mon-Fri 11-4, Dinner Mon-Sat 4-11. AE,DC, MC,V.* **793-6167.**
Nestled along the boulevard, this venerable Verona haunt has a striking view of the river from a glass-enclosed diningroom. Italian cuisine. Lunch/Dinner $7-$14.

#### Paule's Lookout
*2627 Skyline Drive, W Mifflin. Tues-Sat 11-9. Sun 12-7. AE,DC,MC,V.* **466-4500.**
Family restaurant high on a hilltop with a panoramic view of the Mon & the Youghiogheny. Seafood, lobster & prime rib. $6.50 up.

#### Veltri's
*Rt 907 & Coxcomb Hill, Plum Boro. Dinner Mon-Thur 5-10, Fri-Sat til 11. Reser. AE,DC,MC,V.* **335-4474.**
Beautiful view of the the Allegheny, romantic atmosphere. Italian-American cuisine, good veal. DJ Dancing Wed-Sat. $7-$18.

### DOCKING ON THE RIVER

#### ALLEGHENY

**Allegheny Marina** *One 62nd St, Lawrenceville. 7 days 24 hrs.* **782-3113.**
At Mile Marker 5. Service, supplies, facilities, showers. **Slips:** 100, guest docking available, overnight $15 up.

**Allegheny River Boat Club** *314 Arch, Verona. 7 days 24 hrs.* **828-7775.**
Power, showers, picnic facilities. Restaurant/bar, public launch $10. **Slips:** 90, 6 free for restaurant patrons, overnight $10 up.

**Aspinwall Marina** *285 River Ave, Aspinwall. 7 days 8am-10pm.* **781-2340.**
Accessible dock, fuel, service, supplies, public ramp $10. **Slips:** 200, 15-20 guest, overnight $20.

**Bell Harbour Marina** *1 River Road, Blawnox. 7 days 10-9.* **828-3477.**
Service, supplies, facilities, showers, snacks. Ramp $10. **Slips:** 55, 5 guest $8-$15, overnight $10-$15.

**Dave's Marina** *Grantham & River Ave, North Shore. 7 days 9:30-9:30, fuel 8-8.* **231-9860.**
Fuel, facilities, ramp $7, snack bar. **Slips:** 95, guest/overnight available.

**Downtown Yacht Club** *Next to Boardwalk in Strip between Veterans & 16th St bridges.* **257-1500.**
Restaurants/disco/patio bar. **Slips:** 60 at Yacht Club, 60 guest slips at Boardwalk free to patrons.

**Dock of the Bay** *River Rd, Sharpsburg. 7 days 8-8.* **782-4176.**
Last marina before Lock #2. Fuel, supplies. **Slips:** 250, guest slips vary, overnight $15.

## Marinas

### PITTSBURGH'S RIVER RENAISSANCE

*Pittsburgh is truly a river town... beautifully situated at the Point of three rivers...where the Allegheny and the Monongahela merge to form the Ohio. The largest inland port in the U.S., Pittsburgh's waterways carry more commercial tonnage (34.3 million in 1992) than any other inland port in the country, far ahead of St Louis, second with 26 million. And Pittsburgh ranks a surprising 17th of all U.S. ports—including deep water coastal and Great Lakes ports. Allegheny County also has one of the largest number of registered pleasure boats in the U.S.—29,289 in 1993, second only to Miami's Dade County. And as new riverfront projects reclaim city waters for recreation and entertainment, Pittsburgh's River Renaissance is here!*

**Fox Chapel Yacht Club** *1366 Old Freeport Rd, Fox Chapel.* **963-8881.** Private club, full-service. **Slips:** 110 members. Free docking restaurant patrons.

**Hunt's Marina** *10 Washington Ave, Oakmont, 7 days 8-8.* **828-1260.** Full service, fuel, power, showers. **Slips:** 140, 10 guest, overnight $20.

**North Shore Marina** *River Ave/Mendota. 7 days 10-8.* **231-2333.** Full service, fuel, supplies, snacks. **Slips:** 100, 4 guest. Stadium docking $7, overnight $20—water/elec $25 extra.

**Outboard Haven** *228 Arch Street, Verona. 7 days 9-9.* **828-4944.** Very accessible dock. Fuel, supplies, facilities, shower, snacks. **Slips:** 250, guest slips vary. Overnight $20-$25.

### MONONGAHELA

**Beach Club Marina** *124 S Union, New Eagle, off Rt 88. 7 days 8-8.* **258-2088.** Fuel, power, facilities, showers, picnic facilities, volleyball, horsehoes. Public launch $5. **Slips:** 170, 10 guest, overnight 50c ft.

**Boat World** *119 River Rd, Speers, near Belle Vernon Bridge. Weekdays 10-7, Sat 10-4, Sun 12-4.* **483-3337.**

Fuel, service, parts, supplies, facilities, picnic area.
**Slips:** 180, 8 for guests, docking fees/overnight vary.

**Engel's Holiday Harbour** *Rt 88 at Ten Mile Crk, Millsboro. 7 days 9-7.* **377-0151.** Fuel/service, facilities/showers, supplies, snacks. **Slips:** 65-70, 4-5 slips overnight only, 50c ft.

**Green Cove Yacht Club** *Rt 88 at Ten Mile Ck, Millsboro. 7 days 9-5.* **377-0184.** Longest pool (lock to lock) on Mon. Fuel, service, supplies, restaurant/snacks, camping; launching weekdays only, $10. **Slips:** 325, unlimited guest, overnight 50c foot, water/elec extra.

**South Side Public Launch** *S Side Riverfront Pk, foot of Birmingham Bridge, at 18th St. 7 days 6am-12am.* **255-2390** Public launch ramp, picnic area.

### Three Rivers Rowing

The Three Rivers Rowing Assn, with home-base and 120-ft dock on the back channel at Washington's Landing, has 300 area members who row year round—indoors in winter on machines. For information call **231-8772.**

9

## Riverwalks

### RIVERWALKS

**Three Rivers Heritage Trail**

Hikers will one day be able to walk 12 miles on Pittsburgh's riverfront along a planned **Three Rivers Heritage Trail**. Beginning at Washington's Landing, the walkway will cross the Allegheny River on a picturesque old Herr's Island railroad bridge to North Shore's riverside walkway in Roberto Clemente Park. It continues past Carnegie Science Center, then over the Mon via the West End Bridge to the South Side. Here it joins Station's Square's proposed riverwalk and industrial artificats museum. Above the 10th St Bridge the Trail becomes a wooded pathway to S Side's Riverfront Park...and hopefully on to Sandcastle.

It's expected to be 80% completed by 1997.

**Current Riverwalks**

**South Side Riverfront Park** 3/4 mile, walking, jogging, biking.
**Boardwalk, On the Water**
1/2 mile, walking, jogging, biking.
**Sandcastle Water Park** Scenic walk, the length of the park, along the Mon.
**Station Square Riverwalk** Mile-long path with industrial artifacts, length of Station Sq from Panhandle Bridge to Ft Pitt Bridge. ('95)
**Washington's Landing** One and a half miles walking, jogging, biking trails circling the island.

**Sandcastle on the Mon** *bet Homestead/ Glenwood Bridges.* **462-6666.**
Docking for patrons with admission fee $2-$12. Food, DJ dancing eves.

OHIO

**B & L Marina** *4621 Royal Avenue, Coraopolis. 7 days 24 hrs.* **269-9569.**
On back channel. Service, facilities, restaurant, launching $10. **Slips:** 25, guest if space.

**C & E Marina** *200 Dawson, Sewickley under Glenfield Bridge. 7 days 9-5.* **741-6810.**

### Clipper Cruises

Best way to see Pittsburgh and appreciate its unique geography is by water. **Gateway Clipper's** 1-3 hour cruises run daily from Station Square dock. You can sail on everything from the Good Ship Lollipop to the 365-ft Majestic. **355-7965.**

Fuel, service, supplies, facilities, shower. Dry-stacking, park/launch. **Slips:** 25, 2 guest—overnght only, $15.

**Groteton Boat Club** *Royal Ave, Neville Isl. Back Channel. 7 days 8-11.* **264-6776.**
Fuel, supplies, snacks, 8 acres picnic grounds, launching $5. Courtesy Marine Exam (CME) for safety Coast Guard sticker. DJ Sat/holidays. **Slips:** Guest slips always available.

**Gr Pgh Aquatic Club** Pine St, Neville Island. Back channel. **264-9978.**
Fuel, elec/water, docking. Members only.

**Vic's Boat Park** *1 River Road, McKees Rocks. Back channel. 7 days 10-10.* **771-DOCK.**
Fuel, service, towing, facilities, supplies, ice/snacks, launching $10. **Slips:** 120, few guest/overnight $25.

## RIVER CELEBRATIONS

### Pgh Three Rivers Regatta
Point State Park. First weekend in August. Celebration on all three rivers opening with downtown Regatta Parade, fireworks, food booths, entertainment, sternwheeler races, "Anything That Floats" contest, hot air balloon races, air show, Intl Formula I Grand Prix speed-boat races. **261-7055.**

### Oakmont Yacht Club Regatta
Oakmont. Last weekend in July. Food, fun, fireworks, boat races on the Allegheny River. **828-9847**

### Head of Ohio Crew Regatta
September. Crews from all over vie in annual Mercy Hospital/Three Rivers Rowing Assn contest drawing national and international oarsmen. **231-8772.**

### Three Rivers Rowing Races
*Washington's Landing*
McAlice Stake Race—around Washington's Landing (July); 3-Rivers Scholastic High-School Sprint (May). **231-8772.**

### Mississippi/Delta Queen
Cruise boats dock at the Mon Wharf, Downtown in July, Aug and Oct creating riverfront excitement. **800-543-1949.**

### Albert Gallatin Regatta
Point Marion, Mem Day Wknd **725-9190.**

### Armstrong Co Regatta
Kittanning. Aug. **548-3226.**

---

### Take a Water Taxi!
You can take a Water Taxi to and from all city/stadium events—and see city sights along the way—in a Three Rivers Charter Service taxi. Boarding at 11 locations:
**Downtown:** Point Park at both Ft Pitt & Ft Duquesne Bridges. Sixth St Bridge (theatre district). Lawrence Convention Center.
**Boardwalk** in the Strip.
**North Shore:** Allegheny Landing–(Warhol Museum). Stadium/Clemente Park. Carnegie Science Center.
**Washington's Landing** Herr's Island at 31st St.
**Sandcastle–Club Wet** and **McKees Rocks.**
(Downtown $1.50, Boardwalk $2.50, Sandcastle $4.50, McKees Rocks to Sandcastle-1 hr $6.50.) Also boat rental. (See Party Rooms). **363-BOAT.**

9

### Beaver Co River Regatta
3rd wknd Aug. **728-0212.**

### Monongahela Riverfest.
Mile 32, 2nd wknd Aug. **258-5988.**

### White Water Rafting
Ohiopyle State Park Apr-Oct. **329-8591.** "Yough Slalom" White Water Boat Races Ohiopyle State Pk. Aug/Sept. **329-8591.**

### Yough River Days
Connellsville. 1st wknd Jun. **628-5500.**

---

### Houseboat For Hire
You can spend a whole day out on the river aboard a 56-foot houseboat/yacht, the **"Sunseeker."** It comes complete with rooftop, hot tub, waterslide, kitchen, wet bar & stereo with crew. Cost $400 & up for a 4-hour cruise. **831-1188.** (See Party Rooms)

### Rent a Boat
You can rent a boat to steer yourself at **Paradise Boat Rental** at the Boardwalk in the Strip dock near Donzi's. Mini-speedboats (for 2-3) $25 a 1/2 hour, mini-pontoons (for 4 to 5) $30 1/2 hour. Large pontoons for 8-9 $70 hour. **655-7272.**

# OUTDOOR CAFES/PATIOS

Outdoor dining spots continue to spring up all over...from busy downtown sidewalks to patios high above the city...enhancing the quality of urban life and the pleasures of summer dining.

## Sidewalk Cafes/Patios

### Abate

*Waterworks, Freeport Rd, Fox Chapel. Sun-Thur 11:30-11, Fri-Sat til 12. AE,CB, DC,MC,V.* **781-9550.**
There's a delightful open sun porch with fans overhead serving a full menu in this Italian seafood house with great pastas, salads, hearth baked pizza. $4-$18. (See Review)

### Alexander's

*5104 Liberty Ave, Bloomfield. Mon-Sat 11-12, Sun 11-11. MC,DC,V.* **682-9824.**
Denizens aren't nonplussed by the traffic breezing by sidewalk tables in this most unlikely spot. But the roped off area provides a good buffer and you can relax of an evening as you dribble tarragon olive oil and Parmesan on crusty Italian bread at every table. Have a refreshing drink and dinner is on. Italian pastas, meats, salads, pizza and grandpa's wonderful tiramisu. $5-$13.

### Antonini's

*2700 Jane St, S Side. Mon-Thur 11-12, Fri-Sat til 2. Sun 5-12. AE,D,DC,MC,V.* **381-9901.**
Courtyard patio for Italian coastal cooking...chicken, veal, steak, pasta, crab, lobster plus sandwiches, salads. $9.95-$26.95.

### Artery

*5847 Ellsworth, Shadyside. Tues-Sun 5-2am. AE,D,MC,V.* **361-9473.**
Umbrellaed brick patio in art gallery/show-case restaurant. Light appetizers to pop-ular mesquite chicken and fish on the outdoor grill. $3-$8.

### Attic

*3609 Forbes, Oakland. Mon-Fri 11:30-10, Sat 10-12am, Bar til 2. AE,D,MC,V.* **682-2050.**
Outdoor patio off 2nd floor room popular with students/locals. Informal sandwiches, Mexican. $2-$8.

---

### Euro Cafe on the Square

#### Garden Cafe/Grand Concourse
*Station Sq. Cont Breakfast, Lunch, Dinner. AE,DC,MC,V. Reser.* **261-1717**
This flower-bedecked, 65-seat open-air pavilion outside the Gandy Dancer was inspired by European cafes. Open in good weather, it has a charm-ing red roof, brick floor, benches and hanging flower pots. Accordion music adds to the atmosphere from 7-10pm. The food's hearty ethnic...mostly Ger-man...bratwurst, knockwurst, spaetzle plus roast chicken, perogis and imported beers/sangria ($6-$11). Great stop for strollers at the Square.

---

### Bentley's

*5608 Wilkins, Sq Hill. Mon-Thur 11:30-10, Fri-Sat til 11. AE,D,MC,V.* **421-4880.**
Neighborhood favorite with awninged sidewalk patio, full menu, good Early Birds. $4-$13.

### Brandy's

*Penn Ave & 24th St, Strip. Mon-Thur 11:15-12am, Fri-Sat til 2am. Sun 3-11. AE,D,DC,MC,V.* **566-1000.**
A brand new concrete outdoor patio for this picturesque eatery. You'll sight the green/white umbrellas, colorful Brandy's mural from the avenue. Outdoor grill, light menu only. Off-street parking on corner. Good late evening stop. $4-$8. (Review)

### Bunznudders

*305 S Craig Street, Oakland. Mon-Thur 7:30-10, Fri-Sat til 11. Sun 9-6.* **683-9993.**
The white tables on the steps at Craig Square Shops are for happy eaters from this neon-lit ice creamery/bakery with homemade ice cream, yogurt, delicious cinnamon buns, meat/cheese croissants, espresso, lemonade. Great break. Inexp.

**10**

## Sidewalk Cafes/Patios

### Cafe Azure
*317 S Craig Street, Oakland. Mon-Thur 11:30-9:30, Fri-Sat til 10:30. AE,DC, MC, V.* **681-3533.**
Classic dining on sleek outdoor terrace, the sophisticated French cuisine tempered by breezy museum/university atmosphere. Cafe Jazz Fri-Sat 8-12, Light Fare 10:30-12am. $6-$20. (See Review)

### Cafe Sam
*5242 Baum Blvd, Oakland. Lunch Mon-Fri 11:30-4, Dinner Sun-Tues 5-10, Wed-Thur til 11, Sat-12. AE,MC,V.* **621-2000.**
A private rooftop patio with blue awnings and umbrellas, complements this charming restaurant. Innovative cuisine at good prices–full dinner menu, late snacks, $4-$13. (See Review)

### Cafe Victoria
*946 Western Ave, N Side. Lunch Tues-Sat 11:30-3, Tea 3-6. Dinner Tues-Sat 6-9. Sun Brunch 10-3, Tea 3-6. D,MC,V.* **323-8881.**
A brick New Orleans garden courtyard winds to the back of Victorian restaurant. White wrought-iron furniture, a profusion of flowers make for delightful dining on refined cuisine. Called the "Angel's Watch," the patio is named for the Tiffany stained glass window in the church across the lane. $4-$19. (See Review)

### Cheese Cellar
*Shops at Station Square. 7 days 11:30-2am. AE,DC,MC,V.* **471-3355.**
A front row seat to watch the Square's horse & buggy go by at this charming sidewalk cafe...romantic at night under lighted trees. Also an atmospheric outdoor area at side. Entrees, fondues, salads, desserts, $6.50-$13.

### D's Riverfront Cafe
*National Steel Ctr, 20 Stanwix, Downtown. Mon-Fri 7am-5. AE.* **281-0422.**
You can breakfast/lunch at this little business eatery with a terrace view of the river along Ft Pitt Blvd. $2-$6.

---

### Al Fresco at the Frick

**Frick Cafe**
*7227 Reynolds St, Point Breeze. Tues-Sat 10-5:30. Sun 12-6.* **371-0600.**
Now you can dine al fresco at the Frick on a French patio amid trees and flowering plants in a small 'summerhouse' across from the Visitor's Center betweem the Frick Art Museum and Clayton. Inside the charming cafe has paned glass views of the grounds. A delightful "tea" menu includes soup, salads, artistic sandwiches i.e. smoked salmon with herb cream cheese, plus pastries, lemonade, coffee drinks. A most refreshing spot!

---

### Dingbat's City Tavern
*Oxford Centre, Downtown. Lunch Mon-Sat 11:30-2, Dinner Mon-Thur 5-11, Fri-Sat til 12. Bar til 2 daily. AE,MC,V.* **392-0350.**
This 'sunken' patio at the foot of Oxford Center has a Rockefeller Plaza atmosphere, lovely outdoor dining at pastel umbrellaed tables by the terraced waterfall. Great day/night menu— entrees, light fare, salads from $3-$13.

### Doc's Grille
*5442 Walnut St, Shadyside. Tues-Fri 4-2am, Sat 12-2am. AE,MC,V.* **681-3713.**
Roof patio atop Doc's Place with inside/outside dining. Entrees, appetizers, grills, sandwiches. Mod.

### Elbow Room
*5744 Ellsworth, Shadyside. Mon-Sat 11-2am. Sun 11-12. D,MC,V.* **441-5222.**
Tree-shaded bricked courtyard behind popular restaurant/bar, a favorite haunt of Shadysiders. Friendly, informal with good prices on soup, burgers, salads, sandwiches from $1.50-$8.

## Sidewalk Cafes/Patios

### El Dolce Cafe
*4525 Liberty, Bloomfield. Mon-Sat 8am-12am. No credit cards.* **681-5225.**
More than a coffee house, this little cafe with sidewalk tables on Liberty & Taylor, has a terrific aura. Wonderful hot/cold sandwiches—eggplant, chorizo sausage sweet peppers—plus perfect antipasta, homemade desserts, delicious tiramisu. $1-$5.

### Foster's/Holiday Inn
*100 Lytton Street, Oakland. Mon-Fri Breakfast/Lunch 6:30am-2, Sat-Sun 7:30-2, Dinner 5-10. Sun Brunch 10-2. AE,D, MC,V.* **682-6200.**
Pleasant, informal patio shielded by greenery from street bustle. Light fare to entrees, great Cajun gumbo, dirty rice. Terrific daily Happy Hour, Jazz Fri-Sun. $4-$19.

### Froggy's
*100 Market St, Downtown. Wed-Thur 4:30-10, Fri til 2, Sat 7pm-1am. AE,DC, MC,V.* **471-3764.**
Small 3rd-floor patio amid city rooftops in popular downtown eatery. Relaxing under bright Cinzano umbrellas...wonderful sundown after-five spot. No food upstairs, just good times, big 4-oz drinks $4 up.

### Harris Grill
*5747 Ellsworth Avenue, Shadyside. 7 days 11-2am. AE,D,MC,V.* **363-0833.**
An easy mix of people at the tables in front of this popular Shadyside hangout—and the owner is interested in them all. Good cafe food from burgers to moussaka $3-$10. Great place for lunch, dinner or 'night break.' Inside the restaurant's three stories are simple rooms in the Greek manner.

### Kane's Courtyard
*303 S Craig Street, Oakland. Mon-Fri 7-5:30, Sat 10-5:30.* **683-9988.**
Charming eatery with little white tables in the courtyard of the Gallery Shops and an indoor skylit patio. Gourmet pastries & coffee—try the jumbo muffins—and some

---

### Outdoor Dining With City View

#### Grandview Saloon
*1212 Grandview Ave, Mt Washington next to Duquesne Incline. Sun-Thur 11-12am, Fri-Sat til 1. Bar til 2. AE,DC,MC,V.* **431-1400.**
There are two outdoor decks overlooking the city in this smashing restaurant with five levels cantilevered over the hillside and a fantastic view of the Point. Mt Washington's first outdoor eatery, it's young, casual with a busy bar on the 1st level. Light dinner, sandwiches, salads from $5-$17.

---

of city's best sandwiches—egg/chicken salad, ham, capicolla on great bread. Also soup, pasta salads, fruit. Take-out too. $2-$5.

### La Charcuterie
*Ellsworth Plaza, Ellsworth & College. Tues-Fri 10-8, Sat til 6, Sun til 4. MC,V.* **661-2262.**
There are a few outdoor tables outside this gourmet food shop. Sandwiches, pate, breads, cheese, smoked meats, coffee bar. $2-$5.

### La Filipiniana
*5312 Butler St, Lawrenceville. Wed-Sun 5-10. AE,MC,V.* **781-8724.**
Dine in a fragrant outdoor flower/herb garden in this city oasis. Fine Filipino cuisine and a warm, beautiful backyard atmosphere. $7-$15. (Review)

### Le Pommier, The Apple Tree
*2104 E Carson St, S Side. Mon-Sat 5:30-10. AE,DC,MC,V.* **431-1901..**
The sidewalk tables serve the same fine French country cuisine as the serene inside. $15-$23. (See Review)

**10**

## Sidewalk Cafes/Patios

### Mallorca
*2228 E Carson St, S Side. Mon-Thur 11:30-10:30, Fri-Sat til 11:30, Sun 12-10. AE,D,DC,MC.* **488-1818.**
Charming enclosed patio in intriguing Victorian restoration with pieces of Pittsburgh's past. Spanish Continental cuisine served with panache under red & green umbrellas. $5-$24. (See Review)

### Mullaney's Harp/Fiddle Irish Pub
*24th/Penn, Strip. Tues-Thur 11:30-12, Fri -Sat til 2. Sun 4-12. AE,D,V.* **642-6622.**
Enjoy the outdoor deck for Irish specialties—smoked salmon, Irish stew and shephard's pie; also salads and deli sandwiches. Rollickin' Irish music inside Tues-Sun. $5-$11.

### Penn Brewery
*Troy Hill Rd, N Side. Across 16th St Bridge. Mon-Sat 11-12am. Sun 2-10. AE,MC,V.* **237-9402.**
In summer the cobblestone courtyard is transformed into a German biergarten with beer taps, long benches, fun in sun and shade. View of the city from deck above. Great German wursts, sauerkraut, spaetzle & beer fresh from brewery. Live music Tues-Sat. $5-$10.

### Piccolo, Piccolo
*1 Wood Street, Downtown. Mon-Fri 11:30-3, Mon-Thur 5-10, Fri-Sat til 11. AE,DC,MC,V.* **261-7234.**
Sidewalk tables front this popular downtown restaurant for outdoor lunch on famous Italian specialties and before/after theatre drinks & appetizers. Continental... you can have your cappuccino outside. $5.95-$10.95.

### Pietro's Italian Chophouse
*Hyatt Regency Pittsburgh, Downtown. Patio Lunch Mon-Fri 11-2. Sun Breakfast Buffet 8-12. AE,DC,MC,V.* **288- 9326.**
Outdoor cafe overlooking city skyline adds a charming touch to lunch in this

---

### A Little Bit of Heaven In Heart of Town

### Heinz Hall Courtyard
*Heinz Hall Plaza, 6th/Penn, Downtown. Mon-Fri 11:30-3. AE,MC,V.* **392-4879.**
This little outdoor cafe is a refuge in the bustling city...complete with murmuring waterfall and greenery. Light lunch at tables with fresh flowers, a variety of soups, salads, desserts, hot entrees, coolers/cocktails from the bar. $3-$8. City living at its best.

---

sleek, contemporary dining room. Fine dining on N Italian cuisine $6-$20.

### Pittsburgh Deli Company
*728 Copeland St, Shadyside. Sun, Tues, Thur 11-10, Wed, Fri, Sat til 12am. No credit cards.* **682-3354.**
Sidewalk tables at charming kosher/vegetarian deli; matzo ball soup, vegetarian chili, hot corned beef, latkes, nova & other stellar sandwiches, 50 domestic/micro-beers. ($1-$6.25).

### Primanti's
*Forbes Pkg Garage, 11 Cherry Way, Downtown. Mon-Fri 6am- 6pm, Sat til 5.* **566-8051.**
You can get a quick bite at outdoor tables at this famous sandwich eatery. $3-$6.

### Promenade Cafe
*Pittsburgh Hilton, Gateway Center, Downtown. Lunch Mon-Fri 11:30-2. 7 days 6:30-8pm. AE,DC,MC,V.* **391-4600.**
This 'cafe on the park' has a lovely vista of Gateway greenery. Luminous light under bright awnings, formally set tables give a garden party feel to one of city's best open-air settings. Elegant light fare, sandwiches/salads $5-$8. Tall cool drinks add to outdoor delight. Restful al fresco.

## Sidewalk Cafes/Patios

### Lunch in the Courtyard

Join the office lunching crowd Mon-Fri in the pleasant USX Plaza courtyard under green/yellow umbrellas. Selections from **Au Bon Pain** (build your own sandwiches), **Fat Frank's** (hot dogs/kolbassi), **Q's Cafe** (ham barbecue, burgers, fresh lemonade). Also pizza. (**$2-$5.**)

### Rosebud
*2600 Smallman. Lunch Tues-Sat 11:30-6. Call for dinner/show schedules. Sun 9pm-2am. AE,D,DC,MC,V.* **261-2221.**
In summer floor length windows are open to an outside table area. Light menu—burgers, salads, pizza, pasta chicken, fish entrees plus coffee/desserts. $4-$14.

### Ruddy Duck
*Ramada Hotel, 1 Bigelow Sq. Mon-Fri 11-2pm.AE,CB,D,DC,MC,V.* **281-DUCK**
Lunch outdoors in busy urban scene at red-umbrelled tables. BBQ from outdoor grill, sandwiches, salads. $7-$9.

### Sammy's Famous Corned Beef
*Manor Complex, 564 Forbes, Downtown. Mon-Thur 7-10, Fri til 11.* **261-7033.**
Tables have sprouted outside this popular little deli tucked behind the County Office Bldg. Great hot corned beef, pastrami, roast beef and big Kosher beef hot dogs $1.99. Also chicken soup, egg salad, slaw, beer. ($3-$4). Busy urban view.

### Suzie's
*130 6th St, Downtown. Mon 11-3, Tues-Fri 11-8, Sat 4-8. No crediit cards.* **261-6443.**
Busy little awninged cafe off bustling sidewalk in true Greek tradition. Everything's special—homemade pasta, breads, authentic Greek cuisine. Lunch/Dinner $4-$13. Real favorite!

### Sweet Basil's
*5882 Forbes, Sq Hill. Sun-Mon 5-9, Tues-Thur 11:30-10, Fri-Sat til 11. MC,V.* **421-9958.**
Pleasant umbrellaed patio in popular local eatery; reasonable dinners, fish, great chicken sandwiches, salads. $3-$14.

### Thai Place
*809 Bellefonte St, Shadyside. Mon 4:30-10, Tues-Thur 11:30-10, Fri til 11. Sat 12-11. Sun 12-9:30. AE,D,DC,MC,V.* **687-8586.**
Complete meals outdoors at these busy tables in the midst of Shadyside...romantic at night. City's best, award-winning Thai cuisine, mild to spicy. $7-$16.

### Tramps
*212 Blvd of Allies, Downtown. Mon-Thur 11:30-10:30, Fri-Sat til 11:30. Bar til 2. AE,DC,MC,V.* **261-1990.**
New addition to this downtown charmer is white-latticed patio off "Dolly's Boudoir," a 2nd-fl party room. Full menu—soups, salads, sandwiches, entrees $2-$14.

### USA Gourmet
*2115 Penn Ave, Strip. Mon-Sat 7-4:30. No credit cards.* **471-6333**
You can take your sandwiches, desserts and cappuccino outdoors to tables in the homey backyard of this popular gourmet shop. $2-$5.

### Whiskey Dick's
*1600 Smallman St, Strip. Mon-Sat 11-2am. AE,D,DC,MC,V.* **471-9555.**
Informal deck dining in fun atmosphere. Burgers, ribs, chicken from the hardwood grill. Salads, sandwiches, great onion rings, big 64 oz drinks. Acoustic/live bands Tues & Thur. $3-$12.

**10**

# OUTDOOR CAFES/PATIOS

## Sidewalk Cafes/Patios

### SUBURBS

#### Augie's American Bistro
*The Galleria, 1500 Washington Rd, Mt Lebanon. Mon-Thur 11-11, Fri-Sat til 12. Sun 12-9. AE,D,DC,MC,V.* **571-1157.**
Gourmet pizza, pasta, soup, salad in bistro setting on huge deck; music, greenery. $4.50-$14.95.

#### Cain's
*3239 W Liberty, Dormont. Mon-Thur 4-12 Fri-Sat 4-1am. AE,D,MC,V.* **561- 7444.**
A large, relaxing 2nd-floor roof deck at neighborhood favorite specializing in ribs, chicken, pizza, $7-$16.

#### Chiodo's Tavern
*107 W 8th Ave, Homestead. Mon-Sat 10-2am. No credit cards.* **461-9307.**
This famous Homestead bar has an outdoor beer garden in true Italian fashion (nestled behind a billboard) for your more outgoing summer nights. Try a 'mystery sandwich'—meats & peppers on a submarine ($2.75 half, $4.95 whole)—and one of 125 beers. Good fun, and host Joe Chiodo himself making sure everyone has a wonderful time. You won't feel lonely.

#### Hideaway Restaurant
*Venango Golf Course, Rt 19, Cranberry.* Lunch Mon-Fri 11:30-2:30, Din Mon-Sat 5-10. Sun 5-8. AE,DC,MC,V. **776-0058.**
Pastoral scene for lunch/dinner, lovely patio overlooking golf course, pavilion for parties. Amer-Cont cuisine. $5-$16.

#### Hohmann's
*Mt Nebo Rd, Sewickley. Exit 20 I-79 Mon-Thur 11-9:45, Fri-Sat til 10:45. AE,CB,D, DC,MC,V.* **741-9968.**
Italian, pasta, seafood, good desserts on big, informal outdoor deck. $7-$20.

#### Hotlicks
*Galleria, S Hills. Mon-Thur 11:30-10, Fri-Sat till 12. Sun 12-9. AE,DC,MC.V.* **341-7427.**
Now you can enjoy your licks outdoors in a patio with arcade games. Famous ribs & chicken, burgers, fajitas, salads, sandwiches, desserts. $4.50-$14.

#### Houlihan's
*300 Mall Blvd, Monroeville Mall. Mon-Thur 11-10, Fri-Sat til 12:30. Sun 10-10. AE,D,DC,MC.V.* **373-8520.**
Patio at colorful, lively eatery. Dinner, sandwiches, appetizers. Happy Hour specials. $6-$14.

#### IKEA Cafe
*2001 Park Manor Blvd, Robinson. Mon-Fri 11-9, Sat 10-9, Sun 10-6. D,MC,V.* **747-0747.**
Big, wooden patio with relaxing view of the countryside at famous furniture store. Hot/cold Swedish delicacies—meatballs, salmon, herring, great desserts. $3-$6.

#### Mad Anthony's Bier Stube
*13th & Merchant, Ambridge. Mon-Sat 11-2am. AE,MC,V.* **266-3450.**
Outdoor courtyard, rustic atmosphere with German food, thick sandwiches, light entrees. Live bands Fri-Sat. $3-$12.

#### The Pour House
*215 E Main St, Carnegie. Mon-Fri 11-1am Sat 4-1am. AE,D,DC,MC,V.* **279-0770.**
Small, fenced-in patio behind little eatery; stews, sausage, light fare. $4-$6.

#### Stone Mansion
*1600 Stone Mansion Dr, Franklin Park. Lunch 11:45-2:30, Dinner Mon-Thur 5-10, Fri-Sat til 11. AE,CB,D,DC,MC,V.* **934-3000.**
Lovely terrace dining overlooking the greenery on stone patio at historic landmark. Beautifully presented Continental cuisine. Lunch $6-$12, Dinner $14-$30.

#### TGI Fridays
*240 Mall Blvd, Monroeville. 7 days 11-2am. AE,D,DC,MC,V.* **372-6630.**
Sunny, outdoor deck at trendy restaurant with menu of 300 items—everything from quiche to sirloin—$5.65-$12.50. Check out the myriad paraphernalia inside.

# BRUNCH/SUNDAY

Sunday Brunch, a popular Pittsburgh pastime, is an economical way to enjoy the city's best cuisine. Most brunches are buffets with limitless servings and savings on gratuities. Many of the larger brunches require reservations. Bars open Sunday at 1pm. Remember...Early Birds get the best brunch!

## Sunday Morning On the Water

### Crewsers

*Boardwalk On the Water, 15th/Smallman, Strip. AE,MC,V.* **281-3680.**
**Hours:** 10-2.
**Cost:** $12.95, 10 & under $6.95.
A fun buffet on Pittsburgh's "jettee" right out on the water. Breakfast—eggs Benedict, bacon, sausage, home fries plus hot chicken Parmesan, baked fish, pasta, veggies, fruit, salad, dessert...and a great view of the city skyline.

### Aussie's Downunder Pub

*4617 Liberty Ave, Bloomfield. AE,DC, MC,V.* **681-2290.**
**Hours:** 11-2.
**Cost:** Menu $5-$6.
Complimentary champagne at lively brunch in Australian theme pub. Pancakes, NY strip & an "Outback Omelet"–peppers, onions, tomatoes, cheese–bacon, eggs to order.

### Blarney Stone

*30 Grant Ave, Etna at Rt 8 & 28. AE,DC, MC,V.* **781-1666.**
**Hours:** 11-3:30.
**Cost:** Menu $8.95; under 12, $5.95; under 2, free.
Hearty home cooking with Gaelic flavour. Juice, salad bowl, delicious Irish date-bread, hearty bean soup plus choice of seven entrees i.e. ham & eggs, chicken a la king, roast lamb, poached salmon, stuffed peppers. Good family fare.

### Cafe Victoria

*946 Western Ave, Allegheny West. D,MC, V.* **323-8881.**
**Hours:** 10-3.
**Cost:** Buffet $12.95 inc bev, under 12 $6.95, under 6, $3.

Dine in Victorian splendor in landmark house filled with saleable antiques. The diningroom table is laden with appropriate dishes...ham with glazed apples, smoked salmon terrine, French omelettes to order, chicken...plus a complimentary mimosa. In fine weather you can take your repast into the garden. Continue antiquing next door at Allegheny Stalls.

### Cheese Cellar

*Station Sq. AE,DC,MC,V.* **471-3355.**
**Hours:** 10:30-2:30.
**Cost:** Buffet $9.95; under 12, 25c a yr.
Delightful brunch in rathskeller atmosphere, outdoors in summer; made-to-order waffles & omelettes, cheese and chocolate fondues, salad/dessert bars. Free champagne mimosa, Bloody Mary or Screwdriver. Good and lively.

### Duranti's

*Park Plaza, 128 N Craig, Oakland. AE,DC, MC,V.* **682-1155.**
**Hours:** 11-2.
**Cost:** Menu $3.95-$7.95.
A tempting array of appetizing breakfast/lunch items—pancakes, French toast, sausage; sandwiches, salads. Good after-church stop.

## Elegant Victorian Brunch

### Victoria Hall

*201 S Winebiddle, Bloomfield. Reser. MC,V.* **363-8030**
The latest in elegant brunch is at this beautiful 1865 Victorian mansion. restored to its original splendour. Now a party/reception hall, it's open to the public Sundays from 10am-3pm for an elaborate buffet brunch in the ballroom. There's a lavish breakfast spread plus smoked salmon, crab claws, jumbo shrimp, salad molds, prime rib, ham...and music on the harp for your enjoyment. $18.95, under 12, $8.95, 5 & under free.

---

### Weekend Dim Sum—Light Chinese Appetizers

#### Chinese on Carson
*1506 E Carson St, S Side. AE,D,DC, MC,V.* **431-1717.**
**Hours:** 11-4 (also Sat)
**Cost:** $1.25-$3.75 an item.
Some 30 items in beautiful surroundings ...Singapore spring rolls, pot stickers (pan fried dumplings), BBQ pork buns, shrimp dumplings, vegetable puff, stuffed chicken wings, sweet rice, desserts.

#### Peking Gourmet Kitchen
*2018 Murray, Squirrel Hill. D,MC,V.* **421-1920.**
**Hours:** 11:30-2 (also Sat).

**Cost:** $2-$10.
Choose from 36 delicacies–baby pork buns, dumplings, hot sesame noodles, spare ribs, steaming pots of tea.

### ...And a Thai Buffet

#### Thai Place
*809 Bellefonte, Shadyside. D,DC.* **687-8586. Hours:** *12-3 (also Sat).*
**Cost:** $2-$6.95 an item.
Delightfully different Thai specialties... shrimp/chicken/fish dumplings, shrimp crepe, pork buns, stuffed wings, fried wonton, salad, tempura, chicken satay, vegetable/beef lomein, taro cake.

---

#### Foster's
*Holiday Inn, 100 Lytton Ave, Oakland. AE,D,DC,MC,V.* **682-6200.**
**Hours:** 10-2.
**Cost:** Buffet $10; seniors $8.95, 6-12, $5.95; under 6 free.
Bright diningroom, patio in summer. Breakfast items plus beef, ham, seafood, salad, desserts... and jazz sound track.

#### Grand Concourse
*Station Square, AE,DC,MC,V.* **261-1717.**
**Hours:** 10-2:30.
**Cost:** $15.95; under 12, $5.95, under 4 free.
Beautiful buffet in elegant setting with live music. Gourmet items—smoked/poached salmon, English trifle, fresh juice, hot breads. Take your plate to River Room for wonderful view. Free coffee/hot doughnuts in Gandy Dancer while you wait. A city favorite.

#### Museum Cafe
*Carnegie Museum of Art, Forbes & Craig. AE,MC,V.* **622-3225.**
**Hours:** 11:30-2 (not in Jun-Aug).
**Cost:** Buffet $9.50 inc bev, 12 & under $4.95.

Very pretty buffet with glass-walled view of fountain, marble tables, pink napkins. Scrambled eggs, waffles, mini-croissants plus pasta, meat, veggie dishes. And for dessert...pastries...fruit...and the museum!

#### Orchard Cafe
*Pittsburgh Vista, Liberty Center, Reser. AE,DC,MC.V.* **227-4470.**
**Hours:** 11-2:30.
**Cost:** $19.95, 6-12 1/2, 5 & under free.
Bountiful repast in bright garden setting with pianist/Dixieland band. Gourmet items i.e. smoked fish, pates, seafood, prime meats, unique salads, health foods plus Belgian waffles, fruit, fabulous desserts...and glass of champagne. Costly, but one of city's biggest, best.

**11**

---

### Bach, Beethoven & Brunch

Watch for **Pittsburgh Center for Arts** classical Sunday brunches from 10 to noon June-July on the lawn at Mellon Park. Bring your own basket or purchase from gourmet booth there $1-$5. **361-0873.**

---

## City

### Pietro's Italian Chophouse
*Hyatt Regency Pgh, Chatham Ctr. Reser sugg. AE,DC,MC,V.* **288-9326.**
**Hours:** 8-12.
**Cost:** Buffet $10, 12 & under $5, 5 & under free.
Hearty North Italian festa begins with appetizer pizzas, antipasto. Eggs to order, fancy waffles, crepes with walnut sauce, ham, chicken, salmon, orange roughy with champagne sauce, great desserts—sundaes, tiramisu. Festive!

### Poli's
*2607 Murray Ave, Sq Hill. AE,CB,DC, MC,V.* **521-6400.**
**Hours:** 11-2.
**Cost:** Buffet $8 inc bev, 10 & under $4.
Stylish buffet in fashionable decor—omelettes to order, bacon, sausage, hand-carved ham, Belgian waffles, bagels with salmon/cream cheese, Scrod Poli style, pasta, chicken, veggies. Additional for smoked salmon, shrimp, Bloody Marys, mimosas. Appetizing spread!

### Reflections
*Sheraton St Sq, AE,DC,MC,V.* **261-2000.**
**Hours:** 10-2.
**Cost:** Buffet $10.95 inc bev, 6-12 1/2 price, under 6 free.
Sunny brunch with spectacular riverfront view; made-to-order omelettes, beef, fish,chicken, pasta, big salad bar. Nice Sunday afternoon.

### Philosopher's Brunch
### Food For the Soul

A unique event takes place Sundays at **La Filipiniana,** 5321 Butler Street in Lawrenceville... brunch from the fine Filipino menu 12:30 to 1:30 followed by inspiring discussions in philosophy 1:30-4:30 conducted by Dr. Lewis Schipper, Chef Teody's husband. Total cost $9.95—food for the body and the soul! For info call **781-8724.**

### Jazz Brunch
### Shadyside Balcony
*Theatre Mall, 5520 Walnut, Shadyside. AE,D,DC,MC,V.* **687-0110.**
**Hours:** 11-3.
**Cost:** Menu $8.95.
The popular Balcony Brunch has a jazz piano/soloist and a wonderful array of food...10 entrees—French toast, eggs Benedict, vegetable frittata, big combo breakfast plus cold buffet with veggies, sweet breads. Sunday meeting place.

### Southern Platter
*6947 Kelly Street, Homewood. No credit cards.* **441-7217.**
**Hours:** 1-6.
**Cost:** Dinner Buffet $8.95 inc bev, 10 & under 1/2 price.
Sunday "soul" buffet—roast beef, Southern fried & smothered chicken, Virginia ham, fish, greens, black-eyed peas, yams, soup/salad bar. Summer barbecue under tent. Homewood tradition.

### The Terrace Room
*Westin William Penn, Mellon Sq. Reser 5 or more. AE,DC,MC,V.* **553-5065.**
**Hours:** 11-2 (also holidays).
**Cost:** Buffet $19.50, 12 & under $11.75, under 5 free.
Glass of champagne/white zinfandel starts off brunch in this splendid room off the grand lobby. Fresh flowers, piano music and an array of 30 gourmet dishes. Eggs Benedict, pates, fresh fruit, smoked fish, roast beef and famous Willam Penn Cheesecake. Elegant.

## SUBURBS

### Abate
*Waterworks, Freeport Rd. AE,D,MC,V.* **781-9550.**
**Hours:** 9-2.
**Cost:** Menu $3-$6. Pleasant brunch inside or on the glass-front patio; pancakes, French toast, all kinds of eggs plus pasta, lunch items.

### Cheat'n Heart Steak House
*Holiday Inn, Wm Penn Hwy, Monroeville. AE,D,MC,V.* **372-1022.**
**Hours:** 10-2.
**Cost:** Buffet $10.95, 6-12 $4.95; Sr Cit $8.95. Breakfast items–Belgian waffles, sausage, bacon, ham–plus hot dishes, pasta, desserts in colorful decor.

### Chestnut Ridge Inn
*Rt 22, Blairsville. Reser sugg. AE,D,DC, MC,V.* **459-7191.**
**Hours:** 11-2.
**Cost:** Menu $10.95, 12 & under $5.95, Sr Cit $8.95.
Belgian waffles with toppings, omelettes, breakfast meats, ham, beef, vegetables, desserts in warm country club setting.

### Dingbat's
*Fox Chapel: Waterworks* **781-7727.** *Robinson Twp: Towne Ctr* **787-7010.** *Ross Park Mall* **369-0440.** *AE,D,DC,MC,V.*
**Hours:** 10-2.
**Cost:** Buffet $10.95, under 12 free. Lavish spread including omelettes, eggs Benedict, pancakes, waffles, chicken,

### Big Holiday Buffets

In addition to their usual Sunday buffets, the **Harley Hotel,** Penn Hills, has festive feasts from 11-7 Thanksgiving, Easter and Mother's Day. Smoked ham, round of beef, lamb, seafood Newburg, salads, desserts $14.95; 12/under $7.95. Sr Cit 10%. Reser. AE,D,DC,MC,V. **244-1600.**

### Brunchin' On the River

#### Misty Harbour
*19th & River Rd, Sharpsburg. AE,D, MC,V.* **781-4222.**
**Hours:** 10-3 Summer.
**Cost:** Buffet $11.95, 12/under $7.95. A unique brunch on 300-ft boat & blue canopied barge with wonderful river view...you can take your plate out on deck. Big spread—omelettes pancakes, ham plus roast beef, salads. Ship ahoy!

crabcakes, shrimp, lox, pastries & cheese cake, A winner!

### Elephant Restaurant & Bar
*5242 Clairton Blvd, Rt 51, Pleasant Hills. Reser sugg. AE,MC,V.* **885-0151.**
**Hours:** 10-2.
**Cost:** Buffet $9.95, 6-12 50c per yr, under 6 free.
Complete buffet in trendy favorite—omelettes, waffles, eggs Benedict, salad, fajitas, ham, beef, chicken specialties plus bottomless glass of champagne—$3.95.

### Fox Chapel Yacht Club
*1366 Old Freeport Road, Fox Chapel. Reser sugg. AE,MC,V.* **963-8881.**
**Hours:** 10-2.
**Cost:** Buffet $13.95; under 10, $7.95. Dining with a pleasant riverview. Vast array of breakfast/lunch items—10 hot including carved beef/ham, 30 salads, fresh veggies, fruit, cheese, 25 desserts. Good Sunday experience.

### Harley Hotel
Off Rodi Road, Penn Hills. AE,D,DC, MC,V. **244-1600. Hours:** 9-2. **Cost:** Buffet $6.95, 10-5, $5.25; 5 & under free. For the breakfast lover...a big buffet in Rivers Three diningroom with pleasant windowfront view. Omelettes, crepes, eggs every way, hash browns, bacon, sausage, pastries.

11

# Suburbs

### Houlihan's
*Ft Couch/Washington Rd, Bethel Pk*
**831-9797**. *300 Mall Blvd, Monrv* **373-8520**. *AE,D,DC,MC,V.*
**Hours:** Sat/Sun 9-2.
**Cost:** Buffet $6.99, chldrn 5-10, $3-$4; under 5 free.
Bountiful buffet with breakfast items inc. omelette bar, Belgian waffles, fresh fruit, plus beef stroganoff, chicken a la king, pastries, puddings.

### Longnecker's
*Holiday Inn, Greentree. AE,CB,D,DC, MC,V.* **922-8100.**
**Hours:** 10-2.
**Cost:** Buffet $14.95, Sr Cit $12.95, 6-12, $5.95, under 6 free.
Big casual, glass-walled room; hearty chicken, carved beef, ham plus eggs to order, salads, dessert bar.

### Max & Erma's
*1910 Cochran Road, Greentree. AE,D, DC,MC,V.* **344-4449.**
**Hours:** 10-2:30
**Cost:** Buffet: $9.95; 5-12, $5.95; under 5 $3.95.
Casual, homey. Ham, chicken, beef, smoked salmon, oysters Rockefeller, peel 'n eat shrimp, salads, mousse, fruit.

### Oxford Dining Room
*Radisson Hotel, Monroeville Mall. AE,DC, MC,V.* **373-7300.**
**Hours:** 9:30-2.
**Cost:** Buffet $11.95; 6-12, $6.25; under 5, $1 yr.
Popular family brunch in warm Colonial room with hot entrees, breakfast goodies, omelettes and steamship round of beef, chicken, seafood, fabulous desserts i.e. mousse, trifle.

### Naples Station
*2723 Stroschein Rd, Monrv. AE,D,DC, MC,V.* **372-1744.**
**Hours:** Breakfast/Brunch 9-3.
**Cost:** $5.95-$8.95, 12 & under $3.95.

Breakfast items til 11:30 followed by buffet—hot/cold pastas, beef, ham, lamb ...and Moia's delicious Italian pastries.

### Papa J's
*200 E Main St, Carnegie. AE,DC,MC,V.* **429-7272.**
**Hours:** 10:30-2.
**Cost:** $8.95, 12 & under, $4.95.
Big breakfast buffet with omlettes, pasta frittata, waffles with brandied peach, cherry, raspberry sauce, eggs, ham, sausage, bacon.

### Pastel's
*Royce Hotel, Thorn Run Rd, Coraopolis, near Airport.* **262-2400.**
**Hours:** 10-2.
**Cost:** $12.95; 5-12, $5.95; Sr Cit $10.95.
Omelettes, waffles, breakfast items plus dinner inc roast beef, ham in lovely mauve/pink decor.

### Pavillion Cafe
*Cranberry Sheraton Inn, Mars. AE,D,DC, MC,V.* **776-6900.**
**Hours:** 10-2.
**Cost:** Buffet $12.95, 6-12 $6.95; under 5 free, Sr Cit $9.50.
Pleasant surroundings, big buffet—ham, beef, spare ribs, seafood newburg, omelettes, Belgian waffles, salads, fruits & ice cream bar.

---

## Festive Buffets

### Servico Holiday Inns
100 Lytton Ave, Oakland **682-6200**. Braddock Hills **247-2700**. Greentree **922-8100**. N Hills **366-5200**. Moon **262-3600**. Meadowlands. Washington **222-6200**. AE,DC,MC,V.
**Hours:** 10-2.
**Cost:** $9.95-$13.95, special rates for Chldrn, Sr Cit. Sunday Brunch a specialty at these Holiday Inn tables laden with breakfast/lunch dishes in pleasant ambience.

# Budget

## Prime House
*Greentree Marriott, Greentree. AE,D,DC, MC,V.* **922-8400.**
**Hours:** 8-1:30.
**Cost:** Buffet $9.95, 12 & under $4.95, under 5 free.
Appetizing breakfast buffet in plush room with fruit, biscuits, omelettes made to order, eggs Benedict, blintzes, bread pudding, pies, mousse.

## River Room
*Sewickley Country Inn, 801 Ohio River Blvd. AE,D,DC,MC,V.* **741-4300.**
**Hours:** 10:30-2.
**Cost:** Buffet $10.95, 6-12 $5.95, under 6 free, Sr Cit $8.95.
Charming atmosphere for roast beef/ham. pasta, waffles, omelettes, sundae bar.

## Shajor
*422 McMurray Road, Bethel Park. AE, MC,V. Reser sugg.* **833-4800.**
**Hours:** 10-2.
**Cost:** Buffet $10.95, under 12 $5.50.
Creative menu in elegant gray-mauve contemporary decor. French toast, waffles, omelettes, bacon, sausage, fish, chicken, pasta, salads, desserts.

## TGI Friday's
*240 Mall Blvd, Monroeville* **372-6630.**
*2800 Oxford Dr, Bethel Pk* **854-5610.**
*5300 Corp Drive, McCandless* **367-1101.**
*AE,D,DC,MC,V.*
**Hours:** 10-3.
**Cost:** Menu $4.99-$7.50, Child $2.49.
Lively brunch in colorful Art Nouveau; croissants, 3-layer omelettes, Belgian waffles, Eggs/Tenderloin Benedict.

## Vernon's
*South Hills Vilg; Ft Couch Rd, Bethel Pk Reser 6/more. AE,D,DC,MC,V.* **531-3688.**
**Hours:** 10-2.
**Cost:** Buffet $9.95; 12 & under 35c yr.
Free Champagne/ Bloody Mary/Screwdriver at big brunch long on breakfast items—eggs, homemade waffles, plus meats, seafood, salad/sundae bar. Also limited menu.

---

### Hot, Hot Brunch

## Mad Mex
*370 Atwood at Bates. Oakland. AE, MC,V.* **681-5656.**
**Hours:** Sat & Sun 11-3.
**Cost:** $5-$6 plus menu.
You can join the urban yuppie scene for weekend brunch at this hot, hot bar/restaurant. They turn out delicious Cal-Mex hueoves rancheros, breakfast burritos, omelettes, French toast and eggs Benedict with spinach & chorizo sausage. Great scene. (See Review)

---

## BUDGET BRUNCH

## Applebee's
*Edgewood Towne Ctr* **731-9782.** *Greentree Rd* **276-9166.** *McKnight Rd, N Hills* **369-8418.** *Lebanon Ch Rd, West Mifflin* **653-9437.** *Rt 19 S, McMurray* **942-4870.**
**Hours:** 10-3.
**Cost:** Menu $2.99-$6.
Lots of good dishes from breakfast platters to spinach & artichoke Benedict $4.79, steak & eggs $5.99. Also French toast, Mexican breakfast, eggs/omelettes. Good spread.

## Bagel Nosh
*5885 Forbes, Squirrel Hill. MC,V.* **521-5834.**
**Hours:** 8-9 pm.
**Cost:** Menu $2-$8.
Brunch on your own from the menu at this popular deli. 12 kinds of bagels—with eggs, cheese, pastrami, corn beef, in French toast, noshes. Full deli menu and cheesecake, of course.

## Eat 'n Park
*43 city/suburban sites. AE,D,MC,V.* **923-1000.**
**Hours:** *Breakfast Buffet 7:30-11, Brunch 11-2.* **Cost:** *Breakfast $4.59, Brunch $6.30, 6-10 1/2 price. 5 & under free.*

**11**

## Budget

Breakfast buffet–scrambled eggs, baked goods, biscuits, fresh fruit...followed by brunch with additional hot entrees–chicken, ham, salads, pasta. Go early.

### Elbow Room
5744 Ellsworth, Shadyside. D,MC,V. **441-5222.**
**Hours:** 11-3.
**Cost:** Menu $1.50-$6.
Informal Shadyside brunch—omelettes, soups, burgers, salads—summer patio.

### Hartner's
*Rt 19, n of Cranberry Mall. AE,D,DC, MC,V.* **931-7999.**
**Hours:** 8:30-11:30 (also Sat).
**Cost:** Buffet $3.95-$7.95, 8 & under 1/2 price.
Breakfast—Belgian waffles, French toast, donuts, bread pudding, fruit, cereal—plus 11:30-2 buffet with hot entrees, ham, pasta, veggies.

### IKEA
*Robinson Twp: Robinson Town Centre. AE,D,DC,MC,V.* **747-0747.**
**Hours:** 10-2 (also Sat).
**Cost:** Buffet $4.99 ; under 10, $1.99.
Brunch with a Swedish touch in popular furniture store's gourmet deli. Bacon, sausage, Swedish meatballs, omelettes, desserts, delicious pastries.

### King's Family Restaurants
*Various suburban sites. Some take credit cards.*
**Hours:** Open 24 hours.
**Cost:** $3-$5.
Good family brunch in cheerful surroundings. Famous for all-day breakfast—waffles, hot cakes, eggs plus dinners.

### Max & Erma's
5533 Walnut St, Shadyside. AE,CB,D, DC,MC,V. **681-5775.**
**Hours:** 11:30-2:30.
**Cost:** $4-$6.95.

---

### For Pancake Lover– City's Best

#### Pamela's
5813 Forbes, Squirrel Hill **422-9457.**
3703 Forbes, Oakland **683-4066.**
5527 Walnut, Shadyside **683-1003.**
No credit cards.
**Hours:** 7 days 7-7, Walnut & Sq Hill Mon-Sat 8-4. Sun 9-2.
**Cost:** Menu $2.95-$6.95. Long lines for breakfast specials at these favorite eateries—best pancakes in town ...walnut, strawberry, banana with whipped cream; sausage, bacon, sandwiches, salads at low prices.

---

Popular, brassy 2nd floor. Omelettes, eggs Benedict, lunch items, sundae, pasta bars.

### Star of India
*412 S Craig St, Oakland. AE,MC,V.* **681-5700.**
**Hours:** 12-3.
**Cost:** $6.95, 12 & under $4.95. Spice up your Sunday with a rare Indian buffet ...chicken tandoori, lamb/chicken curry, tarka daal (lentils & garlic), raita (yogurt & cucumber), wonderful breads, other aromatic Indian dishes.

### What's Cookin' at Casey's
*608 Allegheny River Blvd, Oakmont. MC,V.* **826-1400.**
**Hours:** 8-2.
**Cost:** Menu $3-$5.
Cozy, country breakfast til 2. Hotcakes, eggs, French toast, omelettes with 3 fillings, corned beef & hash plus lunch menu.

# Open On Sunday

Included are restaurants in major city areas. Also check Best of the Suburbs.
B–Brunch, L–Lunch, D–Dinner, LS–Late Supper. Inexp–$10/under, Mod–$10-$20,
Exp–$20/over.

| | Address | Phone | Cuisine | Price | B | L | D | LS | Hours |
|---|---|---|---|---|---|---|---|---|---|
| **DOWNTOWN/STRIP** | | | | | | | | | |
| Brandy's | Penn & 24th | 566-1000 | Amer | Mod-Exp | | | D | LS | 3-11 |
| Chinatown Inn | 522 Third | 261-1292 | Chin | Inex-Mod | | | D | LS | 2-10 |
| Crewsers | 15th/Smallmn | 281-3680 | Amer | Mod | B | L | D | LS | 10-12 |
| Orchard Cafe | Vista Hotel | 281-8162 | Eur-Am | Mod | B | L | D | | 6:30-10 |
| Jakes Above Sq | 430 Market | 338-0900 | Cont | Mod-Exp | | | D | | 4-10 |
| Liang's Hunan | Vista Hotel | 471-1688 | Chin | Mod-Exp | | L | D | | 11:30-10 |
| Mick McGuire's | Market Sq | 642-7526 | Irish | Inex-Mod | B | L | D | | 10:30-7 |
| Morton's | 625 Liberty | 261-7141 | Amer | Exp | | | D | | 5-10 |
| Pietro's | Hyatt Pgh | 288-9326 | Ital | Mod-Exp | B | L | D | LS | 6:30-11 |
| Primanti's | 46 18th St | 263-2142 | Amer | Inex | B | L | D | LS | til 5am |
| Promenade | Hilton Hotel | 391-4600 | Amer | Mod | B | L | D | | 7-5 |
| Roland's | 1904 Penn | 261-3401 | Amer | Inex-Mod | | L | D | | 11-10 |
| Ruddy Duck | Bigelow Apts | 281-3825 | Amer | Mod | B | L | D | LS | 7-12 |
| Ruth's Chris | PPG #6 | 391-4800 | Amer | Exp | | | D | | 5-9 |
| Seventh St Grille | 130 7th St | 338-0303 | Amer | Inex-Mod | | L | D | LS | 12-2am |
| Spaghetti Whs | 2601 Smallmn | 261-6511 | Ital | Inex-Mod | | L | D | | 12-10 |
| Sterling's | Hilton Hotel | 391-4600 | Cont | Mod-Exp | | | D | | 5-11:30 |
| Terrace Room | Wm Penn | 553-5235 | Cont | Mod-Exp | B | L | D | LS | 6-11 |
| Top Triangle | USX Bldg | 471-4100 | Amer | Mod-Exp | | | D | | 4-9 |
| **STATION SQUARE** | | | | | | | | | |
| Bobby Rubino's | Commerce Ct | 642-7427 | Amer | Inex-Mod | | L | D | | 11-9 |
| Cheese Cellar | Freight Hse | 471-3355 | Amer | Inex-Mod | B | | D | LS | 10:30-11 |
| Gandy Dancer | Landmark Blg | 261-1717 | Amer | Inex | | L | D | LS | 2:30-10 |
| Gr Concourse | Landmark Blg | 261-1717 | Amer | Mod-Exp | B | | D | | 10-9 |
| Houlihan's | Freight Hse | 232-0302 | Amer | Mod | B | L | D | LS | 11-11 |
| Kiku's | Commerce Ct | 765-3200 | Jap | Mod | | L | D | | 12-10 |
| Reflections | Sheraton Hotel | 261-2000 | Amer | Mod-Exp | B | | | | 10-3 |
| River Cafe | Freight Hse | 765-2795 | Amer | Mod | | L | D | | 12-9 |
| Sesame Inn | Freight Hse | 281-8282 | Chin | Mod | | L | D | | 12-9 |
| Tequila Junct | Freight Hse | 261-3265 | Mex-Am | Inex-Mod | | L | D | | 12-10 |
| Waterfall Ter | Sheraton Hotel | 261-2000 | Amer | Mod | B | L | D | LS | 6am-12 |
| **MT WASHINGTON** | | | | | | | | | |
| GeorgetownInn | 1230 Grandview | 481-4424 | Amer | Mod | | | D | | 4-10 |
| Grandview Sal | 1212 Grandview | 431-1400 | Amer | Inex-Mod | | L | D | LS | 11-12 |
| LeMont | 1114 Grandview | 431-3100 | Cont | Exp | | | D | | 4-9:30 |
| **OAKLAND** | | | | | | | | | |
| Ali Baba | 404 S Craig | 682-2829 | Mid-E | Inex | | | D | | 4-10 |
| Cafe Sam | 5242 Baum Blvd | 621-2000 | Con/Am | Mod | | | D | | 5-10 |
| Duranti's | 128 N Craig | 682-1155 | Amer | Mod | B | | | | 11-8 |
| Foster's | 100 Lytton | 682-6200 | Amer | Mod-Exp | B | L | D | LS | 7:30-11 |
| Khalil's | 4757 Baum | 683-4757 | Mid-E | Inex-Mod | | | D | LS | 4:30-11 |
| Mad Mex | 370 Atwood | 681-5656 | Mex | Inex | B | L | D | LS | 11am-1am |
| More | 214 N Craig | 621-2700 | Cont | Mod-Exp | | | D | | 5-9 |
| Museum Cafe | 4400 Forbes | 622-3225 | Amer | Inex-Mod | B | | | | 12-2 |
| Samreny's | 4808 Baum | 682-1212 | Mid-E | Inex-Mod | | | D | | 4:30-9:30 |
| Star Of India | 412 S Craig | 681-5700 | Indian | Mod | | | D | | 5-10 |

**11**

# Open on Sunday

| | Address | Phone | Cuisine | Price | B | L | D | LS | Hours |
|---|---|---|---|---|---|---|---|---|---|
| **NORTH SIDE** | | | | | | | | | |
| Billy's Bistro | 1720 Lowrie | 231-9277 | Amer | Inex-Mod | | L | D | LS | 11:30-10 |
| Cafe Victoria | 946 Western | 323-8881 | Amer | Mod-Exp | B | L | | | 10-6 |
| Max's Tavern | Middle/Suismon | 231-1899 | Ger | Inex-Mod | | L | D | | 11-8 |
| Park House | 403 E Ohio St | 231-055l | Amer | Inex | | | D | LS | 5:30-2am |
| Penn Brewery | Troy Hill Rd | 237-9402 | Ger | Inex-Mod | | | D | | 2-10 |
| Warhol Cafe | 117 Sandusky | 237-8310 | Amer | Inex | | L | D | | 11-6 |
| **SOUTH SIDE/DORMONT** | | | | | | | | | |
| Abruzzi's | 52 S 10th | 431-4511 | Ital | Mod | | | D | | 4-9 |
| Antonini's | 2700 Jane | 381-9901 | Ital | Mod-Exp | | | D | LS | 5-12 |
| Cafe Allegro | 51 S 12th | 481-7788 | Fr/Ital | Mod | | | D | | 4:30-9:30 |
| Cafe Giovanni | 2302 E Carson | 481-6662 | Ital | Mod-Exp | | | D | | 4:30-9 |
| Chinese/Carson | 1506 E Carson | 431-1717 | Chin | Mod | | | D | | 4-10 |
| City Grill | 2019 E Carson | 481-6868 | Amer | Mod | | | D | | 4:30-10 |
| Davio's(Bchvw) | 2100 Broadway | 531-7422 | Ital | Mod-Exp | | | D | | 4-9 |
| 1889 Cafe | 2017 E Carson | 431-9290 | Amer | Inex | B | L | | | 8:30-2 |
| Hunan Gourmet | 1209 E Carson | 488-8100 | Chin | Inex-Mod | | | D | | 2:30-9:30 |
| Mallorca | 2228 E Carson | 488-1818 | Span | Mod-Exp | | L | D | | 12-10 |
| Margaritaville | 2200 E Carson | 431-2200 | Mex | Inex-Mod | | L | D | LS | 12-2am |
| Paparazzi | 21st/Carson | 488-0800 | Ital | Mod | | L | D | LS | 11-11 |
| Pgh Steak Co | 1924 E Carson | 381-5505 | Amer | Mod | | | D | LS | 4-11 |
| Rumors | 1828 E Carson | 431-4500 | Amer | Mod | | | D | | 4-10 |
| 17th St Cafe | 75 S 17th | 431-9988 | Ital | Mod | | | D | | 5-10 |
| **SHADYSIDE** | | | | | | | | | |
| Artery | 5847 Ellsworth | 361-9473 | Amer | Inex-Mod | | | D | LS | 5-11 |
| Cappy's | 5431 Walnut | 621-1188 | Amer | Inex | B | L | D | LS | 10-2am |
| China Palace | 5440 Walnut | 687-7423 | Chin | Mod | | | D | | 2-9 |
| Cozumel | 5507 Walnut | 621-5100 | Mex | Inex | | L | D | | 12-9 |
| Elbow Room | 5744 Ellsworth | 441-5222 | Amer | Inex | B | L | D | LS | 11-12 |
| Harris Grill | 5747 Ellsworth | 363-0833 | Gr/Amer | Inex | | | D | LS | 11-2am |
| Hot Licks | 5520 Walnut | 683-2583 | Am/Ribs | Inex-Mod | | | D | | 4:30-9 |
| La Feria | 5527 Walnut | 682-4501 | Peruvn | Inex | B | L | | | 9-2 |
| Jimmy Tsang's | 5700 Centre | 661-4226 | Chin | Mod | | | D | | 3:30-9 |
| Max & Erma's | 5533 Walnut | 681-5775 | Amer | Inex | B | L | D | | 11:30-1 |
| Pamela's | 5527 Walnut | 683-1003 | Amer | Inex | B | L | | | 9-2 |
| Pasta Piatto | 736 Bellefonte | 621-5547 | Ital | Mod | | | D | | 3-9 |
| Pgh Deli Co | 728 Copeland | 682-3354 | Deli | Inex | | L | D | | 11-10 |
| Shadyside Balcony | 5520 Walnut | 687-0110 | Amer | Inex-Md | B | | | | 11-3 |
| Sushi Too | 5432 Walnut | 687-8744 | Japan | Inex-Mod | | L | D | | 1-9 |
| Thai Place | 809 Bellefonte | 687-8586 | Thai | Mod | | L | D | | 12-9:30 |
| Szechuan Gourm | 709 Bellefonte | 683-1763 | Chin | Inex-Mod | | | D | | 4:30-10 |
| **SQUIRREL HILL** | | | | | | | | | |
| Bagel Nosh | 5885 Forbes | 521-5834 | Deli | Inex | B | L | D | | 8-8 |
| Gullifty's | 1922 Murray | 521-8222 | Amer | Inex-Mod | B | L | D | LS | 10-12 |
| Pamela's | 5813 Forbes | 422-9457 | Amer | Inex | B | L | | | 9-2 |
| Peking Kitchn | 2018 Murray | 421-1920 | Chin | Inex-Mod | B | L | D | | 11-9:30 |
| Poli's | 2607 Murray | 521-6400 | Amer | Mod-Exp | B | L | D | | 11-9:30 |
| Rhoda's | 2201 Murray | 521-4555 | Deli | Inex | B | L | D | LS | 7-11 |
| Siamese Ktchn | 5846 Forbes | 521-0728 | Thai | Mod | | | D | | 4:30-9 |
| Suzie's | 1704 Shady | 422-8066 | Greek | Inex-Mod | | | D | | 4-9 |
| Sweet Basil | 5882 Forbes | 421-9958 | Amer | Inex-Mod | | | D | | 5-9 |

**12**

Budget eats are the latest food fashion. Pittsburghers are eating out more... but at more reasonable prices. Surprisingly some of Pittsburgh's best restaurants offer budget eats—Early Bird dinners at reduced rates and nightly specials under $10. We've also included lots of other eateries with substantial food from $5-$10.

# Early Birds

## EARLY BIRDS

*You can savour some of the city's best cuisine at these 'Early Bird' dinners with special prices on complete meal...usually at earlier hours. A great way to eat the best for less!*

## Bentley's
*5608 Wilkins Ave, Sq Hill. AE,D,MC,V.* **421-4880.**
**Hours:** Mon-Sat 4-6.
**Cost:** $7.95 inc bev.
Full dinners i.e. pasta, chicken marinara, linguine with clam sauce, chicken breast, liver & onions, scrod with two sides—soup, salad, veg, potato & dessert.

## Del's Bar & Restaurant
*4428 Liberty, Bloomfield. AE,D,MC,V.* **683-1448.**
**Hours:** Mon-Thur 2-8, Fri-Sun 2-5.
**Cost:** $4.50-$5.50.
Pasta, seafood, chicken, veal inc soup, salad, side, ice cream/bev. Lots of food.

## Gandy Dancer
*Landmarks Bldg, Station Sq. AE,DC, MC,V.* **261-1717.**
**Hours:** Mon-Thur 11:30-11pm, Fri til 1.
Fabulous seafood 1/2 price weekdays. Check for bargains on tub of mussels, shrimp, oysters, clams, fish sandwich, $3 up. And fun besides. (See Review)

## Economy—First Class

Accolades to **Duranti's,** 128 Craig St, for better-than-average cuisine at super prices for the Oakland apartment set. Good lunches $3.95-$6, dinners $7.95-$11 and $7.95 dinner specials 7 days from 5-9 make for economical eating. Satisfying traditional dishes—chicken, short ribs, old favorites i.e. Turkey Devonshire, Hot Beef/Turkey Sandwich, homemade soups, old-time jello salads. Delivery to immediate area 2-5 pm. Order before 4pm. **682-1155.**

## Rare Sunday Bird

### Pasta Piatto
*736 Bellefonte St, Shadyside. AE,MC,V.* **621-5547.**
**Hours:** Mon-Fri 4:30-5:45, Sun 3-4:30.
**Cost:** $9.95 & under.
One of the city's best, a unique Sunday—and weekday—"presto pranzo" (early dinner). Entrees change daily...pasta, veal, chicken, seafood...with choice of appetizer, salad & fresh Italian bread. A must!

## Grand Concourse
*Landmarks Bldg, Station Sq. AE,DC,MC, V. Reser.* **261-1717.**
**Hours:** Mon-Sat 4:30-6, Sun 4:30-9.
**Cost:** $9.95-$16.
Elegant dinner with appetizer/salad/soup, dessert & beverage at one of city's top restaurants with choice of four fish, nine other entrees—plus sunset river view. (See Review)

## More
*214 N Craig St, Oakland. AE,MC,V,DC.* **621-2700.**
**Hours:** Mon-Thur 4:30-5:45.
**Cost:** $7.50-$8.50.
Great atmosphere for excellent dinner bargains—choice of 4 entrees—fish, beef, chicken with soup, salad, veg/potato.

## Poli's
*2607 Murray Ave, Sq Hill. AE,DC,MC,V.* **521-6400.**
**Hours:** Tues-Fri 3-5:30.
**Cost:** $8.50-$12.95.
Seafood lovers crowd these early birds. Choice of six entrees with seafood items i.e. lemon sole, scallops, shrimp plus chicken, veal, filet mignon, salmon—with soup, salad, vegetable. Good value. Call **Early Bird Hotline 594-4473** for daily menu. (See Review)

## Minutello's
*226 Shady Ave, Shadyside. AE,D,MC,V.*
**361-9311.**
**Hours:** Mon-Fri 3:30-5:30.
**Cost:** $4.95-$6.95.
Economical daily specials at big oldtime family favorite—pasta, chicken, fish, veal, beef with salad/cole slaw/apple sauce, ice cream, beverage.

## Pleasure Bar
*4729 Liberty Ave, Bloomfield. AE,D, MC, V.* **682-9603.**
**Hours:** Mon-Thur 3:30-7.
**Cost:** $4.95.
Six entrees—pasta, fish, chicken, shrimp, stuffed shells, eggplant with soup, salad, pasta/veg, ice cream, bev. Good deal!

### EARLY BIRDS - SUBURBS

## Birdie's Bar & Restaurant
*4733 Wm Penn Hwy, Rt 22E Monroeville. All credit cards.* **372-9878.**
**Hours:** Mon-Fri 4-5:30.
**Cost:** It pays to eat early here with $2 off every menu item (except the specials) at this popular eatery; big menu—entrees, sandwiches, salads.

## Gino's
*Bourse Shops, Greentree Rd, Scott. AE,D,DC,MC,V.* **279-1414.**
**Hours:** Mon-Thur 4-5:30.
**Cost:** Menu $8-$12.
Six to seven choices of seafood, veal, fowl inc. soup, salad and brunch.

---

## Thursday Special

### Per Favore
*Royal York, 3955 Bigelow Blvd,* Oakland. **681-9147.**
Every Thursday from 4-10 you can sample food from this prestigous restaurant for $25 a couple. Choice of 6-7 entrees, 5 courses—appetizer, side dish, vegetable, dessert. Good buy, great atmosphere.

---

## Rodi Grille House
*204 Rodi Road, Penn Hills. AE,D,MC,V.*
**241-1730.**
**Hours:** Mon-Fri 3-5:30.
**Cost:** $7.95.
Great values at this super fish house featuring fresh fish, chicken, pasta, beef. Includes soup/salad, veg/potato, famous house sour dough bread & sherbet.

## MEALS UNDER $10

### Apollo Cafe
*429 Forbes Ave, Downtown. Mon-Fri 7am-3pm. No credit cards.* **471-3033.**
Unique gourmet fast food—quiche, soup, great shish-kabob, sandwiches, desserts $5-$7. Breakfast $2 up.

### Dave's Lunch
*237 Third Ave, Downtown. Mon-Fri 6:30am-5:30pm. No credit cards.*
**391-2409.**
Favorite downtown lunchroom, $2.50 breakfast. Good soup, chili, burgers with onions & hot peppers. $1.65-$4.

### Federal Building Cafeteria
*2nd fl, Grant/Liberty, Downtown. Mon-Fri 6:30am-4pm. No credit cards.* **261-3660.**
Breakfast, lunch with lots of choices—soup, sandwiches, salad bar, entrees with soup/salad, potato, veggie $3-$4.50.

### First Presbyterian Church
*320 6th Ave, Downtown. Mon-Fri 11am-2pm.* **471-3436.**
Popular business lunch—homemade soups, salads, sandwiches, cakes, pies 75c-$2. Daily hot entrees $3. Great buy!

### Gateway Cafeteria
*Gateway #2, lower level, Downtown. Breakfast 7-10, Lunch 11-2.* **261-9671.**
Underground favorite with workers/shoppers. Delicious breakfast/lunch, hot/cold entrees, sandwiches, salads, homemade desserts, $1-$4. Daily specials $2.95.

**12**

# Meals Under $10

### Best Sandwich In City

Our candidate for the best sandwich in town is the **Seafood Sub** at 40 popular **Subway** outlets all around town. No frills but a delectable mixture...lightly mayonnaised Alaskan King crab & white fish on a tender, freshly-baked Italian bun...we like it with everything—cheese (American white), shredded lettuce, tomato, green peppers, onions, black olives and jalapenos, drizzled with Subway oil/vinegar dressing. A meal in itself with a tingly clear Mountain Dew. 12" sub $4.99, 6" $2.99. Also great-tasting bacon sub, other subs, salads, breakfast buns. $1-$4.29. Most open 11-11. No credit cards.

### Max's Allegheny Tavern

*Middle/Suismon St, N Side. Mon-Thur 11-11, Fri-Sat til 12. Sun 11-8. AE,DC, MC,V.* **231-1899.**
Marvelous German fare in atmospheric old tavern; wursts, sauerbraten, sweet/sour cabbage, great beers. ($4.25-$10) (See Review)

### Original Oyster House

*20 Market Sq, Downtown, Mon-Sat 9am-11, Sit down 10-6* **566-7925.** *Also 801 Liberty, Mon-Fri 10:30-7, Sat 10:30-5* **566-9630.** *No credit cards.*
Historic old saloon with city's best fish sandwich $2.85. Seafood Platter with shrimp, fish, crab, fries & slaw–a meal in itself–$4.75, Oysters, clams, buttermilk and beer. Old Pgh at its best. Eat outside in Market Square.

### Park House

*403 E Ohio St, N Side. 7 days 11:30-2. . AE,DC,MC,V.* **231-0551.**
Old-time barroom, good food—the highest at $6.99. Shrimp, nachos, appetizers, salads, soups, hot/cold sandwiches; good selection of imported beer, coffees.

### Penn Brewery

*Troy Hill Rd, N Side, nr 16th St Bridge. Mon-Sat 11am-12am.AE,MC,V.* **237-9402.**
Believe it or not—wurst plates, pork chops, potato pancakes all well under $10...delicious with wonderful German sides, beer/band fun Tues-Sat. (Review)

### Primanti Brothers

*46 18th St, Strip. Mon-Sat 24 hrs. Sun til 5am.* **263-2142.** *3803 Forbes, Oakland. Mon-Thur 10am-3am, Fri-Sat til 4am, Sun noon-3am.* **621-4444.**
A legend in its own time, favorite of Strip workers, late-nighters. Famous hearty food including meal-in-one sandwich with kolbassi, pastrami, fries and slaw in the sandwich. Good antipasto, chili. $2.75-$6.

### Rosebud

*1650 Smallman. Tues-Sat 11:30-6. Sun 9am-2am. AE,D,DC,MC,V.* **261-2221.**
Also Times Bldg, 336 Fourth Ave, Downtown. *Mon-Fri 7-3. AE,M,V.* **261-0735.**
Coffee/desserts plus full menu—big salads, sandwiches, pizza and entrees from the wood-burning oven at spacious, mod cafe $3-$10. Breakfast/lunch with frittatas, soups, salads at downtown location.

### Spaghetti Warehouse

*2601 Smallman, Strip. Mon-Thur 11-10, Fri-Sat til 11. Sun 12-10. AE,CB,D,DC, MC,V.* **261-6511.**

### Attention Vegetarians!

### East End Co-op Cafe

*7516 Meade St, Pt Breeze. Mon-Fri 11-4, Sat til 5. Sun 12-4.* **242-3598.**
This little cafe run by the East End Co-op natural foods store, is a haven for vegetarians & healthy eaters. You can breakfast, lunch & early sup on whole grain foods, soups, lentel/tofu burgers, salad, carrot cake, organic coffee, herbal

Popular Italian dishes at popular prices in big, fun restaurant with lots of memorabilia, trolley car, brass bed settings. Pasta veal/chicken Parmesan, pizza, antipasto. $3.25-$5.95.

### Richest Restaurant
*140 6th, Downtown. Mon-Sat 9-9, later for Heinz Hall events. AE,D,DC,MC,V.* **471-7799.**
Favorite downtown deli. Blintzes, hot pastrami, Reubens, great corned beef, matzo ball soup, $3-$6. Platters $5.25 & Early Bird dinners from 4-8, $7.15.

### Suzie's
*130 6th St, Downtown. Mon 11-3, Tues-Fri 11-8, show nights Sat 4-8. No credit cards.* **261-6443.** *1704 Shady, Sq Hill. Mon-Thur 11:30-10, Fri & Sat til 11, Sun 4-9. MC,V.* **422-8066.**
Homemade Greek...delicious moussaka, spanakopita, chicken salad with grapes—all under $10. Great food! (See Review)

### Tic-Toc
*1st fl, Kaufmann's Dept Store. Store charge only.* **232-2680.**
Some of the best coffee shop food in town. 99c breakfast, great ham salad, chopped olive/cheese, delicious ice cream, unique coffee soda; also light meals Mon-Thur. $1-$5.

### Trinity Episcopal Church
*325 Oliver. Mon-Fri 11-2.* **232-6404.**
Open since 1914, this church lunchroom offers daily home cooking i.e. veal Parmesan, salisbury steak, meatloaf with vegetables $3.20. Soups, sandwiches, homemade desserts $1-$2

### EAST END

### Alexander's
*5104 Liberty Ave, Bloomfield. Mon-Sat 11-12, Sun 11-11. MC,DC,V.* **682-9824.**
Family Italian—good pasta, crusty Italian bread, Grandpa's delicious homemade tiramisu. Outdoor tables in summer. Lots of dishes under $10. ($5-$13).

---

## For Soda Fountain Fans

### Kennilworth Pharmacy
*5700 Centre, Shadyside. MC,V,D (Cred cards min $10.)* **361-1999.**
**Hours:** Mon-Fri 8-7:30, Sat 8:30-5. Shades of the past at this neighborhood drugstore with an oldtime formica soda fountain/grill and booths in the back. Breakfast 99c. Good soup, sandwiches, meals i.e. spaghetti, chicken, stuffed cabbage —with potato, vegetable—only $2.69! Old time desserts & ice cream sodas (made with pop). Deja vu!

### Ali Baba
*404 S Craig, Oaklnd. Lnch Mon-Fri 11:30-2. Dinr 7 days 4-10.AE,D,MC,V.* **682-2829.**
City's favorite Mid-East fare, a mecca for students, vegetarians; bargains galore at lunch/supper—under $9.95—Shish-ke-bab, hummus, kibbee, Greek salad, falafil, aromatic Arabic coffee. $2.50-$9.

### Bagel Nosh
*5885 Forbes, Sq Hill. Mon-Fri 6:30-9, Sat 8-9, Sun 8-8. D,MC,V.* **521-5834.**
All kinds of bagels plus French toast, pancakes, waffles for $2; sandwiches, salads, eggplant lasagna and chicken—stuffed, barbecued or Parmesan $4-6.

### Bloomfield Bridge Tavern
*4412 Liberty Ave, Bloomfield. Mon-Sat 11-1. AE,D,DC,MC,V.* **682-8611.**
Neighborhood-bar decor, hearty ethnic food—kielbasa, perogi, haluski, kluski, pigs in blanket, 100 imported beers. Inexp—$5.95's the highest.

### Bobby O's
*3716 Forbes, Oakland. 7 days 10-10, Fri-Sat til 12am. No cred cards.* **621-1962.**
Big, friendly place, 3 flrs, with hearty char-grilled chicken sandwiches, burgers, 'wild wings,' big salads, 75c basket of fries. All under $4. Good upscale 'fast' food.

**12**

# Meals Under $10

### D'Amico's
*4744 Liberty Ave, Bloomfield. 7 days 11-10. D,MC,V.* **682-2523.**
Neighborhood treasure, big, pleasant with real homemade pasta, Italian specialties, sandwiches, pizza, gelato. $4.50-$14.

### Eat 'n Park
43 locations, most open 24 hrs. AE,D, MC,V. **923-1000.**
'Fast' family eatery cut above the rest. Breakfast anytime, burgers, salads, entrees in $4-$5 range. Soup/Salad Bar $4.29. Free Smiley cookies for kids. Sun Brunch 11-2 $6.29.

### Hemingway's
*3911 Forbes, Oakland. 7 days 11-2.* AE,DC,MC,V. **621-4100.**
Good, inexpensive fare in busy university atmosphere; great pastas (try sausage diablo), chicken. Daily features Mon–pasta, Tues–steak...and poetry, Fri–crab, fancy desserts. $4.25-$12.

### Howard Johnson
*3401 Blvd of Allies, Oakland. MC,V.* **681-6300.**
Dependable for locals, travelers. Great blueberry pancakes, hot dogs on toasted buns, famous ice cream, $3-$9. All you can eat Seafood Buffet—fish, clams or shrimp Wed, Fri, Sat $6.99. Great deal! Patio in good weather.

### Italian Oven
*5859 Ellsworth, Shadyside* **361-6836.** *1700 Penn, Strip* **765-2440.** *Edgewood Towne Ctr* **241-6960.** *Loehmann's Plaza, Monrv* **373-6836.** *Shops Station Sq* **261-2111.** *Ross Towne Ctr, N Hills* **366-1800.** *Century Sq, W Mifflin* **653-9333.** *Sun-Thur 11-10, Fri-Sat til 11.* AE,D,MC,V.
Bright, popular eateries with black/red Italian theme, 23 pastas, crisp flavorful pizzas from wood-fired brick oven, chicken, fish, soups, salads—terrific vegetable, chicken/pepper salad. $4.25-$8.50. Kids love it!

### Foster's, Holiday Inn, Univ
*100 Lytton Ave, Oakland.* **682-6200.**
One of the city's best-kept secrets is the terrific Hungry Hour at **Foster's** in Oakland's Holiday Inn. With a beverage you can get wonderful food for $1 a plate at a 5-7 Happy Hour Mon-Fri. And what a line-up! **Mon:** Mexican tacos/rice. **Tues:** Italian pasta/antipasto. **Wed:** BBQ Wings/ Ribs. **Thur:** Beef/cheese sandwich, potato salad. **Fri:** Peel 'n Eat Shrimp ...marvelously spiced...plus great New Orleans gumbo, dirty rice. You can't go wrong here. And in summer, a breezy outside patio!

### La Feria
*5527 Walnut Street, Shadyside (above Pamela's). Mon-Fri 10-9. Cappuccino bar Sun 9-2. D,MC,V.* **682-4501.**
Authentic Peruvian/Latin Amer food—black beans, salads, sandwiches, vegetarian and extraordinary light lunch/dinner in the midst of intriguing Peruvian emporium. (See Review)

### Mad Mex
*370 Atwood St, Oakland. Sun-Wed 11-11, Thur-Sat til 1. AE,MC,V.* **681-5656.** *7905 McKnight Rd, Ross. 7 days 11-1.* **366-5656.** *2000 Smallman, Strip.* **261-6565.**
They come from all over for terrific Cal-Mex cuisine...including enchalada/ burrito plates with salad, sour cream, guacamole for $6-$7. Wonderful beers. (See Review).

### Moscow Nights
*1722 Murray Ave, Sq Hill. Mon-Thur 11-10, Fri & Sat til 11-12. AE.* **521-5005.**
There are lots of unique dishes at this charming Russian/Israeli eatery. Cold salads, delicious soups (best borscht in town!), meat/cheese blintzes under $5 & dinner under $10. (See Review).

## Pamela's
*3703 Forbes, Oakland* **683-4066.** *5527 Walnut, Shadyside* **683-1003.** *5813 Forbes, Sq Hill* **422-9457.** *Mon-Sat 8-4, Sun 9-2. Oakland 7 days 7-7.*
Casual East End breakfast/lunch favorite. Good low prices for best hot cakes in own; sandwiches, light fare. $2-$5.

## Paski's
*2533 Penn Ave, Strip. AE,DC,MC,V.* **566-2782.**
Big Fri nite Fish Fry 5:30-10. All-you-can-eat broiled/fried with potatos, slaw $5.95.

## Pittsburgh Deli Co
*728 Copeland, Shadyside. Sun, Tues, Thur 11-10, Wed, Fri, Sat til 12am. No credit cards.* **682-3354.**
Kosher sandwiches, matzoh ball, chicken noodle soup, sides, knishes, big bowls of great vegetarian chili—a meal in itself; wonderful raspberry mundle (75c). $2-$7.

## Rhoda's
*2201 Murray, Sq Hill. Sun-Thur 7-11, Fri-Sat til 12.* **521-4555.**
Real deli food, homemade soup, potato pancakes, Reuben platter, stuffed kishke, chicken, under $5. Kids Menu $2 & under.

## Ritter's Diner
*5221 Baum Blvd, Bloomfield. 7 days 24 hours. No credit cards.* **682-4852.**
A Pgh tradition for good solid food around

---

## Bagel Mania

### Brueggers Bagels
*Downtown, Oakland, Sq Hill, South Hills, North Hills. Mon-Sat 6am-8pm, Sun 8am-6pm. No credit cards.*
An interesting way to meal—on bagel sandwiches at these hot new bagel shops, 9 locations. Bagel sandwiches in many different versions...chicken & tuna salad, garden vegetable, lox & turkey, flavored cream cheeses. Also soup, desserts in casual cafe atmosphere. Eat in, take-out. Under $3.

---

## As The Chicken Turns

### Boston Chicken
*5889 Forbes, Sq Hill* **521-8550,** *5200 Baum Blvd, Shadyside* **683-9752,** *4826 McKnight Rd, N Hills* **369-7750.** *3776 Wm Penn Hwy, Monrv* **373-7010,** *1736 Washington Rd, Upper St Clair* **854-5840.** *Sun-Thur 11-9, Fri-Sat til 10. MC,V.*
The rotisserie chicken craze has hit Pittsburgh with a bang...particularly **Boston Rotisserie** with meals well under $5. Side dishes include scrumptious butternut squash, stuffing, cornbread, cranberry/walnut relish, real mashed potatoes and a very good pot pie. Also chicken salad, sandwiches. Meals $4-$6. (P.S. Many loyal fans still prefer the popular **KFC's Kentucky Fried Chicken** all over town. They have their own version of Rotisserie Gold plus quick drive-in service.)

---

the clock. Breakfast bargains—buck-wheat cakes plus hearty meat/potato entrees, daily specials, sandwiches, salads. $2-$5.

## Tessaro's
*4601 Liberty Ave, Bloomfield. Mon-Sat 11-12am. AE,D,DC,MC,V.* **682-6809.**
Fans have found you can eat budget here if you watch the menu. Wonderful burgers, salads, barbecue chicken, chili, famous sandwiches in the $5-$10 range. Try Mon Mexican specials! (See Review.)

## Union Grill
*413 S Craig St, Oaklnd. Mon-Thur 11-11. Fri-Sat til 12. AE,D,DC,MC,V.* **681-8620.**
Handsome, cheery bar/restaurant with good buys on burgers, appetizers and hearty $5-$6 salads, entrees under $7 with good meat, pasta, garlic potatoes.

**12**

# Meals Under $10

MEALS UNDER $10 - SUBURBS

### Abate Seafood Co
*Waterworks, Freeport Rd, Fox Chapel. Sun-Thur 11:30-11, Fri-Sat til 12.. AE,CB, DC,MC,V.* **781-9550.**
Good buys on select items at this super Italian/seafood house. Famous Fish Sandwich with slaw $4.95, super-size $5.95. "Piccolo" pasta $5.95-$7.95 and big house salad $2.95 (great low-cal dressing). Hearth-baked pizzas $5.75-$6.50. Special prices on Wed Shrimp Feast. (See Review)

### Armstrong's
*Galleria, 1500 Washington Rd, Mt Lebanon. Mon-Sat 11-11, Sun 12-8. No credit cards.* **341-9460.**
Long lines at this door for great prices. Big menu of soups, salads, sandwiches, hoagies, calzones plus steak, chicken, veal, seafood, pasta. $4.25-$8.95.

### Clara's Pittsburgh Pierogies
*2717 Library Road, Rt 88 off 51, Castle Shannon. Mon-Fri 7-5, Sat 10-5. No credit cards.* **882-3555.**
Taste some of the city's best ethnic food at this little 28-seat restaurant famous for perogi, stuffed cabbage, haluski, kielbasa & sauerkraut. Also stuffed peppers, potato pancakes, soups, sandwiches and homestyle breakfast. ($2-$5).

### Old Country Buffet
*Southland Shop Ctr* **653-2422.** *N Hills Village* **364-5060.** *Gr Southern Shop Ctr* **257-8640.** *Mon-Thur 11-8, Fri-Sat til 9. Sun 8-9.*
Old-fashioned home-style buffet—chicken & dumplings, country fried steak, lasagna, homemade rolls, salad bar, ice cream machine. $5-$6.69. Sat-Sun breakfasts 8-11, $5.29. Good buy.

---

## Senior Discounts For 55 & Over

Many restaurants feature discounts to seniors 55 & over...but often you have to ask.
**10% off:** Chili's, Damon's (also 20c coffee/tea), Howard Johnson, Long John Silver, most McDonald's, Ponderosa Steak House, Wendy's. Roy Rogers (Wed only). Hoss's 20% Mon-Sat 1:30-4. Chi-Chi's $1 off.
**Special Menu/Reduced Portions:** Bob Evans, Eat 'n Park, King's Family Restaurant.
**Discount Card:** Elby's (62 & up), Old Country Buffets.

---

### What's Cookin' at Casey's
*608 Allegheny River Blvd, Oakmont. Mon-Thur 7am-9, Fri-Sat til 9:30. Sun 8-8. D,MC,V.* **826-1400.**
Country cozy, big variety sandwiches, casseroles, pizza, strombolis. Big on breakfast. $4-$10. Worth the stop.

**For more meals under $10 check the Oriental/Asian section and Mexican and Mid-Eastern restaurants.**

# COFFEEHOUSES/TEAS

**13**

The coffeehouse craze has hit the Burgh with a bang! Gathering places for singles, students, young, old, they spill out onto the sidewalk adding a new dimension to the city's social scene. They're great places in which to read in private or strike up a conversation. Happily most serve light fare along with coffee/tea, pastries and desserts. Expect no credit cards.

## Coffeehouses

### Arabica
*733 Copeland St, Shadyside* **621-4401.**
*5887 Forbes, Sq Hill* **422-2226.** *420 S Craig, Oakland* **621-2233.** *1501 East Carson, S Side* **381-8330.** *Sun-Thur 7-12am, Fri-Sat til 1.*
It's pronunced ara-BE-ka and they're springing up all over. Informal, crowded, they're student favorites with fast turnover, art on the walls; good values in cappuccino espresso–99c to $2.75 for a mocha coffee-milk. veggie salads, delicious biscotti, pastries.

### Beehive Coffee House
*14th & Carson. S Side. Sun-Thur 8:30am (Sat-Sun 9am) til 1am, Fri-Sat til 3.* **488-4483.**
The granddaddy of them all with a loony-toon touch, psychedelic tables, chairs by local artists. Fabulous coffee/teas (try the rich Kenya) terrific cheesecake, desserts. Lots of local color over chess, parchesi, poetry, occasional happening.

### Beehive Oakland
*3807 Forbes, Oakland. Mon-Thur 7-12am, Fri til 1. Sat 8:30-1. Sun 8:30-12.* **687-9428.**

---

### Coffee At the Warhol

#### All In Good Taste
*Warhol Museum, Lower level, 117 Sandusky, N Side. Wed & Sun 11-6, Thur-Sat 11-8. MC, V.* **237-8310.**
A lovely respite after doing the 7-story museum...or for light dining ...in this avant garde cafe as innovative as the museum. A gourmet menu by Robert Sendall (former Greenbrier/Heinz family chef) is surprisingly economical. Relax to the strains of Sinatra as you enjoy grilled focaccia, green & grain salads, fresh fruit, chef's desserts (luscious apple bundt cake!) with your coffee. Coke in the original bottle, cookies & milk for the kids!

---

### Book Lovers Cafe

Book lovers can stop for a bite from breakfast to dusk as they browse amid the 100,000 books at the Barnes & Noble super bookstore at 6th & Smithfield (old Gimbel's building), entrance on Smithfield. The **Espresso Cafe** is open during store hours Mon-Fri 7am-9pm, Sat 9-9, Sun 11-6. **742-4324.** There's another big new two-story Barnes & Noble superstore & cafe at 1723 Murray Ave, Squirrel Hill, open 7 days from 9am to 11pm. **521-3600.** Both serve light food along with coffee & desserts.

---

In the heart of Oakland's student/urban scene...it's always buzzin'. The castle-like old firehouse has two floors with study & conversation upstairs and culture on the first level—poetry/play reading Thur & Sun nights and an art/classic cinema where you can sip 'n eat while you watch a film. Coffees plus veggie snacks, cheesecake. espresso, $1-$3.

### Bunznudders
*305 S Craig St. Sun-Thur 8am-10pm, Fri & Sat til midnite.* **683-9993.**
Wonderful coffees, cappuccino, ice cream, yogurt (some low-cal), croissant sandwiches. Homemade lemonade and the best sticky buns in town. Try a cinnamon swirl ($1.35) with a double cappuccino $2.25. Freshly-made breads including long French loaves. Quieter, nice vista.

### Caffe Zio
116 S Bouquet St, Oakland. Mon-Fri 7-6. **621-7440.**
Fans from Oakland's medical center swear by this little cappuccino/espresso bar, a La Prima outlet. No seating but you can enjoy paintings from two long stand-up counters; also pastry, focaccia sandwiches, pizza, biscotti. $1.25-$3.

# Coffeehouses

## Coffee Tree

*5840 Forbes, Sq Hill. Mon-Thur 7-12am, Fri til 1. Sat 8-1. Sun 8-12am.* **422-4427.**
A more serene taster's choice with old-fashioned dark wood decor. They roast all their own coffees (80c-$2.75) for smooth cafe mocha. Pastries plus delicious, fat-free cinnamon-raisin briegels; super sandwiches (chicken in light mayonnaise, crusty bread $3.99), soups. Outdoor seats in the shade.

## El Dolce Cafe

*4525 Liberty/Taylor (acr from Tessaro's), Bloomfield. Mon-Sat 8-12am.* **681-5225.**
A pleasant, hunter-green room with hardwood floors, an old-fashioned aura and an atmospheric front window view. Homemade Italian pastries, lovely tiramisu, hot/cold sandwiches—sweet peppers, sausage, chicken Parmesan prosciutto—choose your bread & ingredients. Also delightful day-long tea with cucumber sandwiches, scones. ($2-$4.50).

## Java Jeff's

*2301 Murray Ave, Squirrel Hill. Sun- Thur 8-12am, Fri & Sat til 1.* **421-5282.**
Pleasant room with a window on Murray and local art for sale; Gourmet coffees/teas 75c-$2.50, specialty—cafe mocha with a dash of chocolate. Gourmet cakes, pastries, croissant sandwiches. Acoustic music Tues-Wed, magic card trading Thur nights.

---

### Washday Brews

#### Always a Monday

*2330 E Carson St, S Side. 7-10 daily.* **481-9274.**
Named for the laundry next door... this is a good place to sip a cup while your clothes spin dry. Also desserts under $3 and video games, juke box & things for the kids to do. Neat trick.

---

### What To Order

We prefer a plain (or double) cappuccino or just a good cup of brew. But here's the typical coffeehouse lineup...almost all available in decaf.
**Espresso** Small cup with a big wallop of strong concentrated coffee with a bitter taste. Sugar optional.
**Cafe Mocha** Cappuccino with a taste of chocolate.
**Cappuccino** Espresso smoothed with steamed, foamed milk. You can shake cocoa or cinnamon on top.
**Caffe Latte** A longer drink of espresso with hot foamy milk.
**Cocoaccino** Chocolate espresso.

---

## La Prima Espresso

*205 21st Strip. Mon-Fri 6:30-4:30, Sat-Sun til 3.* **281-1922.** *602 Liberty, Downtown* **471-4590.** *Galleria* **341-6620.** *Greater Pgh Intl Airport* **472-5080.**
Italian-style espresso bars all over town with the city's finest coffees. Pastries inc. delicious mele—freshly sliced apples in puff pastry and focaccia with eggplant & sweet pepper ($1.50-$2.50). Most are stand-up with 'coffee carts' at USX Tower, CMU campus. Great espresso.

## Mystery Lovers Bookshop Cafe

*514 Allegheny Rv Blvd, Oakmont. Mon, Wed, Fri 10-7, Thur 10-8, Sat-Sun 9-5. MC,V.* **828-4877.**
Small tables inside and out for a mystery book browser's break...sometimes with the mystery writers themselves. Coffee drink specials and pastries from La Charcuterie. Under $5.

## Rosebud

*2600 Smallman. Tues-Sat 11:30-6. Sun 9am-2am. AE,D,DC,MC,V.* **261-2221.**
An in-vogue arts/music center with a full-blown menu, Rosebud's atmosphere is still a good venue for coffee and

**13**

## Coffeehouses

conversation. It's glass front opens to outdoor tables in summer. Great array of coffees, teas, terrific desserts plus full menu—dinner, salads, appetizers. $3-$10.

### 61C
*1839 Murray Ave, Sq Hill. Mon-Thur 7-11, Fri & Sat til 12:30. Sun 10-5.* **521-6161.** This big, sunny room is right on the 61C bus route...you can sit in the green chairs in the side patio and wait for the bus to pick you up! A calming spot on the bustling avenue, it has an all-ages clientele and some interesting reading materials along with exotic coffees (try the rich Ethiopian), teas, good crunchy sandwiches, all kinds of desserts. ($1.65-$2.50).

### Sip, Shadyside
*238 Shady Ave, Shadyside. Mon-Sat 8am (Sun 10am) to midnite.* **361-4478.** Refreshing alternative—moody laid-back ambience in glass-fronted first floor with dark walls, quixotic touches; nooks for private talks, serious habituees. Coffee, exotic teas, pastries plus big choice of Mediterranean/vegetarian salads, soups. $1-$5. Mellow hangout.

### The Strip Bar
*1814 Penn Ave, Strip. Mon-Sat 8-6, Fri-Sat reopens 8pm-4am.* **471-1043.** You can relax on a sofa, eat from scattered tables in this 'livingroom' with coffee plus, desserts, Mediterranean snacks...books and board games. $1-$5.

### Tuscany Premium Coffees
*Forbes, Oakland, Mon-Fri 6:30-6* **682-5354.** *One Mellon Bk Ctr, Mon-Fri 6:30-5* **261-0299.** *Two Mellon Bk Ctr, Mon-Fri 7-5* **281-9669.** Billed as a "true coffee house" with real "baristas"—coffee bartenders schooled in the fine art of perfect cappuccino. Handsome, burnished room with long counters and a jazz/classical track. Desserts, great lattes—coffee drinks with milk. Meat/veggie focaccia sandwiches $4.95 to $5.95 for lunch/pasta specials.

### "Soho" Bistro

#### Luciano's
*1023 Forbes Ave, Uptown. Mon-Wed 10-10, Thur 10-2, Fri-Sat 5-1am, Sun 9-2. MC, V.* **281-6877.** A student haunt across from Duq U. this Soho-style bistro has coffees, desserts, pastries plus $2.95 lunches, sandwiches, salads and dinner $2-$8.50. It also has a bar downstairs, art shows, a running local theatre Fri-Sat nights at 7:30 and occasional rock/punk groups. Drinks: Inexp.

### Vie de France Bakery/Cafe
*5808 Forbes, Squirrel Hill. Mon-Fri 7am-9pm. Sat-Sun 9-9.* **521-1138.** The inviting aroma of freshly baked croissants, French bread and pastries wafts across this cafe as you feast on special teas, coffee drinks plus salads, soups, hot/cold sandwiches. $2-$5. Charming country French decor makes it a welcome neighborhood addition. Vive la difference!.

**13**

Who takes tea? An old tradition–tea time–is returning with its civilized charm and late-afternoon goodies that have made it a continental institution. It's a wonderful way to relax and become aware of the many Pittsburgh pleasures around us. Tea for you too!

## Teas

### Cafe Victoria
*Torrance Hse, 946 Western Ave, Allegheny West. D,MC,V.* **323-8881**
**Hours:** Sun-Fri 3-6.
Enjoy "delectables & collectables" as you take tea in this quaint house, antiquing as you go. Most of the Victorian items are for sale and there are more antiques next door. A modest tea and dessert in a great setting indoors or in a charming courtyard. $3-$5. (See Review)

### Cathy's Windsor Tea Room
*515 Locust Place, Sewickley. MC,V.*
**Hours:** *Mon- Sun 11-4.* **741-6677.**
Luncheon Tea in the British tradition in elegant Victorian house with homemade scones, British biscuits, tea sandwiches, desserts, $7. Lovely High Tea with shining silver service, fine china, scones, tea sandwiches, shepherd's & meat pies, unlimited dessert, $14. You might run into owner Cathy Milton, well-known TV personality and British buff. Browse amid English/Amer antiques at Cathy's Corner on the second floor.

### Classroom
*133 Camp Lane, McMurray off Rt 19, Peters Twp. AE,D,MC,V.* **942-4878.**
**Hours:** Mon-Fri 2-4:30.
Quaint tea in old one-room schoolhouse with chalkboard, wooden flooring, loft seating for smokers. Luscious desserts—pineapple cheesecake, strawberries Romanoff, creme caramel, scones plus tea sandwiches, soups/salads $2.75-$5.95. (Lunch 11:30-2, Dinner 5-10.)

### Frick Cafe
*7227 Reynolds, Pt Breeze. AE,MC,V.* **371- 0600.**
**Hours:** Tues-Sat 2-5:30.
A most delightful tea in artistic suroundings on the wooded grounds of the Frick Museum and Clayton. Seating indoors and on the French patio amid trees and flowering plants for freshly baked scones with Devon cream/jam and assorted tea sandwiches ($2.95). "High Tea"...sandwiches, scones, pastries...$8.95. Loverly!

---

### Holiday Tradition- Year 'Round

### Westin Wm Penn Hotel
*Downtown, AE,DC,MC,V.* **553-5235.**
**Hours:** 7 days 2:30-4:30
Holiday tea at the William Penn is a Pittsburgh tradition in the chandeliered Palm Court Lobby of this grand hotel—elegant atmosphere, gleaming silver service and music on Andre Previn's grand piano. Choice of three items from tea sandwiches, scones, gateau or Greek pastry with your tea/coffee. An affordable luxury at $8.25 person.

---

### Johnston House
*907 Rt 228, Mars. D,MC,V.* **625-2636.**
**Hours:** Wed/Sat 11am & 1pm by reserv.
An exquisite English tea party in a charming Victorian house. Warm/cold tea sandwiches, scones, clotted cream...indoors or on the porch. Browse in Victorian gift shop. $13 person. Worth the ride!

### Promenade Cafe
*Pgh Hilton, Gateway Ctr. AE,DC,MC,V.* **391-4600. Hours:** *2-5.*
No set teatime but delightful afternoon snacking in the glass-walled diningroom on Gateway Center park or on the green and white umbrellaed patio. Light sandwiches, yummy desserts. $3-$7.

### Shadyside Balcony
*Theatre Mall, Walnut St, Shadyside. AE, D,DC,MC,V.* **687-0110.**
**Hours:** Mon-Sat 3-5.
Modern tea & conversation on the Balcony overlooking Walnut Street for a well-earned shopping break. The whole lunch menu to choose from—appetizers, salads, soup/salad/quiche combinations, sandwiches and delicious desserts. How about ice cream with your own pitcher of chocolate sauce—all from $2-$6. Lovely way to while away an afternoon!

14

Where do Pittsburgh executives/professionals dine in their on-the-job hours? At a handful of traditional restaurants, generally with comfortable, club-like settings conducive to a working lunch or a relaxing  business dinner...or in executive dining rooms and private membership clubs. At night many of these restaurants take on a more festive air.

### Baum Vivant

*5102 Baum Blvd, Oakland. AE,D,CB, DC,MC,V.* **682-9446.**
An impressive choice for a high-powered dinner is this sparkling little restaurant with a band-box look...the creation of Toni Pais (maitre d' of the former La Normande). You can let Toni do the worrying as you relax over the fine Portuguese/Italian cuisine and enjoy special house touches–the complimentary pate, almond liqueur, delicious herbed cream cheese. There's exceptional fish, seafood, steak and chop entrees with haute cuisine touches and some beautiful desserts. And you're not far from downtown.
**Dinner:** Mon-Thur 5:30-10, Fri-Sat til 11. ($17-$27).

### Brandy's

*2323 Penn Avenue, Strip District. AE,DC, MC,V.* **566-1000.**
A unique decor, brick & hanging greenery and an out-of-city feel make this a business favorite for relaxed dining. There's a bar with real Pittsburgh flavour and private 'board rooms' for larger meetings in a warm, informal atmosphere. An added plus to the veal/seafood menu are delicious Brandyburgers and liqueur ice-cream desserts. A good place to further business friendships. (The Brandy Van picks up groups from downtown by reservation).
**Lunch:** Mon-Sat 11-4 ($4-$8).
**Dinner:** Mon-Thur til 12, Fri-Sat til 2, Sun til 11. ($12-$16).

### The Carlton

*One Mellon Bank Center, Downtown. AE,D,DC,MC,V. Reser.* **391-4099.**
This is a handsome, burnished room with lots of private space, a quiet, unruffled atmosphere for confidential conversations. At night it takes on a more festive air...with free limo service to and from Heinz Hall and Benedum Center by reservation. The menu is traditional— grilled meats, chops, seafood, with business

luncheon specials. Free dinner parking in One Mellon Bank Center.
**Lunch:** Mon-Fri 11:30-2:30. ($8-$16).
**Dinner:** Mon-Thur 5-10, Fri & Sat til 11. ($16-$24).

### Christopher's

*1411 Grandview Avenue, Mt Washington. Reser. AE,D,DC,MC,V.* **381-4500.**
The right site for decision-making at the highest level with the lighted city for background and inspiration. Superb views from glass walls on three sides, an entire wall made of coal, a Sports Hall of Fame and a mini-museum of Pittsburgh memorabilia provide a showcase for Pittsburgh products. Visitors leave with a wonderful impression of the city. Valet parking.
**Dinner:** Mon-Thur 5-10, Fri-Sat til 11. ($16-$35).

### Curzon's City Club

*119 6th St, Downtown. AE,MC,V.* **391-3300.**
This downtown athletic club's Cafe Restaurant, open to the public for lunch, is a private setting for a quick repast for businessmen/women. For members it's a convenient stop after a noonday workout. The serene two-level room has a unique glass-wall view of the club pool and courts. There's an inexpensive salad bar, soup, sandwiches...and 25 imported beers. You can continue your talk at the bar (open til 10:30 in the evening).
**Lunch:** Mon-Fri 11:30-4. Light Menu 4-8 ($3-$7).

### The Colony

*Greentree & Cochran Rds, Mt Lebanon. Reser. AE,D,DC,MC,V.* **561-2060.**
One of the best steaks in town—and an atmosphere for relaxing—or business talk—by the open grills of this informal room. It's mellow, comfortable, an ideal site for beginning or finishing up business ...then relaxing with nightly entertainment in the Lounge. A weary executive will appreciate the thought.
**Dinner:** Mon-Thur 5-10, Fri-Sat 5-11. Sun 4-9. ($20-$29).

## Common Plea

*308 Ross Street, Downtown. Lunch reser suggested. AE,DC,MC,V.* **281-5140.**
An interesting second floor room with a Renaissance atmosphere—heavy wooden tables, high backed chairs, a rococo decor—and lots of comfort for leisurely dining, a favorite haunt of Pittsburgh's legal profession. The cuisine—especially the seafood and veal—is top-flight.
**Lunch:** Mon-Fri 11:30-2:30. ($7-$10).
**Dinner:** Mon-Sat 5-10. ($16-$25)

## Consigliere

*425 Cherry Way, across from Kaufmann's parkng garage. AE,D,DC,MC,V.* **281-0003**
Favorite haunt of uptown lawyers— "consigliere" in Italian—this little eatery has excellent pasta, chicken, veal, steak, seafood and a relaxing atmosphere.
**Lunch:** Mon-Fri 11-4. ($6-$9). (Soup/ Salad Special $6.95.)
**Dinner:** Mon-Sat 5-9. ($13-$22.50). Happy Hour hors d'oeuvres.

## Davio's

*2100 Broadway, Beechview. Up West Liberty, right at Pauline (at Rohrich's Cadillac) left to Broadway. 10 min from town. No credit cards. No liquor.* **531-7422.**
Executives who know Pittsburgh dining are taking their guests to this delightful hideaway...perfect cuisine in a warm, relaxing trattoria setting, a deceptively simple charmer. Pittsburgh's famed Chef David Ayn's creativity is lovingly applied to fine Italian dishes, delicious breads, superb salads. You can't go wrong—from the "maestro's" signature dishes in the high $20's to simple 'peasant' cuisine— the food is sure to please. Remember to take cash/check and your own wine. Worth the trip!
**Lunch:** Mon-Fri 12-3. ($5.95-$11).
**Dinner:** Mon-Sat 4-11, Sun 4-9. ($10-$29).

## D'Imperio's

*3412 William Penn Highway, Wilkins. AE,DC,MC,V. Reser.* **823-4800.**
A businessman's favorite, this restaurant's fine cuisine and calm ambience draws executives from all over. Famous six-course dinners—trout, sole, veal, steak impeccably served in gracious surroundings with special attention to business needs and international dishes for corporate guests. Perfect for the serious gourmet.
**Lunch:** Mon-Fri 11:30-3. ($7-$11).
**Dinner:** 7 days 5-11. ($15-$27).

## Grand Concourse

*Station Square. AE,DC,MC,V. Reser.* **261-1717.**
Still the grandest location to impress visiting executives with the big changes in Pittsburgh. This magnificently restored P&LE Station, with its soaring stained glass ceiling, is a fitting place for a luncheon or dinner feast. While you're there take the opportunity to look around Station Square.
**Lunch:** Mon-Fri 11:30-2:30. ($6.50-$12).
**Dinner:** Mon-Thur 4:30-10, Fri & Sat til 11, Sun 4:30-9. ($11-$25 ).

## The Harvest

Pittsburgh Vista Hotel, Liberty Center, Penn Ave, Downtown. Reser sugg. AE, D,DC,MC,V. **227-4480.**
Warm elegance—glass, brass, a genial comfortable bar—greet you in this intimate room, sure to be a favorite of your international visitors. The decor's Edwardian and the menu's American/ Continental changing seasonally with the finest of ingredients—fish, steak, duck, chicken, veal, fresh fruit and vegetables. This is a relaxing mileau for busy executives with matchless service by a European-trained staff. Your visitors from near and far will be delighted!
**Lunch:** Mon-Fri 11:45-2:30. ($9-$14).
**Dinner:** Mon-Sat 5:30-10:30. ($14-$26).

14

## Jake's Above the Square

*430 Market Street, Downtown, 2nd level.*
*Reser sugg. AE,DC,MC,V.* **338-0900.**
Jake's offers diners a sweeping view of
Market Square in stylish surroundings. A
great spot for important business lunches,
it specializes in North Italian and regional
American cuisine—grilled seafood and
homemade pasta and pastries. Nightly
piano adds to dining pleasure.
**Lunch:** Mon-Sat 11:30-5. ($8-$13).
**Dinner:** Mon-Thur 5-11, Fri & Sat til 12,
Sun 4-10. ($17-$33).

## Le Mont

*1114 Grandview Avenue, Mt Washington.*
*AE,D,DC,MC,V.* **431-3100.**
An impressive place to take visitors for
Continental cuisine and a spectacular
view of the city from banquette seating
facing a sheer glass wall. The decor is
plush and dramatic—for those who like to
do business with a flair. Valet parking.
**Dinner:** Mon-Fri 5-10:30, Sat til 11:30,
Sun 4-9:30. ($11-$35).

## Le Pommier, the Apple Tree

*2104 E Carson Street, South Side. Reser.*
*AE,DC,MC,V.* **431-1901.**
This fine little Country French restaurant
is a disarming choice for a special guest.
Connoisseur diners and women
executives will appreciate its simple
charm and outstanding cuisine. Perfect
setting for a private business tete-a-tete.
**Dinner:** Mon-Sat 5:30-10. ($15-$23).

## More

*214 N Craig Street, Oakland. AE,DC,*
*MC,V.* **621-2700.**
Famous for its food, this Oakland standby is always a reliable executive choice.
The fine cuisine—seafood, veal, fish,
salads, pasta—won't disappoint. The
surroundings are comfortable, relaxing,
the service is good and the drinks superb.
**Lunch:** Mon-Fri 11:30-2:30. ($4.50-$7.50).
**Dinner:** Mon-Sat 5-10, Sun 5-9.
($9.50-$20).

## Morton's of Chicago

*CNG Tower, 625 Liberty Ave, Downtown.*
*AE,CB,D,DC,MC,V.* **261-7141.**
One of the famous Chicago chain, a
beautiful burnished restaurant with lots of
polish and executive opulence and
seamless service. Famous prime aged
steaks, Maine lobster, seafood...and for
dessert...Grand Marnier, chocolate and
lemon souffles or fresh raspberries/
strawberries with sabayon. A must for
steak lovers, the zenith for the executive
connoisseur!
**Lunch:** Mon-Fri 11:30-2:30. ($7-$18).
**Dinner:** Mon-Sat 5:30-11, Sun 5-10.
($16-$29).

## Per Favore

*Royal York, 3955 Bigelow Blvd, Oakland.*
*Reser sugg. AE,DC,MC,V.* **681-9147.**
Here's a bright, hospitable room for
business talk and North Italian specialties—veal, chuck roast braised in barolo
wine, pasta, intriguing pizzas. Your visitor
will feel at home. Piano at dinner Thur-
Sat. Valet parking.
**Lunch:** Mon-Fri 11-4. ($3.95-$7.95).
**Dinner:** Mon-Thur 4-10, Fri & Sat til 11.
($10.95-$21.95).

## Piccolo Mondo

*Foster Plaza, Greentree. 15 min from*
*Airport. Reser. AE,D,DC,MC,V.* **922-0920.**
Rico Lorenzini of North Hills Rico's fame
has taken over this beautiful restaurant
atop the hills of Greentree, the perfect site
for a relaxing repast out of the city.
Renowned for its French & North Italian
cuisine and special service to business
clients, it serves some of the city's best
fish, veal, rack of lamb in a lavish decor.
Nearby hotel limos offer service to the
door. Impressive experience.
**Lunch:** Mon-Fri 11:30-3:30. ($5-$10.50).
**Dinner:** Mon-Thur 4-10, Fri-Sat til 11.
($12-$25).

## Pietro's Italian Chophouse

*Hyatt Pittsburgh at Chatham. AE,DC, MC,V.* **288-9326.**
Spacious, two-level room with modern decor, glass walls and patio looking out over the city. Good Uptown meeting place for fine North Italian dining, fabulous Sunday Brunch "Festa." Good place for power breakfast.
**Breakfast:** Mon-Fri 6:30-11, Sat & Sun til 11:45. ($3.95-$15).
**Lunch:** Mon-Fri 11-3,Sat-Sun 11:45-3. ($6-$13).
**Dinner:** Sun-Thur 6:30-10:30, Fri & Sat til 11. ($11-$20).

## Ruddy Duck

*Ramada Hotel, Bigelow Square Downtown. Reser sugg. AE,DC,D,MC,V.* **281-3825.**
This warm club-like room centered around a big brass bar is a gracious setting for an early breakfast or executive lunch. There's traditional grilled fish & meat plus creative variations on duck—hence its name. Handy to city business. A real favorite. (Parking in Ramada garage).
**Breakfast:** Mon-Fri 6:30-11. ($1.50- $7).
**Lunch:** 7 days 11-4. ($5.50-$8).
**Dinner:** 7 days 4-10. ($9-$16).

## Ruth's Chris Steak House

*6 PPG Place, Downtown. AE,DC,MC,V. Reser sugg.* **391-4800.**
One of the famous national chain, a comfortable, sophisticated room in which to wine and dine your clients—a must for steak lovers. Also delicious lobster, chicken and chops. Good lunch bargain. Free evening parking in PPG garage from Third or Fourth Ave.
**Lunch:** Mon-Fri 11:30-3. ($6-$13).
**Dinner:** Mon-Thur 5-10:30, Fri & Sat til 11, Sun 5-9. ($16-$22).

## Scoglio

*Fifth Ave Place, 5th & Stanwix, Downtown. AE,D,DC,D,MC,V.* **391-1226.**
*Reser. Also Law & Finance Bldg, 429 4th.* **263-0545.**
Unique rooms with elegant touches, fine North Italian cuisine. Calming atmosphere, business, before-theatre favorite. Same fine cuisine at **Scoglio Updown**, a lawyer's haunt.
**Lunch:** Mon-Fri 11:30-2. ($7-$9).
**Dinner** Tues-Sat 4-9. ($8.95-$15).

## Sterling's

*Pittsburgh Hilton, Gateway Center. Reser sugg. AE,DC,D,MC,V.* **391-4600.**
A handsome hotel grill with an exclusive feel and lots of privacy for business discussions. Seafood, steak, Continental cuisine...good executive/traveler's retreat. Valet parking.
**Dinner:** 7 days 5-11:30. ($15-$27).

## Tambellini's

*860 Saw Mill Run Blvd, Rt 51 near the Liberty Tunnels. AE,DC,MC,V.* **481-1118.**
Famous for seafood in Pittsburgh. They come from all over to this big, spacious restaurant for stellar Seafood Louis, fish, lobster, veal, chicken and pasta. A repast here can turn a business meeting into a convivial gathering.
**Lunch:** Mon-Fri 11:30-3:30. ($6-$8.25).
**Dinner:** Mon-Sat 4-11. ($9.75-$25).

## Terrace Room

*Westin William Penn, Mellon Square, Downtown. AE,DC,MC,V.* **553-5235.**
An elegant room restored to its 1916 splendour, this Pittsburgh landmark is a tradtional favorite for executive breakfast, lunch, dinner. Its ornate ceiling, sparkling chandeliers and fine service make an impressive setting for seafood, steak, best prime rib in town. Good choice for hearty beef lovers.
**Breakfast:** 7-11:30. ($4-$9).
**Lunch:** 11:30-2. ($11-$17).
**Dinner:** 6-11. ($13-$24).

**14**

# Private Membership Clubs

## Top of the Triangle
*USX Tower, 600 Grant. AE,D,DC,MC,V. Parking in bldg.* **471-4100.**
A spectacular view of downtown Pittsburgh from the 62nd floor makes this an outstanding choice for visiting VIPs. With traditional offerings, fine service and relaxing music in the Lounge, it's a good place to unwind when business is done. Beautiful day/night views.
**Lunch:** Mon-Fri 11:30-3, Sat 12-3 ($5.95-$13).
**Dinner:** Mon-Thur 5:30-10, Fri-Sat til 11, Sun 4-9. ($16-$24). Lounge Mon-Sat til 2.

## PRIVATE MEMBERSHIP CLUBS

## The Allegheny Club
*Three Rivers Stadium, Fourth Level.* **323-0830.**
**Membership:** Open. 1400 members. Established 1970.
Dinner for major events and after daylight football games. The glass-walled dining-room overlooking the Point has a marvelous terrace view of Pirate/Steeler games. Private facilities for member-sponsored functions.
**Hours:** Lunch Mon-Fri 11:30-2, Sat & Sun 2 hrs before games. "4th Inning Menu" on Game Days.

## The Duquesne Club
*325 Sixth Avenue, Downtown.* **391-1500.**
**Membership:** By sponsorship. 2600 members. Established 1881.
The brass lions outside this familiar, awninged brownstone guard Pittsburgh's oldest and most exclusive club. Prestigious leaders meet to eat, work and relax in its 56 meeting/dining rooms, health club, barber shop, corporate suites, overnight guest rooms.
**Hours:** 7 days, 24 hours.
Breakfast/Lunch/Dinner: Mon-Sat 7am-10pm.

## Curzon's City Club
*119 6th Street, Downtown.* **391-3300.**
**Membership:** Open. Established 1981.
Modern health club with restaurant/cafe, conference room; full health club facilities— racquetball, squash, nautilus/free weights, jogging track, whirlpool, swimming pool, aerobic studio, pro shop.
**Hours:** Mon-Fri 6am-10pm, Sat 9-7. Sun 9-3. Breakfast/Health Food Bar Mon-Fri 7-9:30. **Lunch:** Mon-Fri 11:30-4, Light Menu 4-8.

## Engineer's Society W Pa
*337 Fourth Ave, Downtown.* **261- 0710.**
**Membership:** Professional sponsorship. 1200 members. Established 1880.
A social and business meeting place for engineers, related professionals and students. Comfortable private dining-rooms, bar and lounge; members' seminars, club functions.
**Hours:** Mon-Fri 8:30-5. Dinner by arrangement.

## The Gateway Center Club
*Three Gateway Center, 24th fl.* **566-1300.**
**Membership:** Open—with references. 900 members. Established 1973.
A luncheon club with a sweeping view of the Point, favorite of Gateway Center executives and Greater Pgh Chamber of Commerce members. Dining facilities, meeting rooms for private parties, office catering.
**Hours:** Mon-Fri 11:30-7:30. Lunch 11:30-2:30.

## Harvard-Yale-Princeton Club
*619 William Penn Place, Downtown.* **281-5858.**
**Membership:** Sponsorship by members, limited to graduates or those listed in Harvard, Yale or Princeton alumni books; associate membership to other university graduates. 600 members. Est. 1930.
Pittsburgh's oldest downtown residential buildings, these charming red brick "houses" off a small courtyard are headquarters for the city's Ivy League alumni. Dining rooms and three private meeting

## Private Membership Clubs

rooms are available for members/
non-members.
**Hours:** Mon-Fri Lunch 12-2, Dinner by
arrangements. Cocktail Lounge 5-8.

### Igloo Club
*Civic Arena, Uptown.* **642-1890.**
**Membership:** Pgh Penguins full-season
ticket holders. 800 members. Established
1967.
This modern/neon two-level club offers
hockey fan members a la carte entrees at
**Icing's** restaurant on the first level and a
bar/buffet on the second floor for pre/
post-game revels. The facility is also
available to members and the public for
private parties.
**Hours:** Two hours before game time.

### Pittsburgh Athletic Association
*4215 Fifth Avenue, Oakland.* **621-2400.**
**Membership:** Sponsorship by member.
2500 members. Established 1909,
opened 1911.
This beautiful five-story Venetian Renaissance building with its ornate frieze is a
second home to Pittsburgh's top business
and professional leaders. It houses one of
the city's most complete athletic facilities
for men/women...a marble/terra-cotta
swimming pool and bowling alleys, an
elegant, rococo first floor diningroom and
smaller private rooms. It also houses
guests—some of them permanent.
**Hours:** Mon-Fri 6:30-10, Sat til 11:30,
Sun til 9. Breakfast/Lunch/Dinner: Mon-Fri
7-11, Sat 8-11:30, Sun Brunch 11-2:30,
Dinner 3-9.

### The Rivers Club
*One Oxford Centre, Downtown.* **391-5227.**
**Membership:** Sponsorship by member.
1000 members. Established 1983.
This sleek health club, on the fourth floor
of Oxford Centre, has a main dining area,
four private dining rooms and first-class
athletic facilities—pool, track, nautilus,
weights, racquetball, squash, sauna,
steam room, whirlpool.
**Hours:** Mon-Fri 6am-9, Sat 9-5. Lunch
Mon-Fri 11:30-2, Dinner Wed-Sat 5:30-10.

### The University Club
*123 University Place, Oakland.* **621-1890.**
**Membership:** College graduates.
Sponsorship by member. 2000 members.
Established 1890.
Facilities include private dining rooms,
largest private library in the city, bowling
alleys and health club—squash, sauna,
whirlpool. Parties, summer dances and
outdoor dining on handsome roof garden
overlooking Oakland. Also member guest
rooms. Reciprocal lunching privileges at
the Downtown Club of Pittsburgh, 62nd
floor, USX Bldg.
**Hours:** 7 days. Breakfast 7-11, Lunch
11:30-2:30, Dinner Sun-Fri 5:30-9, Sat
til 10.

**14**

# GOURMET TO GO

Whether it's a brown bag for office workers, a festive box for picnickers, or a sumptuous gourmet take-out meal...Pittsburghers are increasingly eating as Europeans do...from movable feasts of bread, fruit and cheese to full meals to eat in city parks, by the riverside or by their own hearths. And you can now have meals delivered to your door.

## Benkovitz Seafoods

*23rd & Smallman, Mon-Thur 9-5,Fri til 5:30, Sat 8-5.* **263-3016.**
People come from miles around for stellar seafood, gourmet seafood salads; super fish sandwich, shrimp bisque, clams, potato pancakes, fish hoagie. $2-$6.

## Catz 'n Kids

*2114 Murray Ave, Squirrel Hill. 7 days 9-8. No credit cards.* **421-9500.**
A yen for kosher food? Here's the real thing. Meats, deli sandwiches, potato pancakes, platters $1.50-$7. Feed a family on Big Jack Sandwich—corned beef, pastrami, salami, swiss on a whole loaf of rye—with fries & slaw. Wry waitresses make for real eat-in experience!

## HoneyBaked Spiral Ham

*Penn Center Blvd, Monrv* **823-1400.** *4780 McKnight Rd, N Hills* **364-1800.** *Wash Rd, S Hls* **835-2400.** *No credit.Mon-Sat 10-6.*
Your guests will rave about this ham, so tender it falls off the bone, uniquely sliced in a spiral, with a delicious crunchy glaze. 6-16 lbs, $27-$70. Also BBQ ribs, turkey, cheeses, salads, cheesecakes and all kinds of mustard.

## Hotlicks

*5520 Walnut, Thtr Mall, Shadysde.* **683-2583.** *Galleria, Mt Lebanon* **341-7427.** *McIntyre Sq, N Hills* **369-7675.** *Mon-Thur 11:30-10, Fri-Sat til 12. Sun Shadyside 4:30-9, S Hills/N Hls 12-10. AE,DC,MC,V.*

---

### Faxing...
### A New Food Fad

Many offices save worktime by faxing lunch orders from a Fax Menu before 10:30am or by 5 the night before for pick-up or delivery next day. Taking fax orders downtown are: **Fat Franks**, USX Bldg **Fax: 471-9677**, **Liang's Hunan,** Liberty Center **Fax: 471-1557**. **Subway** 401 Wood **471-7279.**

---

### Dinner For Two

How about a **McGinnis Sisters'** dinner right on your own hearth. You can pick up the makings of Surf 'n Turf for 2—fresh lobster tail, filet mignon, Idaho potatoes, broccoli, 1/2 lb fresh mushrooms to cook in your own home. $60 for 3 to 4-oz tails, $75 for 6 to 8-oz. Call to order. Pick up at 3825 Saw Mill Run Blvd **882-6400** or Penn Ctr, Monrv. **824-6330.** MC,V.

---

Great ribs, wings, sandwiches—mesquite & Cajun chicken, smoked turkey to go—$4.50 up. Catering. Good eatin'.

## Kiku Express

*229 S Highland Ave, Shadyside. Mon-Sat 11-10. Sun 12-9. DC,MC,V.* **661- 5458.**
A-1 Japanese 'fast food.' Indoor, patio plus take-out; Teriyaki, sukiyaki, other delicacies and sushi—shrimp, vegetable, fish, California roll $3-$5.

## La Charcuterie

*Ellsworth Plz, Ellsworth/College. Tues-Fri 10-8, Sat til 6, Sun til 4. MC,V.* **661-2262.**
Take out extraordinaire from famed local chefs Michael and Candy Uricchio...with a few stand-up & outdoor tables, Gourmet foods, pastries, breads, smoked meats, imported cheeses, pate, sandwiches, coffee bar. Upscale but deliciously worth it!

## Fat Franks

*USX Tower. Mon-Thur 10:30-6:30, Fri-Sat til 8. MC,V.* **471-3388.**
Great Buffalo Wings with terrific sauce make a great party with celery/blue cheese $2.99 dz. Also hoagies, kiellbasa, hot dogs with slaw, baked beans. Tables, take out. Limited delivery.

**15**

# Picnic Baskets/Boxes

## Pittsburgh Gourmet— Perogi Feast

Give a Pittsburgh flavour to your party with a "halftime special" from **Clara's Pittsburgh Pirogies**, 2717 Library Road, Castle Shannon (Rt 88 off 51). How about a whole/half pot of pierogi–nine varieties-$25-$35. Plus stuffed cabbage, haluski, kielbasa & sauerkraut $13-$19. Call ahead or buy them by the dozen at Clara's drive-thru window! Also hot sausage, rigatoni, meat balls, chicken, potato, salads...much more at this ethnic restaurant. **Att: Pgh Clubs.** Shipping anywhere in US—10 doz perogi for $85 incl shipping. No credit cards. **882-3555.**

## Fresh Fish House

*2102 Murray Ave, Sq Hill Mon-Fri 11-7, Sat 11-4, Sun 11-5.* **422-FISH.**
The place is small but the fish is stellar... for eating at high stools with an avenue view or first class take-out. Fresh from fish store next door—scallops, smelts, oysters, shrimp in basket (fried in peanut oil), soup & sides. $2.25-$5.95. Also fried/broiled fish to go $5.95 lb.

## McGinnis Sisters

*3825 Saw Mill Run, S Hls. Mon-Sat 9-7. Sun 9-5.* **882- 6400.** *Penn Ctr, Monrv Mon-Sat 9-7, Sun 9-5* **824-6330.** *MC,V.*
Three sisters–Bonnie, Sharon, Noreen—gourmet cooks all—are a local legend for their succulent hams, Amish chicken, Black Angus beef, Foley's Boston seafood, salads, baked goods, deli cheeses/meats. $3 up. Free delivery on a "working lunch."

## Rania's To Go

*100 Central Square, Mt Lebanon. Mon-Fri 10-7, Sat til 3pm. MC,V.* **531-2222.**
Little gourmet shop with sunny service. Soups, salads, sandwiches, gazpacho,

SW grilled chicken with black beans & corn salad. Five hot specials i.e. lasagna, moussaka. Desserts/pastries. $1-$6.

## Rhoda's

*2201 Murray Ave, Sq Hill. Sun-Thur 7-11, Fri-Sat til 12. No credit cards.* **521-4555.**
Restaurant/deli items to go. Delicious noodle kugel, potato salad, chopped liver, smoked salmon, pickled herring, matzo ball, latke (potato pancakes) chicken soup, sandwiches made to order, and their famous corned beef. $3-$10.

## Ruggeri's

Northumberland, Sq Hill **521-0718.** 196 N Craig, Oklnd. **621-4544.** Mon-Fri 8-7, Sat 9-3. Full deli, 3-4 homemade soups, entrees, salads, full bakery from Breadworks, USA Gourmet. $1.25 up. Dinner for 2 $8.95.

## Shadyside Market

*Mineo Bldg, 5414 Walnut St, Shadyside. Mon-Fri 9-6, Sat 9-5.* **682- 5470.**
Menu varies daily, gourmet versions of chicken, veal, beef, pasta, soups, desserts, fresh scones. $2-$10.

## Simply Delicious

*1200 Old Freeport Road, Fox Chapel. 7 days 7:30am-4pm. AE,MC,V.* **963-0636.**
You can eat in a peach/white parlor behind the deli counter at this creative gourmet house...or take out their wonderful goodies. Gourmet sandwiches, hot/cold soups, salads, hot casseroles and desserts—how about Peach Schnapps Ice Cream? From $1.50 to 'sky's the limit' depending on your imaginative appetite.

## USA Gourmet

*2115 Penn Ave, Strip. Mon-Sat 7-4:30. No credit cards.* **471-6333.**
Fantastic-looking, great-tasting food—chicken/ham salad, quiche, fruit salads. Wonderful desserts–raspberry/vanilla/chocolate cheesecake, tarts, brownies, you name it. $1-$7.

# Picnic Boxes/Baskets

## Meal Delivery To Your Door

### Wheel Deliver
Call in Mon-Fri 10:30-10, Sat & Sun 12-10. **421-9346.**
An idea whose time has come, this restaurant home delivery service is a boon to busy careerists and the homebound. Customers in East End, South Side and Fox Chapel areas can place lunch/dinner orders from a Wheel Deliver menu of some 40 restaurants. Meals are delivered by a tuxedoed driver usually within 45 minutes. You can order anything from sandwiches to gourmet feasts (minimum $10, 15% delivery charge) for the luxury of eating in your own home.:

**East End:** Alexander's Pasta Express, Ali Baba, The Attic, Bentley's, CJ Barney's, Darbar, Dave & Andy's, The Fishery, Hemingway's, Hotlicks, India Garden, Kiku Express, Mad Mex, Minutello's, More, Peking Gourmet, Rib House, Shadyside Balcony, Siamese Kitchen, Silky's, Suzie's, Sweet Basil, Tai Pei.
**South Side:** Blue Lou's, Chinese on Carson, City Grill, Excuses, Kiku, Margaritaville, Mario's, Nick's Fat City, Sesame Inn, River Cafe, Tequila J
**Fox Chapel:** Abate's, Crow's Nest, Dingbat's, Thai Pei.

### Wholey's
*1711 Penn Ave, Strip. Mon-Thur 8-5:30, Fri 8-6pm, Sat til 5.* **391-3737.**
Really fresh seafood—jumbo fish sandwich, shrimp in basket, deviled crab, soups, meat, poultry, complete deli ($1.99-$3.50). Cookware upstairs plus seating on the "Captain's Deck."

## PICNIC BOXES, BASKETS

### Apple Cookie & Chocolate
*411 Smithfield., Downtown. Mon-Fri 7-5:30.* **261-2277.**
**Box Lunch:** To eat in downtown parks or by the riverside. Sandwiches, salads, desserts, croissants, brownies & fine cheesecake. $5-$6.

### Blarney Stone
*30 Grant Ave, Etna. Tues-Thur 11- 9, Fri-Sat til 11. Sun 10:30-9. AE,MC,V.* **781-1666.**
**Baskets:** Fried chicken with roast or corned beef on croissant or biscuit plus cole slaw, Italian macaroni salad, cheese, fruit, brownie. Basket with tablecloth & utensils. $8 person. Handy for Hartwood picnics.

### Brown Bag Deli
*Triangle Bldg, Downton* **566-1795.** *Kossman Bldg* **355-0270.** *411 Wood* **391-0806.** *220 Grant* **261-9697.** *Chatham Ctr* **471-3354.** *625 Stanwix* **281-3403.** *Union Trust Bldg* **263-2120.** *Liberty Center* **261-5111.** *Mon-Fri 7-5.*
**Bag Lunch:** Sandwiches, soups, salads, snacks, fruit, ice cream. $1.99-$3.59.

### Fluted Mushroom
*109 S 12th St, South Side. Mon-Fri 9-5. No credit cards.* **381-1899.**
**Picnic Boxes:** Posh picnics, elegant goodies in little white boxes tied with a green ribbon. Min of 10, delivered to home/office. Gourmet salads i.e. grainy mustard chicken salad, shrimp with red peppers, Italian veal meatloaf, Black Forest ham/brie sandwich. Maryland crab cakes, cole slaw, potato salad, fruit cup, chocolate brownie. $10-$13 person.

### Food Gallery
*5550 Centre Ave, Shadyside* **681-1500.** *Fox Chapel Plza: Freeport Rd* **781-4424.** *1082 Bower Hill Rd , Mt Lebanon* **279-8645.** *Valley Brook–Rt 19 4 mi S of S His Vlg* **942-0600.** *Mon-Sat 8-10, Sun 9-6.*

**15**

# Picnic Boxes/Baskets

**Picnic Trays**: Meats, cheeses, veggies, dip, fruit, salads, rolls. $2.50-$4.95 person, 48-hr notice. **Box Lunches:** Fried chicken, salad, roll, fruit & brownie $5.99.

## Kane's Courtyard

*303 S Craig Street, Oakland. Mon-Fri 7-5:30, Sat 10-5:30.* **683-9988.**
**Box Lunches:** Some of the city's best sandwiches—choice of meat, cheese, bread—plus pasta salad, cookie, bev. $5.75.  Free delivery to East End.

## McGinnis Sisters

*3825 Saw Mill Run, S Hills. Mon-Sat 9-7, Sun 9-5* **882-6400.** *Penn Ctr, Monrv. Mon-Sat 9-7, Sun 9-5* **824-6330.** *MC,V.*
**Box Lunches:** Croissant sandwich— choice of baked ham, lean roast beef, NY style corned beef, gourmet turkey breast. Choice of cheese, salad and brownie carrot/apple cake. Utensils/napkins. $5.50.

## Rania's To Go

*100 Central Sq, Mt Lebanon. Mon-Fri 10-7, Sat til 3pm. MC,V.* **531- 2222.**
**Box Lunches:** 14 different combinations- tasty, homemade sandwiches, salads, fruit, soups, terrific desserts. $6.65- $12.50. Deli trays.

## Salim's

*4705 Centre Ave, Oakland. Mon-Sat 10-8. Sun 11-6.* **621-8110.**
Some of the city's best Mid-East/Greek take-out. Spinach/meat/cheese pies, tabouli, gyros, falafel, hommus and baba ganooj, Greek salad, baklava. $1-$3.

## Simply Delicious

*1200 Old Freeport Rd, Fox Chapel. 7 days 7:30-4. AE,MC,V.* **963-0636.**
**Bag Lunches:** Choice of chicken salad/ tuna/roast beef/turkey/ham sandwich $4, on croissant $4.75. Also fruit, cole slaw, quiche.
**Picnics Boxes:** Bring in your  hamper/ box at least a day ahead and they'll fill it with your favorite goodies.

## Picnic Boxes Under the Stars

You can enjoy food with your music at **Star Lake's** exciting outdoor amphitheatre on Rt 18 May-Sept. Call ahead for Gourmet Picnic baskets available to box seat ticket holders. Deluxe Barbecue Basket for 6— Southern Style Chicken BBQ, Ribs, Peel 'n Eat Shrimp, red-skin potato salad, sourdough bread, sweet butter, cheddar cheese & crackers, fresh strawberries, beer nuts plus dessert tray with homemade brownies, cookies & an 8" Granny Smith apple pie ($75-$90). Alternate—Shrimp by Dozen, Fruit & Pepperoni for 6, Antipasto & Hoagy picnic baskets. 48 hours notice. Or you can eat on the lawn from food booths there. Call **947-7415.**

## USA Gourmet

*2115 Penn Ave, Strip. Mon-Sat 7-4:30. No credit cards.* **471-6333.**
**Box Lunch:** Choice roast beef/cheddar, Virginia ham/Amer cheese or smoked turkey breast/Swiss with potato salad, cole slaw or pasta primavera and cookie. Condiments, paperware. $6.50 per.

**16**

One of the city's fastest growing, most popular cuisines is exotic Asian/Oriental food. Here are fifty of the city's favorite Chinese... Japanese, Thai, Indian, Vietnamese and even a Filipino restaurant with exciting new tastes. Many new Asian eateries boast smashing decors.

## Chinese

### Charley Ung's Tea Garden
*5929 Baum Blvd, E Liberty. Tues-Fri 12-9:30, Sat 12-10. Sun 12-9. AE,D, MC,V.* **661-0511.**
Old fashioned Chinese, Pgh's oldest—70 years—'best egg rolls in city,' Cantonese/Szezhuan. $6-$20. Inexp-Mod.

### China Palace
*5440 Walnut, Shadyside. Mon-Thur 11:30-10:15, Fri-Sat til 11:15. Sun 2-9* **687-7423.** *Jonnett Plaza, Wm Penn Hwy, Monrv* **373-7423.** *409 Broad, Sewickley* **749-7423.** *Mon-Thur 11:30- 9:30, Fri-Sun til 10:30. AE,MC,V*
Above-average Szechuan, Hunan, Mandarin in tasteful surroundings. Great sampler Pu Pu Platter—grill your own & saute in spicy sauce. Excellent "Happy Family"—beef, pork, broccoli. Mod-Exp.

### Chinatown Inn
*520 Third Ave, Downtown. Mon-Fri 11-10, Sat 12-10, Sun 2-10. AE,DC,MC,V.* **281-6708.**
Favorite downtown lunching spot, one of the last vestiges of Pittsburgh's old Chinatown. All the regulars & excellent Kung Pao Chicken and Fung Mei Har—shrimp in bacon with sweet sour sauce. Mod.

### Chop Stix
*1034 Freeport Rd, Fox Chapel. 7 days 11:30-10, Fri-Sat til 11. AE,MC,V.* **782-3010.**

---

### Chinese on Carson

*1506 E Carson, S Side. Mon-Thur 11-10, Fri-Sat til 11. Sun Brunch 11-4, Dinner 4-9. AE,DC,MC,V.* **431-1717.**
A rarity in Chinese restaurants, a modern room in lavendar, black & neon, one of city's handsomest. Great Szechuan, Cantonese, Burmese; chicken curry, unique Lobster Egg Rolls, braised duck with seafood. Mod-Exp.

---

### Elegant Oriental

#### Liang's Hunan
*Liberty Center, Downtown. Sun-Thur 11:30-10, Fri-Sun til 11. AE,D,DC, MC,V.* **471-1688.**
Elegant Downtown room, smashing Oriental decor; gourmet Hunan, Szechuan—asparagus prawns, smoked duck, pheasant, venison, rabbit, frog's legs. Delicious crispy whole fish $19.50. Mod-Exp.

---

On site of former Anna Kao's. Szechuan, Hunan, Peking dishes including "30 Minute Duck" and pork in bean sauce. Buffet Sun-Tues 5:30-8:30 8.99. Mod-Exp.

### Coral Garden
*Edgewood Towne Ctr, S Braddock. Mon-Thur, Sat 11-10, Fri & Sun til 10:30. D,MC,V.* **731-1101.**
Art gallery decor, low-salt, low-cholesterol Szechuan, Hunan, Cantonese. Lunch $3-$7, Dinner $5.50-$10. Daily specials $7.95, Wed Dinner Buffet $9.95 and Sun Lunch Buffet 12-3:30, $6.95.

### Dynasty Express
*633 Smithfield, Downtown. Mon-Fri 10:30-8pm. No credit cards.* **281- 9818.**
Small eat-in/take-out place, favorite of office workers; Hunan, Mongolian beef/chicken. Szechuan chicken, Inexp.

### Empress
*Waterworks, Fox Chapel. Mon-Thur 11:30-9:30, Fri til 10:30, Sat 12-10:30. Sun 12-9. AE,D,MC,V.* **781- 3727.**
Spacious good-looking room with authentic Szechuan cuisine, chicken, beef; Potato Basket with shrimp, lobster, scallops & vegetables. Inexp-Mod.

### Golden Palace
*206 Shiloh, Mt Washington. Mon-Thur 11-10, Fri-Sat til 11, Sun 4-10. AE,MC,V.* **481-8500.**

Casual, modern with good vegetarian dishes, great eggplant with garlic sauce, bean curd. Inexp.

### Great Wall
*Pines Plaza, 1130 Perry Hwy, Ross. Mon-Thur 11:30-10, Fri-Sat til 11. Sun 3-9. AE,DC,MC,V.* **369-5858.**
Full Mandarin menu, Szechuan, Peking, Kwonton in modern decor. Seafood special—crabmeat, shrimp, scallops; also seafood with lobster sauce, sizzling rice & chicken. $6-$13. Mod.

### Jade Chinese Restaurants
*4450 Wm Penn Hwy, Murrysville.* **733-2281.** *Jade Garden, 6022 Saltzburg Rd, Verona* **793-9937.** *Jade Palace 10636 Perry Hwy, Wexford* **934-0555.** *Mon-Thur 11:30-9:30, Fri-Sat til 10:30. Sun 12-9:30. (Saltzburg closed Mon.) AE,DC MC,V.*
Comfortable, modern American rooms; good General Tso Chicken, Seafood in Bird Nest. $5.50-$13. Inexp-Mod.

### Jimmy Tsang's
*Kennilworth Apts, 5700 Centre, Shadyside. Mon-Thur 11:30-10, Fri-Sat til 11. Sun 3:30-9. AE,DC,MC,V.* **661-4226.**
Big, busy restaurant with fancy-to-casual dining, city's favorite for wide variety of Chinese/Korean—"over 100 best-loved Peking, Szechuan, Shanghai, Cantonese dishes." Detailed menu explains cuisine, helps in ordering. Mod- Exp.

## Kosher Chinese

### King David
*2020 Murray, Sq Hill. Mon-Thur 11-10, closed Fri-Sat summer, open Sat in winter 1 hr after sundown til 12 am. Sun 2-10. AE,D,DC,MC,V.* **422-3370.**
How about Kosher Chinese, a most unusual mix...and some Amer food too! Soup & Egg roll, hot Chinese vegetable platter, sesame chicken. $1.50-$14. Also take-out. Phone greets you with "Shalom."

## Four Chinese Stars

### Mandarin Gourmet
*YWCA Bldg, 305 Wood St, Downtown. Mon-Sat 11-9. AE,D,DC,MC,V.* **261-6151.**
One of Harold & Mrs Jou's four fabulous "gourmet" houses...excellent Mandarin, Cantonese, Hunan. All-day Dim Sum. Try Dragon Phoenix—half chicken, half lobster with veggies... mmm! Inexp-Mod.

### Hunan Gourmet
*1209 E Carson, S Side. Mon-Thur 11:30-10, Fri-Sat 11:30-11. Sun 3-9:30. AE,D,DC,MC,V.* **488-8100.**
Serene room with all-day Dim Sum outstanding shrimp/scallops in garlic sauce, best Gen Tso's Chicken in town. Mod.

### Cathay Gourmet
*4812 McKnight Rd, N Hills. Mon-Thur 11:30-10, Fri-Sat til 11, Sun 3-9:30. AE,D,DC,MC,V.* **366-9111.**
One of city's best, renowned beef, pork, great Dragon-Phoenix Soup, Pu Pu Platter $9 for 2. Mon Buffet $8.95. $4.50 to $18.95 for lobster. Mod.

### Szechuan Gourmet
*709 Bellefonte St, Shadyside. Mon-Thur 11-10, Fri-Sat til 11. Sun 4:30-10. AE,D,DC,MC,V.* **683-1763.**
Longtime favorite, same great "Gourmet" dishes; special Szechuan Chicken, big vegetarian menu. Mod.

**16**

### King Wu
*304 Plaza Mall, Monrv. Sun-Thur 11:30-10, Fri-Sat til 11. AE,D, MC,V.* **373-5464.**
Spacious Chinese modern for Szechuan, Mandarin, Hunan. Good wonton chips, Peking Duck, Pu Pu Platter. Lunch Buffet $6.95. $3.25-$14. Inexp-Mod.

# Chinese

## Sesame Inns

### Sesame Inns
*Shops at Station Sq, Balcony* **281-8282**. *715 Washington Rd, Mt Lebanon* **341-2555**. *Mon-Thur 11-10, Fri-Sat til 11. Sun 12-9 (Mt Leb 4-10). AE,DC,MC,V.*
Good Szechuan, Hunan cuisine in lovely atmosphere. Try the fried dumplings, cold noodles with sesame paste, Orange Beef, Seafood Supreme, Gen Tso's Chicken, Sesame/Walnut Shrimp. $8-$15.

### Mark Pi China Gate
*Galleria, 1500 Washington Rd, Mt Lebanon. Mon-Thur 11:30-10, Fri-Sat til 11. Sun 12-9.* **341-8890**.
Exquisite decor, contemporary atmosphere. Excellent Szechuan, Mandarin, Hunan specialties. Sesame Beef, Hunan Shrimp, Dragon & Phoenix—prawns, scallops, chicken, lobster, scallop rumaki. Good date place. Inexp-Mod.

### Me Lyng
*428 Forbes, Downtown. Mon-Sat 11-9. AE,MC.V.* **642-2922**. *Also 213 W 8th Ave, Homestead. Mon-Thur 11-9:30, Fri til 10, Sat 4-10. Sun 3-9.* **464-1477**.
Simple elegance with pink/white tables, friendly service. Good Viet/Chinese incl Song Sing Chicken, Tangy Scallops/Shrimp, Sesame Chicken. $5.25-$15.95. Inexp-Mod.

### New Dumpling House
*2138 Murray, Sq Hill. Mon-Thur 11-10, Fri-Sat til 11. Sun 1-10. AE,MC,V.* **422-4178**.
Soothing, pleasant, elegant touches; tinted vegetable flowers enhance fine cuisine—dumplings in bamboo box...try Szechuan in hot sesame sauce (8 for $3.50). Orange flavored chicken, Dragon

Phoenix Lobster in Szechuan sauce. $4.50 to $26 for whole duck. Inexp-Mod.

### Sichuan Houses
*1900 Murray, Sq Hill. Mon-Sat 11:30-10. Sun 2-10. AE,MC,V.* **422-2700**. *Va Manor Mt Lebanon. Mon-Fri 11:30-10, Sat 4:30-11. Sun 4:30-10. MC,V.* **563-5252**. *1335 Freeport Rd, Fox Chapel. Mon-Fri 11-10, Sat-Sun 12-10. AE,MC,V.* **967-0789**.
Some of city's most creative Chinese, mild to spicy, good portions at moderate prices. Specialties Gen Tso's Chicken, Sea Delight. Great Peking Duck for 2 $24.50. Inexp-Mod.

### Peking Gourmet Kitchen
*2018 Murray Ave, Sq Hill. Lunch Mon-Fri 11:30-2:30. Dinner Sun-Thur 2:30-9:30, Fri-Sat til 10:30. Dim Sum Sat-Sun 11-2:30. D,MC,V.* **421-1920**.
Favorite for delicious eight-course Peking Duck feast ($16.90) and Chinese Pancakes for 4 ($28). Mandarin, Szechuan, Hunan. Inexp-Mod.

### Sichuan Palace
*Penn Hills Shopping Center, Mon-Thur 11:30-9:30, Fri-Sat til 10:30. Sun 12-9:30. MC,V.* **241-7110**.

## Cafeteria, Chinese Style

### Yum Wok
*400 S Craig, Oakland. Mon-Sat 11-8.* **687-7777**. *124 Sixth St, Downtown. Mon-Sat 11-8.* **765-2222**. *No credit cards.*
A unique idea, a Chinese cafeteria! Off Craig Street in a very tasteful setting—tile tables, high-backed chairs, great food (mostly Cantonese), wonderful prices. You can snack cheap on 50c rice & noodles and $3.55 lunch specials—Cashew Chicken/ Crab Rangoon, Honey Pineapple Chicken, Moo Goo Gai Pan. You'll see lots of Asian patrons. $2-$6.75. Inexp. Also Downtown.

### JAPANESE
### SUSHI—WHERE TO GET IT

## Terrific Take Out

### Zaw's Asian Food
*2110 Murray Ave, Sq Hill. Mon-Thur 11-9:30, Fri-Sat til 10:30. Sun 12-9. No credit cards.* **521-3663.**
It's take out only—and some of the best in the city—at this energetic little place. You can watch as it's cooked to order—try Szechuan Eggplant, Malaysian Coconut Soup, Chicken with Broccoli—all under $6. Big portions $4.50-$11.50. Inexp.

### Hana Japanese Rest/Sushi Bar
*Graeme St, Market Sq, Downtown. Mon-Fri 11:30-2:30, 5-9:30. Sat 5-9:30. AE, MC,V.* **471-9988.**
2nd-fl room with stellar reputation for sushi, tempura, noodles, sukiyaki steak, sesame chicken, shrimp flambee. Inexp.

### Kabuki
*635 Brown Ave, Turtle Creek. Lunch Mon-Fri 11:30-1, Dinner Mon-Sat 5:30-9. AE,DC,MC,V.* **823-0750.**
Authentic Japanese in spare, serene setting; first sushi in Pgh. Seating at tables or floor cushions in tatami room. Mod.

Small, graceful room with Szechuan, Hunan. Mongolian beef, lobster and steak cubes, seafood. $7-$12. Inexp-Mod.

### Silk Pagoda
*4070 Beechwood Blvd, Greenfield. Mon-Thur 11:30-10, Fri-Sat til 11. Sun 12-10. AE,D,DC,MC,V.* **521-8620.**
Modern apricot/gray decor, serene lighting, fabric ceiling. Mandarin, Hunan, Szechuan cuisine from Liang family father, Hsiao Mei Liang, chef of 50 years. Soups, dumplings, great fish, famous whole red snapper. $4.95-$15. Inex-Mod.

### Kiku of Japan
*Station Sq. Lunch Mon-Sat 11:30-2:30, Dinner Mon-Fri 5-10:30, Fri-Sat 3-11:30. Sun 12-10. AE,DC,MC,V.* **765-3200.**
Sushi bar and table service. Full Japanese menu, fabulous swordfish teriyaki, great broiled Hijiki seaweed. Mod-Exp.

### Tai Pei
*Freeport Rd , Fox Chapel* **781-4131.** *Bourse, Greentree* **279-8811.** *Mon-Thur 11:30-10, Fri-Sat til 11. Sun 11:30-9:30. AE,D,DC,MC,V.*
Light, airy, comfortable room with Hunan lamb, Gen Tso's chicken, seafood, Peking Duck, good spring eggplant. Mod.

### Reffy's
*256 N Craig St, Oakland. Lunch Mon-Fri 11:30-2, Dinner Mon-Sat 5-10. MC,V. Reser sugg.* **681-9883**
Small sushi bar, table service...and sushi by ace Johnnie from old Anna's Place, Downtown. The Korean Bulgoki—beef/sprouts/egg—can't be beat. American sandwiches, beer, wine. Call ahead for sushi on weekends. Inexp.

### Yen's Gourmet
*4219 Murray, Sq Hill. Mon-Fri 11:30-10, Sat-Sun 4:30-10. AE,D,DC,MC,V.* **421-5500.**
Good Twin-Tasted Chicken, $8.95. Triple Sizzing Delight—shrimp, scallops, chicken over sizzling rice, $10; Precious Seafood in Bird Nest $14. Inexp-Mod.

## Sushi To Go

### Kiku Express
*229 S Highland , Shadyside. Mon-Sat 11-10. Sun 12-10. MC,V.* **661-5458.**
Main dishes and sushi & maki to go or eat in at this bright Japanese eatery... at wonderful prices. Tuna sushi, California roll plus shrimp, teriyaki, miso, Tokyo ribs, Katsu bowl pork & rice...under $6.

**16**

## Indian

### Indian Lunch Buffets

Newest Asian trend is the Indian Lunch Buffet offered by five E End restaurants: **Darbar** 4519 Center, Oakland. 7 days 11:30-2:30. $6.95.
**Delhi Grill** 320 Atwood, Oakland. Mon-Sat 11:30-3. $4.99.

**India Garden** 328 Atwood, Oakland. 7 days. 11:30-2:30. $6.95
**Star of India** 412 S Craig, Oakland. Mon-Wed 11:30-2:30, Sun 12-3. $6.95.
**Taste of India** 4320 Penn, Bloomfield. Thur-Sat 11-2:30. $6.50.

### Samurai Japanese Steak House

*2100 Greentree Rd, Greentree Mon-Thur 11:30- 9:30, Fri-Sat til 11. Sun 4:30-8:30. AE,DC,MC,V.* **276-2100.**
Dramatic dining at habachi tables with performing chefs; great decor, steaks, seafood, tropical drinks. Mod-Exp.

### Shogun

*8 Tech Dr, near Monrv Mall. Mon-Fri 11:30-2:30, 5-9:30, Fri-Sat til 10:30. Sun 3-9. AE,DC,MC,V.* **372-0700.**
Japanese chefs perform at your table in this handsome restaurant. Also sushi & sashimi. Lunch/Dinner $4.50-$24.

### Sushi Too

*5432 Walnut St, Shadyside. AE,D,MC,V. Mon-Fri 11:30-3, Sat til 10:30, Fri-Sat til 11:30. Sun 1-9.* **687-8744.**
Bright Japanese decor/music; sushi bar & traditional cuisine—seafood, teriyaki, tempura. Private tatami-mat dining room. $4.95-$20. Inexp-Exp. (See Review)

### Tokyo Japanese Food Store

*Ellsworth/College, Shadyside. Mon-Sat 10-8, Sun 10-7. No credit cards.* **661-3777.**
Food store with city's best sushi/sashimi, big selection of exotic fish, vegetable rolls. Call ahead for take-out.

### Young Bin Kwan

*4305 Main, Bloomfield. Mon-Fri 11-10:30, Sat-Sun 1-11. AE,DC,MC,V.* **687-2222.**
Sushi/Japanese/Korean/Chinese standards plus exotic Asian dishes, tableside cooking. Atmospheric private Japanese tatami rooms, wishing bridge. Mod-Exp.

## INDIAN

### Darbar

519 Centre Ave, Oakland. 7 days. Lunch 11:30-2:30, Dinner 5-10, Fri-Sat til 10:30. Sun 5-10. AE,MC,V. **687-0515.**
Pleasant neighborhood room with mostly North Indian Punjab cuisine; excellent paneers, curries and biryanis with saffron rice. Inexp-Mod.

### Delhi Grill

*320 Atwood, Oakland. Mon-Sat 11:30-3, 5-10. D,MC,V.* **681-8855.**
Casual, Indian music, N & S cuisine—good tandoori, masala dosa—rice, potatoes, lentils. $4.99. Buffet $5.75-$11.

### Dosa Hut

*4141 Old Wm Penn Hwy, Monroeville. Mon-Fri 11-8 (closed Tues), Sat-Sun 10-9. No credit cards.* **373-5581.**
Small, family Indian/vegetarian. $4-$6.

### India Garden

*328 Atwood St, Oakland. Mon-Sat 11:30-2:30, 4-10. Sun 4-10. AE,D,DC, MC,V.* **682-3000.**
Indian music, decor. Sophisticated N Indian from Chef Didar Singh. Famous for tandoori chicken, vegetarian dishes, all-you-can-eat $6.95 Buffet. Inexp-Mod.

### Star of India

*412 S Craig St, Oakland. Lunch 11:30-2:30, Dinner Sun-Thur 5-10, Fri- Sat til 10:30. AE,MC,V.* **681-5700.**
Excellent cuisine in pleasing room, vegetarian thali, mixed grill tandoori, paneer & bhartha—herb spiced eggplant;

## Thai/Vietnamese

ndian breads. Great Lunch Buffet
Sun-Wed $6.95. Mod. (See Review)

### Shish Mahal
*155 Wm Penn Hwy, Monrv. Tues-Fri
:30-9:30. Sat-Sun 12-9:30. AE,MC,V.
73-6699.*
Hyderabab Indian cuisine; specialties
lamb curry, chicken, desserts. Inexp.

### Taste of India
*320 Penn Ave, Bloomfield. Lunch Mon-
Sat 11-2:30. Dinner Sun-Thur 5-10,
Fri-Sat til 11. AE,DC,V. 681-7700.*
little eatery specializing in N Indian—
andoori, chicken jal frezi, shrimp kabob,
Mod-Exp.

## THAI/TIBETAN/CAMBODIAN

### Himalayan Tibetan Restaurant
*531 Forbes, Oakland. Mon-Thur 11- 8,
Fri til 9. Sat 12-9. D,MC,V. 687-6550.*
City's only Himalayan; informal, unusual
menu—vegetable dishes, soups, moo
moo (dumplings), curries. $4-$8. Inexp.

### Phnom Penh
*10 First Ave, Downtown. Mon-Sat 11-4.
No credit cards. 261-4166.*
Homestyle Cambodian, Thai, Chinese—
noodle soup, chicken with lemon, basil
and pineapple/ginger, green curry. $5-$6.

## Top Thai

### Thai Place
*809 Bellefonte St, Shadyside. Mon
4:30-10, Tues-Thur 11:30-10, Fri til
11, Sat 12-11. Sun 12-9:30. AE,D,
DC,MC,V. 687-8586.*
Pittsburgh's Thai fans are enthused
over this warm, stylish room, rated
one of "top 25" Thai restaurants in
the country. Great seafood platter,
tiger prawns in red curry sauce, crispy
fish. Smiling service, delightful sidewalk tables in summer. Inexp-Mod.

## Tropical Delight
## Teody's La Fillipiniana
*5321 Butler St, Lawrenceville. Wed-
Sun 5-10. No credit cards. 781-8724.*
Charming little tropical oasis with a
soothing decor and four-star Phillipine
cuisine, a delightful blend of Thai,
Indian and Spanish. Unusual marinated Adobo chicken, delicate curries,
trout in banana leaves, appetizers,
desserts. $7-$13. (See Review)

### Rama
*346 Atwood, Oklnd. Mon-Sat 11:30-2:30,
4:30-9:30. AE,D,DC,MC,V. 687- 8424.*
Little place specializing in great Dap Thai
noodles, seafood. $5-$10. Inexp.

### Siamese Kitchen
*5846 Forbes, Sq Hill. Tues-Thur 11:30-3,
4:30-9:30, Fri & Sat til 10:30. Sun 4:30-9.
AE,D,DC,MC,V. 521-0728.*
Very pleasant 2nd-fl room, Thai curry,
satay chicken, lemon grass soup. Mod.

## VIETNAMESE/CHINESE

### Kim's Coffee Shop
*5447 Penn, Garfield. Tues-Thur & Sun
11:30-9:30, Fri-Sat til 10:30. MC,V. No
liquor. 362-7019.*
Popular Vietnamese/Mandarin; try crispy
chicken wings stuffed with shrimp & crab.
You can get really spicy here! Inexp.

### Me Lyng
*213 W 8th , Hmstd. Mon-Thur 11- 9:30,
Fri-Sat til 10. Sun 3-9. AE,MC,V.464-1477.*
Casual Viet/Chinese. Sour Soup with
homemade eggrolls, crispy beef. Inexp.

### Thai Binh
*Century III Mall, Mon-Thur 11-10, Fri-Sat
til 11. Sun 12-9. AE,D,MC,V. 655-4044.*
Thai binh—"peace" in Vietnamese—has
good sweet/sour soup, shrimp with bean
sprouts & seafood bird nest. $9.95-$17.

**16**

# PARTY ROOMS

Whether it's a boat, train or a magnificent museum...beautiful and unique sites for private/business parties abound in the Pittsburgh area. Here are some of the city's best...with exciting atmosphere and that element of surprise that transforms a gathering into a celebration making *you* a successful party-giver!

## The Benedum

Hold a business/social meeting at the resplendent Benedum Center for the Arts—home of the city's opera, ballet, dance and Broadway shows. The restored grand lobby is a glamorous setting for a wedding or reception with the promenade and mezzaine, rehearsal studios and downstairs galleries all available for parties.
**Capacity:** 20-400.
**Cost:** Varies, smaller rooms $3.75 pers, more hors d'oeuvres, sitdown meals.
**Contact:** Adm Office—**456-2600**.

## Brandy's Restaurant
*Penn Ave & 24th St, Strip.*
A good in-city site for receptions, meetings and parties is Brandy's new "party house" adjoining their concrete patio. Two L-shaped, green carpeted rooms can accommodate large events of up to 180—an additional 60 with the patio in summer. A second upstairs room shares the restaurant's stained-glass, oakwood decor and accommodates up to 50. Private bar, fireplace and dance floor make it an ideal site for informal

---

## A Floating Party On Pittsburgh's Rivers

The Gateway Clipper's six vessels are unique settings for weddings, private parties, business and social events. You can tie the knot with the Point Fountain in the background and a salute from the Captain's horn. Or celebrate by releasing many-coloured balloons over the water! The vessels can be chartered for up to 3 hours—the Liberty Belle or River Belle accommodates up to 240, the Party Liner up to 400, and the elegant 265-foot Majestic up to 700. The Clipper will cater anything from a $5.95 box lunch to a $32 buffet or $43 for a sit-down dinner. They'll also arrange for music, magic, entertainment. **355-7965**.

---

office revels, football parties, rehearsal dinners.
**Cost:** Party House $100, Upstairs Room $50. Catering $7-$22.
**Contact:** Larry Patterson/Brett Geibel— **566-1000**.

## Cafe Victoria
*Torrance House, 946 Western Ave, Allegheny West.*
Charm your guests in this restored home, its quaint rooms overflowing with Victorian antiques...a unique setting for small business/private parties. Best space is the William Morris-style front parlor with blue & gold wallpaper, fireplaces, fringed lamps, intriguing antiques. A dusky upstairs garret has a 'courtin' settee' and a 'Do Not Disturb' sign...a delightful place to pop the question or for an intimate party or business 'assignation.'
**Capacity:** Two to 65 for the entire house.
**Cost:** No room cost. Catering from menu $7 up, or by arrangement.
**Contact:** Harrison Booth—**323-8881**

## The Carnegie
*4400 Forbes Avenue, Oakland.*
Some of the city's most magnificent interiors are available for private celebrations at the Carnegie Museum. Imagine your guests in the Music Hall's ornate gilt and marble foyer, dancing or banqueting beneath the gold baroque ceiling...a spectacular site for a sumptuous private party. Or in the marble Hall of Architecture, the huge architectural casts an imposing background for a special event. Or–imagination soars– your gathering in the Museum of Art's graceful Scaife foyer overlooking the beautiful Sculpture Court and fountain... a lovely space by day...enchanting on a summer's eve as guests wander amid the Court's illuminated trees and statues...the golden lights reflected in the Gallery's sheer glass walls. If you have it—what a better way to spend!
**Capacity:** Music Hall—2000 reception, 500 for banqueting; Hall of Architecture—

**17**

400 reception, 250 banquet; Museum of Art foyer, 500 reception.
**Cost:** Music Hall, $1950 base rental for 3 hours; Hall of Architecture $960 base rental; Museum of Art foyer $1200 base rental. Museum catering available.
**Contact:** Eileen Dewalt—622-3360.

## Carnegie Science Center
*North Shore, next to Three Rivers Stadium.*
Pittsburgh's famed Science Center is a unique party facility with a great river view, adaptable for everything from seminars to black-tie events. Multiple areas available for rental include the Overlook Diningroom and outdoor dining terrace. You can dazzle your guests with an Omnimax performance or a special exhibition for an out-of-the-ordinary event.
**Capacity:** 20-2500.
**Cost:** Rental $500-$15,000. Catering $10-$50 a person.
**Contact:** Kelly Hardon, Mgr Special Events—237-3431.

## Flaugherty House
*147 Flaugherty Run Road, Moon Twp. (5 min from Pgh Airport).*
Perfect setting for a picturesque wedding ...with a horse and carriage for the bride and groom...in this beautifully restored New Orleans-style mansion fronted by two Georgian pillars. It's on six and a half wooded acres with a private bridge, gazebo and a meandering creek...a

### Japanese Party
A bright idea for those who love Japanese cuisine are the traditional tatami rooms at **Sushi Too,** 5432 Walnut St in Shadyside. Complete with low tables and low cushioned chairs, they're a perfect site for a unique party. No charge for the room, order from regular or special menus. Sliding doors open up space to accommodate 6 to 60. Call Misa —687-8744.

### Party at the Warhol
A sleek new Pittsburgh party space, the new **Warhol Museum,** 117 Sandusky Street, N Side, is a sophisticated setting amid the colorful Warhol collection. The graceful high-tech design is light, soothing... perfect for an office party, reception, small wedding. And the catering— delicious gourmet from the museum's All In Good Taste cafe.
**Capacity:** Up to 200.
**Cost:** Rental $4000-$5000. Cocktails to sitdown $6.50-$75 pers.
**Contact:** Greg Bruchard. 237-8300.

romantic setting for an outdoor wedding. Also ideal for showers, graduations, picnics, business meetings.
**Capacity:** Mansion house 125 guests, Ballroom 450, Gazebo 300.
**Cost:** From $10 person for shower up to $35 for grand dinner.
**Contact** Clark Johnson. 457-1100.

## Gulf Tower
*707 Grant Street, Downtown.*
Your guests can enjoy a great view high above the city as you party from the tower of this famous Pittsburgh landmark. The elegant former Gulf board meeting room on the 30th floor is an impressive meeting site. And an open room on the 26th floor is perfect for cocktails. There's also a 45-seat tiered theatre on the 3rd. All are available from Mon-Fri from 8-5.
**Cost:** $50 an hr, $150 1/2 day, $250 for whole day. No catering.
**Contact:** Mary Jo Vaciro—263-6000.

## The Mansion
*657 S Pittsburgh Rd, Rt 8, Butler.*
The beautiful, chandeliered old T. W. Phillips mansion is a gracious setting for wedding receptions and larger parties. You have your choice of the East Wing...white linen walls, mauve and burgundy accents...or a West Wing

opening into a delightful garden patio. The 1924 mansion (the elegant old Ernie's Esquire) boasts stunning black/white fireplaces and marble floors, paned glass windows and two bar areas.
**Capacity:** Up to 250. No catering.
**Cost:** East Wing $500, West Wing $1500; combined facilities $2000.
**Contact:** Kay Freehling—**586-6171**

## Fountainview Room
*2nd Level, Sheraton at Station Square.* This romantic room, decorated in teal, salmon and dusty rose, has a splendid view of the city skyline. It's plush decor ts the scenery—a superb place for a wedding, rehearsal dinner, cocktail party.
**Capacity:** 100.
**Cost:** Room charge varies. Cocktails $8 erson up, Lunch $8.95 up, Dinner 15.50 up.
**Contact:** Sales Dept—**261-2000.**

## Fox Chapel Yacht Club
*366 Old Freeport Road, Fox Chapel.* An unconventional conference center with relaxing view of river greenery and the ub marina, full audio-visual facilities and mous cuisine to keep your attendees appy. It's an out-of-city favorite for orporate affairs, seminars, retirement nners, small or large parties. And the

---

## Have A Zoo Doo!

### Pittsburgh Zoo
*Highland Park, East Liberty.*
You can talk to the animals as you party in this adventuresome setting. Get a taste of the jungle in the **African Overlook**, a thatched hut for 20-75 people ($100). Or be a "party animal" in the **Tropical Forest** Exhibit Hall (up to 200 for $1500). Or party outdoors under the 6000 sq-ft Party Tent which seats 500 ($250). Get your guests "in the swim" in the The **Aqua Zoo,** a thrilling setting for 200 people ($1000.) Or take over the Main Visitor's Plaza, 300 people ($250) or Lecture Hall for 250 ($400.) Classrooms can accommodate smaller parties from 35-75 ($75-$100). Catering available for breakfast, lunch, dinner, cocktail parties, business meetings 7 days. Best time to see the animals is during zoo hours (additional $3 adm. charge).
**Contact: Special Events-665-3639.**

---

big, pale gray ballroom has an outside deck overlooking the river—ideal for weddings, business and social events.
**Capacity:** 10 to 1500.
**Cost:** Room cost varies. Catering $7.95-$32.50 person.
**Contact:** Paula Meisner–**393-8881**.

## Grand Concourse
*Station Square*
The 'grand hotel' atmosphere of this famous restaurant can't be beat for an elegant wedding breakfast or anniversary party. Tables are separated in the main diningroom but marvelous atmosphere and gracious service prevail for first-class partying.
**Capacity:** 20-200.
**Cost:** No room charge. Hors d'oeuvres $3.75 up, Lunch $10.50-$15, Dnr $19-$25.
**Contact:** Stephanie Highley—**391-3474.**

---

## Pittsburgh Party

### Chiodo's Tavern
*107 W 8th Avenue, Homestead.*
How about a real Pittsburgh party in the back room of this famous neighborhood tavern...or in the Italian beer garden outside in summer. One hundred beers will flow, Joe will serve his famous 'mystery sandwiches' and regale your guests with tales of the city. Here's to good friends. They'll wonder why *they* never thought of it! **Capacity:** 50-75.
**Cost:** Reasonable.
**Contact:** Sam—**461-9307.**

**17**

## Hartwood

*Saxonburg Blvd, Rt 8, Allison Park.*
A garden party on the beautiful lawn of this impressive Tudor Mansion under spacious yellow & white striped tents is a rare experience. Your guests can also tour the impressive Tudor mansion and grounds. Bring your own caterer.
**Capacity:** 75 people.
**Cost:** Varies by season.
**Contact:** Del Cook—**767-9200.**

## Heinz Hall

*Sixth Avenue & Penn, Downtown.*
The possibilities here are endless. Imagine a reception or wedding in the grand marble lobby with its plush gold, white and red decor...or a summer cocktail party under the stars in the outdoor plaza—available on non-performance nights. There's also the Grand Tier and Overlook bars, Mozart Room and downstairs Regency Room...for everything from large corporate parties to very small receptions.
**Capacity:** 25-350.
**Cost:** Varies from budget to lavish depending on group size and catering.
**Contact:** Terry Neugebauer/Jean Ross—**392-4879.**

## Hyeholde Round Room

*Coraopolis Heights Road, Moon Twp. 10 min from Airport.*
Here comes the bride...down the beautiful curved staircase, a dramatic entrance into this elegant stone/glass room. Connected to the restaurant's Tudor mansion by an art-lined gallery, it has a two-story glass wall overlooking two acres of woodland. Spring/summer parties can spill out onto the lawn, a romantic setting for a wedding, reception, cocktail or business function. And guests can revel in Hyeholde's fine cuisine.
**Capacity:** 20-150.
**Cost:** No rental cost for room (excp Sun). Lunch $7-$13, Dinner from $17.50.
**Contact:** Debbie Fajerski—**264-3116.**

## Party—by the Riverside

Party on the floating Boardwalk, On the Water in the Strip. The handsome glass-walled **Riverwatch** banquet hall on the second level, has space for 250-300, an outer deck and a great topside river view. Call Barb **281-3900.**

## La Filipiniana

*5321 Butler St, Lawrenceville.*
A little bit of heaven in the city...soothing surroundings and flavourful, exotic cuisine make this a unique place for wonderful parties in cozy indoor rooms or outdoor garden. A secret favorite of university/professional groups, ideal for office and private parties. You'll love the food and chef/owner Teody's warm welcome and attention to detail.
**Capacity:** 60, 100-150 wth garden.
**Cost:** Lunch $5.95-$10. Dinner $12-$25.
**Contact:** Teody Schipper—**781-8724.**

## L C Simpson's

*3220 W Liberty Ave, Dormont.*
The elegant, chandeliered party rooms of this Dormont restaurant are favorite South Hills party sites. Soft shades of peach and seafoam green are pleasing background for a shower, reception, private party.
**Capacity:** 10-150.
**Cost:** No rental fee. Catering $6-$20 per.
**Contact:** Debbie—**531-0666.**

## Lawrence Convention/Expo Ctr

*1001 Penn Avenue, Downtown.*
Pittsburghers often forget the 25 rooms on the third level of the Convention Center—many with spectacular views of the Allegheny. They're ideal for everything from business meetings to wedding receptions. There are also two full-service lounges with outdoor terraces...ideal for cook-outs on a summer's night. In-house catering, audio-visuals, tele-conferencing.
**Capacity:** 10 to 4000.
**Cost:** Varied rentals, waived for events.
**Contact:** Sales Dept—**565-6000.**

## Max's Allegheny Tavern
*Middle & Suismon Streets, N Side.*
A unique Pittsburgh place, this historic tavern has the atmosphere of a German gastehaus. Four connecting 2nd floor rooms with fireplaces, Victorian wall-paper, lace curtains are just right for an informal party, business meeting, rehearsal dinner. And the food's unique too.
**Capacity:** 10-80.
**Cost:** $50 rental for catering costs under $400.
**Contact:** Karen McCulloch—**231-1899.**

## Metropol/Rosebud
*1650 Smallman, Strip District.*
Perfect get-together space for everything from small meetings to big social/civic/cultural events and parties; uniquely pleasant space for wedding receptions. Stunning multi-level night club plus delightful decor in adjoining coffee house. State-of-the-art audio visuals for multimedia events. Hors d'oeuvres to full-service catering.
**Capacity:** Up to 2000; Rosebud 700, Metropol 1400.
**Cost:** Flexible, depending on event.
**Contact:** Glenn Rizzelli—**261-2221.**

## Morton's of Chicago
*CNG Tower, 625 Liberty Ave, Downtown.*
This famous restaurant's "Boardrooms" are a business favorite—perfectly appointed for everything from a serious board meeting to a bachelor party, informal "cigar dinner" or holiday fete. The decor—rich wood, marble topped buffets, Oriental carpets—carries over the restaurant's handsome burnished look. The audio-visuals are state-of-the-art and Morton's famous steak and Classic Club Bar add a distinctive flavour to your entertaining.
**Capacity:** 10-70.
**Cost:** No room cost. Hors d'oeuvres $5-$8 up per person. Dinner $19.95-$42.95.
**Contact:** Peggyann Cullen—**261-7141.**

### TRAVELING PARTIES

### In A Super Coach...
Travel in style and party at the same time...in a deluxe $325,000 custom built motor coach (not a bus!) from Executive Transportation Co. Equipped with everything from sofas to a galley, bar, TV and a stereo system for a little travelin' music, the car rents for $2.50 a mile (or $800 a day), a bargain shared by groups of 20. You can hire a hostess or bartender and 'lay back' and enjoy fun all the way to your destination. Call month ahead. Jim/Patricia West—**242-6267.**

### In A Railroad Car
You can host daylight parties for up to 15 guests in a refurbished antique railroad car (built in 1926 by Pullman Standard for Louisville/Nashville RR). Stationary at the Conrail yard office in Sharpsburg, the car has hosted movie stars and government officials. It's replete with lounge, four state-rooms sleeping eight, showers, all-electric kitchen, formal diningroom and observation platform from which to watch the scenery. It's a great way to see the USA anywhere that Amtrak goes. What a wonderful way to go!
**Capacity:** 8-15. **Cost:** Price varies. Stationary around $400. **Contact:** John R. Owen—**531-3652.**

### Or By Balloon
How's this for a thrilling party... transport your guests to the skies for a fantastic hot air balloon ride with **Ragge & Willow Enterprises,** 2 min. from Westmoreland Mall. The 45-60 minute flights, at sunrise and a few hours before sunset, include complimentary breakfast and a traditional Champagne Party on landing. Year round 7 days. Reser 3 weeks ahead. **Capacity:** 25 guests. **Cost:** $150 person. **Call:** **836-4777.**

17

# Wedding Scenes

## UNIQUE WEDDING SCENES

### Heinz Memorial Chapel
A jewel of a wedding site, this exquisite Gothic chapel on the Pitt campus is open to Pitt students, alumni, relatives and employees. Capacity 450. Available Fri & Sat.
**Cost: $395. 624-4157.**

### National Aviary in Pittsburgh
The lush foliage of the Tropical American Marsh Room is a unique background for nuptials with exotic, multicoloured birds swooping nearby.
**Cost:** $300 fee, limit 50 guests.
**Contact: 323-7235**

### Phipps Conservatory
The perfect wedding...or party scene... you choose the room...the flower arrangements are magnificent! Accommodates 35-200 guests under glass or outdoors during non-show times.
**Cost:** $250 & up. **622-6906.**

### Pittsburgh Parks
Outdoor "I Do's" in the greenery of city/county parks–Schenley, Hartwood, North/South among them. Consider a back-up shelter in case of rain and be sure to get a permit.
**Cost:** City Shelters $40-$175 **255-2370.** County $75-$275 **392-8455.**

## Penn Brewery
*Troy Hill, N Side. Across 16th St Bridge.*
This authentic German beer hall, the historic old Eberhart & Ober Brewery, is a fun setting for an exuberant party. You can accommodate up to 60 in the Rathskeller daytime Mon-Sat and Mon and Thur nights. Or celebrate upstairs in the cheery beer hall (Mon only) with its high windows, wooden beams and a view of copper-kettle beer-making through a glass wall. Or take your party outdoors into the atmospheric cobblestoned courtyard. The entire facility is available on Sunday. A beer and German food lovers delight!
**Capacity:** Rathskeller 60. Beer Hall 110, Entire facility 100-200. Beer Garden 75.
**Cost:** Reasonable—varies with room.
**Contact:** Mary Beth Pastorius—237-9402.

## The Pennsylvanian
*1100 Liberty Ave, Downtown.*
One of the city's best kept secrets is the beautiful party space in the magnifcent Concourse of the restored Pennsylvania RR Station—now a fashionable downtown address. Your guests make a grand entrance from beneath the familiar rotunda into the Concourse's breathtaking space...lofty skylight ceiling, marble floors, restored wall paintings...an elegant setting for everything from private weddings to huge corporate parties and fund-raising balls.
**Capacity:** 150-2500.
**Cost:** Rental $5000.
**Contact:** Carol Gamble—391-6730.

## The Priory
*614 Pressley Street, North Side.*
This Victorian in-city inn, a charmingly restored abbey, is a delightful choice for secluded meetings and parties. The diningroom and courtyard are romantic background for a wedding/reception and the Inn's quiet rooms are perfect backdrops for business and private parties. Large groups can extend into the hall, sitting room, elegant library and, in good weather, to the charming courtyard.
**Capacity:** 42 seated, 60 stand-up, 100 with courtyard.
**Cost:** Meetings $200, Parties $300, Weddings $600, add $50 for ceremony.
**Contact:** Michael Johnson—231-3338.

# Children's Parties

## CHILDREN'S PARTIES

### The Carnegie
Make your child's next birthday a unique adventure with a Carnegie museum party. Choose Polar World and African Safari (ages 6-9) or Dinosaurs (ages 6-10) Sat & Sun only from 1:30-3:30. Invitations, favors, ice cream, cake, beverages are included. **Cost:** Members $10 child, $12 non-members. Reserve far in advance, there's a long waiting list. **Contact:** Anne Walters—**622-3289.**

### The Factory
*7501 Penn at Braddock, East End.*
Kiddies love this mall full of games:
**ShadySkates PartyLine:** A supervised party for 4 and older—roller skating, gymnastics, sports, beauty parlor—and for eats...pizza. $165 for 15 children 4 & up. **731-4937.**
**Gymkhana's Infant/Toddler Gym**
Supervised parties for tots 3 & younger with child-size gym equipment—miniature trampolines, tree house, trapeze. $95 for 20 tots (1-3 yr olds). **247-4100.**

### Good Ship Lollipop
*Gateway Clipper Fleet, Station Sq.*
Take your party aboard the colorful Lollipop for a one-hour Birthday Cruise on Pgh's rivers. Included are hot dogs, cupcakes, balloons and entertainment with Lolly the Clown! Kiddie favorite. Or you can rent the whole boat for $450 an hour for a private party. **Capacity:** Up to 100. **Cost:** $10.95 person. **Contact:** Maria Kehlbeck—**355-7965.**

### Hartwood Hayride
*Saxonburg Blvd, Rt 8, Allison Park.*
What better site for a party than a good old-fashioned Hayride on a summer's day or eve. Guaranteed fun!
**Cost:** Price varies for 1-hour ride for 20 children/16 adults. **Contact: 767-9200.**

### Kennywood Park
*West Mifflin.*
A novel idea—for both kiddies and adults—is a birthday/special event at Kennywood Amusement Park. For 25 persons or more you can get discounts off the ride-all-day admission price. Bring your own picnic or have the park cater hot dogs, hamburgers and watermelon or charbroiled steak & potatoes served in an outdoor pavilion. It's a trip down memory lane for adults who remember their wonder years. **Capacity:** 25 to 1000 or more. **Cost:** Admission $10.50-$17.50. Catering $5.80-$7.30 person. **Contact:** Bob Henninger/Andy Quinn—**464-9931.**

### Sandcastle on the Mon
*Rt 387, West Homestead.*
Your guests will never forget their summer evening along the Pittsburgh riverfront at this fantastic water park. They can be transported to a Hawaiian Luau, an Island Buffet or a Beach Party (Mon & Tues after park closing) to enjoy the giant hot tubs, volleyball courts, music, dancing, fun.
**Capacity:** Minimum of 100 to 2000.
**Cost:** $8-$27 per person.
**Contact:** Bob Henninger/Andy Quinn—**464-9931.**

### Tramps
212 Blvd of Allies, Downtown. **261-1990.**
What better spot for a party than Dolly's Boudoir or Madame's Room on the 2nd floor of this charming downtown restaurant—the site of one of Pgh's first bordellos. Small, intimate upstairs rooms with quaint touches. Two full bars, patio are ideal for business meetings, cocktail parties or a unique bachelor party.
**Capacity:** 70.
**Cost:** No charge for room. Hors d'oeuvres $5-$11, sit-down $9.95-$15.
**Contact:** Debbie Bradley—**261-1990.**

17

### Shiloh Inn

*123 Shiloh Street, Mt Washington.*
A well-kept secret...high above the city in this mellow restaurant with a Civil War flavour are two small drawing rooms with an atmosphere perfect for small parties.
**Capacity:** 10-75.
**Cost:** No room charge. Food costs vary.
**Contact:** John Edgos—**431-4000.**

### Victoria Hall

*201 S. Winebiddle St, Bloomfield.*
Fulfill your romantic dreams in this "high Victorian" hall (former Ursuline Academy) ...worthy of an elegant wedding, reception. After the ceremony in the chapel with its 19th Cent stained-glass windows you can greet your guests in the conservatory and celebrate in a splendidly restored 1860 dining room...crown moldings, 15 ft ceilings (seats 50-100). Then dance the night away in the palatial grand ballroom.
**Capacity:** Up to 250. Chapel 165. **Cost:** Up to $150 room. Catering $15 up per.
**Contact:** Tom Walsh—**363-8030.**

### Have A Ball On the Belles

You can charter your own boat to your own river destination with **Three Rivers Charter Service**...a perfect setting for memorable parties, weddings, sales meetings, fun/family cruises...or a small romantic, couples' cruise. Party from 3 hours to overnight—in one of the four Belles...Freedom, Merry, Lady and Momma Belle. Cash bar, catering, DJ dancing, entertainment available.
**Capacity:** 6-149 passangers.
**Cost:** $13.50 person for 3 hrs ($16 for special events/holidays). (Min 50 people.) Food—$2 munchies to $13-$18 dinners.
**Contact: 363-BOAT.**

### Party On Your Own Houseboat

A dream of a party...rent your own 56-ft houseboat, the luxurious Sunseeker of **Three Rivers Cruises, Inc.** The boat is equipped with a hot tub for 15, water slide, stereo, wet bar and full galley with a microwave to heat up your own or catered eats. A relaxing milieu and a real change of scene for your next sales meeting, corporate party, wedding, birthday or just a 'friendly' celebration. **Capacity:** One to 60.
**Cost:** $400-$700 base rate for 4 to 6 hr cruises (off-season Oct-Dec $350-$450) plus captain/fuel fees.
**Contact:** 3 Rvs Cruises—**831-1188.**

## PARTY IN THE PARK

You bring the food and fun for a party in one of the City/County parks. Facilities vary from open air shelters to renovated barns and ski lodges, among them Frick, Schenley, Riverview, Grandview, North, South, Boyce and Hartwood. Permits are necessary for formal events i.e. weddings, receptions. Make arrangememts well in advance.

**Pittsburgh Citiparks** has everything from a small shelter in Frick for up to 40 people ($40-$60) to a large shelter at Riverview for 300 ($125-$175). Permits are necessary for formal events. $25 permit for alcohol. **255-2370.**

**Allegheny Co Parks** has picnic shelters in the $10-$15 range with various packages with or without catering. Attractive shelters includes Boyce Park Ski Lodge (in-house catering only) and renovated barns & buildings ($75-$275). Or you can rent a large weatherproof tent to party on Hartwood's beautiful grounds. **392-8474.**

Pittsburgh ribs are second to none! You can check them out at the annual Allegheny Rib Cook-Off on Labor Day weekend when rib-makers from all over compete with local chefs. For information call 392-8455.

18

# Stand up...Sit down...Take out

### Blue Lou's
*1510 E Carson, S Side. Tues-Sat 11-1:30am. AE,DC,MC,V.* **381-7675.**
Tangy pork ribs in fun eatery. Slab $13, half $10, mild to hot. Chicken, platters.

### Bobby Rubino's
*Shops at Station Sq. Mon-Thur 11-10:30, Fri-Sat til 12:30. Sun 1-9.* **642-RIBS.**
Mellow rib dinners in posh decor. Steel City—2 slabs $17.95 1 slab $15 with baked potato/fries; great onion ring loaf $2-3.50. Sit down, take out.

### Damon's
*Waterworks, Freeport Rd, Fox Chapel. Mon-Thur 11-12, Fri-Sat til 1 am, Sun til 11. AE,DC,MC,V.* **782-3750.**
Handsome eatery, full menu & meaty, pungent ribs. Slab $13.95, half $10.95 with salad, baked potato. $5.95 Rib Lunch. Sit down, take out.

### Hotlicks
*Theatre Mall, 5520 Walnut, Shadyside.* **683-2583.** *Galleria, S Hills* **341-7427.** *McIntyre Sq, N Hills* **369-7675.** *Mon-Thur 11:30-10, Fri-Sat til 12. Sun 4:30-9, (S Hills, N Hills 12-10). AE,DC,MC,V.*
Big favorites, popular gathering places. $14.95 rack, $8.95 1/2 with slaw. Sweet mild, smoky med, or Screamin' Killer-Willer. Eat in, take out.

### House of Sauce
*4707 Centre Oakland. Mon-Sat til 2am.* **682-9888.**
The real thing! Hot & spicy, great tastin'. Slab $19.60, 1/2 $10.55, sandwich $7; BBQ chicken, potato salad, sweet potato pie. Sides 50c-65c. Stand up, take out.

### King James BBQ
*1697 Laketon Rd, Wilkinsburg.Tues-Thur 11-11, Fri-Sat til 2am, Sun 1-7.* **242-5477.**
Real soulfood. Mild or hot "in sauce we trust." Slab $18, 1/2 $10.50. Rib sandwich $6. Sides. Take out only.

### Original Hot Dog Shop
*3901 Forbes, Oakland. 7 days 10am-4am.* **621-0435.** The Big "O" is into zesty ribs mild to hot, $8.80 a slab with cole slaw & potato. Sit down, take out.

### Mr P & P's Ribbs
*1501 Fifth/Pride, Uptown. Tues-Thur 11-11, Fri til 2:30am, Sat 3-2:30 am, Sun 1-7. No credit cards.* **566-2773.**
Open-pit, rack of 12—$17.85, 1/2 $9.25. Chicken, Texas toast, great baked beans, cakes/pies. Eat in, take out, delivery.

### Red River Bar-B-Que
*Holiday Ctr, Monrv* **372-2500.** *Perry Hwy, Wexford* **935-9200.** *Mon-Sat 11-10. AE,DC,MC,V.*
Full menu plus award-winning hickory smoked baby back or pork spare ribs. Double $13.95, single $8.95 with 2 sides; mild, hot, dare-devil. Sit down, take out.

### Rib House
*2125 Murray Ave, Sq Hill. Tues-Thur 4-10:30, Fri-Sat 3-10:30, Sun 3-9.* **521-8827.**
Pungent—mellow to extra hot. Rack $14.82, half $7.93; smoked potatoes, sides. Good wings, dinners. $4-$8. Sit in, take out.

### Time Out Half Time Cafe
*20810 Rt 19, Cranberry. 7 days 11-11. No credit cards.* **772-1930.**
'93 Rib Cook-Off winners, zesty ribs. Slab $13.95, 1/2 $7.95, 1/4 $4.50 with salad, chips/fries, salad. Also great wings.

### Wilson's Bar-B-Q
*700 N Taylor & Buena Vista, N Side* **322-7427.** *3404 Penn, E Liberty* **683-1616.** *Mon-Sat 12-12.*
Pungent, hot & tangy, some say city's best. Slab $17.25, plates $6-$9, greens $1.30, sides 90c. Outdoors in summer. Stand up, take out.

### Woodside
*7610 Frankstown, Homewood . Mon-Wed 11am-12, Thur-Sat til 1:30.* **371-1949.**
Secret open pit recipe—hot or mild. Slab $18.50, 1/2 $8.85. Take out only.

### ...and some fabulous wings
**Fat Franks,** USX Tower. Mon-Fri 6am-4pm.. MC,V. **471-3388.**
Hidden treasure for some of best Buffalo Wings in town. Wing Basket with terrific, tangy sauce regular or super hot—with celery/blue cheese $2.99-$5.98. Dogs, burgers. Downtown delivery.

xciting and unusual restaurants are continually opening around
ttsburgh beckoning both suburban and urban diners to discover new
uisine outside the city. Here are the best of the suburbs...many with
stful country settings...plus popular family eateries with food and party
mosphere that children love.

**19**

### SUBURBS NORTH

### Abate Seafood Co
*Waterworks, Freeport Rd, Fox Chapel. Sun-Thur 11:30-11, Fri-Sat til 12. AE,CB, DC,MC,V.* **781-9550.**
Bona fide Italian/seafood house, all kinds of fish, great hearth-baked pizzas, fish sandwich, key lime pie. Lunch/Dinner $4-$18. Friendly, casual.

### Arrostaria Restaurant
*110 Coventry Sq, Allison Pk. Mon-Thur 11:30-10, Fri-Sat til 11. Sun 11:30-9. AE,DC,MC,V.* **487-3900.**
Stone-hearth roasting; chicken, great pastas. Tuscan bread. $4.95-$8.50.

### Blarney Stone
*30 Grant Ave, Etna. Tues-Thur 11-9, Fri-Sat til 11. Sun 10:30-9. AE,MC,V.* **781-1666.**
Irish/Amer cuisine, authentic Irish stew, corned beef & cabbage, pastries by Irish chef. Gaelic entertainment Fri-Sat, Sun Brunch; dinner theatre. $4-$18.

### Bruster's Ice Cream/Yogurt
*2569 Brandt School Rd, Wexford & Wexford Flats. 7 days 11-11.* **934-0840**
Fabulous 'old fashioned' rich ice cream, yogurt, Italian ice. Outside tables, browsing at farm market next door.Real treat!

### Cathay Gourmet
*4812 McKnight Road, N Hills. Mon-Thur 11:30-10, Fri-Sat til 11. Sun 3-9:30. AE,D,DC,MC,V.* **366-9111.**
Renowned Chinese cuisine. Delicious beef, pork, lobster, great Dragon-Phoenix Soup, Pu Pu Platter for 2. Mon Buffet $8.50. Lunch/Dinner $4-$9.

### Chili's Grill & Bar
*7404 McKnight Rd, N Hills. Mon-Thur 11-11, Fri-Sat til 12. Sun 11-10. AE,DC, MC,V.* **364-5678.**
Big, good-looking; tasty Tex-Mex burgers, ribs, steak and, of course, chili. First-class fajitas, delicious baked onion. $4-$15. Close to the real thing!

### Chop Stix
*1034 Freeport Rd. Sun-Thur 11:30-10, Fri-Sat til 11. AE,MC,V.* **782-3010.**
Szechuan, Hunan, Peking dishes, "30 Minute Duck," house special pork/bean sauce, $5.50-$24. Buffet Sun-Tues $8.99.

### Country Crossroads Cafe
*Hardies Wildwood Rd off Rt 8. Mon-Tues 9-4, Wed-Sun til 9. D,MC,V.* **486-9841.**
Country casual with homemade gifts, crafts for sale. Hearty sandwiches, soup, under $5. Visit Wildwood Collection—17 Victoriana boutiques downstairs.

### Cranberry Hall
*Rt 19, Crider's Corners. Mon-Sat 4-8:30. Sun Dinner 12-8. MC,V.* **776-9930.**
Good family fare, American home cooking—baked ham/raisin sauce, fried chicken, rainbow trout, great Strawberry Ice Cream Meringue. $13-$18.

### Cross Keys
*599 Dorseyville Rd, Fox Chapel. Tues-Fri 11:30-10, Sat 5-11. Sun 3-9. Reser wknds. D,MC,V.* **963-8717.**
Charming little inn, an old stagecoach stop. Delicious steaks, veal, seafood. Lunch $4-$8, Dinner $13-$22.

### Damon's
*Waterworks, Fox Chapel. Mon-Thur 11-12, Fri-Sat til 1. Sun 11-11. AE,DC, MC,V.* **782-3750.**
Great barbecue ribs, chicken, full dinners, sandwiches in pleasant decor; four big TV screens for sports fans. $4-$14.

### Dingbat's
*Waterworks* **781-7727;** *Ross Park Mall* **369-0440.** *Mon-Thur 11:30-12am, Fri-Sat til 1. Sun 10-12. AE,D,DC,MC,V.*
Bright, trendy with fun foods, good portions; big variety of sandwiches, steaks, pasta, specialty drinks. $7-$13.

### Five Sisters New American Grill
*3932 Rt 8, Hampton. Mon-Tues 11:30-1/2am, Wed-Sat til 2am. Sun 5-10 (12-8 football season). AE,D,MC,V.* **487-1755.**

Informal pub atmosphere with cozy wood paneling; sandwiches, unusual dinner specials, homemade soups, super desserts. $3.75-$10.95. Big favorite!

## Fox Chapel Yacht Club
*1366 Old Freeport Rd, Fox Chapel. Lunch Mon-Sat 11-3, Dinner Mon-Thur 5-9 (summer til 10), Fri-Sat til 11. Sun 5-9. Reser sugg. AE,MC,V.* **963-8881.**
Fashionable room with riverfront view, trio Fri. Veal, chicken, seafood, pasta. Lunch/Dinner $4.95-$28.95.

## Franco's
*Fox Chapel Plaza, Freeport Rd. Mon-Thur 11:30-10, Fri-Sat til 11. Sun 3-9. AE,MC,V. Reser sugg.* **782-5155.**
Chef Franco, originator of downtown's Bravo! Franco, holds forth in this polished room with delicious veal, seafood, pasta, tableside renditions. And his fans have found him! $5-$17.

## Grant's Bar
*114 Grant Ave, Millvale. Mon-Fri 11-11, Sat 4-11. Sun 3-8. CB,MC,V.* **821-1541.**
Neighborhood landmark for sandwiches, dinners, jumbo butterfly shrimp. $6-$12.

## Great Wall
*Pines Plaza, 1130 Perry Hwy, Ross. Mon-Thur 11:30-10, Fri-Sat til 11. Sun 3-9. AE,DC,MC,V.* **369-5858.**
Casual, modern with tasty Mandarin, Szechuan, Peking. Good seafood, sizzling rice & chicken. $6-$13.

## Hamfeldt's
*Freeport Rd, Aspinwall. Mon-Fri 11:30-2am, Sat 12-2am. Sun 4-12. AE,D,MC,V.* **782-0444.**
Comfortable neighborhood tavern with great steak and lobster in dining room, sandwiches, ribs in the bar. $4-$25.

## Hampton Inn
*Rt 8, Allison Park. Mon-Sat 11-1am. Sun 11-10. AE,D,DC,MC,V.* **486-5133.**
Multi-paged menu, 100 sandwiches $2-$9. Design one & they'll name it for you!

18 dinners $6 up—seafood platter $16; best selection of imported beer. Fun!

## Hideaway Restaurant
*Venango Golf Course, Cranberry. Mon-Sat Lunch 11:30-2:30, Dinner 5-10. Sun 2-7. AE,MC,V.* **776-4400.**
Great atmosphere, fireplaces, beautiful view; good steak, fish, veal, pasta. Patio. Lunch $5-$7, Dinner $11-$16.

## Hohmann's
*Mt Nebo Rd, Exit 20 I-79. Mon-Thur 11-9:45, Sat til 10:45. Reser sugg. AE,D, MC,V.* **741-9968.**
North Hills favorite, reserved, relaxed, smooth service; great pastas–try Pasta d'Mer. Seafood, daily specials. Big outdoor deck. $8.95 up.

## Hotlicks
*8300 McKnight Rd, McIntyre Sq. Sun-Thur 11:30-11, Fri-Sat til 12. AE,D,MC,V.* **369-7675.**
Black/white decor and red hot! Ribs mild to killer, great chicken nachos, grills, salads, sandwiches on dark harvest bread; super vegetarian fare. $3-$15.95. Kids Sun menu 83c. Outdoor deck.

## Hotel Saxonburg
*Main St, Saxonburg. Lunch Tues-Sat 11:30-4, Dinner Mon 5-9, Tues-Thur 4-10, Fri-Sat 4-11. Sun 4-9. AE,MC,V.* **352-4200.**
Casual dining in charming 19th C inn, old stagecoach stop. Full menu $8-$25.

## Iron Bridge Inn
*Rt 19 N, 5 mi south of Mercer. Sun-Thur 11-10:30, Fri-Sat til 11:30. Sun Brunch 11-3. AE,DC,MC,V.* **748-3626.**
A real experience—old lamp shades, moose heads, polar bears. Tangy Cajun seafood, tender prime rib. $2-$16.

## Jergel's
*3855 Babcock Blvd, Ross. Mon-Sat 11-2am, Sun 1-11. AE,D,MC,V.* **364-9902.**
Casual, upbeat, good family homestyle. Sandwiches to surf 'n turf, Cajun, veal, seafood. Wknd entertainment. $3-$21.

**19**

# North

### Jimmy G's
*225 Commercial Ave, Aspinwall. Mon-Thur 11:30-10, Fri-Sat til 11, Bar til 2. AE,D,DC,MC,V.* **781-4884.**
Traditional American cuisine in paneled room; good steak, veal—and burgers too. Sat eve tableside entertainment $5-$22.

### Juno Trattoria
*Ross Park Mall, off McKnight Rd. Mon-Thur 11:30-10, Fri-Sat til 11. Sun 12-7. AE,D,DC,MC,V.* **366-2737.**
Good Italian food and atmosphere, tile-topped tables, interesting art; homemade pasta in piccolo/uno servings, excellent sauces, wine. Lunch/Dinner $3-$13.

### Kangaroos Outback Cafe
*4550 McKnight Road. 7 days 11- 2am. AE,D,MC,V.* **931-3370.**
Casual Australian, 'home of the velcro wall.' Inflatable Sumo wrestling Wed nights. Great roo (sweet potato) chips accompany sangers (sandwiches). Grills, beers, munchies; kids menu. Singles jump on weekends. $3.95-$10.95.

### Kaufmann House
*Main St, Zelienople. Mon-Thur 7am-9, Fri-Sat til 10. AE,DC,MC,V.* **261-2024.**
Friendly room, outstanding kitchen; great broiled seafood platter, Alaskan King crab legs, homemade desserts...try peanut butter pie! $2.50-$17.

### Kleiner-Deutschman
*643 Pittsburgh St, Springdale. Mon-Sat 5-10. AE,MC,V.* **274-5022.**
Adventures in German eating—wine, beer, music, great atmosphere; authentic pork, veal dishes. $8.50-$22.

### Kretzler's
*2240 Babcock Blvd. Mon-Sat 11-2, Sun til 1. AE,D,MC,V.* **821-1606.**
Good basic food, good prices; fresh seaood, steaks, chicken, sandwiches, finger foods. Prime Rib $9.95 wknds. $3.95-$14.

### McSorley's
*2198 Babcock Blvd. Mon-Sat 11:30-9. AE,DC,MC,V.* **821-2138.**
Casual, reasonable, attracts older crowd. Daily specials from stuffed pork chops to Virginia spots. $5.95 up.

### Mardi Gras
*634 Camp Horne Rd, Ohio Twp. Mon-Thur 11:30-10, Fri-Sat til 11. Sun 1-9. AE,D,MC,V.* **369-9916.**
Noisy popular N Hills meeting place. Big oak bar, tables, lots of plants. Cajun/Creole, great seafood gumbo. $7.95 up.

### Misty Harbour
*19th/River Rd, Sharpsburg. Tues-Sun 11-11, Bar til 2. AE,D,MC,V.* **781-4222.**
Unique dining, river view on a tugboat & barge on the Allegheny; chicken, pasta, veal, seafood, steak plus big Sun Brunch ($11.95). DJ/live bands Fri-Sun. $8-$17.

### Montemurro
*1822 Main, Sharpsburg. Mon-Thur 11-11, Fri-Sat til 12. AE,D,DC,MC,V.* **781-6800.**
Pleasant room with big Italian family menu; beautiful banquet room; seafood, pasta, veal $8-$20.

### Perrytowne Tavern
*1002 Perry Hwy, Perrysville. Mon-Sat 11-12, Sun 2-12. DC,MC,V.* **367- 9610.**
Casual atmosphere, great beers, terrific wings, beer-batter fish sandwiches, pasta, seafood. $5-$12.

### Pines Tavern
*Old State Rd, Gibsonia. Mon-Sat Lunch 11-3, Dinner 5-10. MC,V.* **625-3252.**
Warm, cozy inn tucked off highway, fireplace/antiques; gourmet cuisine, casual bar. Great turtle soup, raspberry pie. $4-$19.

### Rico's Restaurant
*Park Pl off Babcock Blvd. Lunch Mon-Sat 11:45-2:30. Dinner Mon-Thur 4-10:30, Fri-Sat til 11:30. AE,DC,MC,V.* **931-1989.**
Fine dining in quaint old hilltop house with getaway feel. Big reputation for seafood, fish, steak. $4-$23. (See Rich Man's) Dining)

### Simply Delicious
*1200 Old Freeport Rd, Fox Chapel.
7 days 7:30am-4pm. AE,MC,V.* **963-0636.**
Small dining area at famed caterer's;
gourmet specialties—filet, great chicken
salad, french fried ice cream, apple muffins. Breakfast to dinner $2-$13.

### Stone Mansion
*Stone Mansion Dr, Franklin Park. Lunch
Mon-Fri 11:45-2:30, Dinner Mon-Thur
5-10, Fri-Sat til 11. AE,D,MC,V.* **934-3000.**
Excellent Continental cuisine in rustic
stone mansion with warm wood, stained
glass. Fresh meat/seafood and light
foods. $6-$30.

### Tai Pei Chinese Restaurant
*124 Freeport Rd, Fox Chapel. Mon-Thur
11:30-10, Fri-Sat til 11. AE,D,DC,MC,V.*
**781-4131.**
Light, airy with Hunan lamb, Gen Tso's
Chicken, seafood, Peking Duck. Lunch
$5.25-$6.50, Dinner $8-$12.

### Tremont House
*Sheraton N, Warrendle Mon-Sat 4-11.
Sun 3-10. AE,D,DC,MC,V. Reser.*
**776-6900.**
Stylish room noted for Fri Seafood Buffet
with lobster tail, hot/cold entrees & Sat
Prime Rib Buffet, both $17. Dinner $8-$25.

### SUBURBS SOUTH

### Amel's
*435 McNeilly Rd, Baldwin. Mon-Sat
11:30-12am. Sun 3-10. AE,D,MC,V.*
**563-3466.**
Favorite Mid-East food; good maza
appetizer sampler, Italian/Amer plus
seafood, homemade desserts. $10-$22.

### Armstrong's
*Galleria, 1500 Washington Rd, Mt Leb.
Mon-Sat 11-11. Sun 12-8. No credit
cards.* **341-9460.**
Long lines for great prices; sandwiches,
salads, chicken, steak, pasta, seafood.
Huge outdoor deck. $4.25-$9.

### Arrostaria
*3351 Washington Rd, Peters Twp. Mon-
Thur 11:30-10, Fri til 11, Sat 1pm- 11.
Sun 12-9. AE,D,MC,V.* **942-3900.**
Another fine Barsotti eatery. Wood-
roasted chicken, ravioli parmigiano
chicken, seafood. Family prices. $6-$10.

### Augie's American Bistro
Galleria, 1500 Washington Rd, Mt
Lebanon. Mon-Thur 11-10, Fri-Sat til 11.
Sun 11-9. AE,CB,D,DC,MC,V. **571-1157.**
European/Amer—pasta, gourmet pizza,
salad; pleasant outdoor deck. $5-$14.

### Bachri's
*3821 Willow Ave, Castle Shannon.Tues-
Thur 4-9:30, Fri-Sat til 10:30. Sun 4-9.
D,MC,V.* **343-2213.**
Great Indonesian and Syrian specialties
in small, cozy quarters. $6.50-$15.

### Bado's
*307 Beverly Road, Mt Lebanon. Mon-
Thur 11-11, Fri til 12, Sat 9-11pm, Sun
9-9. No credit cards.* **563-5300.**
Pizza parlor extraordinare; all-you-can-eat
pizza (Mon) & spaghetti (Tues) $5.25.
Great Sat-Sun breakfasts. $2-$7.

### Cafe Georgio's
*24 Donati Road, Bethel Park. Mon-Thur
11:30-10, Fri til 11. Sat 5-11 or 12. AE,
CB,DC,MC,V.* **833-7000.**
Lively room with funky touches, eclectic
menu. Good homemade flatbread, pasta,
beef, veal, chicken, seafood. $5-$20.

### Candle Keller
*94 Center Church Rd, McMurray. Tues-
Thur 5-10, Fri-Sat til 11. Sun 4-9. Reser
wknds. AE,D,MC.V.* **941-8424.**
Excellent Euro-American food in quaint
rathskeller. Homemade schnitzel, wurst,
great potato pancakes. $8.50-$19.

### Century Inn
*Scenery Hill, Rt 40. Mon-Sat 12- 3. Mon-
Thur 4:30-7:30, Fri-Sat til 8:30. Sun
12-6:30. No cred cards. Reser.* **945-6600.**
Charming trip to Colonial past in 1794 inn;
traditional fare—roast turkey, pork. $5-$24.

**19**

# South

### Classroom Restaurant
*Camp Ln off Rt 19, Washington. Mon-Sat 11:30-2, 5-10. AE,D,MC,V.* **942-4878.**
American style food in old 1907 schoolhouse with real chalkboard menu by Chuck Davis (formerly Angel's Corner); fine seafood, pork, chicken. $4-$17.

### Colony
*Greentree/Cochran Rds. Scott. Mon-Sat 5-10:30. Sun 4-9. AE,DC,MC.V.* **561-2060.**
Warm, elegant atmosphere around open brick grill where suburbanites enjoy best in steak. $20-$29. Piano lounge. (See Rich Man's Guide)

### Craver's
*500 Lewis Run Rd, Pleasnt Hills. Mon-Fri 7:30-4.* **469-6979.** Little place with homemade sandwiches, salads; Sun Br 10-3, gazebo courtyard. $2-$7.

### Davio's
*2100 Broadway, Beechview. Lunch Mon-Fri 12-3, Dinner Mon-Sat 4-11. Sun 4-9. No credit, no liquor. Reser.* **531-7422.**
Italian trattoria with casual feel; superb food from Chef David Ayn—pasta, chops, fish $5.95-$29. More casual **Palio's** bar/restaurant next door. (See Review)

### DeBlasio's
*Va Manor Shops, 1717 Cochran Rd, Mt Lebanon. Mon-Thur 11-12, Fri-Sat til 1am. Sun 12-12. AE,DC,MC,V.* **531-3040.**
Italian—Pittsburgh style—from pasta to lobster. Big favorite. $3-$25.

### Elephant Bar
*5242 Clairton Blvd, Pleasant Hills. Mon-Thur 11-10, Fri-Sat til 12. Sun 10-10. Bar til 1:30. AE,D,MC,V.* **885-0151.**
Safari atmosphere, big Mexican, Italian, Creole menu with lots of fresh fish, pasta, fajitas plus waffle/juice bars.

### Fajita Grill
*580 Old Clairton Rd, Pleasant Hls. Lunch Mon-Fri 11-2, Dnr Mon-Thur 5-9, Fri til 10, Sat 3-9:45. Sun 3-9. AE,D,DC,MC,V.* **653-7230.**

Small eatery, authentic Mexican fajitas, chili relleno; good margaritas. $3-$10.50.

### The Forest—Redwood Inn
*Banksville Rd/Potomac, Dormont. Mon-Fri 7am-2, Sat 8-12, Dinner 5:30- 9:30. Sun 8-1, AE,D,DC,MC.V.* **343-3000.**
Veal, beef, fresh seafood. Bar. $7-$20.

### Gino's
*Bourse Shops, Greentree Rd. Dinner Mon-Sat 4-11. AE,D,DC,MC,V.* **279-1414.**
Classic Italian by Gino (formerly Park Schenley). Seafood, veal, tantalizing desserts. Early Bird Mon-Thur. $11-$30.

### Houlihan's
*Fort Couch/Washingyon Rd, Bethel, Mon-Thur 11:30-10:30, Fri-Sat til 12. Sun Brunch 9-2, dinner til 10. AE,CB,D,DC, MC,V.* **831-9797.**
Casual dining, fun surroundings; great fajitas, chicken, beef, onion soup. $9-$12.

### Jose & Tony's
*1573 McFarland Rd, Mt Leb. Mon-Thur 11-12am, Fri-Sat til 12:30. Sun 4-10. No credit cards.* **561-2025.**
Little take-out/eatery packs a Mexican wallop. 'Big Joe Dinner'—taco, tamale, refried beans, Spanish rice, chili, cheese enchilada $7.25! Bargain tacos, tamales.

### Klay's Cafe
*3105 Banksville Pllaza. Mon-Thur 11-10, Fri-Sat til 11. Sun 3-9. AE,DC,MC,V. Reser.* **341-3200.**
S Hills favorite, excellent Greek/American food; big selection. Casual. $3-$16.

### Living Room
*1778 N Highland Rd, Up St Clair. Mon-Sat 5-2am. AE,D,DC,MC,V.* **835-9772.**
Sophisticated hideaway with good dinners, nightly piano bar. Italian specialties, exceptional cuisine $10-$25.

### Mark Pi's China Gate
*Galleria, 1500 Washington Rd. Mon-Thur 11:30-10, Fri-Sat til 11. Sun 12-9. AE, MC,V.* **341-8890.**

Excellent Szechuan/Hunan/Mandarin specialties; 3 Moon combo—sesame beef, moo goo gai pan, Hunan shrimp. $4 to $25 for whole duck.

## Naples
*3600 Saw Mill Run Blvd, Brentwd. Tues-Fri 11-11,Sat 3-11.Sun 3-10. V.* **884-4899.**
Fans rave about the homemade cooking here (family of famed old Naples downtown). Big portions–chicken, pasta, veal, seafood. Pleasant setting. $4.50-$17.

## New Orleans Inn
*4131 Brownsville Rd, Brentwood. Mon-Thur 11-11, Fri-Sat til 12. Sun 2-8. AE, MC,V.* **881-1112.**
Amer seafood, steak, chicken in warm, wood setting; old-fashioned bar. $4-$13.

## Paule's Lookout
*2627 Skyline Drive, W Mifflin. Tues-Sat 11-9. Sun 12-7. AE,DC,MC,V.* **466-4500.**
Good family restaurant with great river view. Seafood, lobster, prime rib. $5 lunch specials. $7-$15.

## Piccolo Mondo
*Foster Plaza—Bldg #7, Holiday Inn Dr, Greentree. Lunch Mon-Fri 11:30-3:30, Dinner 4-10, Fri-Sat til 11. Reser sugg. AE,D,DC,MC,V.* **922-0920.**
Beautiful room with sweeping view, elegant cuisine, service. Noted for fish, veal. Lunch $6-$10, Dinner $13-$23. (See Rich Man's Dining)

## Prime House
*Pgh Greentree Marriott. 7 days 6:30-2, 5-11. AE,CB,D,DC,MC.V.* **922-8400.**
Elegant room, top service; fine prime rib, inventive Amer cuisine. Seafood, veal, daily specials, tempting desserts. $15-$20.

## Ritz
*928 McLaughlin Run Rd, Bridgeville. Mon-Fri 11-11, Sat til 10. MC,V.* **257-2210.**
Down home cookin' in small old hotel; famous fish sandwiches, chicken, fish, pasta; big portions. $5-$14.

## Ruby Tuesday
*Galleria, 1500 Washington Rd, Mt Lebanon. Mon-Thur 11:15-10, Fri-Sat til 12. AE,D,DC,MC,V.* **343-6855.**
Casual, light fare, dinners; good childrens' menu. Mod.

## Sante Fe
*25 McMurray Rd, Upper St Clair. Mon-Thur 11-12, Fri-Sat til 2. Sun 1-9. AE,MC, V.* **833-7075.**
Big, open room; heaping portions of Tex-Mex dishes—grills, fajitas, appetizers, great ribs. Dinner $8-$16

## Samurai Japanese Steak House
*2100 Greentree Rd, Greentree. Mon-Thur 11:30-10, Fri 5:30-10, Sat 5:30-11:30. Sun 4:30-9. AE,DC,MC,V.* **276- 2100.**
Dramatic dining at hibachi tables, performing chefs; steaks/seafood, tropical drinks. $5.75-$22.

## Sesame Inn
*715 Washington Road, Mt Lebanon. Mon-Thur 11:30-10, Fri-Sat til 11. Sun 4-10. AE,DC,MC,V.* **341-2555.**
Authentic Chinese i.e. Gen Tso's chicken, orange beef, sesame shrimp. $6.50-$15.

## Shajor
*922 McMurray Rd, Bethel Park. Dinner Mon-Thur 5-10, Fri-Sat til 11. Sun 5-9, Brunch 10-2. AE, MC,V.* **833-4800.**
Upscale Amer/Continental, smoked fresh seafood, veal and beef from their own smokehouse $10-$26. Cocktail lounge.

## Sichuan House
*1717 Cochran Rd, Mt. Lebanon. Sun-Fri 11:30- 9:30, Sat til 10:30. Sun 4:30-9:30. AE,MC,V.* **563-5252.**
One of the city's best Chinese. Try the Sea Delight, Chicken/Shrimp/Vegetables & Gen Tso's Chicken. $7.50-$17.

## Tai Pei Chinese Restaurant
*Bourse Shops, Greentree Rd. Scott. Mon-Thur 11:30-10, Fri-Sat til 11. Sun 11:30-9:30. AE,D, DC,MC,V.* **279-8811.**
Comfortable, good Hunan lamb, Gen Tso's Chicken, Peking Duck. $5-$15.

**19**

## East

### SUBURBS EAST

### Angie's
*111 Middle Ave, Wilmerding. Wed-Thur & Sat 4-10, Fri 12-11. No credit cards. No liquor.* **829-7663.**
A small, secret find with great prices on delicious homemade pasta, gnocchi, veal, seafood, spinach calzones. $4.50-$12.

### Birdie's
*4733 William Penn Hwy, Monrv. Lunch Mon-Sat 11-4. Dinner Mon-Thur 4-10, Fri-Sat til 11. Sun 4-9. All CC.* **372-9878.**
Intimate with good service. King-size cocktails, seafood, veal, steak, great garlic toast. Specials off every menu item from 4-5:30pm. $8-$26.

### Chelsea Grille
515 Allegheny Ave, Oakmont. 7 days Mon-Thur 11:30-10, Fri-Sat til 11. Sun 4-8. AE,D,DC,MC,V. **828-0570.**
Adjacent to Hoffstot's. Popular hardwood grill—seafood, steak, chops. Mod.

### China Palace
*Jonnet Plaza, 4059 Wm Penn Hwy. Mon-Thur 11:30-9:30, Fri-Sat til 10:30. Sun 3-9 Reser 6 or more. AE,MC,V.* **373-7423.**
Above-average Szechuan, Mandarin, Hunan; good Pu Pu Platter $9.95 for 2. Great Gen Tso's Chicken, lobster, many specialties. $8-$15.

### Dick's Diner
*Rt 22, Murrysville. Sun-Thur 6:30am-10pm. Fri-Sat til 12. No CC.* **327-4566.**
A Pgh institution; big, modern, informal with wonderful family fare, good prices. Fabulous hot roast beef sandwiches, homemade pies. $2-$7.

### D'Imperio's
*3412 William Penn Hwy, Wilkins. Lunch Mon-Fri 11:30-3, Dinner 7 days 5-11. Reser. AE,CB,D,DC,MC,V.* **823-4800.**
Gracious dining at city's finest; famous seafood, lamb, fish $15-$27. Lunch $7-$11. (See Review)

### Eastwood Inn
*4268 Verona Road, Penn Hills. Mon-Sat 4-10. MC,V.* **241-4700**
Old favorite famous for soft shell crabs year around, good pasta, steak, veal, desserts, $8-$24.50, average $12-$15. Good bet!

### Hoffstot's Cafe Monaco
*533 Allegheny Ave, Oakmont. Mon-Thur 11:30-10, Fri-Sat til 11. Sun 3:30-9. Reser. AE,D,DC,MC,V.* **828-8555.**
Euro/Italian cafe with family flavour, lounge, good prices. Fish sandwiches, dark beer, 50 dinner items. Deserves it's accolades.

### Hotel Benedict
*400 2nd Street, Pitcairn. Mon-Fri 11:30-9, Sat 4-9. AE,MC,V.* **372-9801.**
Comfortable, casual. Famed steak salad, lobster, prime rib weekends. Dinners $10-$27. Specials everyday.

### Houlihan's
*Monroeville Mall. Mon-Thur 11-10, Fri-Sat til 12. Sun Brunch 9-2, Dinner til 9. AE,D, DC,MC,V.* **373-8520.**
You may see your favorite sports star at this lively place. Good eclectic menu, sandwiches, steak, prime rib, pastas. Lunch/Dinner $5-$14. Happy Hour,disco.

### Lone Star Steakhouse/Saloon
*Jonnet Plaza, 4097 Wm Penn Hwy, Monrv. Sun-Thur 11-10, Fri-Sat til 11. AE, D,MC,V.* **373-7233.**
Texas roadhouse fun atmosphere; ribs, seafood, chicken, hand-cut USDA choice steaks $5-$18.

### Me Lyng Restaurant
*213 W 8th, W Homestead. Mon-Fri 11-9:30, Sat 4-11.Sun 3-9. AE,MC.V.* **464-1477.**
Beautiful Chinese/Vietnamese dishes—shrimp, duck, fish, pork—110 in all. Lunch $4-$5. Dinner $7-$13. Take out.

## Naples Station
*2723 Stroschein Rd, Monroeville. Mon-Thur 11-11, Fri-Sat til 12. Sun Brunch 10-3, dinner 3-9. AE,DC,MC,V.* **372-1744.**
Big local favorite. Casual dining in railroad car decor. Veal, pasta, seafood, steaks cut at tableside. Outdoor deck. $4-$24.

## Nick Marie's
*4000 Wm Penn Hwy, Monroeville. Mon-Fri 11-10:30. Sat 4-10:30. Sun 4-9. AE, D,DC,MC,V.* **372-4414.**
Good Italian—seafood, pasta, shrimp, veal. $4-$9 & up. Early Bird 4-7 daily.

## Oxford Dining Room
*Radisson Hotel, Monrv Mall Blvd. Sun-Thur 6:30-10, Fri & Sat til 11. Sun Brunch 9:30-1:30. All CC.* **373-7300.**
Romantic atmosphere, fireplaces. Fri prime rib/pasta, Sat Italian buffet $17-$18. Lunch $6-$13, Dinner $13-$20.

## Penn Monroe Grill
*3985 Wm Penn Hwy, Monrv. 7 days 10-2am. Sun 11-1am. AE,DC,MC,V.* **373-1180.**
Casual dining, homemade soup, sandwiches $1.50-$4.50, authentic Italian— meatballs to steak, $5-$10. Rigatoni Mon $1.89. Sing-a-longs Sun, Tues.

## Rivers Three
*Harley Hotel, off Rodi Rd, Wilkins. Lunch 7 days 11-2, Dinner Sun-Thur 5:30-10, Fri-Sat til 11. AE,D,DC,MC,V.* **244-1600.**
Quiet, elegant—hilltop view, dinner music, extra touches. Seafood, prime rib, steak. Sun Breakfast Buffet 9-2. $5.50-$18.

## Rodi Grille House
*204 Rodi Rd, Penn Hills. Sun-Thur 11-10, Fri-Sat til 11. AE,D,MC,V.* **241-1730.**
Big, roomy restaurant with great fresh seafood, fish, specialty steaks, prime rib; chicken, veal, pastas, good San Francisco sourdough bread. $9-$16. Early Bird 3-5:30 Mon-Fri $7.95.

## Shogun Japanese Steak House
*Monroeville Blvd opp Racquet Club. Lunch Mon-Fri 11:30-2:30. Dinner Mon-Thur 5:30-9:30, Fri-Sat til 10:30. Reser sugg. AE,DC,MC.V.* **372-0700.**
Delightful Japanese, hibachi-style steak, seafood, sushi prepared at table. Entrees with shrimp appetizer $9 to $24 for scallop/steak/lobster combo.

## Sichuan Palace
*Penn Hills Shopping Center. Mon-Thur 11:30-9:30, Fri & Sat til 10:30. Sun 12:30-9:30. AE,DC,MC,V.* **241-7110.**
Light, airy, gracious service, good cuisine. Popular Gen Tso's Chicken on huge menu. Daily specials. $3.25-$13.

## Spadaro's
*Rt 22, Murrysville. Mon-Thur 11-10, Fri-Sat til 11. Sun 12-8. AE,CB,DC,MC.V.* **327-5955.**
'Italian garden,' gazebo, stained glass. Excellent seafood, crab cakes; super hot/cold luncheon salad bar $3-$7. Wed-Thur Prime Rib $10.$4-$25.

## Station Brake Cafe
*500 Station St, Wilmerding. Lunch Mon-Fri 11-3, Dinner Mon-Sat 5-10. Sun 4:30-9. AE,DC,MC,V. Reser wknds.* **823-1600.**
International cuisine, wild game in warm dining room, fireplace, lots of surprises. Fancy seafood, veal, lamb, beef. Lunch $5-$10, Dinner $9-$28 but 30 items under $15. Deli next door.

## TGI Friday's
*240 Mall Blvd, Monrv. 7 days 11:30-2am. Sun Br til 3. AE,D,DC,MC.V.* **372-6630.**
Colorful Art Nouveau, brass, greenery, summer patio, long menu a la carte to dinners $2-$14. Nightlife at big brass bar.

## Tivoli Restaurant
*419 Rodi Rd, Penn Hills. Lunch Tues-Fri 11-3. Dinner Tues-Sat 4-11. Sun 3-9. Reser wknd AE,D,DC,MC.V.* **243- 9630.**
Light, bright Mediterrean setting for good food; veal, pasta, seafood, flambeed desserts $3-$18.

**19**

# East/West

### Uno Pizzeria
*Penn Center, Wilkins. Mon-Thur 11-11, Fri-Sat til 12:30. Sun 12-10. AE,D,MC,V.* **824-8667.**
Sassy, upbeat place for famous Chicago deep-dish pizza. Also pasta, ribs, salads, sandwiches, appetizers $2-$10. Five minute lunch $5.

### Veltri's
*Rt 909 & Coxcomb Hill, Plum. Dinner Mon-Thur 5-10, Fri-Sat til 11. Reser. AE,DC,MC.V.* **335-4474.**
Romantic dining, beautiful river view. Italian-Amer, great veal Parmesan. $7-$21. DJ at Nikki's Lounge Wed-Sat.

### Village Inn
*551 Wildwood Rd, Verona. Tues-Fri 11:30-10:30. Sat-Sun 2-10:30. No credit cards. Reser sugg.* **828-8714.**
A taste of Italy, cozy, popular. Pasta, seafood, Veal Romano, real tortellini Trentina. $2-$11.

### Winchester Room
*1728 Lincoln Hwy, N Versailles. Mon-Thur 5-10, Fri-Sat til 11. Sun 4-8. Reser sugg. AE.,D,DC, MC,V.* **823-9954.**
Famous for great steak; fresh fish, pasta to lobster in popular, busy rooms. $8-$23.

## SUBURBS WEST

### Beef & Burgundy
*Holiday Inn Airport, 1406 Beers School Rd, Coraopolis. Mon-Sat 6am-2, 5-11. Sun Brunch 10-2, Dinner 5-10. AE,D,DC, MC,V.* **262-3600.**
Warm, elegant room with fresh seafood, chef's specials. $5-$22. Dinner dancing.

### Cathy's Windsor Tea Room
*515 Locust Place, Sewickley. Tues-Sun 11-7. Reser sugg.* **741-6677.**
Traditional tea in charming "British" house with pasties (meat pies), scones, gourmet breakfast. Luncheon Tea $7. Formal Tea with shepherd/meat pies, unlimited desserts $14. Some Ital dishes. ($2-$17).

### Dingbat's
*200 Park Manor Drive, Robinson. Mon-Sat 11:30-2am. Sun Brunch 10-2, Dinner til 1am. AE,D,DC,MC,V.* **787-7010.**
Casual fun, specialty menu—sandwiches, pasta, char-broiled steaks, fish, oyster bar. Greenhouse patio dining. Happy Hour 4:30-6:30. $4-$15.

### Hyeholde
*Coraopolis Hgts Rd, Moon Twp. Lunch Mon-Fri 11:30-2, Dinner Mon-Sat 5-10. AE,D,DC,MC.V. Reser sugg.* **264-3116.**
Warm Elizabethan mansion—flagstone floors, fireplaces, tapestries. Romantic dinner by candlelight. DiRoNa fine dining award for elegant American cuisine. $7-$29. (See Rich Man's Guide)

### IKEA Cafe
*Robinson Town Center. Mon-Fri 11- 9, Sat 10-9. Sun 10-6. D,MC,V.* **747-0747.**
Hot/cold Swedish delicacies—meat balls, salmon, herring, great desserts in popular furniture store's sleek cafe. Outdoor deck. Sun Brunch 11-2. $3-$6.

### Mad Anthony's Bier Stube
*13th/Merchant, Ambridge. Mon-Sat 11-2am. AE,MC,V.* **266-3450.**
Rustic room with outdoor courtyard, live bands Fri-Sat. German dishes, good

sandwiches, salads, beers $3-$12. Great stop after touring nearby Old Economy.

### Maggie Mae's Creekhouse

*288 W Steuben, Crafton. Mon-Thur 11-11, Fri til 12. Sat 4-12. Sun 4-9. AE,D, DC,MC,V.* **922-1662.**
Charming Victorian-style renovated 1890 bridge-house. Fun food/dinners, casual atmosphere. Try 'taste of honey' fried chicken, Cajun. $7-$12.

### Mario's Family Restaurant

*926 Broadhead Road, Moon. Mon-Sat 4-11. AE,D,DC,MC,V.* **262-3020.**
Good home-cooked Italian; veal, chicken, pasta, seafood & steak, traditional desserts—tiramisu, spumoni. Economical $6.50 to $30 for lobster.

### Papa J's

*200 E Main, Carnegie. Mon-Thur 11-10, Fri-Sat til 11. Sun 10:30-9. AE,CB,DC, MC,V. Reser sugg.* **429-7272.**
Tempting seafood grills, pasta, veal in European cafe atmosphere. Lunch $4-$6, Dinner $10-$20.

### Pastels, Royce Hotel

*1160 Thorn Run Rd Ext, Coraopolis. 7 days Breakfast/Lunch Mon-Fri 7-2, Dinner 5-11. AE,D,DC,MC,V.* **262-2400.**
Minutes from Airport. Continental cuisine, soothing peach decor. Sun Brunch 10-2. Lunch $6-$7, Dinner $12-$23.

### La Primadonna

*801 Broadway Ave, McKees Rocks. Mon-Sat 4-11, Lounge til 12. AE,CB,DC,MC,V.* **331-1001.**
Neighborhood eatery making gastronomic waves for hearty Italian dishes—mouth-watering pasta, seafood, chicken, veal at wonderful prices. No reser but worth the wait. $10-$19. (See Review)

### Red Bull Inn, Robinson

*5205 Campbell's Run Rd. Mon-Fri 11-11, Sat 4-12. Sun 4-9. AE,D,DC,MC,V.* **787-2855.**
Famous for prime rib, lobster pot, salad bar. Pasta, veal, chicken, steak. Happy Hour Mon-Fri 5-7 1/2 off appetizers. Piano Bar in Lounge Friday. Srs 20% off from 2-5:30. $9-$16. Chldrn $2.95.

### River Room

*Sewickley Country Inn, 801 Ohio River Blvd. Mon-Sat 6:30am-10pm. Sun 6:30-9. AE,D,DC,MC.V.* **741-4300.**
Warm, comfortable setting for veal, seafood, pasta. $4-$17.

### Tambellini Bridgeville

*413 Railroad St, Bridgeville. Mon 11-9, Tues-Thur til 10, Fri til 11, Sat 4-11, Sun 4-9. AE,DC, MC,V.* **221-5202.**
Fine dining in handsome rooms; specializing in veal, seafood. Lunch $4.25-$8, Dinner $8-$24.

### Wooden Angel

*West Bridgewater, Beaver. Tues-Fri 11:30-11. Sat 5-12. AE,D,DC,MC,V.* **774-7880.**
Award-winning wine cellar, American wines & cuisine in intimate rooms, classical music; veal, seafood. Lunch $5.50-$15, Dinner $16-$30. (See Rich Man's Guide)

### Wright's Seafood Inn

*1837 Washington St, Heidelberg. Mon-Thur 11-10, Fri-Sat til 11. Sun 4-9. AE,D, DC,MC.V.* **279-7900.**
Big sprawling restaurant with some of city's best seafood—lobster, crab, Norwegian salmon $17, great bouilla-baisse. Lunch $4-$7, Dinner $8-$22.

# Family Chains

### Bob Evans

*Sun-Thur 5am-10, Fri-Sat til 11:30. MC,V. Century III Mall, Coraopolis, Harmarvlle, Monroeville, N Hills, Warrendale, Washington Mall, N Huntingdon,*

Casual, country-style, famous sausage with eggs, gravy, grits; good ribs, BBQ chicken, peanut butter pie, dinners $1-$6. Child/Seniors discounts.

### Chi-Chi's Mexican Restaurants

*Mon-Thur 11-11, Fri-Sat til 12. Sun til 10. AE,DC,MC,V. Washington Rd 833-8886. Greentree 937-0818. Wm Penn Hwy, Monrv 856-8860. McKnight Rd, N Hills 364-2414. Clairton Blvd 653-6000.*

Popular, bustling Tex-Mex—tostados to special chimichangas—all under $8. Children's $2 menu opens into sombrero! Mexican beer, desserts.

### Chuck E. Cheese

*7 days 11-9, Fri-Sat til 11. MC,V. Wm Penn Hwy, Monrv 856-5044. Wash Pike, Bridgeville 257-2570. Lebanon Ch Rd , 655-8840. Perry Hwy, Wexford 364-6292.*

Birthday favorite—kids have time of their lives—puppet show, video games, big mouse Chuck E Cheese himself. Burgers, pizza $6-9; salad bar $3.29. Beer/wine for grown-ups.

### Eat 'n Park

*7 days, many 24 hrs. 57 sites. AE,D, MC,V. 923-1000.*

Favorite family place for big Soup 'n Salad bars, Sunday Buffets, great breakfasts, economical meals, famous strawberry pie, free Smiley cookie to kids. Bakeries—good sticky buns. $3-$7.

### Ground Round

*Mon-Sat 11-1, Sun 12-12. AE,MC,V. Narrows Run Rd, Coraopolis 269-0644. Wm Penn Hwy, Monrv 856-0385. Washington Rd, Mt Leb 833-7580. Greentree Rd 561-2187. Wexford 935-4290.*

Kid's delight, fun decor, old time flicks some locations. Varied menu—beef, chicken, fish, spaghetti, Mexican. $4-$12. Kids 1 cent a lb Thur. Sr discounts.

### HOSS'S Steak & Sea House

*Sun-Thur 10:30-9:30, Fri-Sat til 10:30. MC,V. Rt 8. Allison Pk 486-9291. Belle Vernon 929-9249. Beaver Grade Rd, Coraopolis. 262-8857. Rt 22, Murrysvle 733-2090. Frankstown Rd, Penn Hills. 241-7522.*

Big family places, good home cooking—chicken, fish, steak, seafood with vegetable/potato, salad bar $6-$11. Sr discounts. Great Sunday stop.

### King's Family Restaurants

*7 days 24 hrs. MC,V. Bridgeville, Coraopolis, Cranberry, Fox Chapel, N Versailles, Penn Hills, Steubenville Pike, Up St Clair. (Monrv 24hr wknds only.)*

Family favorite, fast service, senior specials. Complete dinners $4-$6, great breakfasts $3-$5, huge sundaes.

### Olive Garden

*Mon-Thur 11-10, Fri-Sat til 11. Sun 11-10. AE,DC,MC,V. Oxford Dr, Bethel Pk 835-6353. Greentree Rd 922-7200. McKnight Rd 369-9686. Monrv Mall Blvd 372-5017. Clairton Blvd 653-5897.*

Popular Italian, pleasing decor, inviting menu; good pasta, veal, chicken, unlimited soup, salad. $4-$12.

### Pappan's

*7 days. Most 9-9. Sun til 7. Alleg Ctr 321-8151. Century III 655-7220. N Hills Vlg 369-8802. Robinson Town Ctr 788-0155. McMurray 942-0401.*

Locally-owned chain with home cooking, good service. Speciality—Chicken Dinner $4.19 to varied menus $6.69. Sr menu.

### Red Lobster

*Sun-Thur 11-10, Fri-Sat til 11. AE,DC, MC,V. Wm Penn Hwy, Monrv 372-5591. Washington Rd, Mt Leb. 831-7373. McKnight Rd 367-2998. Rt 30, Robinson 788-8700. Clairton Blvd, Pleasant Hills 653-3552.*

Seafood lover's haven—fish, lobster, crab legs any way you like. Informal, friendly. $4-$21

# INDEX

# Share Your Love of Pittsburgh!

## PGH PLACEMAT/PRINTS

Favorite well-loved scenes of old and new Pittsburgh from "Pgh Pleasures" calendars' spectacular photographs by Herb Ferguson. Glossy, laminated finish, 12x16 1/2. View from Ft Pitt Bridge, Point, Incline, Fireworks. Beautiful framed.

## PGH GUIDE/WALKING MAP

Discover city's hidden secrets ...places to go, best restaurant values, romantic hideaways, riverside eateries, Pgh foods, sightseeing in bright new 250p guide PLUS unique 4-color "Pgh Walking Map" with mini-guide, 400 bldgs, parking right ON the map. Save on gold-ribboned gift pair with "Pgh Lovers" tag. A wonderful gift!

## PITTSBURGH PLEASURE EVENTS CALENDAR

Plan your social schedule with this beautiful calendar listing 850 wonderful things to do in the Pittsburgh area day by day...month by month. A collector's item with 13 spectacular color photos of the city. Perfect for friends, employees, customers, students, Pittsburghers away from home.

## Beautiful Pittsburgh Scenes

### NOTECARDS

Favorite Pittsburgh notecards. Brilliant color photo scenes of the Point/Golden Triangle, View from the Incline, Phipps Flower Show, Univ of Pgh. 10 cards (2 each of 5 scenes). Fold to 4 1/4 x 5 1/2.

### POSTCARDS

12 full-color photos, favorite Pgh scenes including Incline, Pitt, Golden Triangle, View from Ft Pitt Tunnels, Regatta, Station Square, PPG Plaza. Wonderful memento of the city.

---

**NEW PITTSBURGH PUBLICATIONS   BOX 81875   PITTSBURGH, PA 15217   (412) 681-8528   681-0601**

Enclosed is a check/money order for:

| | | |
|---|---|---|
| _____ | "Perfect Pair" Guide/Map Gift Sets $14.95 ea. | |
| _____ | "Rich/Poor Man's Guide to Pittsburgh" at $12.95 ea | _____ |
| _____ | "Pgh Walking Map & Guide" at $2.95 ea | |
| _____ | "Pittsburgh Pleasures Events Calendar" at $10.95 ea | _____ |
| _____ | Pittsburgh Placemat/Prints at $3.50 ea. Set of 4-$12 | _____ |
| _____ | Boxes Beautiful Pittsburgh Notecards at $5.99 ea | _____ |
| _____ | Boz Postcards, 12 cards assorted $4.20 doz | _____ |

| **Shipping/Handling** | |
|---|---|
| $2.50-$4.99 | $1.60 |
| $5-$15 | $2.50 |
| $16-$25 | $3.50 |
| $26-$50 | $4.00 |
| $51-$100 | $4.50 |
| Add $1.50 for each separate address. | |

_____ Shipping
_____ Sub-Total
_____ 7% Sales Tax (PA residents

========= TOTAL  AMOUNT ENCLOSED

PLEASE SHIP TO: _____Date: _____

Address: _____

City/Zip _____Phone:_____
　　　　　　　　(If gift specify "Gift card to read")

_____ Please send me information on business bulk rates, imprinting

# I Love Pittsburgh!
## Sightseeing Guide
# I Love Pittsburgh! Downtown

## Famous Addresses

Business decisions made in Pittsburgh are heard around the world. 7th largest corporate headquarters, the city is home base to 20 Fortune 500 & Forbes firms. Famous downtown bldgs are: **USX Tower,** 600 Grant St–64 steel stories, tallest bet NY & Chicago. **Westinghouse Bldg,** Gateway, home of world-famous logo. **Alcoa Bldg,** 425 Sixth Ave, 30-story aluminum showcase. **PPG Industries,** 4th/Mkt– 6 shimmering Gothic towers. **One Mellon Bank Center,** Grant, **CNG Tower,** Liberty Ave, **Gulf Tower,** Grant/7th with its pyramid top weather beacon & **Koppers Bldg,** 436 7th Ave with fine art deco lobby.

## **Quaint Old Pittsburgh

One of town's few remaining residential bldgs–picturesque (1894)Harvard-Yale-Princeton Club, Wm Penn Way/7th, its flagstone courtyard, red brick facade untouched by city bustle. Nearby is narrow, arcaded Strawberry Way.

## *Civic Arena

Uptown. dome home of Penguins hockey, concerts. Steel roof ...world's largest re-tractable...rolls back on balmy nights-moving sight.

## View From the Bluff

High above city off Forbes is Duquesne U, famed for music, law, Mies van der Rohe's Mellon Hall. Panoramic view from Bluff—on a clear day you can see far down river.

## Mellon Square

A shady in-city parklet across from Westin Wm Penn. Closest thing to a Pittsburgh promenade as office workers stroll, meet and eat around fountain.

## Market Square

Off 5th/Forbes below Wood. This famous square, site of Pgh's old marketplace, is a grassy park...benches, friendly pigeons in midst of bustling shops, towering PPG complex.

Grant/Ross. One of world's finest examples of masonry architecture, this 1888 landmark is the masterpiece of famed architect H H Richardson. The Romanesque stone 'castle' with massive towers, chain-linked iron posts, 10 Commandments in stone is connected to County Jail by 'Bridge of Sighs.' Hidden courtyard parklet (off Forbes or 5th) can be viewed from 2nd fl corridor. Up Grant is amazing Gothic tracery of **Two Mellon Bank Center** with its 11-story rotunda..one of city's best interiors.

## ***Allegheny Courthouse

## Window Shopping

Pgh—like Paris—is a walking city, with shopping in compact 12-block area. On Smithfield bet 5th/6th are Kaufmann's, Saks & Brooks Bros. Near Gateway are Lazarus Dept Store & 5th Av Place shops. Station Sq's a block away.

## Gateway Center

City's first Renaissance I development, newly refurbished **Gateway Center,** has fountained plaza...six buildings joined to **Equitable Plaza** by walkway across Blvd of Allies.

## ** Point State Park Block House-Museum

Follow Point Park signs under wide archway for lovely stroll in park and relaxing close-up of **Point Fountain.*** This is where it all began. You're standing at strategic **Gateway to the West**—where swift Allegheny (rt) and muddy Monongahela (lft) form the Ohio. Here two centuries ago France & England battled for control of Amer frontier. **Ft Pitt Blockhouse,** on original site, is all that re-imains of Ft Pitt, built by victorious British in 1764 on ruins of French Ft Duquesne. **Museum** tells story of pioneer/Indian life, how city grew up around Fort as merchants/traders provisioned flat-boats & wagons going west. **Blockhouse/Mus** Tues-Sat 10-4:30, Sun 12-4:30. **281-9284.**

*Allegheny River*

*Monongahela River*

**\* Worth Seeing  \*\*Really Worth Seeing  \*\*\*Don't Miss!**

# I Love Pittsburgh!
# Sightseeing Guide

$3.00

## ☆☆☆ Visitor's Special ☆☆☆
### Five Easy Ways to Fall in Love with the City

### Renaissance II Bldgs

Explore downtown's spectacular new bldgs...starting at PPG's glass palace, 4th/Market...on to 5th Ave Place, Stanwix/Liberty. Then past Heinz Hall Plaza to CNG Tower... straight ahead to Liberty Center/ Vista. Up on Grant are One Mellon Bank Ctr at 5th, Oxford Ctr at 4th.

### Station Square Shops

S Side at Smithfield St Bridge. Walk, ride the "T" subway or take a Wood St bus to city's famous mall in splendidly restored RR station. Enjoy shops, eateries, beautiful Grand Concourse restaurant, outdoor Bessemer Ct Museum. Great river views, Gateway Clipper dock. Shops til 9. Food til 12. A must. **281-3145.**

### Scaife Gallery

Carnegie Museum, Forbes/Craig, Oakland. Don't let visitors leave town without slipping out to classic modern glass & granite Scaife Gallery, dazzling Hall Minerals/ Gems, Dinosaur Hl. Dine at cafe. You can't miss Cath of Learning, Pitt's 42-fl Gothic home nearby.

### Gateway Clipper

The best way to experience Pittsburgh— the Gateway to the West—is from famous three rivers. Sail past spuming Point Fountain. Imagine Indian, settler past in looming hills. Discover city of bridges (573—most in US), working tugs, barges, steel mills, new riverfront parks, marinas. Daily cruises from Station Sq dock. $7.95, chd $4.95. Kiddie cruise, $5.95-$3.95. Shuttle to/from Stadium games 1.25. **355-7980.**

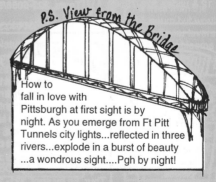

### Duq. Incline

Ride 400 ft up the Duquesne Incline, S Side for panoramic view of the Golden Triangle - breathtaking day/night from Mt Wash observation pods. Daily 5:30am-12:45am (Sun from 7am). **381-1665.**

### P.S. View from the Bridge

How to fall in love with Pittsburgh at first sight is by night. As you emerge from Ft Pitt Tunnels city lights...reflected in three rivers...explode in a burst of beauty ...a wondrous sight....Pgh by night!

### *Worth Seeing **Really Worth Seeing ***Don't Miss

Pull Out!